The
COAST OF MAINE
Book
A Complete Guide

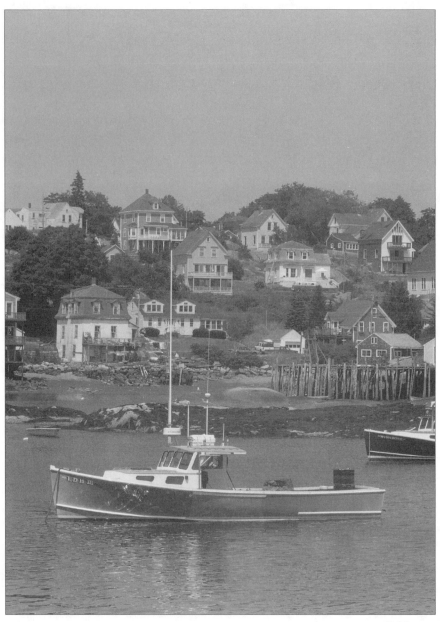

Stonington Harbor

THE
COAST OF MAINE
BOOK

A Complete Guide

Fourth Edition

Rick Ackermann and Kathryn Buxton

Berkshire House Publishers
Lee, Massachusetts

On the Cover and Frontispiece:
Front Cover: *Early morning at Pemaquid Light, Pemaquid Point, Maine;* photo © Paul Rezendes.
Frontispiece: *The harbor at Stonington, Little Dear Isle, Maine;* photo © Herb Swanson.
Back Cover: Authors' photo by Herb Swanson.

Excerpt on p.143 from
Calvin Trillin, *Alice, Let's Eat*
Ticknor & Fields, New York © 1989 Calvin Trillin

Excerpt on p.146 from Sarah Orne Jewett, *The Country of the Pointed Firs,* Houghton Mifflin, Boston

The Coast of Maine Book: A Complete Guide
Copyright © 1992, 1996, 1997, 1999 by Berkshire House Publishers
Cover and interior photographs © 1992, 1996, 1997, 1999 by credited photographers

Library of Congress Cataloging-in-Publication Data

Ackermann, Rick, 1948-

The coast of Maine book : a complete guide / Rick Ackermann and Kathryn Buxton. — 4th ed.
      p.   cm. — (The great destinations series, ISSN 1056-7968)
Includes bibliographical references (p.) and index.
ISBN 1-58157-006-6
  1. Maine—Guidebooks. 2. Atlantic Coast (Me.)—Guidebooks. I. Buxton, Kathryn, 1958-
II. Title. III. Series.
F17.3.A25   1999
917.4104'43—dc21   98-53100
                                          CIP

ISBN: 1-58157-006-6
ISSN: 1056-7968 (series)

Editor: Susan Minnich. Managing Editor: Philip Rich. Design and layout: Dianne Pinkowitz.
design for Great Destinations™ series: Janice Lindstrom. Cover design: Jane McWhorter.
Maps: Mirto Art Studios.

Berkshire House books are available at substantial discounts for bulk purchases by corporations and other organizations for promotions and premiums. Special personalized editions can also be produced in large quantities. For more information, contact:

Berkshire House Publishers
480 Pleasant St., Lee, MA 01238
800-321-8526
E-mail: info@berkshirehouse.com
Website: www.berkshirehouse.com

Manufactured in the United States of America

10 9 8 7 6 5 4 3 2

No complimentary meals or lodgings were accepted by the authors and reviewers in gathering information for this work.

Berkshire House Publishers'
Great Destinations™ travel guidebook series

Right on the money.

. . . a crisp and critical approach, for travelers who want to live like locals.

Great Destinations™ guidebooks are known for their comprehensive, critical coverage of regions of extraordinary cultural interest and natural beauty. The authors in this series are professional travel writers who have lived for many years in the regions they describe. Each title in this series is continuously updated with each printing, in order to insure accurate and timely information. All of the books contain over 100 photographs and maps.

Neither the publisher, the authors, the reviewers, nor other contributors accept complimentary lodgings, meals, or any other consideration (such as advertising) while gathering information for any book in this series.

Current titles available:
The Adirondack Book
The Berkshire Book
The Charleston, Savannah & Coastal Islands Book
The Chesapeake Bay Book
The Coast of Maine Book
The Hamptons Book
The Monterey Bay, Big Sur & Gold Coast Wine Country Book
The Nantucket Book
The Newport & Narragansett Bay Book
The Napa & Sonoma Book
The Santa Fe & Taos Book
The Sarasota, Sanibel Island & Naples Book
The Texas Hill Country Book
Wineries of the Eastern States

If you are traveling to, moving to, residing in, or just interested in any (or all!) of these enchanting regions, a **Great Destinations**™ guidebook is a superior companion. Honest and painstakingly critical, full of information only a local can provide, **Great Destinations**™ guidebooks give you all the practical knowledge you need to enjoy the best of each region. Why not own them all?

Contents

CHAPTER ONE
From the Ice Age to Lobster Rolls
HISTORY
1

CHAPTER TWO
How to Get Here and Get Around
TRANSPORTATION
19

CHAPTER THREE
Where the Beaches Are
SOUTH COAST
31

CHAPTER FOUR
Where the Rocky Coast Begins
MIDCOAST
113

CHAPTER FIVE
Where the Mountains Meet the Sea
DOWN EAST
194

CHAPTER SIX
Blueberry Barrens and the First Sunrise
EAST OF SCHOODIC
241

CHAPTER SEVEN
Practical Matters
INFORMATION
261

Acknowledgments

Over the years, family and neighbors have proved reliable scouts, telling us about a great restaurant here or a wonderful B&B there. The sum of their recommendations has been essential to this, the fourth edition of *The Coast of Maine Book.*

In particular, we'd like to thank Herb Swanson, our photographer, who is also a connoisseur of coastal fast-food joins. Also Wendy Keeler and Cynthia Hacinli for getting us off to a good start; Ken and Kathryn Buxton for their fingers on the pulse of Belfast and Camden; Barbara Ackermann for her birding advice; Shari and Aric Wauzzinski for liking Popham Beach; Kate Woodsome for her invaluable contributions; Mike White for his surfer's tips; Romaine Simenson, our island expert; Bill Sweet for his historical expertise; Deb Dalfonso, Bill Connor, Arthur Kirklian, Joan Ackermann, Elizabeth Edwardsen, Tim Beidel, and Greg Clement for their help in finding some of the best places to eat and stay on the coast; our dog Argos, who still knows a good beach when she sees one; and our daughter Jane, who has introduced us to a new class of childproof inns and restaurants.

Finally, we'd like to say thanks to Philip Rich, Susan Minnich, Carol Bosco Baumann, Mary Osak, and Jean Rousseau at Berkshire House. Philip, he's as goodnatured and patient an editor as two writers could hope for. Susan, thanks once again for being so dogged and thorough.

Introduction

Half of all Mainers vacation in the state. When they're not vacationing, they're getting away, in Maine, for the weekend. That's why so many cars in our Portland neighborhood have bike or ski racks on the back, an Old Town canoe or a sea kayak on top, and fishing gear, sail bags, extra battens, camping, or beach equipment (including lobster bib) in the trunk. We suspect many have several of the above ready and waiting to go at a moment's notice. Car-wise, it's hard to tell a Mainer from an out-of-stater.

Of course, vacationing is not a way of life suited to everybody. Some cars that pass through the state look as if the only thing that's ever been in them are people. Every year more than four times as many people as live in Maine visit Acadia National Park. Most of them, after a brief detour to L.L. Bean, go home again. And every year a small group of visitors decides to give up whatever it was they were doing and move here. Many open new restaurants, which is fine, since in addition to vacationing, Mainers love to eat. More than just a few of them are busy cooking up things as exciting as the best of what's served in much larger cities. Others among the newly relocated open bed & breakfasts or inns. Traveling the coast we have met an investment banker, a pilot, a state department official, a social worker, and a psychologist, all enjoying their new occupations. One woman, from Houston, had looked out her snow-covered window at sunset a few days earlier and cried. She said she cried not out of frustration with Maine's winter, which can be long, but because she was "so happy to be here."

She came for the same reason people as far back as the Abenaki Indians and European settlers came — for a better life. They came for the rocky coast, ocean storms, fog thick enough to stuff a pillow, wildflowers in spring, and vast sandy beaches at low tide. Visitors and new residents on Maine's coast come so that every day they can look out on the pen-and-ink lines of fish weirs in Johnson Bay off Lubec. They like watching the colors change during fall in the Camden Hills. They want to be able to cross-country ski the carriage paths in Acadia — one of the great off-season joys of the coast.

People are not only taken with the coastal Maine landscape and all it has to offer, but with the way of life. The state tourism office bottled this phenomenon with the slogan "Maine. The Way Life Should Be." — a phrase ridiculed among residents and recent transplants for its obviousness. Maine is a place people come to change — to slow down and try something new — and Mainers encourage this kind of behavior. People here are highly independent and extremely resourceful, and it is not rare to know someone who has done what may seem impossible — taken up mountain climbing at 80, started an opera company in a tiny seaside village, written a novel, or captured the coastal light on canvas.

Life here — and vacations — represent an ethic different from most other parts of the country. Small, family-run operations are the rule. Big shopping malls and chain restaurants are the exception (in fact, they are virtually non-existent east of Portland, the state's largest city). Shops, inns, and restaurants are run by individuals who are unremitting in their quest to offer good value. That comes from a particularly Yankee characteristic, which is to get the most out of something.

That's why almost everybody in Maine, rich or poor, knows two things: how to conduct a yard sale and how to shop at a yard sale. Someone's discarded sofa easily becomes someone else's treasured antique. Likewise, old wooden lobster boats or vintage friendship sloops, once popular coastal working boats, now are prized by weekend sailors, and sea captains' homes are made over into inns. Recycling and rejuvenation take on new meanings here.

Rick Ackermann and Kathryn Buxton
Portland, Maine

THE WAY THIS BOOK WORKS

ORGANIZATION

This book is divided into seven chapters, each with its own introduction. If you are interested in one chapter or another, you can turn to it directly and begin reading without losing a sense of continuity. You also can take the book with you on your travels and skip around, reading about the places you visit as you go. Or you can read the entire book through from start to finish. If you're interested in finding a place to eat or sleep, we suggest you first look over the restaurant and lodging charts in the Index (organized by area and price); then turn to the pages listed in the general index and read the specific entries for the places that most interest you.

The central chapters — Chapters 3–6 — each cover one of four regions of the coast: "South Coast," "Midcoast," "Down East and Acadia," and "East of Schoodic." (A map showing these regions appears at the end of the introduction and at the end of the book.) Sections within each of the four chapters cover lodging, dining, food purveyors, recreation, and shopping available along that part of the coast.

Some entries, most notably those in the lodging and dining sections, include specific information (telephone, address, hours, etc.) organized for easy reference in blocks in the left-hand column. The information here, as well as the phone numbers and addresses in the descriptions, were checked as close to publication as possible. Even so, details change with frustrating frequency. It's best to call ahead.

PRICES

For the same reason, we have avoided listing specific prices, preferring instead to indicate a range of prices. Lodging price codes are based on a per-room rate, double occupancy, in the high season. Low season rates are likely to be 20–40 percent less. Again, it's best to call.

Restaurant prices indicate the cost of an individual meal including appetizer, entree, and dessert, but not including cocktails, wine, tax, or tip. Restaurants with a prix-fixe menu are noted accordingly.

Lodging rates generally increase close to Memorial Day when the summer season begins, and they are highest from July 4 weekend through the fall foliage season in mid- to late October. Special packages are often available for two or more nights' stay, and frequently there are even better values during the off-season. If breakfast and/or dinner is included with the price of a room, we do not alter the rate category, we just note that the room rate includes one or more meals. These lodging rates exclude required room taxes or service charges.

Price Codes

	Lodging	*Dining*
Inexpensive	Up to $65	Up to $10
Moderate	$65 to $125	$10 to $20
Expensive	$125 to $180	$20 to $30
Very Expensive	$180 or more	$30 or more

Credit Cards are abbreviated as follows:

AE — American Express	DC — Diner's Club
CB — Carte Blanche	MC — Master Card
D — Discover Card	V — Visa

AREA CODE

There is one telephone area code for Maine: 207.

TOURIST INFORMATION

The best sources for year-round tourist information are: **www. visit maine.com, Maine Tourism Association** (P.O. Box 2300, Hallowell, ME 04347; 207-623-0363 in Maine; 800-633-9595 out-of-state and Canada; E-mail, metainfo@mainetourism.com), and the various chambers of commerce listed in Chapter Seven, *Information*.

WELCOME CANADIANS / BIENVENUE AUX CANADIENS

We hope this book will give Canadians an idea of all the good things there are to do on the Maine coast. We have kept our northern neighbors in mind and have tried to provide pertinent information.

Nous voulons que ce livre donne aux Canadiens une idée de tous les endroits où on peut s'amuser sur la côte du Maine. Nous apprécions la visite de nos voisins du nord, et nous essayons de leur fournir des renseignements pertinents sur cette partie du Maine. Il y a beaucoup d'aubergistes et de restaurateurs sur la côte qui parlent français. Si vous êtes en train de planifier un séjour sur la côte du Maine et vous aimeriez consulter quelqu'un qui peut vous renseigner en français, communiquez avec le Maine Tourism Association (P.O. Box 2300, Hallowell, ME 04347; 207-623-0363 au Maine; 800-633-9595 au Canada; www.visitmaine.com; E-mail, metainfo@maine-tourism.com). Ce service publie plusieurs brochures en français.

The
COAST OF MAINE
Book
A Complete Guide

CHAPTER ONE
From the Ice Age to Lobster Rolls
HISTORY

We'd like to welcome you to the fourth edition of *The Coast of Maine Book,* and to take a few sentences to update travelers on interesting developments, advances, changes, and "news" about life on the coast since we last wrote.

Case in point: the recent historical record says a great deal about Maine. Politically, the state continues to demonstrate its particularly bewildering brand of individualism that runs the gamut from salt-of-the-earth, pocket-book conservatism to slightly left of liberal. In the 1994 presidential race, a greater percentage of Mainers voted for H. Ross Perot than in any other state. In 1998, voters here elected the nation's first of two independent governors, Angus King. This is, we believe, also the only state where the Green Party has earned a place on the state ballot.

The state has set up shop on the information superhighway. The Maine web page offers a current listing of business opportunities, as well as some information from the state tourism office. Maine's internet address is **www.state.me.us.** If you are just looking for travel information, try **www.visitmaine.com.**

Above all, Maine remains a wonderful place to visit and live; one survey distinguished Maine as the safest state in the union (the crime rate here is virtually non-existent compared to more populous places to the south), while another found that this is one of the top ten healthiest places to live in the country. No wonder we like it so much.

Finally, travelers will find eating and drinking in Maine more healthful. In the spring of 1999, the state legistalture voted to ban smoking in Maine restaurants and bars. Bon appétit!

Long before Europeans discovered the New World, tribes of the Algonquin nation came every summer to the coast of Maine where the sun was tempered by cool ocean breezes. "Down East," as 19th-century sailors termed the land governed by the prevailing west winds, is a place to come back to. Mainers built and sailed the wooden ships that traded with the world and rode those westerly winds "Down East" to their homes on the Maine coast.

People still come here to cool off and to trade. Today, the major trading route connecting the Maine coast to the rest of the world has shifted inland to coastal Rte. 1. Tourism is second only to the paper industry in total revenues for the state. Visitors shop Maine's outlets and relax by its inlets. Many of the old working harbors have been transformed into pleasure harbors. Visitors from all over the world come to sail windjammers on Penobscot Bay, peep at

The village of Lubec near the border with Canada.

the autumn leaves on Rte. 182 north of Ellsworth, cross-country ski on the carriage roads in Acadia National Park, and bed and breakfast in old sea captains' homes. For many Canadians, the south coast of Maine is the closest beach.

What visitors find is a coast that has much in common with the Maine coast of the 19th century. Artists are still intent on capturing the region's fugitive colors. Mainers today have to work just as hard to make a living.

All Yankees, and especially those who live along Maine's coast, have a reputation for keeping to themselves. Mainers are a people of few well-chosen words — all delivered with an accent flat as a clam bed at low tide. Underneath this crusty exterior, they are adventurous, inquisitive, and have a great sense of humor, as Benedict Thielen discovered 30 years ago writing for *Holiday* magazine: "They never seem to look at you," he mentioned to an acquaintance. "Oh, they do, sideways, or when your back is turned," the man replied. "That fellow, he's probably off around the corner right now, looking at the license plate of your car."

The writer E. B. White once wrote to his wife, Katharine, about the apparent indifference he found frustrating but infinitely attractive. "Dear K, Santayana, whom I read on the train last night, holds out little hope for our achieving any satisfactory relationship with the Maine people." The Whites ended up spending the second half of their lives on the Blue Hill peninsula among these laconic people. Like the Whites, people "from away" find the coast a place they want to come back to year after year. Maine is not a fashionable place, but it is one where you find delicious traditions such as the four-decades-old lobster festival in Rockland. It's also a place to enjoy some of nature's most enduring pleasures, such as Ogunquit's broad sandy beach, Acadia National Park's rocky headlands, and the dramatic 18-foot tides at Cobscook Bay.

NATURAL HISTORY

TOPOGRAPHY OF MAINE

Visitors are astounded by the topography of the Maine coast. Enormous tides expose rocky headlands that rise abruptly from the ocean. Two thousand to three thousand islands dot its length; inlets and fingers of land provide infinite variety. To understand what forces created the "rocky coast of Maine," you have to look at its geologic past.

ROCKS OF THE ROCKY COAST

Sand and shingle beach at Roque Bluffs State Park.

Herb Swanson

According to the plate tectonics theory of continental drift, the European and North American tectonic plates began to collide about 450 million years ago. The impact caused the edges of both plates to buckle and crack as the ocean floor separating the two plates began to slide under the North American plate. Tons of rock were forced upward into huge mountains. Rivers of magma forced their way through cracks and formed volcanoes. In some places, magma pushed its way through cracks in the hardened granite crust to form what geologists call "black dikes." Today you can see black dikes cutting through the pink granite at Schoodic Point at the far eastern reach of Acadia National Park.

The geologic past is also evident in the makeup of Maine's islands. Look at the mostly long, skinny southern coastal islands, and you'll see the remnants of the mountains that were formed when the two tectonic plates pushed together and forced the coastline to crumple. Further up the coast, islands such as Monhegan and Mount Desert are distinctly rounded mounds. These were created when molten magma forced its way up through the plate and formed volcanoes.

The two plates continued to slide together, and, about 390 million years ago, the coastal lands' layers of sedimentary materials were transformed into metamorphic rock by the immense pressure and heat. The collision created a diverse collection of rock formations and minerals along the Maine coast —

sandstone, shale, and limestone in the south; shale, slate, and impure lime-stone in the north. The European and North American plates eventually began to drift apart, and 70 million years ago the Atlantic Ocean was formed. Today the continental plates continue to shift and the ocean to expand at the hardly perceptible rate of one inch every year.

THE DROWNED COAST

Roy Zalesky

Cadillac Mountain in Acadia National Park. At 1,530 feet, it is the tallest coastal mountain in the eastern United States and affords splendid views of the bay.

The most prominent feature of Maine's coast is a consequence of the Ice Age. Twenty thousand years ago great glaciers covered much of the northern hemisphere, including Maine. Weighed down by thousands of tons of ice, the coastal plains and many of the bordering mountains were forced downward. Water from the melting glaciers rushed into the ocean and the rising waters poured into the depressed valleys and lowlands of Maine, forming what is now called the drowned coast.

The glaciers have disappeared, and coastal lands have bounced back, at least partially, to their pre-glacial elevation. Still, much of Maine's coastal lowlands, marshes, and wide sandy beaches, part of a giant alluvial plain that once stretched the entire length of New England, now lie hidden by Gulf of Maine waters. The result of the lingering glacial depression is a meandering line where land meets water. The state's coastline stretches for 2500 miles from Kittery to Eastport — a distance that is only 225 direct miles or 290 miles by car. Several major rivers empty into the ocean in Maine: the Piscataqua at the Maine-New Hampshire border; the Saco River between Biddeford and Saco in the south; the Androscoggin between Brunswick and Topsham; the Kennebec at Bath; the Penobscot near Bucksport; and the St. Croix at the border between the U.S. and Canada.

The coast has hundreds of deepwater approaches and safe ports protected by thousands of islands. Some islands are small piles of rocks that appear at low tide. Others are larger, like Mount Desert Island, which is the second-largest island in New England. It has 17 mountains, several towns and villages, and the eastern United States' only fjord.

Major Bays of Maine

Casco	Dyer
Merrymeeting	Narraguagus
Sheepscot	Pleasant
Muscongus	Western
Penobscot (by far the largest)	Chandler
Isle au Haut	Englishman
Blue Hill	Machias
Union River	Cobscook
Frenchman	Passamaquoddy

THE ICY LABRADOR CURRENT

The Atlantic Ocean gives the coast much of its character. The waters off Maine's shore are kept cold by the icy Labrador Current that runs from the northeast, over the Grand Banks off Newfoundland, southwest past Nova Scotia, and through the Gulf of Maine before veering east off Cape Cod.

The ocean is also responsible for two other Maine coast phenomena: fog and tide. Fog, which frequently enshrouds the coast and islands between May and September, occurs when warm moist air traveling overland from the southwest encounters cooler ocean temperatures. The air is cooled and moisture in the air condenses to form low-lying clouds — or fog. Maine's tidal range increases dramatically as you head east: the tide at Kittery is about nine feet; at Eastport it reaches nearly twenty feet as the sea rushes in and out of the Bay of Fundy's narrow confines.

VERY BIG PINES

The coast of Maine and its islands are home to more than 300 types of birds, which make the coast a birder's paradise. It's not unusual to see an eagle on Mount Desert Island or further Down East. Herring gulls are common, as are terns, great cormorants, snowy egrets, blue herons, sandpipers, osprey, and Canada geese. Mergansers dive in the ocean for fish. Teals swim on the rivers. Puffins, nicknamed "sea parrots," and once near extinction, nest on Matinicus. Visitors also frequently meet with other Maine wildlife, including black bears, deer, and moose.

Hundreds of wildflowers are found along the coast and its islands, including the spiky purple wild lupine, white Queen Anne's lace, yellow goldenrod, orange Turk's-cap lily, pink rhododendron and laurel, and pale green jack-in-the-pulpit. Wild blueberries stain the hillsides and coastal mountaintops from Ellsworth to Eastport (in the fall, the blueberry barrens Down East turn bright red).

There are 76 species of trees in Maine. Softwoods like the white pine, balsam fir, white spruce, and hemlock account for only 14 species, but make up more than 89 percent of the forest. And, even today 80 percent of the state is forested.

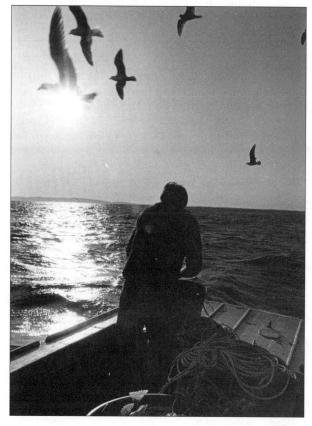

Fishing the rich waters Down East. The barrel contains sea urchins, one of the many edible forms of sea life found off the coast of Maine.

State Development Office

The most famous of the state's trees is the white pine. Maine takes its nickname, "The Pine Tree State," from the tall and stately coniferous tree that grew in abundance near the shore when the first Europeans arrived in the 1600s. The British crown government had all pines more than 74 feet tall with a diameter 24 inches and greater marked with the King's Arrow and reserved for use in the making of masts for his navy. The colonists often — in defiance of the crown — exploited the white pine for their own purposes, and in Pre-Revolutionary Maine homes you often could find broad white pine beams, floor boards, and clapboards. Later, paper manufacturers cut the pine for use in pulp mills. As a result, few of these great trees, many of which measured 6 feet around and stood 200 feet tall, remain today. The pine that do exist are not the abundant virgin forests the early explorers saw lining the coast, but second and third growths on land once cleared by coastal farmers.

The balsam fir is an easily recognized denizen of the coastal forests. It is the tree seen most often growing in the thin topsoil on the islands and near the coast. On a cool, moist day in late summer or early fall you can smell its fragrant aroma as you drive or walk through a grove of balsams.

The white birch grows in the state's northern reaches and along the easternmost shore. Coastal Native Americans used to make their canoes from birch

---

Tidal Pools

The importance of tidal pools cannot be underestimated. They are a miniature saltwater empire, and reveal a great deal about life in the ocean at large. The food chain in a tidal pool is much the same as it is in the ocean. Hermit crabs take over empty snail shells and dine on smaller animals. Clams bury themselves in the sand and at low tide you can see airways leading down to their hiding places. Mussels and barnacles cling to rocks and ocean debris with periwinkles, starfish, kelp, rockweed, Irish moss, and hundreds of other plants and animals.

The Maine coast has an abundance of tidal pools, from the small puddles left at low tide to Biddeford Pool, which is a mile in diameter. Another great place to

 observe the ocean community at work is at Two Lights Park in Cape Elizabeth, where the receding waters expose hundreds of small saltwater pools and the marine organisms that make them hop.

Discovering nature in a tidal stream, Washington County.

Herb Swanson

bark. Coast white cedar and butternut is found in York County, but as a rule not further north. Maples and fast-growing aspens are abundant. The American elm was once so plentiful around the city of Portland that it was called "Forest City." The trees, which had survived two devastating fires that raged through the city, fell prey to Dutch elm disease during the middle of this century.

Maine's waters are home to hundreds of species, including cod, haddock, flounder, whiting, yellowtail, pollock, lobster, mussels, oysters, and clams. Wild Atlantic salmon occasionally are found in the waters of Merrymeeting Bay near Bath. More often the salmon one finds has been farm-raised in aqua-culture pens near Vinalhaven and Eastport. Whales also frequent the coast. Pilot whales sometimes become stranded near the South Coast's beaches, because they follow squid too far into shore. Humpbacks and finbacks visit late in summer after warmer water temperatures lure the fish they feed on close to shore. Seals are as numerous as boats in many Maine inlets.

SOCIAL HISTORY

RED PAINT AND OYSTER SHELL PEOPLE

Remains from the first known inhabitants of Maine date from approxi-mately 4000 B.C. to 3000 B.C., well after the glacier's ice began to recede from the coast. These early Native Americans were well developed in their ability to make and use implements. Spears, knives, and fire-starting tools fashioned from stone indicate that the first known human residents of Maine were hunters who eventually evolved into farmers and fishermen. Found among their remains were heavy woodworking tools, including adzes, gouges, and axes. They had elaborate rituals, including the practice of burying their dead in graves lined with a mix of clay and iron oxide. For that they have been named the "Red Paint People." To collect the iron oxide, they had to travel inland to Katahdin, Maine's highest peak. Their grave sites have been found near Blue Hill and Ellsworth, as well as at several locations inland.

The Red Paint People have provided the basis for a great deal of speculation and romanticizing among historians and archaeologists. For a long time it was believed they were a lost race washed away by a huge tidal wave or erased by some other natural catastrophe. While scholars speculated, no archaeological record was uncovered to support the theory. Today most historians believe the Red Paint People are ancestors of the Native American tribes Europeans found when they first came to Maine. It is believed that their burial rituals — like their reliance on wildlife and game for food — changed with time.

The next archaeological record of Maine's native population occurs around A.D. 80 to 350. Giant piles of oyster and clam shells were left in waste heaps near rich oyster-breeding grounds. The largest of these middens, or collections of everyday "kitchen" waste, was called the "Whaleback Heap," and was removed in the 1900s. Today several smaller middens remain, measuring up to 400 feet in length and almost 25 feet high. They can be seen near Damariscotta on Rte. 1 in the Midcoast region.

Few Native American artifacts have been found among the oyster, clam, and mussel shell mounds. The implements that were discovered — spoons of copper and well-formed pottery — indicate that the Oyster Shell People, like their predecessors the Red Paint People, were sophisticated in their use of tools and natural resources.

THE FIRST SUMMER VISITORS

Members of the Micmac tribe in Bar Harbor at the turn of the century.

Courtesy of Penobscot Marine Museum

By the time of the Oyster Shell People, life had developed a rather peaceful rhythm for Maine's natives. They summered in relatively large colonies on the coast and sometimes on its islands. When the cold weather arrived, they dispersed to smaller communities inland. That seasonal way of life was carried on by the Oyster Shell People's successors, the Abenakis, or "people of the dawn."

The Abenakis, a branch of the Algonquin nation, were divided into four distinct tribes: the Androscoggins, the Kennebecs, the Penobscots, and the Passamaquoddies. In summer they tended gardens of beans, squash, and corn. They also picked wild berries and harvested and dried fish and shellfish. During the winter they hunted game, fished the rivers and inland lakes and, as winter turned to spring, made maple syrup.

When the Europeans "discovered" the New World in the 15th century, historians estimate there were approximately one million Native Americans living in North America. Some 3,000 of the more fortunate of those — the Abenakis —lived along Maine's coastal region.

FROM AWAY

A bout A.D. 1000 Vikings may or may not have sailed down Maine's coast. They even may have landed, but contrary to popular opinion, there is no proof they did.

The first European documented to have landed on the Maine coast was an Italian in the service of an English king during the late 1400s. King Henry VII hired Italian navigator and explorer John Cabot (his unAnglicized surname was "Caboto") to sail up and down the northeastern seaboard and explore endless rivers to find a passage to the Indies. All Cabot found was dense forest, much of it in Maine, but he drew a map later used by England as the basis for its claim to North America.

After Cabot, the exploration of the land was left mostly to the French. They were not only interested in treasure, but also in the establishment of a New France. French King Francis I hired another Italian explorer, Giovanni da Verrazano, to explore and chronicle the prospects of the new world. Although Verrazano reached Maine's coast in 1524, he had no great interest in what he found. On a subsequent trip Verrazano was eaten by natives on a beach in Guadeloupe.

Maine also held little attraction for the Spanish explorer Gomez, who arrived one year later. Nor did it promise enough riches to hold the interests of several other explorers who set ashore here during the 1500s. The Frenchman Jean Allefonsce did stay long enough to explore a cape and river he called "Oranbega," which in native Abenaki means "stretch of quiet water between two rapids." He probably described the land near the mouth of the Penobscot River.

Sometime during the 1500s, "Norumbega" achieved notoriety in Europe as a city filled with precious minerals and gems and inhabited by wealthy, regal Indians. One of the first to write extensively about Norumbega was David Ingram, an Englishman who in 1568 sailed to the New World on a pirate ship. He was left ashore in the Gulf of Mexico, and claimed to have walked to Maine, where he said he saw the fabled city. He found a ride home on a French trading ship and wrote a book documenting his adventure and perpetuating the myth.

Several other Frenchmen came and went, but the team of Samuel de Champlain, Pierre du Gast, and the Baron de Poutrincourt left the era's most notable mark. In 1604, after Champlain and du Gast already had spent considerable time exploring the Atlantic coast, they established a settlement with de Poutrincourt on an island at the mouth of the St. Croix River (which now forms the border between Maine and Canada). While his partners built their new town, Champlain toured the nearby coast. He sailed into what is now known as Frenchman Bay, saw an island with ancient treeless mountains and named it *L'Isle des Monts Deserts*, or Mount Desert Island. Today it is the most visited spot in all of Maine.

A WEALTH OF FISH

Ironically, European fishermen looking to fill their nets had been rummaging about the Gulf of Maine for years. They camped ashore for months at places such as Pemaquid Point, drying their catch and co-existing peacefully with the Abenakis. These fishermen didn't keep records. Finding a good fishing hole is not something a smart fisherman boasts about, and the Gulf of Maine may have been the best fishing spot in the known world. In 1604, Champlain claims to have met one industrious boat captain along the coast who had made more than 40 fishing trips across the Atlantic. By the 1600s more than 300 fishing boats were harvesting Maine fish to feed Spain, Italy, France, England, Portugal, and Scandinavia.

In 1605, Captain George Waymouth explored the New England coast. Returning home, he convinced King James I of England of what the French already knew: this was a region worth more than gold; it was worth developing. To make the king feel a part of the exploration, Waymouth kidnapped five Native Americans and brought them with him to England. This did not endear the English to the Native Americans. More of that later. The king backed Waymouth's bid for future colonization.

FRENCH AND ENGLISH SETTLERS

The French and English were eager to colonize the coast, although the French at first were less aggressive than the British. The French tended to learn the languages and try to fit in with the local tribes in order to foster a profitable fur trade. A few Frenchmen came to spread their religion. In 1613, nine years after Champlain gave Mount Desert its name, a group of Jesuits established a religious community there.

One month later, the British razed the Mount Desert settlement and set the Jesuits out to sea. This marked the beginning of a long and bloody feud between the two nations. The region that is now Maine was, in fact, part of two overlapping territorial claims established by both nations. The territory played heavily in the struggle for supremacy that continued until the Peace of Paris in 1763, when France gave up its claim to the vast timberlands, excellent deepwater harbors, and potential fur trade.

DREAMS FOR "THE MAIN"

In 1606, James I granted a charter for southern Maine to the Plymouth Company. In 1607, the same year the British established a permanent settlement at Jamestown, Virginia, a group of British settlers established the Popham Colony (they called it St. George) at the mouth of the Kennebec, in what is today Phippsburg. This was the start of British colonization in New England (the Popham Colony preceded the settlement at Plymouth,

Massachusetts, by 13 years). Although the colonists endured only one long and unusually harsh winter, this is where Maine's famed shipbuilding history began. In 1608 the colonists built the fifty-foot pinnace *Virginia* to take them back to England. The *Virginia* was much hardier than the colonists who had built it; it sailed the Atlantic for many years.

The first permanent European settlements in Maine were at Monhegan in 1622, Saco in 1623 and Agamenticus (later York) in 1624. In 1629 the Pilgrims of the Plymouth Colony in Massachusetts established a trading post at Bagaduce, on the Penobscot peninsula. From there they sent their English sponsors furs and other goods to pay off the debt for their New World voyage. The French didn't like the English being in what they considered their territory. Forty years later Baron de St. Castin took it by force.

In 1635 King Charles I of England, assuming it was his to give, gave Maine to Sir Ferdinando Gorge and named him "Lord of New England." Sir Gorge chose Agamenticus, which had grown into a small village, as the center of his empire. Five years later, he named it after himself, Gorgeana. Sir Gorge's hopes to develop "the main" — or the mainland and later "Maine" — were never realized. His heirs sold out his dream in 1677, and Gorgeana was reorganized as the town of York.

PRELUDE TO THE FRENCH AND INDIAN WARS

Uneasy relations between the French and English continued for years before formal war was declared. The coastal lands of Maine, particularly those east of the Penobscot River, were in a fairly constant state of dispute.

Although the French controlled most of the area east of the Penobscot, the English had managed to establish two trading centers there — one at Machias and one at Penobscot village. The French raided the posts in 1634 and 1635, and the English retook them in 1654. In 1664, the Duke of York was granted the lands between Pemaquid Point and the St. Croix River. In 1667, the English King Charles II surrendered his claim on lands including Nova Scotia, Acadia, and Penobscot to the French under the Treaty of Breda. At that time, Baron de St. Castin established himself in Penobscot and proceeded to protect France's interest while trading with both the English and the Native Americans. He remained there until Sir Edmund Andros, the governor of New York and Massachusetts, forcibly took the town for the English.

Official hostilities between the two countries lasted from 1675 to 1763. In the British colonies it was known as the Indian War. Saco, Scarborough, and Casco were the first towns to be attacked in September 1675. The Native Americans perhaps were still angry with Waymouth's kidnapping of their five kinsmen 70 years earlier. Certainly they were threatened by the English colonials' encroachment on their land. They sided with the French, who largely had left them and their ancestral claim to the land alone. The acrimonious 88-year struggle preoccupied the small native and colonial populations of Maine and

Archaeological dig done in the late 19th century under the direction of antiquarian John Henry Cartland uncovered British officers' quarters at Fort William Henry, Pemaquid Point, first built in 1692.

R.L. Bradley. Courtesy, Maine Historic
Preservation Committee

was the reason why colonization nearly halted during that time. Following the defeat of the French at Quebec in 1759, English colonists began to settle on the coast in larger numbers.

By 1790 the few Native Americans who had survived the French and Indian Wars were made wards of the Commonwealth and confined to two reservations — one at Old Town, near Bangor, and the second at Perry, near Eastport. They had no documents on which to base their claims to the land, no guns, and were highly susceptible to diseases that had crossed the ocean with the Europeans. "In the end," writes historian James MacGregor Burns, "the less numerous and less sophisticated [Native American] society crumbled before the aggressive expansion of history's largest migration."

In 1953, Native Americans were given voting rights. In 1977 the Penobscot, Passamaquoddy, and Maleseet Indians sued the state claiming that all treaties granting land to Maine were null and void, because they were never ratified by Congress. They asked for $25 billion and 12.5 million acres of land. In 1980 they received a settlement of $81.5 million, but no land.

THE REVOLUTIONARY WAR

In the mid-18th century, Maine was still very much a part of Massachusetts. Whereas Bostonians threw tea into the harbor, a Falmouth (now known as Portland) mob seized the Imperial tax stamps in 1765. Still, many residents along the coast of northern Massachusetts were actively doing business with the British. Although Boston was the capital of Maine, Mainers valued above all their independence from London and Boston.

Once the Revolutionary War started, Mainers refused to ship their highly prized masts to the British fleet. The Royal Navy bombarded the city then called Falmouth and burned much of it to the ground. Before that, zealous Maine patriots claimed the first naval victory of the war when in 1775 colonists captured the British cutter *Margaretta* in Machias Bay, a battle James Fenimore Cooper called the "Lexington of the seas."

The first colonial warship, *Ranger*, was built at Kittery in 1777. Two years later the colonies suffered a disastrous setback when 19 armed ships and 24 transports with more than 1,300 soldiers and marines were lost to the British at Castine. At the war's end in 1783 the Treaty of Versailles established Maine's most easterly border at the St. Croix River.

POSTWAR PROSPERITY AND THE WAR OF 1812

After the Revolutionary War, Maine prospered and grew. The era of logging began. Maine became a center for production of lumber for houses, barrels for trade, masts for ships, and wood for fuel. Ships from safe harbors all along the coast established trade routes around the world. Maine began to think about breaking away from Massachusetts.

Then France declared war on England in 1793. Short of men, England's navy began boarding American ships and impressing sailors with naval duty under pretense they were still subjects. For this reason President Jefferson finally ordered an embargo in 1807 disallowing trade with any foreign country. The embargo was particularly tough on the people and ports of Maine.

Many of the region's maritime businesses turned to smuggling. Eastport, just south of Canada, became the busiest port in the country. When the United States went to war against England in 1812, Mainers at first offered little resistance to the British, who were their best customers. People along the coast also continued trading with their own government. Worse, for the British, they continued building ships used by the American navy. The British set up a blockade and captured Castine and the surrounding towns.

With the Treaty of Ghent in 1814, the war ended as did England's blockade. The people of Maine started thinking again about breaking off from Massachusetts. In 1820, Maine was granted statehood as part of the Missouri Compromise. The separation papers were signed at the Jamestown Tavern in Freeport (the tavern still operates today down the street from L.L. Bean). The 23rd state to join the union established its current-day capital inland at Augusta 12 years later.

WOODEN SHIPS

"There are still any number of working lobster boats, plenty of yacht yards, and even a few deep-sea fishermen. . . . These are inadequate compensations, though, for anyone brought up in the knowledge of Maine's deepwater supremacy, those great times when Maine skippers were admired from the

Elbe to the Amazon, and Maine-built ships were the world's criteria of seaworthiness. In those days, local prodigies like the stupendous six-masted schooner *Wyoming* were legends of the sea," wrote Jan Morris in *New England Monthly* magazine.

By 1850, Maine was considered the preeminent shipbuilding capital of America. By 1860, one fifth of the state's population were mariners, 759 of them masters of ships. Ten percent of the nation's deepwater shipmasters lived in Searsport at the top of Penobscot Bay. Bath, midway up the coast, was the United States' fifth busiest port. A little farther up the coast, Wiscasset was the busiest international port north of Boston.

Maine's romantic era of wooden shipbuilding ended with a complex set of economic events that came just before the Civil War. The invention of ironclad ships didn't help. Foreign trade moved to other ports. Maine businessmen began looking for other industries to bank on; they didn't have to look far. Forests that once supplied timbers for masts and lithe hulls now are devoted almost entirely to the production of paper.

Fisheries were among the industries that flourished, with fishermen reaping a bounty from the cold waters off northern New England, including the fish-rich St. George's Bank. At its peak in 1902, the state landed and processed 242 million pounds of cod, cusk, hake, haddock, ocean perch, mackerel, halibut, pollock, crabs, clam, shrimp, mussels, lobster, herring, and sardines. Canneries built during the height of this fishing boom, now abandoned, are still in evidence from Yarmouth to Eastport. The canning industry fell on hard times. The nation's hunger for canned herring and sardines slaked with the advent of refrigeration and the easy transport of fresh fish at the turn of the century. Other popular whitefish species, such as cod, halibut, haddock, and pollock, have become scarcer as fishermen have overfished the waters off Maine's coast.

ARTISTS "DISCOVER" MAINE'S COAST

Painting the landscape near Somesville on Mount Desert Island.

Herb Swanson

In 1844, Thomas Cole, founder of the Hudson River School of painting, visited Bar Harbor, loved what he saw and spread the word around the art community. He also told his wealthy patrons. More than 200 lavish summer "cottages" were built. Grand hotels appeared. Developers were quick to claim Mount Desert Island's thick fogs were "as healthy for the body as basking in the sun." Bar Harbor became as well known as Newport, Rhode Island.

The Maine Almanac, compiled by the *Maine Times*, reports that in 1870 "Tourists begin arriving in Maine." Not only did they come to see Maine's rocky coast, they came to see and be near the rich people who lived on the coast. Then in 1912 Leon Leonwood Bean invented the Maine Hunting Shoe, an ugly duckling of a shoe, half-leather, half-rubber that nevertheless has made many a hunter happy. "L.L.," as Freeport residents and shop clerks still call him, might as well have invented shopping. The shoe, and the store that grew up around it, eventually turned the little village of Freeport into the second most popular place in Maine.

THE BIRTH OF ACADIA

The most visited place in Maine was also being established about the same time. A group of wealthy Mount Desert "rusticators" decided to donate large parcels of land to be used for a national park. Today Acadia is a public

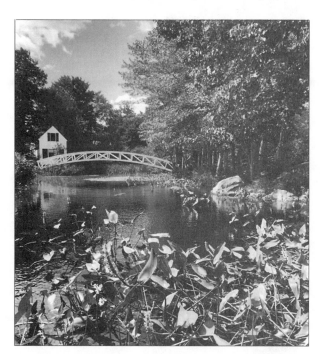

Somesville on Mount Desert Island.

Herb Swanson

toe-hold on a coast that is 98 percent privately owned. In 1947 much of Bar Harbor was destroyed in a forest fire. The French paper *Le Figaro* mistakenly reported the peasants of Maine had struck a blow against feudalism. The town's year-round residents did not like being called peasants.

The fact is there are no aristocrats in Maine. It is a place where millionaires and lobstermen — Yankees who above all value self-reliance — talk about politics, the weather, and their boats over pie and coffee in homespun diners. The beauty of the coast and the ocean is considered more important to the people who live and visit here than what is being worn on the streets of Boston or New York. "We are hardly fashionable," wrote Frances Fitzgerald, whose family members have been longtime summer residents of Northeast Harbor, in the August 1989 *Vogue.* "You might say we are consistent to the point of atavism."

CHAPTER TWO
How to Get Here and Get Around
TRANSPORTATION

Sections of coastal U.S. Rte. 1 in Maine, which today runs from Kittery to Fort Kent by way of Rockland, Ellsworth, and Machias, follow ancient Native American trails. Settlers marked the trails during the 1600s and named the resulting road the King's Highway. The route first was used by mail couriers traveling from Boston to Machias; later, as settlements grew up along the coast, the public highway was traversed by horse-drawn vehicles.

Herb Swanson

Swans Island Ferry leaving from Bass Harbor on Mount Desert Island.

The first stagecoach began operating between Portland and Portsmouth in 1787. The 90-mile journey took three days. Keep that slow crawl in mind as you're creeping across the Carlton Bridge east of Bath. (Later in this chapter we will tell you about some of the most famous bottlenecks along the coast, including the Carlton Bridge; we'll also suggest ways to avoid them.)

Despite the early full-fledged "highway," most of the coast was serviced by roads that were muddy and impassable during much of the year. Because this is a coast, the preferred method of travel then was by sea; ships and shipping were the industries that made Maine.

By the 1850s, 246 sailing vessels and 12 steamships called regularly on the port of Portland while 31 different railway lines carrying lumber and passengers crisscrossed the state. At the turn of the century electric trolleys carried tourists from Boston up the coast to Kennebunkport and Bar Harbor.

With the creation of the Interstate Highway System during the 1950s, suddenly half the populations of the United States and Canada were within a day's drive of the Maine coast. Today, most visitors come by highway.

The biggest change on Maine's transportation scene since we last wrote is a state-of-the-art electronic toll taking system on the *Maine Turnpike*. Hopes are it will help eliminate toll booth bottlenecks on busy summer days. The turnpike will soon have a *new exit for the Portland Jetport*, the state's largest and busiest airport. It is likely it will be completed within the year and before the next edition of this guide is due.

The Bluenose no longer makes daily runs in season between Bar Harbor and Nova Scotia. In its place is *The Cat*, a sleek new, high speed ferry that travels the route in a fraction of the time.

Plans for eliminating one frequent traveler's jam spot, on *Carlton Bridge over the Kennebec River in Bath*, are underway. A new, wider bridge is being built, but probably will not be completed until our next edition, so be forewarned. The traffic there can truly challenge your patience, particularly when the shift ends at the Bath Iron Works shipyard. Check out "Shortcuts" at the end of this chapter where we show how to avoid the bridge altogether.

In other transportation news, the train still doesn't come to Portland but local businesses, individuals and the Maine Department of Transportation continue to lay the rhetorical rail line that will bring an extension of the *Amtrak* line to the southern coast of Maine and link Portland and points south to Boston. Reports are that despite cutbacks in Amtrak's budget, the train will stop in Portland — eventually.

Finally, we'd like to mention that smoking is no longer allowed on *Casco Bay Lines*, the ferry service that connects Portland to the nearby islands. Ahh, the island air feels cleaner already.

TRANSPORTATION TODAY

Airports at Boston, Portland, and Bangor service domestic and international airlines with direct flights from Canada and Europe. Smaller airports, including Rockland and Bar Harbor, serve as connecting points for air travelers. Passenger train service to Maine ended during the 1950s, and as we mentioned at the beginning of this chapter, the battle continues to open an extension of Amtrak that would connect Portland with Boston and New York. Car ferries run regularly between the maritime provinces of Canada and Bar Harbor and Portland, including the new high speed Cat out of Bar Harbor.

GETTING TO THE COAST

BY CAR

From Connecticut, New York, New Jersey and South: I-95 goes right across the Piscataqua River separating New Hampshire and Maine and into Kittery, the first and oldest town on the coast.

From New York: I-95 runs along the coast of Connecticut, up through Providence, Boston, and Portsmouth. For a more direct route take I-95 to New Haven, I-91 north to Hartford, I-84 northeast until you get on the Mass. Pike at the Sturbridge entrance. Take the Westborough exit and follow I-495 northeast to where it joins I-95, just south of the New Hampshire border.

From Boston: Although this route adds a few more miles, it is faster than fighting your way up Rte. 1. Take I-93 north to Rte. 128 east until it rejoins I-95. On the way home there's also the added benefit of saving the Tobin Bridge toll — and avoiding traffic.

From Montreal: AAA recommends you take Rte. 10 to Magog; 55 south to the international border just north of Derby Line, Vermont. Pick up I-91 at the border and follow to Rte. 2 in St. Johnsbury. Continue east on Rte. 2 through Gorham, New Hampshire, and on to Bethel, Maine.

If your destination is the Midcoast or South Coast region, pick up Rte. 26 in Bethel and follow to Portland.

For the Down East/Acadia and East of Schoodic regions, continue on Rte. 2 from Bethel to I-95 near Newport, Maine, and follow to Bangor. From there you can take Alternate Rte. 1 to Stockton Springs and Belfast. Or you can take Rte. 1 south to Ellsworth and points east.

From Quebec City: Take Rte. 73 to Rte. 173 and the border, about 10 miles south of Armstrong. Pick up Rte. 201 at the border and follow all the way to Skowhegan, Maine. To access the South Coast and Midcoast regions, continue on Rte. 201 to Waterville where you pick up I-95 south. If you're headed to the Midcoast or Down East, pick up Rte. 2 east of Skowhegan. It connects with I-95 near Newport, Maine, and goes to Bangor. From there you can take Alternate Rte. 1 to Stockton Springs and Belfast. Or you can take Rte. 1 south to Ellsworth and points east.

From Saint John or Fredericton: Take Rte. 1 from St. John to the international border at St. Stephen, then south to Calais, Maine. Continue on Rte. 1 toward Machias and points south. Rte. 190 in Perry veers off toward Eastport. An alternate route to the Midcoast and South Coast regions is to follow Rte. 1 to Rte. 9 near Calais. Follow Rte. 9 to Bangor.

From Toronto: You have the choice of traveling north or south of Lake Ontario. Both routes take approximately the same amount of time. The southern route is super highways — and tolls — most of the way. The northern route is smaller roads and no tolls.

Traveling north around the lake, take Rte. 401 east to Cornwall, just north of the international border. Pick up Rte. 37 in Rooseveltown, New York, and follow that east to Malone. Take Rte. 11 East to Swanton, Vermont, where you get onto I-89 south. Take this highway to Montpelier. Pick up Rte. 2 east and follow all the way through St. Johnsbury on to Bethel, Maine.

If your destination is in the Midcoast or South Coast region, pick up Rte. 26 in Bethel and follow to Portland.

For the Down East/Acadia and East of Schoodic regions, continue on Rte. 2

from Bethel to I-95 near Newport, Maine, and follow to Bangor. From there you can take Alternate Rte. 1 to Stockton Springs and Belfast. Or you can take Rte. 1 south to Ellsworth and points east.

Traveling south around Lake Ontario, take the QEW to the international border. Take 190 through Niagara Falls, New York, to I-90. Follow I-90 to the connection with the Mass. Pike. Take the Mass. Pike to the Westborough exit and follow I-495 northeast to where it joins I-95, just south of the New Hampshire border.

BY BUS

*G*reyhound (800-231-2222 or www.greyhound.com) will take you as far as Boston, but from there **Vermont Transit** (207-772-6587 or 800-451-3292) goes as far north as Bar Harbor. From Boston, the bus stops in Portsmouth, NH; Portland, Brunswick, Lewiston, Augusta, Waterville, Bangor, and Bar Harbor. Sticking to the coast, **Concord Trailways** (207-828-1151 or 800-639-3317 or www.concordtrailways.com) leaves from Boston for Portland, Brunswick, Bath, Wiscasset, Damariscotta, Waldoboro, Rockland, Camden, Rockport, Lincolnville, Belfast, Searsport, and Bangor. Concord also offers an express bus from Boston to Bangor with one stop in Portland. There is no direct bus link to points in Canada.

BY PLANE

If you are not traveling by car, you most likely will arrive in Maine via plane. There are major airports in Portland, Augusta, and Bangor, all with connecting flights to smaller airports in Rockland and Bar Harbor. Many choose to fly into Boston's Logan Airport, only 1.5 hours to Kittery and 2.5 hours to Portland by car. All of the large airports are served by the major airlines. In addition, there are several small coastal and island airports with independent air services that have connecting regular and charter flights.

Augusta State Airport — 207-626-2306; Continental Connection.

Bangor International Airport — 207-947-0384; Business Express, Continental Express, Delta, Northwest, US Airways Express.

Hancock County/Bar Harbor Airport, Trenton (near Bar Harbor) — 207-667-7329; Continental Connection.

Knox County Regional Airport, Owls Head (near Rockland) — 207-594-4131; Continental Connection.

Portland International Jetport — 207-774-7301; Business Express, Continental, Continental Express, Delta, United, US Airways.

Maine Turnpike

To find out what the weather or traffic is like on the turnpike, call 800-675-PIKE. Following is a list of Maine Turnpike interchanges and their numbers.

Exit No.	Location
1	Kittery, York
2	Ogunquit/Wells
3	Kennebunk
4	Biddeford
5	Old Orchard, Saco
6	Scarborough
6A	Portland/I-295
7	South Portland
8	Portland/Westbrook
9	Falmouth Spur, Freeport, Yarmouth
10	Portland North
11	Gray
12	Auburn
13	Lewiston
14	Gardiner
End	Augusta

GETTING AROUND THE COAST OF MAINE

BY CAR

There are three ways to drive up the coast: the fast way on I-95; the medium-fast way on U.S. Rte. 1; and the slow-and-easy way on smaller state highways and roads that often turn out to be the fastest of all. Which route you take depends on your destination — or how serendipitous you want to be.

One of the best ways of exploring coastal waters.

Tom Hindman

MAINE ACCESS

The chart below gives miles and approximate driving times from the following cities to Portland:

City	Time	Miles
Albany	5.5 hours	237
Boston	2.5 hours	109
Hartford	4 hours	200
Montreal	6 hours	255
New York	7 hours	317
Philadelphia	9.5 hours	424
Quebec	6.5 hours	278
St. John	7 hours	309
Toronto	14 hours	621
Washington, D.C.	12.5 hours	557

The chart below gives you miles and approximate driving times from the following cities to Bangor.

City	Time	Miles
Montreal	7.25 hours	306
Quebec	5.75 hours	236
St. John	3 .5 hours	163
Toronto	13.25 hours	609
Yarmouth	19 hours	850
Boston	5.5 hours	249
New York	9 hours	452

The three most-visited spots in Maine and on the coast are: Acadia National Park, L.L. Bean in Freeport and Old Orchard Beach. Depending on your intentions and schedule, you may wish to see — or avoid — all three.

Acadia is one of the most beautiful parks in the national park system. To get to Acadia, take Rte. 1 or Rte. 1A to Ellsworth, which is in the center of the Down East/Acadia region. From Ellsworth take Rte. 3 to Bar Harbor. The park is less than a mile from Bar Harbor. Bar Harbor is 211 miles from Kittery, 122 miles from Eastport, and 46 miles from Bangor. The portion of Acadia on the Isle au Haut can be reached by ferry from Stonington. Most of Acadia's 5 million yearly visitors speed up or down I-95 to Augusta or Bangor before heading coastward along Rte. 3 or Rte. 1A. Once they arrive, they drive the famed Park Loop Road, a 20-mile winding road through the 35,000 acre park, which culminates at the top of 1,530-foot Cadillac Mountain with views of Blue Hill, Penobscot, and Frenchman Bay. In recent years, the number of vehicles on the loop has been so heavy that there have been traffic jams.

To reach Freeport, most visitors opt for Exit 17 or Exit 19 off I-95 (the coastal extension that begins as Rte. 295 in South Portland and leads to Topsham before rejoining the Maine Turnpike). The signs from the highway lead directly into Freeport, home of L.L. Bean and a growing community of factory outlets.

To get to Old Orchard Beach, most travelers take Exit 5 off I-95, which leads to Rte. 5 and Old Orchard Beach. The town is home to a seven-mile long beach — one of the state's most significant sand beaches and the closest to Canada. During July more than 80 percent of the vacationers in Old Orchard Beach are French Canadian.

Then there is the rest of the coast. A small road sign leading off Rte. 1 on the right reads "Friendship." The whole Penobscot peninsula gets a similar simple sign or two. If you opt to heed one of these signs and turn off — and deciding which one or two to take can be the hard part, since any one could be considered a vacation destination — most likely you will find other tourists. You won't find nearly as many tourists as you will find in Acadia, Freeport, and Old Orchard Beach. You could also find a place like Jonesport, where fishermen's houses are piled around the waterfront like lobster traps.

The best way to see the area is by car. Given the relatively long distances between towns on the coast be sure to plan carefully before you leave. Many secondary routes that access towns along the coast are narrow, two-lane roads, and they make travel slower than you might expect. For example, it takes a full hour to get from Rte. 1 at Orland to Stonington via Rtes. 175 and 15.

If you want help getting around the coast, and you're a member, check in with AAA. They can map various routes to your particular destination. Their offices on the coast are:

Portland — AAA Maine
425 Marginal Way
207-774-6377
Mailing address:
P.O. Box 3544
Portland, ME 04104
www.aaanne.com

South Portland — AAA Maine
443 Western Ave.
So. Portland, ME 04106
207-775-6211
www.aaane.com

CAR RENTALS

If you are flying into Boston, Portland, Bangor or Bar Harbor, chances are you will rent an automobile to explore the coast. It is best to call well ahead of your visit to reserve a rental car, particularly during the busier season between Memorial and Labor days.

Alamo Rent A Car: 800-327-9633 (1000 Westbrook St.., Portland; www.goalamo. com; 207-775-0855). Pick up at the airport.

Avis: 800-331-1212 (Portland Jetport, 207-874-7500; Bangor Airport, 207-947-8383).

Budget: 800-527-0700 (Portland Jetport, 207-772-6789; Bar Harbor Airport, 207-667-1200; Augusta Airport, 207-622-0210; Bangor Airport, 207-945-9429; Rockland Airport, 207-594-0822).

Enterprise: 800-RENT-ACAR (Portland Jetport, 207-854-0560; Bangor Airport, 207-990-0745; with other offices in Portland, Saco, Brunswick, Rockland, Lewiston and Augusta).

Hertz: 800-654-3131 (Portland Jetport, 207-774-4544; Bar Harbor Airport, 207-667-5017; Bangor Airport, 207-942-5519).

National Interrent: 800-227-7368 (Portland Jetport, 207-773-0036; Bangor Airport, 207-947-0158; Rockland, 207-594-8424; www.nationalcar.com).

BY PLANE

A fast way to get around the coast is by air. Following is a list of air charter services that fly on the coast.

Acadia Air Inc., Bar Harbor Airport
    207-667-5534; www.acadia.nt/acadia-air; E-mail, acadiaair@acadia.net
Ace Aviation, Belfast Airport
    207-338-2970; www.aceaviation.com
Down East Flying Service, Portland Jetport, Sanford Airport
    800-290-9401
Maine Aviation Corporation, Portland Jetport 207-780-1811; www.maineavia-tion.com; E-mail, info@maineaviation.com
Penobscot Air Service, Rockland Airport
    207-596-6211/800-780-6071; stationair@aol.com
Snug Harbor Airways, Bangor Airport
    207-947-0824

COASTAL TOWN ACCESS

Here are approximate distances between selected cities and towns within the state. The time it takes to travel these distances varies widely, depending on time of year, traffic conditions and the route traveled. The highway speed limit in Maine is 55 mph in populated areas, 65 mph in rural regions.

From Kittery to:	Miles	From Eastport to:	Miles
Old Orchard Beach	37	Machias	44
Portland	50	Bar Harbor	122
Freeport	66	Belfast	141
Brunswick	76	Camden	160
Augusta	107	Rockland	167
Boothbay Harbor	109	Boothbay Harbor	207
Rockland	131	Brunswick	217
Camden	135	Freeport	227
Belfast	153	Portland	243
Bangor	183	Old Orchard Beach	262
Bar Harbor	211	Kittery	293
Machias	249		

Others:	Miles
Bangor to Bar Harbor	46
Augusta to Rockland	42
Augusta to Belfast	47

BY FERRY

One of the advantages of visiting the coast of Maine is that you have so many opportunities to ride a ferry. Island residents live with their inner clocks set to the ferry schedule, and so will you when you plan to visit one of the coastal outlands. For information on ferries statewide, write to or call the *Maine State Ferry Service*, P.O. Box 645, 517A Main St., Rockland 04841; 207-624-7777. Their Rockland number is 207-596-2202; their e-mail is www.state.me.us/mdot/mainhtml/feryinfo.htm.

Rockland to Vinalhaven: Year-round service between Rockland and Vinalhaven on the *Governor Curtis* and the *Charles Philbrook* (207-863-4421); 15 miles; crossing time: one hour and 15 minutes.

To North Haven: Year round on the *Captain Neal Burgess* (207-867-4441); 12.5 miles; crossing time: one hour and 10 minutes.

To Matinicus: Ferry service one day a month in winter; three days a month in summer. The ferry carries supplies to the islanders as well. Best to call in advance. For a taste of Maine (and whether you go or not), it's a phone call well spent. On the *North Haven* (207-596-2202); 23 miles; crossing time: two hours and 15 minutes.

Lincolnville to Isleboro: Year-round service on the *Margaret Chase Smith* (207-789-5611 or 207-734-6935); 3 miles; crossing time: 20 minutes.

Bass Harbor to Swans Island: Year-round service on the *Captain Henry Lee* (207-526-4273); 6 miles; crossing time: 40 minutes.

To Frenchboro: Year-round service on the *Captain Henry Lee* (207-244-3254); 8.25 miles; crossing time: 50 minutes.

Portland to Peaks, Great Chebeague; Long, Great and Little Diamond, and Cliff islands, with seasonal service to Bailey Island: Year-round service on *Island Holiday, Island Romance, Maquoit II, Machigonne II,* by Casco Bay Lines, P.O. Box 4656 DTS, Portland 04101 (207-774-7871; www.cascobay.com/islands/ferry/ferry.htm); 17 minutes to Peaks; 30 minutes to Long Island; one hour and 15 minutes to Chebeague. Ferry leaves Ferry Terminal at Commercial and Franklin streets. This is America's oldest ferry service.

Portland to Eagle Island: Daily service from late June to Columbus Day. Leaves Long Wharf on Commercial St., Portland. Coastwatch Tours and Guiding Light Navigation Company (207-774-6498); 90-minute stopover on island.

Freeport to Eagle Island: Ferry service runs daily between Memorial and Columbus Day. Atlantic Seal Cruises, 25 Main St., South Freeport 04078 (207-865-6112); one-hour stopover on island.

Portland to Yarmouth, Nova Scotia: Regular car and passenger service on the *Scotia Prince* from May through October with occasional "no-sail days." Prince of Fundy Cruises, P.O. Box 4216, Portland, 04101-0416 (207-775-5616 in Portland; 800-341-7540 in U.S.; www.princeoffundy.com); 11 hours. Leaves from the International Ferry Terminal, Commercial St., Portland. Children under 5 travel free. Vehicle and cabin rates extra. Tractor-trailer trucks often take this boat to save driving 850 miles. Once offshore you can gamble and shop duty free. Proof of citizenship required.

Cousins Island to Great Chebeague Island: Year-round service on the *Big Squaw* and *Islander*; Chebeague Transportation Co., Chebeague Island 04107 (207-846-3700). No transient parking available at Cousins Island. Parking and shuttle bus service available from Cumberland Center.

Boothbay to Monhegan: Daily service early June to late September on the *Balmy Days II* with Capt. Bob Campbell, P.O. Box 535, Boothbay 04538 (207-633-2284; www.maineguide.com/boothbay/balmy; E-mail, diane@lincoln.midcoast.com); one round trip per day. Weekends in the off season. Leaves from Pier 8, Commercial St., Boothbay.

Port Clyde to Monhegan: Daily service from May through October on the *Laura B* and the *Elizabeth Ann* with Capt. James Barstow, P.O. Box 238, Port

Waiting to cross the border into Canada at Calais.

Herb Swanson

Clyde 04855 (207-372-8848; www.monheganboat.com); one hour, 10 minutes. Ferry operates three times a week in winter.

New Harbor to Monhegan: Daily service mid-June through Columbus Day, on the *Hardy III*, Capt. Al Crocetti, P.O. Box 326, New Harbor 04554 (207-677-2026 or 800-278-3346; www.gwi.net/~hardy; E-mail, hardy@gwi.net). Reservations recommended.

Stonington to Isle au Haut and Duck Harbor: Five trips daily from mid-June through early September on the *Mink*, or *Miss Lizzie*, RR 1, P.O. Box 709, Stonington 04681 (207-367-6516); 45 minutes. Leaves from Seabreeze Ave. Dock, Stonington.

Northeast Harbor to Sutton Island (on request), Great Cranberry Island, and Islesford: Six trips daily late June through Labor Day on the *Sea Queen* and *Double B*, operated by Beal & Bunker, P.O. Box 33, Cranberry Isles 04625 (207-244-3575).

Bar Harbor to Yarmouth, Nova Scotia: Daily service June through October on the *The Cat*, operated by Bay Ferry, 121 Eden St., Bar Harbor; www.nfl-bay.com (207-288-3395 or 888-249-7245, in continental U.S.); 2 hours, 45 minutes. Leaves Ferry Terminal, Bar Harbor. Car and passenger ferry. Children under 5 travel free.

SHORT CUTS

Bottlenecks are common on the coast because there is one main thorough-fare, Rte. 1, that stretches the entire length. (I-95 follows the coast only between Kittery and Brunswick.) Rte. 1 in Maine is a two-lane highway, with few exceptions, and often it becomes packed.

Sometimes traffic jams are unavoidable. Freeport is intolerable on a rainy day. Shop, if you can, when the sun shines. Rte. 1 between Kennebunkport and Ogunquit is almost always busy. The Park Loop at Acadia National Park is packed during the summer and empty before Memorial Day and after Labor Day. (The loop closes at the first snowfall and reopens in late spring. Cross-country skiers "own" the loop during the winter.) If you want to travel through Bath on your way up coast, the slowdown at the Carlton Bridge is inevitable, particularly when workers change shifts at Bath Iron Works. (We give you a good alternate for this area, below.) The bridge over the Sheepscot River at Wiscasset is another trouble spot. Traffic here is often halted by a single, unyielding light, although in recent years the town has stationed a policeman at a key intersection to urge traffic on.

Below are some shortcuts we've found. They are routes that will take you off the beaten track — and most of the time get you back on your way faster. If you don't want to miss the action, take Rte. 1 one way and the shortcut the other. Many of these shortcuts are just as scenic as, if not more than, more heavily trafficked routes.

South Coast

• To avoid downtown Ogunquit en route to Perkins Cove. As you travel north on Rte. 1 take a right onto Pine Hill Rd. Follow to Shore Rd. and take a left. You'll come out at Perkins Cove.

Midcoast

• To miss the slow moving traffic one Rte. 1 in Brunswick, continue on I-95 to Rte. 196 (exit 24) and follow south through Topsham to Rte. 1.
• To avoid bottlenecks at Carlton Bridge to the east of Bath, as well as the Wiscasset bridge. Take I-95 north to the Gardiner exit. Go east on Rte. 126 until you reach Rte. 32. Follow Rte. 32 south until you reach Rte. 1 in Waldoboro.
• To eliminate the heavily trafficked section of Rte. 1 through Rockland. Take Rte. 90 off Rte. 1 in West Warren. It leads you into Rockport, just south of Camden, and can save you up to 30 minutes on a busy summer day.

EAST OF SCHOODIC

• To avoid the long jog in Rte. 1 through Hancock, Sullivan, Gouldsboro, Steuben, and Milbridge. Take Rte. 182, 4 miles east of Ellsworth, to Cherryfield. It is a few miles shorter than Rte. 1 and the Rte. 1A section from Milbridge to Harrington and is faster and much less crowded. It winds through the hills and is one of the most scenic roads in New England.

CHAPTER THREE
Where the Beaches Are
SOUTH COAST

Most of Maine's just more than million residents live and work along the South Coast. Why? The sea, the long, flat beaches, the proximity to Boston, the mountains to the west, and, of course, Down East, make it irresistible. Depending on what direction you're coming from, Maine begins or ends in **Kittery**, Maine's first city, incorporated on Oct. 20, 1647. The Warren Lobster House, on the banks of the Piscataqua River, displays the first or last of

Herb Swanson

Walker's Point, former president Bush's summer home and one of the most popular sites on the south coast of Maine.

many giant red lobster signs used to woo visitors along a several hundred mile long strip. Ships for the Civil War were built here, so was the nation's first submarine. The shipyard, which is open to the public and sits on Seavey Island in the middle of the Piscataqua River, is actively functioning today.

Recently Kittery has shifted to a retail economy that is based around factory outlet and discount designer stores. This is the beginning — or end — of a long stretch of what could be called the "shopper's coastline." The oldest residential part of town is in the pretty area called **Kittery Point**, which can be reached by Rte. 103, a winding, wooded state road that intersects with U.S. Rte. 1 and leads on toward Rte. 1A and York.

The Yorks are a group of small villages — **York Village, York Harbor, York Beach,** and **Cape Neddick** — that were among the first areas of the coast to be settled during the 1600s.

York has a well-preserved historical district. The Old Gaol Museum at the heart of York's "living history district" is the earliest example of stone architec-

ture in the U.S. For most people, though, the Yorks have other charms. Some of the coast's best beaches are right here. Cape Neddick was one of the state's first summer resorts. Today York's coastal routes and shoreline are marked by an eclectic mix of stately homes, antique shops, working lobster boats and striking stretches of fine white sand.

During the high season in July and August, **Ogunquit** and **Wells** have almost a carnival-like atmosphere and are packed with visitors from New York, Boston, Montreal, and Quebec who come for the cool ocean breezes, good restaurants, healthy cultural calendar — and great beaches. Wells and Ogunquit together have about seven miles of beachfront, roughly the same amount as Old Orchard.

Once a fishing village, Ogunquit, which in Algonquin means "beautiful place by the sea," was discovered by artists during the mid- and late 1800s. These days, you still can see painters with easels perched at the side of the road trying to capture the elusive southcoast light as it plays on Bald Head Cliff, which rises a sheer 100 feet from the ocean. This area is a favorite vacation spot for artists of all kinds and for tourists who come to shop quaint Perkins Cove and walk Marginal Way, the mile-long coastal footpath.

While Ogunquit caters to an art-minded crowd, Wells, with a beach rimmed with shops and family-style restaurants, is a favorite stop for travelers with children. Birders and naturalists also flock here to visit the Rachel Carson Wildlife Refuge, 1600 acres of fragile coastal wetlands, a haven for an amazing number of migrating birds during spring and summer.

The summer home of former president George Bush, the affluent community of **Kennebunkport** has all the makings of a resort town: winding country roads, acres of coastline, stately pines, gracious inns, interesting restaurants, shops, boutiques and galleries, sandy beaches, and the sea.

First settled in the 1620s, the area's early history was peppered with Native American raids. The **Kennebunks** evolved into fishing and shipbuilding towns, and many of the historic captains' mansions are now handsome inns. This area became known as a summer "watering place" in Victorian times, when city folk arrived by train to take in sea air and rusticate.

Kennebunkport is the most often visited. Dock Square, a lively hub of shops and restaurants, is a major draw, as is Ocean Avenue, which snakes past **Cape Arundel** and the Bush estate at Walker's Point. To the south, Kennebunk Beach offers fine sand and a sheltered cove. A short drive north on Rte. 9 to **Cape Porpoise** gives one a glimpse into the past. The Cape is still very much a fishing village, and its harbor is a working one. The waters are so thick with lobster traps, it is almost impossible for pleasure boats to anchor anywhere near shore.

To the west, Kennebunk itself is a period piece. Eighteenth and nineteenth century homes offer a primer of architectural styles from Colonial and Greek Revival to Federal and Victorian. Best known is the Wedding Cake House, so named because of its icing-like embellishments, a sterling example of Victorian excess. The bell swinging in the steeple of the First Parish Church was cast by Paul Revere and the steeple itself designed by Christopher Wren.

A good drive is Rte. 9, which was the main road to Bangor before Interstate 95. It starts in the Kennebunks and travels through Cape Porpoise, **Pine Point,** and past the wealthy seaside community of **Biddeford Pool**.

Visitors returning to **Old Orchard Beach** after a long absence will be impressed by the city's efforts to class up this seaside hot spot. We're pleased to report that although there is a fresh coat of paint and new Victorian-styled park benches all around, this remains one of the best places on the Maine coast to get a good dose of wholesome honky-tonk and a boardwalk meal of fried clams, fried dough, and French fries.

Americans call it the "Maine Riviera" for its summer population, 60 percent of which is French-speaking Canadian. Old Orchard is also called the "Coney Island of Maine" for its predominance of asphalt and its honky-tonk, boardwalk atmosphere.

French-speaking Canadians don't care what Old Orchard Beach is called — many consider it the capital of Maine. Since the 1850s, when the Grand Trunk Railroad opened between Montreal and Portland, French Canadians have flocked to Old Orchard Beach and its centerpiece — a 7.5 mile sandy beach — the closest to Montreal and Quebec City. In the old days, only wealthy French Canadians came to Old Orchard, and they came for weeks at a time. After World War II, working-class Canadians had money to spend and vacation time. Old Orchard was where they headed.

Today wealthier French Canadians favor tonier Ogunquit and Kennebunkport to the south, where there are no amusement parks, where hotels, not motels, are the rule and where shops are boutiques — and don't sell T-shirts with messages like "It's Not How Deep You Fish, It's How You Wiggle The Worm."

There's still a devoted French-speaking following for Old Orchard Beach with its 4,000 campsites, 90 motels, 350 cabins, 120 restaurants, and 15 arcades. They come for the beach, one of the most spectacular and well-groomed stretches of sand in New England.

Old Orchard Beach does all it can to make French Canadians feel at home — perhaps because so many year-round residents of Old Orchard and nearby **Biddeford** and **Saco** are of French ancestry. Everywhere is the sign, "Ici on parle français." Restaurants feature bilingual menus. You can buy a cup of coffee at Dunkin' Donuts on Elm Street in nearby Biddeford and hear fellow patrons trade thoughts on politics and the weather — in French. St. Margaret's Catholic Church on Old Orchard St. holds a mass in French every Sunday. Many of the corner stores sell French-language newspapers from back home in Quebec and Montreal.

These days, both French- and English-speaking Canadians have another reason to visit Old Orchard Beach — shopping. The exchange rate has been very favorable in recent years. There's also the "TPS," or "GST" — 7 percent tax levied on all goods and services purchased in Canada since 1991. Visitors from the province of Quebec also pay an 8 percent sales tax on top of the TPS, making Maine's 6 percent state sales tax seem quite reasonable, indeed.

Old Orchard Beach has plenty of inexpensive electronics. Old Orchard St., the town's center strip, has at least nine electronic/T-shirt stores — a popular combo here — in its several downtown blocks, offering bargains for Canadian shoppers.

If there is one city on the coast that is an anomaly, it is **Portland**. Outsiders may not be able to understand this at first. To the rest of Maine, Portland is considered more a suburb of Boston than the state's largest city and home to one fifth of Maine's approximately one million inhabitants.

Maybe that's because of its big city ways. Boutiques. Ethnic food. More restaurants per capita than all but one other U.S. city (San Francisco). A full-time, professional symphony orchestra. The I. M. Pei-designed Portland

Museum of Art. An international ferry (to Nova Scotia) and an international airport. And, of course, the Old Port, the old waterfront commercial district that has been made over into a mecca for shoppers and business people who eat lunch here. A writer for *The New York Times* once described it as the "San Francisco of the East."

The city sits on a moderately hilly peninsula framed by the Fore River to the west, the Presumpscot River to the East, and Casco Bay to the north. With its working waterfront and underneath its big city ways (only a Mainer would call this cosmopolitan), it is the latest incarnation of a 19th-century seaport.

There are hundreds of islands large and small in Casco Bay (several of which have become bedroom communities for working Portlanders) that are interesting to explore, as well as good swimming, biking, and walking ground.

A newcomer to **Freeport** will certainly note that this town was built for shopping. Rte. 295 off the Maine Turnpike deposits the traveler on a two-lane road leading right through town. For the most part, the view from the car window is good enough to eye the buttons on a Ralph Lauren shirt or catch the winsome line of a canoe bow at L.L. Bean.

Way back before there were factory outlets, and before there was even an L.L. Bean, this was a favored stopping place for the British navy. His Majesty's ships would berth and pick up the famous Maine white pine the Royal Navy used to make their masts. Even today, two major landmarks commemorate this early trading route — Upper Mast Landing and Lower Mast Landing where the mast pines were collected before being shipped.

Until 1981, there was L.L. Bean and the kind of stores you'd find on Main St. in any small town. Now it is wall-to-wall factory outlets. But the true beauty of Freeport isn't in the great bargains to be found there. It's that the town has retained much of its feel as a New England village and knowing that only two minutes' drive east on Bow St. and you're out in the country. There you get a sense of the way this part of the coast used to be: hilly, green pastures, tidy 18th- and 19th-century farmhouses, country lanes, pines, and firs.

SOUTH COAST: LODGING

R omantic is the word that best describes the Maine coast's lodging industry. Centuries of seagoing travelers made their homes here. Many of these grand houses have been turned into inns and bed and breakfasts, and are now used by travelers who live in faraway places. There are so many of these stately homes with widow's walks and the wonderful carpentry of renowned Maine ships' carpenters that all the sea lore can seem a bit passé to year-round and returning seasonal residents. A surprising number of these lodging houses are run by people from away — men and women who have visited the coast and found innkeeping a good opportunity to come back and enjoy it full time.

The lodgings we recommend in this survey represent places we either have stayed at or visited and toured. We also include a few others that have been recommended and written up by well-traveled friends and family. They are by no means the only places to stay on the coast (there are more than 300 inns and B&Bs in Bar Harbor alone), but a reliable list of those places we know that provide a good resting place. Some are quiet and beautiful enclaves where it might be worth staying for two or more nights to absorb all the peace the place has to offer. Others are well situated for sightseeing and recreational opportunities. Several inns listed have restaurants; when possible, we have included them in *Dining,* later in this chapter.

For alternative listings, you can contact the ***Maine Tourism Association*** (P.O. Box 2300, Hallowell, ME 04347; 207-623-0363 in Maine; 800-533-9595 out-of-state and Canada; E-mail, metainfo@mainetourism.com). Every year they publish the *Guide to Inns & Bed & Breakfasts,* a list of inns and B&Bs by region. All of the listings are written and paid for by the owners, so you should take them with a grain of salt. The ***Maine Innkeepers Association Food & Lodging Guide,*** with advertising from hotels, motels and inns throughout the state, is available at most tourist information centers, or from the association (305 Commercial St., Portland, ME 04101; 207-773-7670; E-mail, info@maineinns.com).

MAINE COAST LODGING NOTES

Rates: Rates can vary widely off season and in season. They generally increase close to Memorial Day and are highest from July through the leaf season in mid- to late October. Special packages are often available for two or more nights stay, and frequently there are even better values during the off season. If breakfast and/or dinner is included with the price of a room, we do not alter the rate category, we just note that the room rate includes one or more meals.

Inexpensive	Up to $65
Moderate	$65 to $125
Expensive	$125 to $180
Very Expensive	$180 and up

These rates exclude Maine state lodging tax or individual hotel service charges that may be added to your bill.

Credit Cards: Several lodging places we recommend in this book do not take plastic. If they do not, they almost always take personal or travelers' checks. Following are credit card abbreviations:

AE — American Express	DC — Diner's Card
CB — Carte Blanche	MC — MasterCard
D — Discover Card	V — Visa

Minimum Stay: Many inns and B&Bs require a minimum stay of two or more nights during the summer season. We have noted minimum stays when possible, but it's best to check when making room reservations.

Deposit/Cancellation: To reserve a room on the Maine coast, it is generally necessary to make a deposit to cover the first night of your stay — and some places may require up to 50 percent of the cost of the intended stay. Cancellations often must be made at least seven to 10 days in advance. Ask about the inn's policy when you make reservations.

Handicap Access: Many of the inns and B&Bs in this book have yet to comply with federal regulations regarding handicap access. We have noted handicap access is available in inns, B&Bs, and hotels where the owners can guarantee at least one room with access.

Other Options: For information on camping, from tents to RVs, see the section entitled "Camping" under *Recreation*. If you plan to camp with an RV, be sure to make reservations well in advance. If you plan on tent camping, most of the national and state parks and national forests campgrounds are available on a first-come, first-serve basis.

Cape Elizabeth

INN BY THE SEA
Innkeeper: Maureen
  McQuade.
207-799-3134.
www.innbythesea.com.
40 Bowery Beach Rd. (Rte.
  77), Cape Elizabeth
  04107.
Open: All year.
Price: Expensive to Very
  Expensive.
Credit Cards: AE, D, MC, V.
Handicap Access: Partial.

This modern-day, gray-shingled inn is not far from where Portland goes to the beach and comes to pick their own during strawberry season. It is a 43-suite complex, each suite featuring Chippendale furniture, TV and VCR packed away in a cherry armoire, and terry-cloth robes in the closet. Many have ocean views. There are four cottages with rocking chairs on their porches. Amble down to Crescent Beach on the wooden walkway bordered by rose bushes. There are tennis courts, shuffleboard courts, a swimming pool, and a restaurant — the Audubon, which looks out on Casco Bay and provides the setting for a romantic interlude. No pets. No smoking at the inn.

Chebeague Island

CHEBEAGUE INN
Manager: Larry
  Beauchamp.
207-846-5155.
Box 492, South Rd.,
  Chebeague Island 04017.
Open: Mid-May to late
  Sept.

On a gently sloping hill overlooking Casco Bay, the Chebeague Inn is the sort of old-style seaside hotel that's fast becoming extinct. The 21 rooms — some are on the small side — are simply done in pale tones. Many have ocean views, as does the dining room, which serves breakfast, lunch, and dinner (See *Dining*). While there's a

Price: Moderate.
Credit Cards: D, MC, V.

public golf course right next door, beaches nearby, and plenty of spots on the island to walk or bike to, more sedentary types will set up camp on the expansive porch with its cane-backed rocking chairs. There's also a comfortable living room with loungers and a stone fireplace should the weather turn chilly. Chebeague Island is a 15-minute ferry ride from Cousin's Island and an hour's ride from Portland.

Freeport & South Freeport

ATLANTIC SEAL BED & BREAKFAST

Innkeeper: Captain Thomas Ring.
207-865-6112 or
877-ATLSEAL
Main St., Box 146, South Freeport 04078.
Open: All year.
Price: Moderate to Expensive.
Credit Cards: None, but they accept personal and travelers' checks.
Handicap Access: None.

The tiny, picturesque village of South Freeport sits on the water; so does the Atlantic Seal. It has since the mid-19th century. Capt. Tom Ring, a tugboat captain who has worked around the world, grew up in this old Cape, and generations of his family have gone to sea and returned with furniture. The house is filled with Ring family treasures, including wonderful seascapes. The four homey rooms, all named after ships, have pumpkin pine floors, hand-hooked rugs, beds with homemade quilts, and private baths. One comes with a private whirlpool bath, another has a window seat overlooking the harbor. When we last visited, Capt. Ring was busy building a stone walkway down to the inn's dock, using cobblestones and granite he salvaged while working on the Casco Bay Bridge. He also was about to complete a deck overlooking the harbor. Breakfast is served on Sunday-best blue Camilla Spode with a silver setting. Breakfast can include lobster omelets or something called "stuffed" French toast, and the mahogany dining table it's served at has been all over the world on a sailing vessel. Tom also offers cruises out to the neighboring islands on the *Atlantic Seal* and the *Arctic Seal*. Ask and he'll give you a short course on lobstering. No smoking. No pets.

HARRASEEKET INN

Innkeepers: The Gray Family.
207-865-9377 or
800-342-6423 out-of-state.
www.stayfreeport.com.
E-mail: harraseeke@ aol.com.
162 Main St., Freeport 04032.
Open: All year.

With 84 rooms and suites, a health club and other features, the Harraseeket Inn offers the kind of amenities you would expect to find in most big hotels. But this is Freeport, and everything here has to be bigger because there's so much shopping going on. Right on the village's main street, this elegant black-shuttered inn is really a series of connecting buildings. The newest was built in 1997; the other two in 1798 and 1850. Many of the rooms

The Harraseeket Inn, comprised of old and new buildings, is luxurious throughout.

Michael Loomis

Price: Expensive to Very Expensive.
Credit Cards: AE, CB, D, DC, MC, V.
Handicap Access: Yes.

have fireplaces, Jacuzzis, steam baths, and all have elegant canopied beds. All have air conditioning and cable TV, and are decorated in tasteful muted florals. The parlor has cushy wing chairs and couches and is accented with gleaming old silver and dark wood antiques — reminiscent of a country estate's drawing room. The dining room has a solid wine list, a growing reputation for inventiveness, and a commitment to using local seafood and produce (See *Dining*). The tavern is more casual. Breakfast is included with the room rate, as well as afternoon tea and hors d'oeuvres. Dinner is additional. Special packages available.

ISAAC RANDALL HOUSE
Innkeeper: Ciny Wellito.
207-865-9295 or
800-865-9295.
www.isaacrandall.com.
E-mail: nkeepa@
cybertours.com.
10 Independence Dr.,
Freeport 04032.
Open: All year.
Price: Inexpensive to
Moderate.

Just down the block from what is now the outlet center of Freeport's shopping district, descendants of Mayflower passengers built this farmhouse; later it was a stop on the Underground Railway and still later a speakeasy during Prohibition. The ten rooms all have private bath, telephones, and air-conditioning. Five of the rooms have fireplaces. They share an upstairs sitting room with a VCR and a common-area kitchen, stocked with cheese, crackers, and soft drinks. Travelers on a tight budget can cook dinner here. There's a

Credit Cards: D, MC, V.
Handicap Access: Very
Limited.

Honeymoon Suite with a king-size wicker bed; a Southwestern room with exposed beams, prints of New Mexico, and an antique copper captain's tub in the bathroom — something male visitors seem to take to; and an Aqua room with a king-sized bed and two twin beds. Kids love the twin set in a small alcove. There's a full breakfast. Items include homemade granola, pancakes, and raspberry coffee cake. There's a pond out back: in the winter they encourage people to bring skates. There's also a caboose out back which has been converted into guest quarters with a queen-sized bed, two stacked singles, and bath with shower. Pets allowed in two of the rooms. No smoking.

Kennebunk

ECONOLODGE
207-985-6100 or
   800-336-5634 (out of state).
55 York St. (Rte. 1 south),
   Kennebunk 04043.
Open: All year.
Price: Inexpensive.
Credit Cards: AE, D, MC, V.
Handicap Access: Yes, but
   call ahead during the off-
   season.

Set against a backdrop of pines minutes away from downtown Kennebunkport, this Econo Lodge has more appeal than most chain motels. That's particularly appreciated in a town where lodging during the high season can be hard to come by and expensive. Wood balconies lend a rustic air to the low-slung brick-and-stucco building, and the rooms are, for the most part, tastefully decorated. Color cable TV, phones, air conditioning, and continental breakfast are among the perks, and there is an outdoor pool. Smoking and non-smoking rooms. No pets.

Kennebunkport

CAPE ARUNDEL INN
Owner: Ann Fales.
207-967-2125.
www.capearundelinn.com.
E-mail: cai@capearundel
   inn.com.
P.O. Box 530A, Ocean Ave.,
   Kennebunkport 04046.
Open: Memorial Day
   weekend to Columbus
   Day.
Price: Moderate to
   Expensive.
Credit cards: AE, MC, V.
Handicap Access: Limited.

Set on a hillside with handsome trees and shrubberies, this forest-green-shingled inn makes the most of its aerie over the Atlantic. The common areas, dining room, and guest rooms (seven at the inn, six at the motel, one in the carriage house) have dramatic panoramas of the sea. Curved windows and turrets add to the cachet. Rooms are decorated in pale tones — cream spreads with dark wood antiques and reproductions. A few of the bathrooms are on the small side, but many have vintage sinks and clawfoot tubs. Country wicker and antiques fill the parlors, while the dining room leans toward early American. Not so the food, which is modern and inventive. Children in the motel only. No pets. No smoking in the dining room.

CAPTAIN LORD MANSION

Innkeepers: Bev Davis and
 Rick Litchfield.
207-967-3141 or
 800-522-3141.
www.captainlord.com.
E-mail: innkeeper@
 captainlord.com.
P.O. Box 800,
 Kennebunkport 04046.
Corner of Pleasant and
 Green Sts.
Open: All year.
Price: Expensive.
Credit cards: D, MC, V.
Handicap Access: Limited.

This is one of the coast's great inns. Seven generations of Lords lived in grand style here before it became an inn. As inn lore goes, old Nathaniel Lord, the captain, built this stately home to keep his ships' carpenters busy during the British blockade in the War of 1812. Today it is an elegant stopping place in the historic district of this handsome seaside town. There are 16 bedrooms on three floors, all with private bath, 14 with gas fireplaces. Most have king- or queen-sized beds. A suite has been added to the mansion, featuring a grand bath with a double Jacuzzi and fireplace. The suite has two pieces of workout equipment and a king-sized canopy bed. The inn is filled to the brim with lovely antiques, most from the Federalist period, oriental rugs, and art. The beautifully restored woodwork and staircases are knockouts. A three-course breakfast includes muesli, fresh fruit and yogurt; homemade muffins, and either French toast, fresh fruit pancakes, quiche, or Belgian waffles. With advance notice, the innkeepers are more than willing to accommodate a guest's special diet. The inn offers guests beach parking passes, beach towels, umbrellas, and mats. They also serve afternoon tea. Children over six. No pets. Totally non-smoking.

GREEN HERON INN

Owners: Charles and
 Elizabeth Reid.
207-967-3315.
www.greenheroninn.com.
E-mail: greenheron@
 cybertours.com.
P.O. Box 2578, 126 Ocean
 Ave. Kennebunkport
 04046.
On Ocean Ave.
Open: All year, except
 January.
Price: Inexpensive to
 Moderate.
Credit Cards: None.
Handicap Access: Yes.

Less than a mile from Dock Square, the Green Heron is a homey stop, just the thing for families. Rooms (there are 10 of them plus a cottage with kitchenette) are cozy with pastel quilts, extra pillows, modern motel-style bathrooms, TV, and air conditioning. Each sleeps four (there's a double plus a trundle). So what if the parlors are a mishmash of summerhouse wicker and hunting camp castoffs? The inn has many of the comforts of home — local and big city newspapers, books, jigsaw puzzles, cards, and games. Breakfast is included with the room, and it's an elaborate one with homemade English muffins, buttermilk biscuits, vegetable frittatas, blueberry pancakes, orange French toast, and Welsh rarebit. Smoking in rooms only. Pets allowed but not in the common rooms. Children accepted.

WHITE BARN INN
Innkeeper: William
  Mozingo.
207-967-2321.
www.whitebarninn.com.
E-mail: innkeeper@
  whitebarninn.
P.O. Box 560 C,
  Kennebunkport 04046.
Beach St., off Rte. 9.
Open: All year.
Price: Moderate to Very
  Expensive.
Credit Cards: AE, MC, V.

It's hard to imagine this as a boardinghouse in 1800. It's too grand: lush landscaping, antiques, and English country floral fabrics. Fresh flowers, robes, and comfortable beds are a given in the 24 rooms, all with air conditioning, telephones, and private baths. Seven suites also have fireplaces, sitting areas, marble baths with whirlpools, and TVs. The parlor, with its claret walls, elegant wing chairs, and garden views, is an ideal spot for an aperitif. The inn now features an outdoor pool for guest use in the summer months. And the restaurant is arguably the best (and most expensive) in town. The local rumor mill tells us that Barbara Bush likes meeting her pals there when she's in town. Breakfast is included in the room rate, along with afternoon tea (dinner is separate). Special off-season packages with dinner are available. Smoking at the bar only.

Kittery

GUNDALOW INN
Innkeepers: Cevia and
  George Rosol.
207-439-4040.
www.innsnorthamerica.
  com/inactive/gundalow
  inn.htm.
6 Water St., Kittery 03904.
Open: All year.
Price: Moderate.
Credit Cards: D, MC, V.
Handicap Access: Limited.

This is a very civilized place to stay, located just across the New Hampshire border and not far from one of Maine's shopping meccas. This carefully renovated brick Victorian offers travelers excellent views of the Piscataqua River from the dining room and four of the six well-appointed guest rooms. All have private baths with lovely restored bathroom fixtures. We recommend breakfast on the patio — if the weather's good. You can watch boats on the river. No pets, children under 16, or smoking.

Ogunquit

HARTWELL HOUSE
Owners: Jim and Trisha
  Hartwell.
207-646-7210 or
  800-235-8883.
www.hartwellhouse
  inn.com.
E-mail: hartwell@
  cybertours.com.
P.O. Box 393, 118 Shore Rd.,
  Ogunquit 03907.
Open: All year.
Price: Moderate to
  Expensive.

With 16 rooms in its two houses, Hartwell House is among the largest B&Bs in Ogunquit. Modeled after the English country inns of Europe, it is also one of the most elegant. In keeping with the theme, they serve a lovely "European" tea every day at 4:30. The rooms are large, full of light, carefully decorated, and furnished with Early American or English antiques. All are equipped with air conditioning and have private baths, and many of the rooms have decks, patios or balconies, and views of the water. Several

Credit Cards: AE, D, MC,
  V.
Handicap Access: Yes.
No children under 12.

extremely large suites include a kitchen and a living area, and are good for families or groups traveling together. Unlike many of the town's inns, the
Hartwell has a good bit of property. Its two buildings flank Shore Rd., and this assures privacy and
plenty of greenery and gardens to enjoy. No TV or
telephones in the rooms. No pets. No smoking in the inn. No children under
twelve.

THE TRELLIS HOUSE
Innkeepers: Jerry and Pat
  Houlihan.
207-646-7909.
www.trellishouse.com.
P.O. Box 2229, 2 Beachmere
  Pl., Ogunquit 03907.
Closed January.
Price: Moderate.
Credit Cards: MC, V.

The Trellis House is the sort of place that
becomes familiar quickly, where guests feel at
home soon after arriving. Originally a summer cottage, the gray-shingled house with the large
screened porch looks friendly, comfortable, and
homey. Inside, the rooms are filled with a mixture
of antiques and collectibles. A fireplace in the living room encourages conversation and mingling,
and there are many private nooks in the house.
There are six guest rooms, including a two-room
suite, all with private baths. There is also a carriage
house near the main house that has been renovated to hold four rooms, all
with private baths. Three of the rooms feature fireplaces. Best of all, the Trellis
House is within walking distance of the village, the beach, Perkins Cove, and
the Marginal Way. So there's no worry about where to park while doing the
rounds. Full breakfast included. No smoking.

Old Orchard Beach

**ATLANTIC BIRCHES
  INN**
Innkeepers: Dan and Cyndi
  Bolduc.
207-934-5295 or
  888-934-5295.
www.nettx.com/atlantic
  birchesinn/index.html.
20 Portland Ave., Old
  Orchard Beach 04064.
Open: All year.
Price: Inexpensive to
  Moderate.
Credit Cards: AE, CB, D,
  MC, V.

This homey inn set in a 1910 Victorian seems out
of place among the strip motels that populate
Old Orchard Beach. The Bolducs have made many
additions and improvements to the inn, ensuring a
more spacious and comfortable stay. There are
three additional rooms with private bath in the renovated small neighboring house. The inn also has
added two one-bedroom kitchenette apartments,
for a total of ten bedrooms. An in-ground pool has
also been a welcome addition to keep guests cool in
the hot summer months. The Atlantic Birches is
located on one of the town's few tree-lined streets.
Guests can relax on the big porch, read, or watch
passersby coming and going from nearby Old
Orchard Street, the town's main strip. The rooms
have flowered wallpaper, oriental rugs, and a

smattering of antique touches. Fresh-baked muffins, fruit salad, cereals, and juices are served every morning in the dining room (breakfast is included in the room rate). Children are welcome. Smoking isn't.

Portland

THE DANFORTH
Innkeeper: Barbara
 Hathaway.
207-879-8755.
www.danforthmaine.com.
E-mail: danforth@
 maine.rr.com.
163 Danforth St., Portland
 04102.
Open: All year.
Price: Moderate to
 Expensive.
Credit Cards: AE, MC, V.

The Danforth is an 1823 Federal-style yellow brick mansion with polished wood floors, spacious rooms, and grand staircases. The nine guest rooms have been fully restored and furnished. Seven have private baths and working fireplaces. Most have deep white carpeting and follow rich color schemes (cool sea green, navy blue, and gold). Rooms No. 5 and 6 are former servants quarters, and are small, but ample, pretty, and share a bath, a good choice for a traveling family. A full breakfast is included with the room and is served in your room or in the sun room. Health club passes are available for the guests. No smoking.

INN AT PARKSPRING
Innkeepers: Lionel and
 Elinor Berube.
207-774-1059.
www. javanet.com/~psinn.
E-mail: psinn@javanet.com.
135 Spring St., Portland
 04102.
Open: Year round.
Price: Moderate.
Credit Cards: AE, MC, V.

The ParkSpring was the first of the city's small, first-rate inns to serve what is Maine's most cosmopolitan city. In a renovated 1839 townhouse on a busy city street, the inn is quiet and private. Each of the six rooms is different. All come with private bath. The walls of the Courtyard room — our favorite — are painted a pretty French blue and a door leads to a city garden where guests may breakfast alone. Otherwise breakfast is at a long table in the sunny breakfast room. The ParkSpring is two blocks from the Portland Museum of Art and not far from galleries, shops, and the Old Port. No children under 12. No smoking.

INN ON CARLETON
Innkeepers: Phil and Sue
 Cox.
207-775-1910 or
 800-639-1779.
www.innoncarleton.com.
46 Carleton St., Portland
 04102.
Open: Year round.
Price: Moderate to
 Expensive.
Credit Cards: D, MC, V.

This is a lovely bed and breakfast in a stately Victorian-style brick townhouse within walking distance (or a short drive) to nearly all of Portland's sights, restaurants, and shopping. Sue Cox is a southerner who has lived in Maine for more than a dozen years. Since she and her husband Phil bought the inn, they have shuffled the period furnishings, uncovered and refinished wide pine floors in several of the tall-ceiling guest rooms, hung paintings and pastels by Maine artists on almost every wall, and added a gorgeous English garden out back. The service is friendly and accommodations comfortable. There are seven guest rooms; four of the rooms have private baths; one bath is a mere postage stamp, and guests will marvel that both a toilet and a shower fit inside. Don't worry, you can apply makeup and shave at the ample sink in the room. The shared baths are all roomy and have clawfoot tubs. A full breakfast — usually homemade waffles, blueberry pancakes with real maple syrup, or quiche — is served in the formal dining room. After dinner in town, stroll along the Western Prom, just down the street. Children ages eight and up are welcome. No smoking; no pets, although there is a resident marmalade cat named Kitty.

The Pomegranate, with contemporary hand-painted walls and its striking collection of antiques, is one of Maine's most unusual inns.

Michael Loomis

THE POMEGRANATE INN
Owner: Isabel Smiles.
207-772-1006.
www.pomegranateinn.com.
49 Neal St., Portland 04102.
Open: All year.
Price: Moderate to Expensive.
Credit Cards: AE, D, DC, MC, V.

Near Portland's Western Prom, this stucco Georgian looks proper from the outside, but one step over the threshold and the visitor will be left breathless. Isabel Smiles was an antiques dealer and interior designer before she and her husband turned their efforts to innkeeping. Guest and common rooms feature handpainted walls with *trompe l'oeil* and other imaginative motifs, along with a collection of original paintings, sculpture, and highly unusual antiques. There are eight rooms, each decorated differently and each with a private bath. Four of them have fireplaces. The carriage house has been converted into a separate, private suite with a kitchen for travelers who might want to cook their own dinner or merely make coffee or tea. Below the suite is a room with a private garden. Breakfast is included.

PORTLAND REGENCY
General Manager: Hillary Spence.
207-774-4200 or 800-727-3436.
www.theregency.com.
20 Milk St., Portland 04101.
Open: All year.
Price: Expensive.
Credit Cards: AE, CB, D, DC, MC, V.
Handicap Access: Yes.

Right in the heart of the Old Port with its boutiques, restaurants, and nightlife, the Portland Regency has a lot of charm for what used to be an old armory. A brick-paved circular drive, marble floors in the lobby, and parlors with Oriental rugs and antiques give this turn-of-the-century, block-long brick building the aura of luxury. The 95 rooms, some of them a little cramped, are done in antique reproductions and muted florals. Several have four-poster beds and standing mirrors. There's also a restaurant, lounge, and health club on the premises.

WEST END INN
Innkeepers: John Leonard and Kelly Gillespie.
207-772-1377 or 800-338-1377.
146 Pine St., Portland 04102.
Open: All year.
Price: Moderate to Expensive.
Credit Cards: AE, MC, V.

This small inn in an immaculate 1871 brick townhouse is located on a quiet residential street in Portland's historic West End. There are six tastefully appointed guest rooms, each with its own modern, spacious bath and cable TV. A full, hot breakfast is included. The inn is within walking distance of the Western Prom and views of the Fore River and the White Mountains. It's also a longer walk (or a short drive) to downtown and the city's Old Port. No children; no smoking.

York

DOCKSIDE GUEST QUARTERS
Innkeeper: Eric Lusty.
207-363-2868 or 800-270-1977.
www.docksidegq.com.
E-mail: info@dockside gq.com.
P.O. Box 205, York 03909.
Harris Island Rd. just off Rte. 103.
Open: All year.
Price: Moderate to Expensive.
Credit Cards: D, MC, V.

This hideaway compound mixes Yankee austerity with renovations and million-dollar views. Harris Island is actually a peninsula that sticks out into York Harbor with the Dockside taking up the better half. Vacationers tend to come back with their families year after year. The Dockside Restaurant is a short walk. People living aboard their boats sometimes move here for the winter. There's a shuffleboard court, croquet, and a sandbox. There are five guest bedrooms in the main house and an elegant white clapboard summer cottage with black shutters. Most have a bath, a porch, and direct access to the level, well-kept lawn. The four cottages are clean and neat. Some have apartments suitable for two to four people. Others are studios for two or three. All of the apartments have private baths and private decks.

York Harbor

EDWARDS'
HARBORSIDE INN
Innkeeper: Jay Edwards.
207-363-3037 or
800-273-2686.
Stage Neck Rd. just off Rte.
1A.
P.O. Box 866, York Harbor
03911.
Open: All year.
Price: Inexpensive to Very
Expensive.
Credit Cards: MC, V.

Come by boat and tie up at the pier. Take advantage of fishing rods made available to guests. This three-story, turn-of-the-century, sprawling, gabled inn looks like a mass of sails in a brisk wind. Inside, the house is immaculately kept, open, airy, and quiet, and opens onto a great stairway. Most of the 10 rooms have a view, TV, and air conditioning. Some have fireplaces, some share baths; others, including the suites, have private baths. All are furnished simply and elegantly. Out front, the well-tended lawn leads to Little Harbor Beach. Breakfast is continental, and a nice feature is afternoon wine and cheese, a great relaxer after a hard day at the beach. No pets. No smoking.

SOUTH COAST: DINING

When we first moved to the Maine coast a decade or so ago, we were amazed by the quantity and variety of good food that could be found here. That has not changed, and we continue to discover many fine places to eat.

There are thousands of restaurants along the coast. Nationally second only to San Francisco in restaurants per capita, the competition among Portland's restaurants has produced enough good places to eat and the promise that the quality of food will remain high. If the homegrown cooks weren't good enough already, the coast has attracted highly skilled chefs "from away." Usually these fine cooks are drawn to the quality of life here, and their happiness is well reflected in their cooking. We all benefit as a result.

Here then is a select list of restaurants, some coastal legends, a few new finds, places we found out about by badgering reluctant residents and neighbors, places we liked, plus places written up and sent in by friends, all experienced or professional eaters. It's a list long enough to get you up or down the coast and back next summer.

We've noted the restaurants' serving times and seasons as they were when we made the final survey for this guide. As with all things, times, phone numbers, and sometimes addresses are subject to change according to the changing seasons and demands of the economy. Call first. If you can, make reservations. Things can get pretty busy at the great places, especially during July and

August. Many restaurants, even white tablecloth ones, don't take reservations, though. So if you're really hungry, plan to arrive early enough to stake a good place in line.

The price range we list is meant to reflect the cost of a single meal, usually dinner, unless the review talks about breakfast or lunch. What we've tried to represent as a typical meal is an appetizer, entree, dessert, and coffee, although several of the places we review are not appetizer places. We do not include the price of alcohol or other drinks in the estimated cost.

Dining Price Code:

Inexpensive	Up to $10
Moderate	$10–20
Expensive	$20–30
Very Expensive	$30 or more

Credit Cards:

AE — American Express	DC — Diner's Club
CB — Carte Blanche	MC — MasterCard
D — Discover Card	V — Visa

Cape Neddick

CAPE NEDDICK INN
207-363-2899.
Rte. 1, Cape Neddick.
Closed: Mon. and Tues. off-season.
Price: Expensive.
Cuisine: Country gourmet.
Serving: D.
Credit Cards: AE, MC, V.
Reservations: Recommended.
Handicap Access: Limited.
Special Features: Art gallery.
No smoking in the dining room.

From the outside, the Cape Neddick looks like a typical country inn. Inside, the decor is clever and rather modern with a split-level dining room, abstract sculptures, expressionistic canvases on the walls, Fiestaware, and funky vintage crockery on the tables. Starters may include Chef Michele Duval's pistachio topped farmhouse cheese, wrapped in grape leaves, then grilled and served with champagne grapes. For entrees we suggest you try the potato-crusted cod on cucumber noodles or the gin and juniper marinated duck breasts in gooseberry sauce.

Chebeague Island

CHEBEAGUE INN
207-846-5155.
John Small Rd., Chebeague Island.
Closed: Mid-Sept.–mid-May.

The Chebeague Inn has an old-fashioned feel. Maybe it's the cane-backed rocking chairs on the porch, a perfect spot to while away a lazy (and hot) afternoon. Or because it's so remote (by ferry

Price: Moderate to
  Expensive.
Cuisine: Continental.
Serving: L, D.
Reservations: Recom-
  mended, even for lunch.
Credit Cards: AE, MC, V.
Handicap Access: Limited.
Special Features: Veranda
  with Casco Bay view.

it's an hour or so from Portland and 13 minutes from Cousins Island). Or maybe it's the food. Old-timey fare like real Maine chowder with potatoes and bacon, baked ham sandwiches on thick warm-from-the-oven bread, tuna with celery and mayo, and homemade lemonade and iced tea. Desserts run along the same lines — a mile-high devil's food wedge is the attention grabber. The dinner menu, which is quite extensive, is a mix of country cooking and continental fare.

Freeport & South Freeport

15 INDEPENDENCE
207-865-1515.
40 Independence Dr.,
  Freeport.
Open daily.
Price: Inexpensive to
  Moderate.
Cuisine: American eclectic.
Serving: L, D.
Credit Cards: AE, D, DC,
  MC, V.
Handicap Access: Yes.

This is one of several area restaurants owned by Walter Loehman and Scott Pelletier. Set in an 1800 farmhouse, it looks conservative from the outside. Inside it is a colorful, relaxed dining room (four dining rooms, actually) where the menu reads like a play-by-play of the latest food trends. Don't be daunted. The portions are quite generous and the food is quite good — although some entrees could be simplified. Lunch served in the deli next door is a bargain.

JAMESON TAVERN
207-865-4196.
115 Main St., Freeport.
Open daily.
Price: Moderate.
Cuisine: American seafood.
Serving: L, D.
Credit Cards: AE, D, DC,
  MC, V.
Reservations: Optional.

The Jameson Tavern has been here practically forever, catering to the masses, most recently shoppers resting up from their L.L. Bean experience. Burgers and sandwiches are served in the Tap Room. The more formal offerings can be found in the pretty, unfrilly dining room. This isn't wildly exciting food: lobster, seafood, quiche, burgers, and sandwiches. But it will fortify you before you head out to the outlets again, and it does offer something for almost everyone. The tavern is a local historical stop, where Maine's founding fathers gathered at the beginning of the 19th century and decided to separate from Massachusetts.

HARRASEEKET INN
207-865-9377 or
  800-342-6423.
162 Main St. (Rte. 1),
  Freeport.
Open daily.
Price: Expensive.
Cuisine: Regional
  American.

The menu here is always good for a surprise or two: local produce, fish, and meat well prepared and in some interesting combinations. The wine list, too, is quite good. Decor is understated — white linens, fresh flowers, and flickering candles. Menus change weekly, and there are nightly additions as well. Service is attentive, yet not as

Serving: B, L, D.
Credit Cards: AE, D, MC, V.
Reservations: Recommended.
Handicap Access: Yes.
Special Features: Tableside cooking.

overbearing as it can be in places of this sort. Start with salmon Napoleon napped with light tarragon cream or potato soup with saffron. Salads, included with entrees, mix greens with edible flowers. Main courses run from rabbit with cider cream and wild mushrooms to lamb brochette with cumin. There are also classic dishes like rack of lamb and chateaubriand carved with great fanfare at your table. There is a good by-the-glass selection of wine, and the wine list is excellent. Dessert is a must — try the sundae with dense homemade chocolate ice cream and caramel and fudge sauce, apple pie with a scoop of rich vanilla, or the Harraseeket's fresh fruit sorbet. For those who prefer dessert a la Francaise, cheese and fruit are also on the roster.

The proper way to demolish a lobster.

Tom Hindman

How to Eat a Lobster

Always with gusto.

Rip off both claws, grab nutcracker, hammer, or rock. Crack open, remove meat, dip in butter, and eat.

Next, grab tail in one hand, body in other, and bend back until it cracks and the meat inside can be removed. Once removed, tear off end flippers, grab fork, or long narrow stick, insert, push out tail meat, and eat.

Next, tear off small claws, suck out the meat, and eat. Next, remove the body from the back, crack open sideways, remove the meat, and eat.

Finally, eat the green tomalley (liver), which many consider the best part.

**HARRASEEKET LUNCH
& LOBSTER**
207-865-4888.
End of Main St., South
   Freeport.
Open: May to mid-Oct.
Price: Inexpensive to
   Moderate.
Cuisine: Seafood.
Serving: L, D.
Credit Cards: None.
Handicap Access: Partial.

Twenty minutes from downtown Portland and ten from downtown Freeport, this is a favorite getaway, serving lobster on the deck with a protected view of boats, pine-topped islands, and Wolf's Neck. During the height of the season the line is long, and the kitchen can get a little overwhelmed, but they always remain cheerful and courteous. Better yet, schedule your visit for anything but the height of the lunch or dinner hour. For those who can make do with just lobster, clams, and corn, there's another window around the side of the shack where there is rarely anyone waiting. All the seafood tastes heavenly, the fries have that nice, dry clean taste, and the corn is worth ordering two ears at a time. The pies are okay; the homemade ice cream is better.

THAI GARDEN
207-865-6005.
233 U.S. Route 1, Freeport
   04032.
Open daily.
Moderate.
Cuisine: Thai.
Serving: L, D.
Credit Cards: AE, CB, D,
   DC, MC, V.
Handicap Access: Yes.
Features: Take-out.

In a strip mall on the southern outskirts of Freeport, you don't really come here for the view or the decor which is no better or worse than most Asian restaurants. We come here for the masaman curry and pad Thai. The menu is large and varied with ample vegetarian entrees. If you like Thai food, you can't do much better than this. We have to admit it that sometimes we go shopping up the road just so we can enjoy *this* Thai food.

Hills Beach

BUFFLEHEADS
207-284-6000.
122 Hills Beach Rd., Hills
   Beach.
Tuesday–Sunday.
Inexpensive–Moderate.
Cuisine: Family seafood.
Serving: B, L, D.
Credit Cards: MC, V.
Handicap Access: Yes.
No smoking.
Features: Deck, take-out.

A friend told us about this place, a wonderful, bright family-style restaurant plunk in the middle of an old summer colony and right on the way to pretty Hills Beach. The service is friendly, the portions generous, and on Tuesdays, you can get two entrees for the price of one (they call it Two-fer Tuesdays). The lobster pie is to die for. If you're traveling with someone who's not up to seafood, take heart. They have pasta, chicken, duck, and the Buffleburger on the menu, as well. The place is named for a chubby little duck that winters nearby in pretty Biddeford Pool. Ask and your waitress will supply a pair of binoculars so you can see if you can spot one for yourself.

Kennebunkport

ALISSON'S
207-967-4841 or
  800-667-2896.
5 Dock Square,
  Kennebunkport.
Open daily.
Price: Moderate.
Cuisine: American.
Serving: L, D.
Credit Cards: AE, D, DC,
  MC, V.
Handicap Access: Yes.
Smoking section.

Alisson's is a neighborhood breakfast establishment and later-day burger joint. Because the neighborhood happens to be Kennebunkport, that means that this place is going to be jammed in the summer. There's a butcher block bar where you can wait and watch. The help is affable and on-the-ball. On the menu, it's burgers, soup, sandwiches, salads, bar appetizers, fried seafood, and daily dinner specials. Some of the names may be too cute, but the burgers make up for it. The French fries and onion rings are good, too. Alisson's also makes a noteworthy raspberry chocolate cake.

Kittery & Kittery Point

**CAP'N SIMEON'S
  GALLEY**
207-439-3655.
Rte. 103, Pepperell Rd.,
  Kittery Point.
Closed: Tues. in winter.
Price: Inexpensive to
  Moderate.
Cuisine: Seafood.
Serving: L, D, SB.
Credit Cards: AE, D, MC, V.
Handicap Access: Yes.
Special Features: Great
  view.

This is the perfect place to pop sweet scallops in your mouth or curl up with a nice French fry and gaze out the window at the sea. That's if you can get a window seat. The lobster — usually brought in earlier in the day to the docks below — may require more concentration, but it's worth it. The interior has the feel of an old boat that has been sealed up tight with yearly coats of shellac. There is nothing fancy going on in here with the food, either. These people know what they're doing and have been doing it for years. The purpose here is to see that you're properly filled full of fresh seafood and side orders, and to go on your way. But not before you're ready to leave.

**CHAUNCEY CREEK
  LOBSTER POUND**
207-439-1030.
Chauncey Creek Rd.,
  Kittery Point.
Open: Mothers Day
  weekend–mid Oct.
Price: Moderate.
Cuisine: Lobster.
Serving: L, D.
Credit Cards: MC, V.
Special Features: Great
  no-frills lobster.

We can't think of any place we'd rather be up the creek. This old-fashioned lobster pond actually sits against the edge of an embankment rising from a creek. Across the way are thick woods, making this like a nice homey treehouse where you can lay waste to a lobster or two (there are no nautical distractions). They start serving at 10:30 a.m., and we've known friends to indulge in a late lobster breakfast now and then. The steaming mounds of clams and mussels are succulent and legendary. The service is to the point, probably because they don't indulge in any frills or side dish fanfare here. You want potato salad. Well, then, bring it yourself. The same goes for beer or wine. Chauncey's is out of the way (thoroughly removed from the shoppers' bustle in nearby Kittery) but well known and, for the crowd that comes back year after year, well worth the side trip.

Ogunquit

ARROWS
207-361-1100.
Berwick Rd., Ogunquit.
Closed: Mondays and
    December to March.
Price: Very Expensive.
Cuisine: Regional
    American with ethnic
    accents.
Serving: D.
Credit Cards: CB, MC, V.
Reservations:
    Recommended.
Handicap Access: Limited.

Arrows has a reputation for being one of the best restaurants in New England, and in our opinion it certainly is one of the best restaurants on the coast. Their menu, which changes daily, is first rate and inventive. Royal Osetra caviar served with fried potatoes, iced vodka, and red onion. Prosciutto cured right there. Most of their greens are grown outside in the garden. They have also been presenting special dinners: the food of old Beijing, what they ate at the palace of the Medicis, the cuisine of Alsace and Lorraine, and repasts of the conquistadors. At most places this would sound like dinner theater. Here it sounds like a delicious adventure. Arrows is set in a manicured 18th century farmhouse surrounded by well-tended, well-lighted gardens, and can be found several miles west of the center of Ogunquit. If you think you've missed it, keep driving. Suddenly you'll see it on the right. Their bottled selection has been praised by *The Wine Spectator*.

HURRICANE
207-646-6348 or
    800-649-6348 in Maine
    only.
Perkins Cove, Ogunquit.
Open seven days a week.
Price: Moderate to
    Expensive.
Cuisine: Seafood and
    American with ethnic
    touches.
Serving: L, D.
Credit Cards: AE, D, DC,
    MC, V.
Reservations:
    Recommended.

Hurricane's chef gets his seafood fresh off the cove's fishing boats. He grills it, and often dresses it in an elegant sauce. It's that simple. The setting, like the food, is simple but dramatic. There are two fireplaces in the dining room and views of the Atlantic from every seat. Appetizers include fresh Maine lobster gazpacho, roasted corn and fresh Roma tomato soup, or the Hurricane House salad — fresh greens, roasted shallots, pistachios topped with a cracked peppercorn dressing. There's an extra effort to make everything fresh here. Three or four varieties of fresh grilled fish are offered daily and may include pan roasted sea scallops with a sun dried tomato cream served over fresh linguine, or plank roasted haddock with black bean and Maine crab calalloo. Hurricane gives chicken, pizza, and beef equally fresh treatment and consideration. (Friends are crazy about the burgers — served only at lunch.)

JACKIE'S TOO
207-646-4444.
59 Perkins Cove, Ogunquit.
Open all year.
Price: Inexpensive to
  Moderate.
Cuisine: American.
Serving: L, D in summer;
  L in winter.
Credit Cards: MC, V.
Handicap Access: Yes.

Jackie's Too is known for the generosity with which they pack their lobster rolls, among the least expensive in town, and a lobster dinner that includes steamed clams, mussels, knockwurst, and corn on the cob. The knockwurst is, we think, not only a brave break with tradition but a savory addition. In the summer, the best seats are on the deck, within a stone's throw of the rocky cove. The atmosphere is casual and comfortable. In the off-season, you get a spectacular, albeit protected, view of the water.

JONATHAN'S
207-646-4777.
2 Bourne Ln., Ogunquit.
Closed Mon. and Tues in
  Jan., Feb., and March.
Price: Moderate.
Cuisine: New England and
  Continental.
Serving: D.
Credit Cards: AE, D, DC,
  MC, V.
Reservations: Yes.
Handicap Access: Yes.

For 18 years this has been a popular stop for area residents and returning visitors. Jonathan's offers a raw bar and an extensive menu that leans toward seafood and pasta but also includes dishes like Jaeger Schnitzel and Tennessee tenderloin of pork. Owner Jonathan West's art collection covers the dining room walls and represents well-known local painters, past and present. If they don't grab you, there's a 600-gallon tropical saltwater reef aquarium in the main dining room. Or you can take in the carefully tended gardens visible through the dining room windows. Jonathan's also provides an old-fashioned bright spot in the local nightlife with a convivial piano bar and nightly sing-alongs.

ROBERTO'S
207-646-8130.
82 Shore Rd., Ogunquit.
Closed: Dec.–April.
Price: Moderate to
  Expensive.
Cuisine: Italian.
Serving: D.
Credit Cards: AE, MC, V.
Handicap Access: Yes.

Roberto's specializes in simple Italian food, red and white checkered tablecloths, and collecting celebrities. This is an all-natural, non-salt, high-flavor Italian restaurant, and the dining room is pleasantly casual and busy. Specials change with the season: lighter in the warm days of summer and heavier in the fall. Garlic bread baked daily. Linguini, lasagna, cannelloni, things parmigiana and marsala, all presented in a restored 1850s farm house. The wine list is limited.

Old Orchard Beach

JOSEPH'S BY THE SEA
207-934-5044.
55 West Grand Ave., Old
  Orchard Beach.

In a town of snack bars and pack-'em-in surf-and-turf joints, Joseph's is where to go for escargots served with native dulse, a wild mushroom torte,

Closed: Nov.–March.
Price: Moderate.
Cuisine: French with
    regional touches.
Serving: B, D, SB.
Credit Cards: AE, MC, V.
Reservations: Suggested.

and fettucini Genovese (fresh pasta with arti-chokes, shitake mushrooms, spinach, raisins, pine nuts, and lemon basil olive oil). Joseph's is known for its Angel Hair Pasta Maison (made with shrimp, scallops, and fish sauteed in sun-dried tomatoes, garlic, herbs, and cream). There's also a Saco Bay soup — scallops, mussels, and local fish in a bouillabaisse. Once a private house, its hard-wood floors and handcrafted white birch arch-ways, awnings, and mantels are well looked after. Most people prefer to eat outside on the screened-in porch, which overlooks a manicured lawn with gar-dens, the dunes, the beach, the ocean, islands, and sky. Our optometrist first told us about Joseph's. She didn't want to let too many others in on one of the region's best-kept dining secrets. We've broken her confidence, I'm afraid. This is too good a place to hide.

Portland

BACK BAY GRILL
207-772-8833.
65 Portland St., Portland.
Closed: Sun.
Price: Expensive.
Cuisine: Regional
    American grill.
Serving: D.
Credit Cards: AE, D, DC,
    MC, V.
Reservations:
    Recommended.
Handicap Access: Yes.

This trendy grill in an untrendy part of town has a devoted following. The menu changes weekly, as do wines by the glass (there's an inter-esting selection); the beer list is not bad, either. The wait staff is extremely knowledgeable and efficient. No hemming and hawing when you want to know exactly what kind of vinegar is in the salad dress-ing. They grill almost everything here, including the vegetables and sometimes a dessert. Creme brulee is a signature finish.

**BOONES FAMOUS
RESTAURANT**
207-774-5725.
6 Custom House Wharf,
    Portland.
Open all year.
Price: Inexpensive to
    Moderate.
Cuisine: Seafood,
    American.
Serving: L, D.
Credit Cards: AE, CB, D,
    DC, MC, V.
Handicap Access: Yes.
Smoking Section.
Reservations: For parties
    over 6.

In the old days, this pier is where we would catch the ferry out to the islands. The ferry terminal has since moved down the street, but the hustle and bustle of coastal comings and goings have not been lost. We like this place for its atmosphere. The outside deck is really the former ferry pier, and it's a good place to hang out on summer dog days because there's always a salty breeze and a cool harbor view. The menu, plain and simple New England seafood, is better at dinner than at lunch, but the service is more efficient earlier in the day. We have found the haddock a little too buttery for our taste and the pie merely adequate. Still, on a hot day, a cold draught at the open air bar, complete with a well-preserved trophy tuna, is sure to make up for any shortcomings.

**COTTON STREET
CANTINA**
207-775-3222.
10 Cotton St., Portland.
Open daily.
Price: Moderate.
Cuisine: Americanized
    Caribbean.
Serving: L, D.
Credit Cards: AE, D, MC,
    V.

What can we say? The servings here are big. That being said, we will gladly admit there are other charms to this popular lunch and after-work hangout. If it's winter, the cheerful iridescent pastels, chunky wooden furniture, and big central fountain in the downstairs dining room almost make you forget the snow piling up outside. If it's summer, be sure to arrive early to grab one of the few outside tables where you can nurse an island cocktail or tumbler of fresh squeezed lemonade. Food? Try the sizable tropical pulled pork burrito or Tampa pan Cubano, an overstuffed Cuban-styled sandwich of Virginia ham, Spanish sausage, pickles and cheese —definitely not for the faint of stomach.

DELLA'S CATESSEN
207-773-2624.
92 Exchange St., Portland.
Open all year.
Price: Inexpensive.
Cuisine: American.
Serving: L, D.
Credit Cards: AE, MC, V.
Handicap Access: Yes.

Visitors order deli style here, but the atmosphere is more like a hip urban diner. The walls are painted in broad yellow and white stripes, and adorned with framed vintage *Life* magazine covers and autographed pictures of Roy Rogers, Dale Evans, and other Western greats. We eat here a lot and aren't afraid to champion our favorites. The meatloaf sandwich with spicy ketchup reminds us of mom's famous meatloaf. The turkey burrito is a lean and filling specialty. The melts are always good. Della herself presides with a smile over the friendly and welcoming staff. Take home dinner, ready to pop into the oven or micro, or choose from a selection of wines, gourmet foods, and regional specialties (Atlantic salmon, salt water taffy, rice noodles, exotic coffee beans). Also, this is the perfect place to pick up a boxed lunch for a day on the islands or a trip up the coast. Make sure one of Della's sinful desserts goes with you. We are particularly partial to the lemon squares and coconut-chocolate Magic Bars.

FORE STREET
207-775-2717.
288 Fore Street, Portland.
Open nightly.
Price: Expensive.
Serving: D.
Credit Cards: AE, MC, V.
Handicap Access: Yes.

Fore Street is a place for sizable appetites and sophisticated tastes. The dining room is large and noisy — sometimes a bit too loud — with all the action centered around an open kitchen and the restaurant's impressive wood ovens. The menu changes daily and includes many items that have been apple wood smoked or grilled. Many of the appetizers and salads come from local farms and gardens in season. We enjoyed the tender hanger steak, grilled to just the right degree, and a braised fish and shellfish ragout. Best of all, we like to stop in here every once in a while for a cocktail or a light dinner in the small, elegant bar located just to the left as you come in door. The chairs are quite comfortable.

KATAHDIN
207-774-1740.
Corner of Spring and High
    St., Portland.
Closed: Sunday.
Price: Inexpensive to
    Moderate.
Serving: D.
Credit Cards: D, MC, V.
Handicap Access: Yes.
Reservations: No.

This is a restaurant not afraid to serve carrots. We come here all the time, usually to get the Blue Plate Special and its accompanying mound of mashed potatoes. There's fun stuff on the walls and in the windows, no-nonsense wait people who know what they're doing, and on any given night, the clientele is a good cross section of Portland, including all the so-called alternative groups. When we're not eating the blue plate, we like the stews or the buckwheat pasta, favored by a nurse friend who suggests a half order. Restaurants come and go in Portland. This one appears to be solidly entrenched.

NORM'S BAR B Q
207-774-6711.
43 Middle St., Portland.
Closed: Monday and
    Tuesday.
Price: Inexpensive to
    Moderate.
Cuisine: Bar B Que.
Serving: L, D.
Credit Cards: None.
Handicap Access: No.
Reservations: No

Ah, if not barbecue in Maine, then where? Actually, at times up here, we all get pretty tired of seafood, which may be why you'll find so many ethnic restaurants hidden away. The only fish you'll find at Norm's is catfish, barbecued catfish. Norm also sells homemade clam cakes, but that's it. The rest is ribs — pork, spare, country style, and beef short — barbecued chicken, meat sandwiches smothered in barbecue sauce, and barbecued duck salad, the chef's one bow to highbrow. Buttermilk biscuits and cornbread are baked fresh. Plus, try Norm's crunchy coleslaw or his fresh baked pies for dessert.

PEPPER CLUB
207-772-0531.
78 Middle St., Portland.
Open: Daily.
Price: Inexpensive to
    Moderate.
Serving: D.
Credit Cards: None.
Handicap Access: Limited.
Reservations: No

Very organic and meatless, except for the hamburgers and an occasional chicken. In fact, the hamburgers are usually what we end up getting. They're big, juicy, and made from organic beef. This is Portland's version of southwestern-meets-Los Angeles — lots of huevos rancheros colors painted in jagged angles on the walls, and big black booths. All items are written in multi-colored chalk on the big blackboard, and are multi-ethnic in origin. They also make a nice pie.

PORT BAKE HOUSE
207-773-2217
205 Commercial St.,
   Portland.
Open daily.
Price: Inexpensive to
   Moderate.
Serving: B, L.
Credit Cards: MC, V.
Handicap Access: Limited.
Reservations: No.

STREET & COMPANY
207-775-0887.
33 Wharf St., Portland.
Open daily.
Price: Moderate.
Cuisine: Seafood, pasta.
Serving: D.
Credit Cards: AE, MC, V.
Special Features: Patio
   dining.
Handicap Access: Yes.
Reservations:
   Recommended.

**THREE DOLLAR
DEWEY'S**
207-772-3310.
241 Commercial St.,
   Portland.
Price: Inexpensive.
Cuisine: American,
   vegetarian.
Serving: L, D.
Credit Cards: MC, V.
Special features: Free
   popcorn.

WALTER'S CAFE
207-871-9258.
15 Exchange St., Portland.
Open daily.
Price: Moderate.
Cuisine: American bistro.

This used be just a lunchtime joint and bakery where the mostly business crowd hunched over a tiny counter and devoured big and tasty sandwiches. They went upscale recently and converted it into a little bistro with an expanded menu full of quiche, some more ambitious entrees, and some of the best soup and sandwiches around. We especially like sipping our soup on the new, second floor patio. The fish soup, when they have it, is quite good and the view of the harbor is one of the best in town.

Garlic from the open kitchen still perfumes the air at the casual, subterranean retreat, which sits on a funky cobblestone alley in Portland's Old Port. Dried flowers, rough wood, and family-sized cans of olive oil and tomatoes give the place an ethnic feel. They serve no red meat here, making Street & Co. a logical choice for visitors to this seaside metropolis. Salmon, swordfish, scallops, and shrimp are constants. There's also a soup of the day and changing specials like tuna Niçoise and sole meuniere. Pastas come with a variety of creative seafood sauces. Recent additions include a second dining room and a wine bar with one of the best wine selections in town.

This Portland landmark ale house moved to spiffy new quarters a few years back and now sits at the heart of the city's working waterfront district. The building is old, and that lends a nice flavor to the alehouse atmosphere. The kitchen here turns out an interesting menu of pub food mixed with a dash of spicy vegetarian. You can bring the kids during the afternoon and enjoy burgers at the long alehouse tables.

This is one of those places so much a part of our routine that we often forget to tell others about it. Exposed brick walls, and views into the open kitchen from the downstairs dining room (there are two more small dining rooms upstairs) — close

Serving: L, D.
Credit Cards: AE, MC, V.

your eyes and you could imagine yourself in almost any urban hot spot. The menu reads like an American melting pot: cool Asian noodle salad; east end pannini; southwest spring rolls; Carolina barbecue. Call us boring, but we harbor a soft spot for their giant grilled burgers and their homemade chips. The service is solidly efficient and the food, reliable and satisfying.

Saco

CORNFORTH HOUSE
207-284-2006.
893 Portland Rd. (Rte. 1),
   Saco.
Closed: Mon. in season; Jan.
   and Feb.
Price: Expensive.
Cuisine: Continental.
Serving: D, SB.
Credit Cards: MC, V.
Reservations:
   Recommended.
Handicap Access: Yes.

The Cornforth House is an elegant sidelight on busy Rte. 1 — the last place you would expect to find a country inn. Once inside, the mood is romantic, with gilt-framed artwork and ornate fireplaces in the several small dining rooms. The service is warm, and maybe too eager. The menu ranges from classics such as steak au poivre, rack of lamb, prime rib, and veal marsala to more creative notions like veal sausage in puff pastry and pecan chicken. Desserts, made fresh daily, include a leprechaun-green creme de menthe mousse cake and a monster ice-cream-filled profiterole with hot fudge.

Scarborough

**CARSON'S FAMILY
   RESTAURANT**
207-883-4400.
433 U.S. Rte. 1,
   Scarborough.
Open year round.
Price: Inexpensive.
Cuisine: Seafood, diner
   food.
Serving: B, L, D.
Credit Cards: D, MC, V.
Handicap Access: Yes.

From the outside Carson's looks like one of those roadside stops that could be either a great find or a terrible mistake. It's a find. Frilly white and pink curtains lend a homey touch to classic diner booths. There's also a breakfast counter. The waitresses call you "honey" and treat everyone with a sisterly kindness. The menu is huge and put together with the traveling family in mind: hamburgers and cheeseburgers for the kids; meatloaf and center cut pork chops for those wanting to experience the cuisine of their childhood; salad plates for the dieter; a 12-oz. prime rib for the big eater, as well as a dazzling selection of fresh seafood. Ask for yours with a side of their great mashed potatoes. The pie and strawberry shortcake are homemade, and good.

**SPURWINK COUNTRY
   KITCHEN**
207-799-1177.
150 Spurwink Rd.,
   Scarborough.

The Spurwink is a low-slung beach bungalow smack dab in the middle of a coastal salt marsh and located near some of our favorite beaches. This is a local favorite, especially among families and

Closed: Mondays; late Oct. through mid April.
Price: Inexpensive to Moderate.
Cuisine: Family.
Serving: L, D.
Credit Cards: D, MC, V.
Handicap Access: Yes.
No smoking.

the older Cape Elizabeth crowd. They serve simple Down East classics, a few light items, a selection of half sandwich and cup of soup, and daily specials that you can rely on week to week. They also offer an occasional surprise, for instance their black beans and rice, which we like. Beer and wine are available by the glass. All desserts are homemade, and the wild blueberry pie is topnotch. The atmosphere is generally peaceful. They also have a kids' menu. Everything is available for take out.

Wells Beach

BILLY'S CHOWDER HOUSE
207-646-7558.
216 Mile Rd., Wells Beach.
Open daily in season; closed Dec. to late Feb.
Price: Moderate.
Cuisine: American, seafood.
Serving: L, D.
Credit Cards: AE, D, MC, V.
Handicap Access: Yes.

Friends of ours, a fisherman and an artist, know people from the Massachusetts' Berkshires who, when they hanker for fried clams or boiled lobsters, come here. Then they go home. All in the same day. Our friends understand this. They tell the story to make a point. The portions are huge. What you can't eat, you can take with you. The fried stuff is delicious and light — a true guilty pleasure that's so enjoyable you have a hard time believing it's bad for you. The service is bustling and efficient. This place has a hard New England beauty that you can't beat. Pine boards inside, wetlands and water outside.

York & York Harbor

FLO'S HOTDOGS
Unlisted phone.
Rte. 1, York.
Open all year.
Price: Inexpensive.
Cuisine: American.
Serving: L.
Credit Cards: None.

It's not the hot dog. It's the sauce, the abuse, the atmosphere, and probably something deeper than all that. Just past Pie in the Sky on Rte. 1, this one-story shack with no real sign is the destination of experienced travelers, rich and poor, who come here from all over the country. There's no real parking lot. You just kind of pull over. Inside, not only is there no view, there are no windows, just a few old yellow wooden swivel stools and an order counter. "Here the customer is never right," says Gail, Flo's daughter-in-law. Ah, delicious.

YORK HARBOR INN
207-363-5119 or 800-343-3869.
Rte. 1A, York Harbor.
Open all year.

This 17th-century white clapboard covered inn offers broiled scrod, milky clam chowder, a cluster of many small dining rooms, and a partial view of the harbor. Heavy wood beams, low ceil-

Price: Moderate to
   Expensive.
Cuisine: American.
Serving: B, L, D.
Credit Cards: AE, MC, V.
Reservations:
   Recommended.
Handicap Access: Yes.

ings, creaky wood floors provide that old new world feel. So does the menu. This is a good place for a dose of classic New England dining.

SOUTH COAST: FOOD PURVEYORS

Direct marketing of vegetables in Arundel.

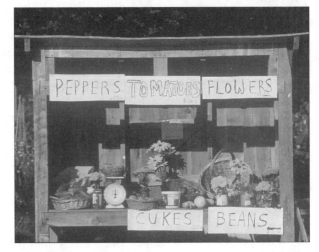

Herb Swanson

We're including a list of food purveyors for each region on the coast. Some are delicatessens that will sell almost anything to go, others are bakeries, gourmet or ethnic food, or beer and wine stores. Visitors will want to note that wine and beer are available broadly, but hard liquor can be harder to find, as liquor stores are not plentiful.

BAKERIES

Bread & Roses (207-646-4227; 28A Main St., Ogunquit). Fresh pastries and bread baked on the spot.

Chase Hill Bakery (207-967-2283; 9 Chase Hill Rd., Kennebunk). An unassuming gray clapboard house with old-fashioned bakery cases and a table or two. They sell comforting chicken pot pies, breads, cakes, and pastries.

Standard Baking Company (207-773-2112; 31 Wharf Street, Portland). Most people like their baguettes the best. We are partial to their sticky buns, spicy ginger cake, and flakey apple tarts.

Whistling Wings Farm (207-282-1146; 427 West St., Biddeford). Berries from this farm and kitchen end up on tables all over the world. The jams, jellies, and syrups contain no preservatives or juice concentrates, and in summer the bakery offers berry sweets for immediate consumption.

BREWERIES

There continues to be an explosion of microbreweries in Maine. D.L. Geary, maker of Geary's Pale Ale, one of the very first microbrews made, is still going strong, and has added a smokey London Porter to their roster. There are so many micros and such an appreciative audience that recently a microbrew (Shipyard Export Ale) sold more beer in Maine than Budweiser. Can you imagine that? If you are looking for a good place to sample the full range of Maine micros, check out *The Great Lost Bear* in Portland (207-772-0300; 540 Forest Ave.).

Allagash Brewing (207-878-5385; 100 Industrial Way, Portland).

Casco Bay Brewing (207-797-2020; 57 Industrial Way). Tours available.

Geary Brewing Company (207-878-2337; 38 Evergreen Dr., Portland). They brew a fine ale here, and if you can't make it to the brewery you can find it at almost any grocery store or gourmet shop in the area. Tours available.

Gritty McDuff's (207-772-2739; 396 Fore St., Portland). This seems like just about everyone's favorite brew pub in New England. They are so popular, they now have a second brew pub (207-865-4321; 183 Lower Main St., Freeport), and they bottle a line of their "best" beers. We like this place, even though we find the brew can be watery.

Kennebunkport Brewing/Federal Jack's Brew Pub (207-967-4322; 8 Western Avenue, Kennebunk). A brew pub and microbrewery at the site of a historic shipyard, and brewer of the aforementioned Shipyard Export Ale. The pub is okay. The beer is better.

Shipyard Brewing Company (207-761-0807; 86 Newbury St., Portland). The "sister" brewery to the Kennebunkport Brewing Co. The big beer guys at Miller were so impressed, they invested in it. This brewery was built on the site where, coincidentally, Henry Wadsworth Longfellow was born in 1807. They brew a fine winter ale in his honor. They also brew Old Thumper Extra Special Ale and more. Tours available.

Stone Coast Brewing (207-773-2337; 14 York St., Portland). There are many in this town who believe that you can't have enough beer or too many brew pubs. This is one of the area's newest brew pubs, but popular both for its beer and for its music. Its stage is one of the busiest on the South Coast.

CANDY & ICE CREAM

Beal's Old Fashioned Ice Cream (207-828-1335; 12 Moulton St., Portland; and 207-883-1160; 161 Pine Point Rd., Scarborough). The name may sound as if it's too good to be true, but it is. Standard flavors run the gamut from vanilla to deep, dark variations on chocolate. They also have someone out back who occasionally comes out with a surprise, like lemon-mint. It's really good.

Ben & Jerry's Ice Cream (207-865-3407; 83 Main St., Freeport). This grew from a one-room shack on the curb outside L.L. Bean to a much larger one room shack, big enough to accommodate long lines in all kinds of weather. Sometimes you need ice cream after a long day shopping.

Browns Apiaries (207-829-5994; 239 Greely Rd., Cumberland). They raise bees here and sell the sweet by-products. Honey, strained and with the comb, in half-pound to one gallon sizes, candles, honey candy, and bee keeping supplies. They're open year round, five days a week, but it's best to call ahead.

The Goldenrod (207-363-2621; York Beach). A vacation at the beach wouldn't be the same without saltwater taffy. They make it right here and call it "kisses." Watch it being made or grab an ice cream soda at their old-fashioned soda fountain.

Harbor Candy Shop (207-646-8078; 26 Main St., Ogunquit). European-style chocolates are made and sold here in a very elegant atmosphere. Their marzipan is out of this world.

Haven's (207-772-0761; 542 Forest Ave., Portland). Every year they hire a new taffy puller and put him in the front window. Usually it's a high school boy, and the girls are hooked for the rest of the summer. Frankly, saltwater taffy is taffy, just about everywhere. Here, you should try the Bangor taffy, a Maine specialty, which has a buttery caramel flavor.

Wilbur's Chocolate Shoppe (207-865-6129; 13 Bow St., Freeport). All-natural chocolate — creams, berry flavors, or rich and dark.

DELIS & TAKE-OUT

Anthony's Food Shop (207-363-2322; 679 Rte. 1, York). Beer, apples, pizza, but best is a selection of great Green Mountain coffees like Columbian Supremo with real cream. There are small sizes for short hops and large sizes for long hauls. If you didn't get a decent cup of coffee for breakfast, stop here and rectify the situation.

Aurora Provisions (207-871-9060; 64 Pine St., Portland). Upscale takeout, such as lamb stuffed with goat cheese and other amazing things. Personally, we like their macaroni and cheese.

Federal Spice (207-774-6404; 225 Federal St., Portland). Tasty, low-fat renditions of the ever-popular burrito. We especially like the pumpkin rice.

Granny's Burrito's (207-761-0751; 420 Fore St., Portland). Sit down and enjoy a burrito at the picnic-style tables or grab one to go.

Hamilton's (207-646-5262; 2 Shore Rd., Ogunquit). Eat-in or take-out available from this deli on the main drag. A favorite breakfast spot for residents.

Hattie's Deli (207-282-3435) in Biddeford Pool. Blueberry pie.

Old Salt's Pantry (207-967-4966; Dock Sq., Kennebunkport). Don't be fooled by its size. This tiny deli offers a huge menu of take-out from sandwiches, subs, and burgers to gourmet tidbits, wine, and beer.

West End Grocery (207-874-6426; 133 Spring St., Portland). Right next door to the Inn at Park Spring, this little neighborhood deli makes fabulous sandwiches and apple cake.

FAST FOOD

Bob's Clam Hut (207-439-4233; Rte. 1, Kittery). Fried clams, sweet and steaming, are served here year round. The ultimate in finger-fast food.

Lobster Cooker (207-865-4349; 39 Main St., Freeport). This is fast food the Maine way. Crisp fried haddock sandwiches, fresh fish chowder, and, of course, lobster rolls — served in a cheery, no-nonsense atmosphere that would make Ray Kroc proud.

Mark's (corner of Exchange and Middle Sts., Portland). Mark is out there through all kinds of weather selling his dogs and smoked sausages from a little red cart. There's a park next door for you to sit in, if it's warm enough.

FOOD FESTIVALS

Yarmouth Clam Festival (207-846-3984). Third week in July. Every year for almost 30 years, the folks in Yarmouth pay tribute to the clam. They eat lots of fried ones, then they go take a ride on the roller coaster at the midway.

GOURMET FOOD STORES

Micucci's (207-775-1854; 45 India St., Portland). A tiny Italian grocer at the foot of Munjoy Hill, they have all the fixings for an authentic Italian feast, including fresh mozzarella on Wednesdays.

Stonewall Kitchen (207-351-2712; 469 U.S. Rte. 1, York and 207-236-8979; 182 Middle St., Portland). Mmmmm. Roasted garlic and onion jam. Ginger peach tea jam. Recently, this award-winning maker of gourmet condiments opened a second store in Portland's Old Port. They've also added a children's line, so now you can get one of their clever peanut butter and jam kits for the little folks back home.

HEALTH FOOD & FARM MARKETS

Portland Green Grocer (207-761-9232; 211 Commercial St., Portland). Terrific fruit and vegetables. Great bakery breads, wine, and an ever-improving selection of cheeses and gourmet deli meats.

Herb Swanson

The Portland Public Market, a great place to put together a picnic.

Portland Public Market (207-228-2000; 25 Preble St., Portland). It's a bit out of the way for most travelers, but worth the side trip. More than 20 vendors selling everything from farm fresh produce and organic beef to fresh flowers, buffalo meat, and wine.

Wolf Neck Farm (207-865-4469; Wolf Neck Rd., off Flying Point Rd., Freeport). Lean, delicious organic beef and lamb raised on a beautiful saltwater farm run by the state university system. They ship to New England and elsewhere, but it's better yet to take the trip down the long dirt road and get a slab to thaw out for a seaside barbecue. This farm has been operating for more than one hundred years and selling natural beef since 1959.

SOUTH COAST: CULTURE

Painters, sculptors, musicians, poets, and writers all have found the Maine coast a place to concentrate on their art. Edgar Allen Beem, a local art critic, has described the attraction of Maine for artists who have always been "mavericks and loners seeking privacy and freedom from influence." The coast, he writes, offers "a sense of authenticity that occurs only when nature and culture are in right relation with each other." That relation has become an elusive balance in most other parts of America these days.

During the late 1800s, Winslow Homer painted at Prouts Neck, a 112-acre point of land stretching into the Gulf of Maine south of Portland (his mother was born in Bucksport). You can find examples of his work, plus some Wyeths, Wellivers, and other well known Maine painters at the Portland Museum of Art.

The most American of poets, Henry Wadsworth Longfellow was born in Portland in 1807, and immortalized the town in his poem "My Lost Youth." He and novelist Nathaniel Hawthorne were classmates at Bowdoin College in Brunswick, both graduating in 1825. Author and environmental activist Rachel Carson, who summered on the South Coast, found Maine a wonderful laboratory for her study of the environment. She wrote *The Edge of the Sea* here.

Today there are dozens of artists and writers who live here year round, many lured by the relatively low cost of living. There are so many writers on the coast that ships arrive with cargoes of Xerox toner and depart laden with manuscripts, cracked humorist Garrison Keillor on a recent stopover in Portland.

The result of all this history of artistic activity is a public that has a deep and healthy appreciation for the visual, written, and spoken arts. It has not been possible to list every historic site and arts organization. For a more complete listing for the area you plan to visit, contact the chamber of commerce for that area (see Chapter Seven, *Information*).

ARCHITECTURE

The earliest buildings built by Europeans making their homes on the coast are believed to have been turf and thatch huts similar to those in England of the same period. It is thought that soon after their arrival settlers began using the abundant lumber from local forests.

Few examples of the structures built by European settlers prior to 1760 remain. Farmhouses, forts, and other early buildings were victims of the ongoing French and Indian Wars, which lasted from 1675 to 1763. One exception is the *Old Stone Gaol* in York, a stone building built in 1653. The old jail house is now a museum and is the oldest stone building still in use in the United States.

Wood continued to be the most popular building material throughout most of the state. Brick became popular in Portland after two fires, in 1775 and 1866, tore through streets lined with wooden structures. Native granite, quarried inland and on several islands off the coast, was primarily used for decorative facades.

The earliest surviving wood-built houses on the Maine coast are similar to those found to the south in New Hampshire and Massachusetts. The design focused on a central chimney and entranceway. A parlor and a dining room usually flanked the entranceway. The kitchen was situated at the rear of the chimney with a small room to either side filling out the basic rectangular shape of the building. Upstairs there were two main bed chambers at the front of the house and two smaller rooms to the rear. Many of the old houses were expanded throughout the years with rooms and a covered walkway connecting to a barn at the back of the house. The exterior of the houses were finished with clapboards (a few were built from brick), and the earliest houses were devoid of outside decoration.

Many examples of the Georgian and Federal styles have survived and seem to have been the preferred architecture for well-to-do residents during the late 1700s and early 1800s. The Greek Revival took hold of Maine during the mid-1800s, a time when the coast was experiencing a great influx of wealth from the shipbuilding and shipping trade. Many of the newly wealthy were ships' captains, and their houses, that line the coast, are rich with elegant woodworking and flying staircases. A good example of the Greek Revival is the *Sarah Orne Jewett House* in South Berwick. The Gothic Revival movement was not as popular, although there are several fine examples that have survived. In Brunswick, there are two Gothic Revival churches: the *First Parish Church* is the more ornate of the two; *St. Paul's* is a more austere example of the trend. In Kennebunk, the *Wedding Cake House* is perhaps the state's most conspicuous example of the Gothic. Portland is home to the state's most outstanding example of the Italianate phase of the Gothic Revival. The *Victoria Mansion,* also known as the Morse-Libby House, was built in 1859 and is rich in Italianate detail.

After the Civil War, the coast became a summer playground for wealthy Bostonians and New Yorkers. Thus the predominate style of architecture during the late 1800s was the grand "cottage," summer homes that were the size of small mansions. Boston architect William R. Emerson made a great impact with the cottages he designed for wealthy patrons on Mount Desert Island — rambling wooden shingled buildings with large airy rooms that also incorporated native granite and stone. Portland architect John Calvin Stevens expanded on Emerson's principles and lined streets throughout the state with stately shingled cottages for both summer and year-round residents.

Since the mid-1600s, the predominant trend in coastal architecture has been simplicity and practicality. That is still seen in the small lobster and fishing shacks that seem to grow out of the rocks and have changed little during the past 100 years, as well as in the new *Maine Maritime Museum* in Bath, I.M.

Pei's **Portland Art Museum,** and perhaps the most famous home in Maine, the **Olson House** in Cushing, made so by artist Andrew Wyeth in his painting *Christina's World.*

For architecture buffs, there is a state inventory of Maine architecture on file at the architectural archives at **Colby College** in Waterville. **The Frances W. Peabody Research Library** at Greater Portland Landmarks (207-774-5561;165 State Street, Portland; E-mail, landmarks@maine.rr.com) is a good place to get a basic education in the region's architectural heritage. The organization offers an excellent walking tour map of the city's historical districts, which include an impressive Victorian residential district with homes of the Italianate, Gothic Revival, Queen Anne, Colonial Revival, and Shingle styles. Walking tour maps are available for a nominal fee, and throughout the summer Landmarks offers a series of guided tours of historically and architecturally significant neighborhoods in Portland and the islands of Casco Bay. Guided walking tours detailing Kennebunk's architectural heritage leave from the **Brick Store Museum;** www.brickstore.com; E-mail, brickstore@cybertours.com. Call 207-985-4802 for information.

Several chambers of commerce, including of course, Portland's, offer maps for self-guided walking tours of local historic districts and buildings. Many of these annotated maps are available at state tourism offices (see Chapter Seven, *Information*). An excellent guide for those embarking on driving survey of coastal architecture is *Maine: A Guide 'Downeast'* published in 1970 by the Maine League of Historical Societies and Museums. Although the book is out of print, it is available in the Maine collections of most local libraries.

GALLERIES

Painters and artists seem to flourish in Maine, so well that often it seems there are as many galleries as lobster pounds. We have culled through the many public, non-profit, and commercial galleries to offer a snapshot of the art scene on the coast. Many of the galleries listed below specialize in the work of Maine artists and that of artists who regularly summer on the coast.

Frost Gully Gallery (207-773-2555; E-mail, frstglly@rr.com; 411 Congress St., Portland). Drawings, paintings, prints, and sculptures by contemporary Maine artists. Mon.–Fri. 12–6.

Institute of Contemporary Art (207-775-5152; www.meca.edu; Maine College of Art, 522 Congress St., Portland). Work by the faculty of this growing art school, plus frequent shows of students' work. This is a good place to find out what's on the mind and in the eye of young artists everywhere. This new building has encompassed the prior Baxter Gallery. Summer; Wed.–Sat. 10–4. Winter; Tues.–Sun. 11–4; Thurs. 11–9.

June Fitzpatrick Gallery (207-772-1961; 112 High St., Portland) Tucked in an old house on a busy street, this tiny gallery often offers a fresh alternative to more "established" art hanging on the walls of the Portland Museum of Art (which is up the street and around the corner).Tues.–Sat. 12–5.

Mast Cove Gallery (207-967-3453; Main St., Kennebunkport). This gallery offers what art critic Gail Glickman calls a "solid introduction to Maine Art." 10–5 daily.

Nancy Margolis Gallery (207-775-3822; 367 Fore St., Portland). Nationally known artists. Features contemporary American crafts, especially textiles, ceramics, and jewelry.

Salt Gallery (207-761-0660; www.salt.edu; 17 Pine St., Portland). Operated by the Salt Center for Documentary Field Studies, this gallery features documentary photographic works by Salt students, alumni, and professional photographers. Wed. and Fri. 2–6; Sat. 10–1.

GARDENS & GARDEN TOURS

Winters on the coast are long. The growing season is short, and the soil, although rocky, is rich. It is little wonder that summer and year-round residents who garden here take so much pride in what they are able to accomplish during the short spring and cool summer (which by the way is an ideal climate for roses). There are several annual garden tours on the coast no self-respecting garden lover would miss. One of those is *Greater Portland Landmarks* (landmark@maine.rr.com) annual house and garden tour which in early summer gains the tourist entrance to a selection of the city's splendid private gardens (207-774-5561). Following are two South Coast gardens open to the public, both of interest to the dedicated gardener.

Hamilton House (Vaughan's Ln., S. Berwick). Overlooking the Pisquataqua River, these are some of the most beautiful grounds in Southern Maine. Open dawn to dusk from June to mid-Oct.

St. Anthony Monastery and Shrines (28 Beach Ave., Kennebunkport). This tranquil retreat is a turn-of-the-century Tudor mansion purchased by the Lithuanian Franciscans in 1949. The gardens and lawns are beautiful. A wooded walkway follows the Kennebunk River and offers fine views of the well-manicured grounds and the ocean. Grounds are open to the public. (207-967-2011; guest accommodations are available, see *Lodging*).

HISTORIC BUILDINGS & SITES

There are hundreds of historic homes and sites that date from Maine's earliest days as part of the Massachusetts Bay Colony and are open to the public. Many of them are the product of the boom times the maritime industry experienced in the late 18th and early 19th centuries. Below, we provide an abbreviated list of notable ones on the South Coast, as well as forts and other coastal history hot spots. Many of these charge a nominal fee for admission (between $1 and $5); others are open to the public free of charge. Be aware that seasons, hours, and admission policies frequently change. When possible we have provided phone numbers for your convenience.

If you are a serious history buff and want to do some additional research, check in with the *Maine Historical Society* (207-774-1822; www.mainehistory.org; E-mail, ncoming@mainehistory.org; 485 Congress St., Portland 04101); the *Maine Historic Preservation Commission* (207-287-2132; E-mail, kirk.mohney@state.me.us; 55 Capital St., 69 State House Station, Augusta 04333-0065); or the *Society for the Preservation of New England Antiquities* (603-436-3205; www.spnea.org; Piscataqua Maine Region, 143 Pleasant St., Portsmouth, NH 03801). The last will provide you with a free visitors' guide to their historic homes in Maine if you send a self-addressed, postage paid envelope (you'll need two first-class stamps).

ADMIRAL ROBERT E. PEARY HOME
207-624-6080.
Eagle Island, Casco Bay.
Season: June–Labor Day, daily 10–6. Accessible by boat.
Admission charged.

Construction of this handsome summer home began five years before Peary discovered the North Pole. The restored home features many striking design elements, including three quartz and fieldstone fireplaces. There are nature trails and a public pier where ferries, tour boats, and visiting sailors can tie up.

FORT McCLARY
207-384-5160.
Rte. 103 (Kittery Point Rd.), Kittery Pt.
Season: May 30–Oct. 1.
Nominal Admission.

The granite fortification that dates back to 1715 saw strategic duty during the Revolutionary War, the War of 1812, the Civil War, and the Spanish-American War. The fort was named for Andrew McClary, a local soldier who died at the Battle of Bunker Hill.

HAMILTON HOUSE
603-436-3205.
www.spnea.org.
Vaughan's Ln., S. Berwick.
Season: June–mid-Oct.; hourly tours Wed.–Sun., 11–5 p.m.
Nominal admission charged; grounds open dawn till dusk year round.

First built for a wealthy merchant during the 18th century, then altered by Boston residents Emily Tyson and her daughter Elise in 1898 to use as a summer home. The two women, friends of author Sarah Orne Jewett, outfitted it in grand Colonial Revival style. Several of the younger Tyson's period photographs are on view, testament to the civilized coastal summer life they enjoyed. The gardens and grounds are lovely, and many visit just to picnic in warm weather or cross-country ski in winter.

J. David Bohl

Overlooking the Pisquataqua River, the Hamilton House has beautiful grounds and gardens.

LADY PEPPERELL HOUSE
Kittery Pt.
Season: Summer: 1–4.
Admission charged.

The 1760 Georgian home of Sir William Pepperell's widow (Sir William was given a baronetcy for his success at the Battle of Louisburg on Cape Breton). The house contains period furnishings and several family portraits — including a portrait of Jane Pepperell, the first painting to be associated with Maine, as well as a good collection of fans and dishes.

NEAL DOW MEMORIAL
714 Congress St., Portland.
Open year round, Mon.–
   Fri., 11–4.
No charge.

Neal Dow was a Quaker who was a leader in social reform during the 19th century. The memorial is the home he and his wife, Maria Cornelia Durant Maynard, built in 1829. Dow was an outspoken advocate for temperance, an abolitionist, Civil War general, two-time mayor of Portland, and candidate for the U.S. presidency on the Prohibition Party ticket. His home, now managed by the Maine Women's Christian Temperance Union, is on the National Register of Historical Places and is a Colonial Revival gem.

NOTT HOUSE
207-967-2751.
Maine St., Kennebunkport.
Season: Open mid-June
through mid-Oct.,
Tues.–Fri. 1–4.

Also known as "White Columns," this beautiful Greek Revival home dates to 1853. It still retains many of its original features and furnishings including wallpapers, carpets, and furniture.

OLD YORK HISTORICAL SOCIETY
207-363-4974.
www.nentug.org/
museums/oldyork.
Lindsay Rd. and Rte. 1A,
Old York.
Season: Mid-June–Sept. 30.
Nominal admission.

A "living history" museum that includes six period village buildings including: the Old Gaol (1719), the oldest public building still in use; the *Emerson-Wilcox House* (1740); the Elizabeth Perkins House (1731); the *Jefferds Tavern* (1750); the *Old Schoolhouse;* and the *John Hancock Wharf and Warehouse.* A good representation of the life and commerce of an 18th-century seaside town. Demonstrations of cooking and maritime crafts; displays of period furniture, china and glass, and the only complete set of the American crewel work in existence (at the Emerson-Wilcox House).

PORTLAND OBSERVATORY
207-774-5561.
www.portlandlandmarks.
org.
138 Congress St., Portland.
Season: Memorial Day to
Labor Day.
Nominal fee.

Built in 1807, this is the last remaining signal tower on the eastern seaboard. The architecture is striking with heavy timbers forming a hexagonal shingled tower that narrows at the top. The views of Greater Portland and the Casco Bay provide a good orientation for the traveler who has just arrived in town. The building is maintained by Greater Portland Landmarks. The observatory will be closed a short time for reconstruction. Call for more information.

SARAH ORNE JEWETT HOUSE
603-436-3205.
www.spnea.org
5 Portland St., S. Berwick.
Season: June 1–Oct. 15,
Wed.–Sun., 11–5; tours
on the hour.
Nominal admission.

This mansion was built in 1718 and later enlarged and remodeled for civic leader Jonathan Sayward who was well known during the Revolution for his Tory sympathies. The owner was wealthy but frugal, and with its small, modest rooms and good, locally made woodwork and furniture, this well-preserved home provides a realistic view of a typical Mainer's lifestyle during the 18th century. The house also has a good collection of Chippendale and Queen Anne furniture, family portraits, and china brought back as booty from the successful skirmish with the French at Louisburg in 1745. Maintained by the Society for the Preservation of New England Antiquities.

Writer Sarah Orne Jewett's home in South Berwick. Jewett is the author of The Country of the Pointed Firs, *an entertaining chronicle of life on the coast during the late 1800s.*

Maine Historic Preservation Commission

SAYWARD-WHEELER HOUSE
603-436-3205.
www.spnea.org.
79 Barrell Ln. Extension, York Harbor.
Season: June–mid-Oct., Sat., Sun. 11–5; hourly tours.
Admission charged.

VICTORIA MANSION
207-772-4841.
www.portlandarts.com/ victoriamansion.
E-mail, victoria@ maine.rr.com.
109 Danforth St., Portland.
Season: May–Oct., Tues.– Sat. 10–4; Sun. 1–5. Open by appointment the rest of the year.
Admission charged.

The 1760 Georgian home of Sir William Pepperell's widow (Sir William led colonial forces at the definitive battle at Louisburg on Cape Breton and was given a baronet for his success). The house contains period furnishings and several family portraits — including a portrait of Jane Pepperell, the first painting to be associated with Maine — as well as a good collection of fans and dishes.

Also known as the Morse-Libby House, the imposing brownstone Italianate villa built for Ruggles Sylvester Morse looks as if it were a set for an episode of *The Addams Family*. Morse was a hotelier between 1858 and 1860, and much of this small mansion is packed with lavish, hotel-sized Victorian details. The house is still in the process of being restored, but is well worth visiting for its seven hand-carved Italian marble fireplaces and mantels alone. Our favorites are the "Turkish" room, where the gentlemen gathered to smoke, and the collection of Confederacy memorabilia.

**WADSWORTH-
LONGFELLOW HOUSE**
207-879-0427.
www.mainehistory.com.
489 Congress St., Portland.
Season: June–Oct.,
Mon.–Sun. 10–4; tours
every half hour.
Nominal fee.

This is the boyhood home of poet Henry Wadsworth Longfellow. Built in 1785 by Henry's grandfather, Gen. Peleg Wadsworth, it is the oldest brick house in Portland, and today contains family artifacts and furnishings dating from 1750 to 1900. This is reported to be the most visited historic home in the state, but don't worry about lines. During warm weather the shaded garden is a wonderful place for a picnic.

LIBRARIES

Dyer Library (207-283-3861; 371 Main St., Saco). Associated with the York Institute Museum, the Dyer is home to genealogical materials, Maine history, city records, and manuscripts of local interest.

Historical Society of Wells & Ogunquit (207-646-4775; E-mail, wohistory@ cybertours.com Rte. 1, Wells). A collection of manuscripts and genealogies pertaining to the two towns and their early residents.

Maine Historical Society Library (207-774-1822; www.mainehistory.org; 485 Congress St., Portland). More than 60,000 monographs and serials published after 1497, including the state's most comprehensive collection of historical documents and printed materials. Open Tues.–Fri. 10–4, and the second and fourth Sat. of every month 10–4.

Ogunquit Memorial Library (207-646-9024; 74 Shore Rd., Ogunquit;). Nannie Connarroe built the library in 1897 as a memorial to her late husband George M. Connarroe. It is on the National Register of Historical Places. Open June–Sept., Mon.–Sat. 9–12, 2–5.

Portland Public Library (207-871-1700 or 800-649-7697; www.portlandlibrary.com; 5 Monument Sq., Portland). One of the largest libraries in the state. The Portland Room houses an excellent Maine collection, including old children's books. Mon., Wed., Fri. 9–6; Tues., Thurs. noon–9; Sat. 9–5.

Rice Public Library (207-439-1553; www.rice.lib.me.us; 8 Wentworth St., Kittery). Housed in its original 1888 building, the Rice has an extensive collection of Maine books and historical materials on Kittery.

Salt Documentary Archive (207-761-0660; www.salt.edu/archive.html; 19 Pine St., Portland). Collection of photographs and tape-recorded interviews detailing the way of life of people in Maine. Home of *Salt* magazine.

LIGHTHOUSES

Lighthouse keepers are no more. Most of the lighthouses in the country have been automated. The historic, whitewashed lighthouse at *Goat Island,* near George Bush's Kennebunkport summer home, was automated in 1990 as a cost-saving measure by the government. With the lightkeeper retired, during the former president's term the island served as an air-sea command center that could warn the Secret Service if a plane was headed toward Walkers Point — that's the huge, black, constantly whirling radar beacon that stands next to the old lighthouse.

All told, there are 60 lighthouses along the coast of Maine. Each has its own legends of shipwrecks, ghosts, drownings, and rescues. Some now serve as museums, private homes, or bed and breakfasts.

For information on the restoration and preservation of these symbols of our maritime heritage, contact the *United States Lighthouse Society* (415-362-7255; 244 Kearny St., Fifth Floor, San Francisco, CA 94108; uslthseso@aol.com). If you'd like to learn more about lighthouses, visit the *Museum at Portland Head Light* in Cape Elizabeth. Following are some of the more prominent South Coast lighthouses that can be visited via automobile.

You can check out *Cape Neddick Light* from Sohier Park (follow the signs leading off Rte 1A in York). Stay for a picnic. This is a lovely park with interesting rock formations and good vantages for bird watching. The lighthouse was built in 1879.

Portland Head Light (207-799-2661; Shore Rd., Cape Elizabeth), constructed in 1791 at the order of President George Washington, is the oldest on the East Coast. The lighthouse and quarters were renovated in 1992 and now are home to the Museum at Portland Head Light. The lighthouse and museum adjoin Fort Williams Park, a pretty seaside park complete with ruins of an old fort built in the late 1800s, tennis courts, and a baseball diamond. The town park is open year round. The museum is open on weekends off season and daily during the summer.

Contrary to its name, the *Cape Elizabeth Light at Two Lights State Park* (Two Lights Rd. off Rte. 77, Cape Elizabeth) is only one working lighthouse. In 1824, two lights were built to mark the spot. In 1874, the lighthouses were rebuilt and only one remains active today. This park is a favorite summer evening cool spot for local residents, and there's a popular lobster pound nearby.

MUSEUMS

There are more than 115 registered museums in Maine, and it is estimated there would be more than 300 if you count all the small private collections of painting, sculpture, memorabilia, ephemera, and historical bric-a-brac that are put on display here. Here is a list of a few museums on the coast.

AUTO MUSEUM AT WELLS
207-646-9064.

Once a private collection, now a nonprofit car-lovers' organization, this museum has a collection of more than 70 restored gas-, steam-, and

1181 Post Rd., Wells.
Season: Mid-June–mid-
Sept.: daily 10–5 p.m.;
Memorial
Day–Columbus Day,
weekends 10–5 p.m.
Admission: $4 adults; $2
children 6–12; under 6
free.

BRICK STORE MUSEUM
207-985-4802.
www.cybertours.com/
brickstore.
117 Main St., Kennebunk.
Open year round except
Dec. 24–Jan. 1: Tues.–Sat.
10–4:30.
Admission charged.

**CHILDREN'S MUSEUM
OF MAINE**
207-828-1234.
142 Free Street, Portland.
Memorial Day–Labor Day,
Mon.–Sat. 10–5, Sun.
12–5. Labor
Day–Memorial Day,
Wed.–Sat., 10–5, Sun.
12–5.
Admission: $5 children and
adults; children under
one free.

DESERT OF MAINE
207-865-6962.
www.desertofmaine.com.
95 Desert Rd. (just off Rte. 1
and I-95), Freeport.
Season: Early May–mid-
Oct., daily 9–6.
Admission: $6.75 adults;
$4.75 ages 14–16; $2.75
ages 6–12; children 5 and
under free.

electric-powered automobiles. Stanley Steamers, Rolls Royces, Fords, and motorcycles, license plates, bicycles, antique toys, and nickelodeons; this is an entertaining look at our motoring past, among other things. Particularly fun are rides in one of the museum's Model T's.

This museum that tells the story of Kennebunk began as a small collection of artifacts on display in the town's old general store. These days it encompasses an entire block and runs changing exhibits that tell about the region's maritime and social history. From June to September, the museum offers guided walking tours pointing out the town's architectural highlights.

The museum moved to its spiffy new quarters next door to the Portland Museum of Art in 1993 and was an instant hit with kids and parents. Not only are there many "hands-on" exhibits covering the science bases, but the museum also pays homage to commerce and business. Among other entertaining experiences are exhibits that show how a bank, a supermarket, a jet, and a farm work. Check out the Camera Obscura at the top, which on clear days offers a bird's eye view of Portland and the islands of Casco Bay.

The first chapter in the history of this geologic oddity occurred during the Ice Age, when glaciers deposited sand and minerals. During the late 1700s and early 1800s a family of farmers came, clearcut the land, grew crops, grazed their animals, and failed to use good farming techniques to prevent erosion of the thin layer of topsoil. What remains is a genuine sand desert smack in the middle of coastal Maine, a favorite local tourist attraction since the mid-1930s. Walking and coach tours available. Gift shop, picnic grounds, and campground on the premises.

KITTERY HISTORICAL AND NAVAL MUSEUM
207-439-3080.
Located near the intersection of Rte. 1 and Rte. 236, next to the Town Office on the Rogers Rd. Extension.
Season: June–mid Oct., Tues.– Sat.10–4, or by appointment.
Admission: $3 adults; $1.50 kids 7–15; those under 7 free; families of 3 or more, $6 max.

Kittery is Maine's oldest town, and this relatively young museum (1976) commemorates the port's history as a shipbuilding town. There is a 12-foot model of the *Ranger*, John Paul Jones' ship that had its keel laid here. There are other exhibits about the accomplishments of the naval yard, the first U.S. shipyard and the one responsible for the building of several Civil War ships, as well as the country's first submarine.

OGUNQUIT MUSEUM OF AMERICAN ART
207-646-4909.
183 Shore Rd., Ogunquit.
Season: July 1–September 1; daily, 10:30–5. Sun., 2–5.
Admission: $4 adults; $3 seniors and students; under 12 free.

Built by the painter Henry Strater, the museum houses a good collection of 20th-century American artists who came here to scramble over the rocks, soak up the summer sun and, of course, paint and sculpt. A late director of the Metropolitan Museum of Art described this as a gem, "the most beautiful small museum in the world." A new wing has been added to house special summer shows and selections from the permanent collection. Works on view are by Walt Kuhn, Marsden Hartley, Rockwell Kent, and others.

PORTLAND MUSEUM OF ART
207-773-2787.
www.portlandmuseum. org.
7 Congress Sq., Portland.
Open Tues., Wed., Sat., Sun. 10–5. Thurs., Fri. 10–9. Mon. 10–6 from Memorial Day–Columbus Day.
Admission: $6 adults; $ 5 seniors and students; $1 youths 6–12; children under six free.

Maine's oldest public museum resides in an impressive granite and brick structure designed by I. M. Pei. Inside exhibit space is open and airy, much like space Pei designed for the East Wing of the National Gallery of Art in Washington, D. C. The permanent collection includes a worthwhile selection of American and European art, including paintings by Van Gogh, Picasso, Degas, and many by Winslow Homer (he painted and lived part of the year at Prouts Neck, about 15 minutes from the museum) as well as a significant holding of Colonial and Federal portraits. The museum also is temporary home to visiting exhibitions. On Fridays after 5 p.m. the doors are opened free of charge.

SEASHORE TROLLEY MUSEUM
207-967-2800.
www.gwi.net/trolley.
E-mail, carshop@gwi.net.
195 Log Cabin Rd.,
    Kennebunkport.
Season: Early May–Oct.
    Daily, 9:30–6. Tours
    10:30–4.
Admission charged.

Back when mass transportation was fashionable, handsome trolleys like the ones on display here carried passengers almost everywhere. If you made your connections right, you could trolley all the way from Washington, D. C. to Portland. This museum has the world's largest and oldest collection — more than 100 vintage cars from Biddeford, Saco, San Francisco, Nagasaki, and Rome. It also operates a two-mile stretch of track for sunset trolley rides and a streetcar workshop where visitors can see a trolley restoration in process. Call or write them for a list of special streetcar events sponsored by the museum throughout the year.

YORK INSTITUTE MUSEUM
207-283-0958 or
    207-283-0684.
www.sacomaine.org.
371 Main St., Saco.
Season: Year round, Tues.,
    Wed., Fri., Sun. 12–4.;
    Thurs., 12–8.
Admission: $4 adults; $3
    seniors; $1 students; $10
    family. Free Thursday,
    4–8.

This regional history and art museum has been a growing concern since 1866. It exhibits paintings, textiles, household items, and furnishings from several periods in American history, including Colonial, Federal, and Colonial Revival. The adjoining gallery hosts changing art exhibits, and the library has an excellent Maine history collection.

MUSIC

We've listed some of the larger and better-known musical organizations found on the South Coast. But be warned, there are many more. If your taste leans more to rock-and-roll, be sure to check local newspaper listings to see if local rock legends **The Rustic Overtones** are playing. For a comprehensive schedule of musical events for the area you plan to visit, contact the local chamber of commerce (see Chapter Seven, *Information*).

CUMBERLAND COUNTY CIVIC CENTER
207-775-3458.
www.theciviccenter.com.
1 Civic Center Sq. (at the
    corner of Spring and
    Center Sts.), Portland.
Open year round.
Tickets: $6–$35, depending
    on event.

The acoustics aren't great, but that doesn't daunt folks who travel from way Down East and the far northern reaches of the state to hear good music. Folk, rock, heavy metal plus the occasional circus, ice show or traveling Broadway hit play here.

**PCA GREAT
   PERFORMANCES**
207-773-3150.
477 Congress St., Portland.
Season: Sept.–June.
Tickets: $10–$50.

Every year this group books a range of traveling talent from perennial favorites like the Canadian Brass Ensemble or the Flying Karamazov Brothers to world-class performers like Isaac Stern and the New York City Opera Company. Concerts are held at the Merrill Auditorium.

**PORTLAND STRING
   QUARTET**
207-761-1522.
22 Monument Sq.,
   Portland.
P.O. Box 11, Portland
   04112.
Season: Oct.–April.
Tickets: $20 single concert;
   $75 season's pass (4
   concerts). Senior
   discount. Free for those
   21 or younger.

This is one of the few classical quartets to endure a quarter of a century rehearsing, touring, and performing together without a single change in personnel. The result is a mature sound that can take on the most difficult work and play it beautifully. The group's music is an impeccably performed mix of classic and new chamber works commissioned for the group. When this talented quartet isn't traveling the world, they perform at Woodford's Congregational Church.

**PORTLAND SYMPHONY
   ORCHESTRA**
207-842-0800.
www.portland.com/symp
hony.
20 Myrtle St. off Congress,
   Portland.
Concerts throughout the
   year.

Portland is the smallest city in the U.S. to have a full-time symphony orchestra, and local audiences are extremely appreciative. The symphony, under conductor and music director Toshiyuki Shimada, performs the classics and pops most of the year in the Merrill Auditorium just down the street from their offices. During the summer, they take to the outdoors with a series of concerts at various locations around the state.

NIGHTLIFE

The Asylum (207-772-8274; 121 Center St., Portland; E-mail, asylum@gate.net). People are becoming "totally committed" to the Asylum with its dance club, sports bar, and restaurant. The club features both live bands and DJs playing Disco, House & Hip Hop, Latino, modern rock, and R&B. Open for lunch and dinner, 11 am to 11 pm.

Bad Habits Live & Zootz (207-773-8187; 31 Forest Ave., Portland). Club where there's more dancing than listening to regional and touring acts. DJ plays eclectic selection. This is Portland's best place to dance.

Big Easy Blues Club (207-871-8817; 55 Market St., Portland). Maine is hardly blues central, but Wednesday through Saturday you'd never know it once you're inside the door here.

The Brunswick (207-934-4873; 39 West Grand Ave., Old Orchard Beach). Music, full restaurant and bar on the beach.

The Club (207-646-6655 or 207-646-2345; 13 Main St., Ogunquit). This is the place to dance on the South Coast.

The Comedy Connection (207-774-5554; www.mainehumor.com; 6 Custom House Wharf, Portland). A barrelful of laughs at Maine's only full-time professional stand-up comedy club. The Connection has had many of their comedians receive nationwide recognition from "The Tonight Show" and "Saturday Night Live," among others. A light fare menu and wait service is available before, during, or after the show at the Waterfront Cafe. Reservations welcomed.

Federal Jack's Brew Pub (207-967-4322; 8 Western Ave., Kennebunk). Live music on the weekend, and the neighborhood brew on tap.

The Front Porch Cafe (207-646-3976; Ogunquit Square, Ogunquit). Listen to the strains of the piano until the wee hours in this piano bar. There is also a restaurant here.

The Industry (207-879-0865; 50 Wharf St., Portland). A hopping dance club for those 18 and older. Serves alcohol and is open Friday and Saturday nights.

Martin's Bistro (207-967-3358; Ocean Ave., Kennebunkport). A place for Bush watchers to relax. Bar, restaurant, live bands.

Marvin's Brick Oven Tavern (207-967-3358 or 207-967-8373; Ocean Ave., Kennebunkport).

Mulligans at Millside (207-284-9283; 23 Lincoln St., Biddeford). Pool, darts, bar, and full menu.

One Soho Square (207-934-4524; 43 West Grand Ave. (the Oceanic Inn), Old Orchard Beach). This subterranean British pub features over 40 different brews, the occasional live band, and a deli.

Stone Coast Brewing Company (207-773-2337; 14 York St., Portland). Restaurant, nightclub, brewery: go from casual dining and pub-fare downstairs to live entertainment and a DJ upstairs. The music varies from night to night with live bands and a DJ playing retro dance music. It's been called the "Best live music venue" around by a local newspaper.

SCHOOLS

In Maine, much of the culture centers around the outdoors, so much that the South Coast has two schools dedicated to teaching an appreciation for things you do in the outdoors.

L.L. Bean Outdoor Discovery Program (207-865-3111 Ext. 6666; www.llbean.com; Casco St., Freeport). An interesting series of low-cost lessons that cover everything from cross-country skiing (on weekends beginning in January) and fly fishing to orienteering and emergency wilderness medicine. The program also offers free evening lectures on topics ranging from survival in the Maine woods to making soap, tanning hides, paddling sea kayaks, building fly rods, and cooking small game.

Landing School of Boat Building and Design (207-985-7976; River Rd., Arundel). Learn how to build your own sailing craft in their program that runs the months from September to June.

SEASONAL EVENTS

A ride at the Cumberland County Fair.

Herb Swanson

Cumberland County Fair (207-829-4182; Cumberland Fairgrounds, Cumberland). Livestock, rides, agricultural and cooking competitions. Mid- to late September.

Harvestfest (207-363-4422; York). An old-fashioned New England harvest festival with old-time entertainment including oxcart races, apple bobbing, and a big-time tug of war. Mid-October.

July 4th Weekend Celebration (207-967-0857; Kennebunk and Kennebunkport). Concerts, picnic, silent auction, and probably a former president.

La Kermesse-Franco Americaine Festival (207-282-1567; Biddeford). Food, entertainment, parade, cultural displays documenting the French-American heritage in Southern Maine. Late June.

Laudholm Trust Nature Crafts Festival (207-646-1555; Wells Reserve at Laudholm Farm, Wells). Juried crafts show by artists and craftspeople. Early September.

Sandbuilding Contest (207-646-2939; Ogunquit). Late July.

Yarmouth Clam Festival (207-846-3984; www.propel.com/clamfest; Main St., Yarmouth). Entertainment, crafts, bike race, midway and, of course, clams. Mid-July.

Local craftsmen display their wares at a Maine coast crafts fair.

Herb Swanson

THEATER

The arts continue to thrive Down East. A new theater is being established in Machias on the top floor of the Howard's Men's Shop. According to store owner Wayne Mallar, the new theater, to be called **The Rubicon,** *will focus on community productions. The inaugural offering will be a mystery entitled* Catch Me If You Can.

The Downeast Coastal Press, Oct. 1, 1991

Theater in coastal Maine is generally an unpretentious experience. Patrons often arrive in jeans and Bean boots to enjoy Shakespeare, Fugard, Mamet, or Pinter. The play is the thing. Here are some of the more established companies on the coast. Call to find out their season schedules, times, and ticket prices.

City Theater (207-282-0849; 205 Main St., Biddeford). Sept.–May.

Freeport Community Players (207-865-6041; Freeport High School, Freeport). Young community theater group that presents three shows annually — in the spring, summer, and winter. Visiting performers welcome to audition.

Mad Horse Theater (207-775-5103, 92 Oak St., Portland). Musical comedies, dramas in the round.

Oak Street Productions (207-775-5103; 92 Oak St., Portland). A young and energetic company that performs a variety of modern and classic works. Year round.

Ogunquit Playhouse (207-646-5511; Rte. 1, Ogunquit). For more than 66 summers they have presented musicals and comedies with big-name performers. June–Sept.

Portland Stage Company (207-774-0465; 25A Forest Ave. Portland). Solid local company that often brings actors up from Boston and New York for bigger roles. Sept.–May.

Vintage Repertory Company (207-774-1376; 35 Brackett St., Portland 04102). This professional touring company, based in Portland, performs classics and European comedies at the Oak Street Theater and in other venues. The company is available for private functions and schools as well.

SOUTH COAST: RECREATION

A view of Nubble Light from York Beach.

Herb Swanson

Fun on the coast used to be a one-season affair. Nineteenth-century tourists came here to enjoy cool breezes when cities to the south — Boston, New York and Philadelphia — sweltered in the summer sun. French Canadians early on discovered Old Orchard Beach, the closest sand beach of note to Montreal and Quebec. Today the Maine coast holds plenty of chances to enjoy yourself the year round. Although most people choose to hike and camp here in the summer, many know to take advantage of the off seasons and avoid the crowds. Leaf peeping has become a popular pastime for autumn visitors. Several resorts and parks have extensive cross-country ski trails. There's even downhill skiing at the Snow Bowl in Camden. Spring is mountain bikes and kayaks and the chance to have Acadia National Park all to yourself.

Whatever season you visit, remember the weather. The outlook often changes quickly, and the combination of ocean wind and water can make 40 degrees Fahrenheit seem much colder. Bring along a good selection of warm clothes and rain gear (See "Climate and What to Wear" in Chapter Seven, *Information*) .

AUTO RACING

The chance to see auto racing is rare on the coast. **Beech Ridge Motor Speedway** (207-885-0111, automated race information at 207-885-5800; www.beechridge.com; 70 Holmes Rd., Scarborough) features four divisions of stock car racing on a 1/3 mile track. Starting time April through September is 6:30 p.m. every Saturday evening. Call for times of special events.

BALLOONING

Most balloon flights originating near the coast are overland. Balloonists talk about one pilot who often dares saltwater flights. He and his passengers have been rescued three times.

Even if the winds are blowing inland, you are almost assured a good view from the White Mountains to the shore. Spring flights are tricky — and often canceled — due to the changeable Maine weather. September and October tend to be the busiest months because of foliage flights, so be sure to make your reservations early. Experienced balloonists say winter flights are the most spectacular, when the air takes on a crystalline clarity. Dress warmly, though; it will be much colder at an 800-foot altitude than it is on the ground.

If you want to see the South Coast by air, you have a few choices. **Balloon Rides** (207-761-8373 or 800-952-2076; 17 Freeman St., Portland;www.hotairballoon.com) boasts of having "Coastal Maine's oldest balloon company." Pilot Bob Schuerer of **Freeport Balloon Company** (207-865-1712; Tuttle Rd., Pownal) offers intimate champagne flights . Also, call **Hot Fun** (207-799-0193; E-mail, brooksdunnballoon@msm.com; Cape Elizabeth) and **Balloons Over New England** (800-788-5562; Kennebunk).

BASEBALL

Win or lose, the **Portland Sea Dogs**, the Double A affiliate of the Florida Marlins, keep Hadlock Field (207-879-9500; 271 Park Ave., Portland) filled to capacity throughout the season. This is a young team with an exceptionally loyal following, including former President George Bush who, when he goes, often is asked to throw in the first ball.

The Sea Dogs are so popular that getting a ticket to witness Eastern League baseball in one of the 6,500 seats is virtually impossible for most games. Monday nights are your best bet. Still we suggest calling well in advance.

BEACHES

Maine's beaches are the crown jewels of the coast. Almost all are flanked by the rugged terrain that gives the coast its distinct beauty and charac-

Relaxing on Goose Rocks Beach in Kennebunkport.

Herb Swanson

ter — jagged outcroppings of metamorphic rock, sheer cliffs and exhilarating Atlantic surf. More than 40 percent of the visitors to the coast make the South Coast their destination. That's where most of the sand beaches are, and *Old Orchard Beach* and the long, broad stretches of sand at *York* and *Ogunquit* are the most famous southern Maine beaches. These beaches have lovely sandy bottoms perfect for swimming. Non-residents often find the water a little cool.

We have our favorites. The swimming is great at *Ferry Beach*, in Scarborough, where water over a long, shallow sandbar warms up early in the summer and is kept protected by Prouts Neck. *Higgins Beach* in West Scarborough is a beautiful, broad stretch of sand bound by a modest, old-fashioned summer village (there is no boardwalk in sight and dogs run free after 4 p.m.).

Below, we've listed the *major* beaches, but not all of Maine's South Coast beaches. Travelers will find dozens of lovely little sand beaches tucked here and there, many of them with public access. Just keep your eyes open.

Crescent Beach State Park; Rte. 77, Cape Elizabeth. *The Maine Times* calls this "one of Maine's best family beaches." Sand and stone beach; 1,560 yds.; picnic tables, snack bar, fishing. Entrance fee.

Crescent and Seapoint beaches; Seapoint Rd., Kittery. Crescent Beach, a 625-yard sand beach and its 550-yard sister beach Seapoint across a small peninsula are nice, but have limited parking.

Drakes Island and Laudholm beaches; Rte. 1 to Drakes Island Rd., Wells. This is really one beach with two names, in addition to being a well-kept secret among South Coast beach goers. It's comparatively quiet here in the height of the summer, even when nearby Moody is jammed. It is 940 yds. with accompanying saltwater farm and nature center; limited parking.

Ferry and Western beaches; Rte. 207 to Ferry Rd., Scarborough. Actually three beaches, including two that wrap around a rocky point and lead up to tony

Prouts Neck. The tide rips right at the point, and at high tide you can almost reach out and touch the lobster boats in the harbor. You can let your dog run free after 4 p.m. Total of more than 1,700 yds.; limited parking, for a fee.

Ferry Beach State Park; Rte. 9, Saco. A fine sand beach that stretches more than 4,500 yds. It is part of a 117-acre state park with all the facilities, including picnic tables, toilets, and bathhouse. Fee is charged at gate. Parking.

Fortunes Rocks Beach; Rte. 208, Biddeford. Long sand beach that's great for swimming; 3,740 yds.; parking limited.

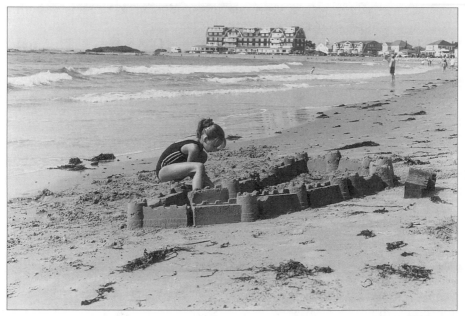

Herb Swanson

A favorite Maine coast pastime.

Gooch's Beach; Rte. 9 to Sea Rd., then left onto Beach Ave. past Kennebunk Beach, Kennebunk. The beach of choice for Kennebunkport residents and summer people including surfers, this is a crescent-shaped sand and shingle beach with a rocky point; 1,300 yds.; parking is limited to those with permits, so take the trolley. It's well worth the ride.

Goose Rocks Beach; Rte. 9 to Dyke Rd., then left onto King's Hwy., Kennebunkport. Lovely beach that attracts both swimmers and birdwatchers (there's a salt marsh at the southeast end); 3,600 yds.; parking limited.

Hills Beach; off Rtes. 9 and 208, Biddeford. An excellent, if short, swimming beach, on a 530-yd. sand spit protecting Maine's largest tidal basin. People like to birdwatch here (see below). Facilities nearby; parking limited.

Kennebunk Beach; Rte. 9 to Sea Rd., then left onto Beach Ave., Kennebunk. Sand and shingle beach popular among families and surfers. It's hard to park here, and illegal if you don't have a sticker; take the trolley instead; 820 yds.

Long Beach; Rte. 1A, York, and **Short Sands**; Rte. 1A, York Beach. Long Beach, at 2,180 yds., and Short Sands, 410 yds., are two of the South Coast's most popular beaches. The surfers like the waves. Parents like Short Sands, because it is near the heart of York Beach, so tired young beach bums can easily refuel with a snack. There are lifeguards and rest rooms at both. Parking is limited, so arrive early.

Moody Beach; Rte. 1 to Bourne Rd., then right onto Ocean Ave., Wells. A couple of years ago in a heated courtroom battle, residents tried to cut off public access to the beach. In a blow to the coastal aristocracy, they failed. Moody Beach is 2,750 yds. and surrounded by a honeycomb of summer cottages; facilities nearby; fee for parking which is none plentiful.

Ogunquit Beach; Rte. 1 to Beach St., Ogunquit. People love the sand here. It's refined, white and abundant (1,620 yds.). One local newspaper describes this as "very popular with the gay community"; another publication says that it is "near summer art colony." We call it fun. Facilities; fee for parking.

Old Orchard and Surfside beaches; Rte. 9, Old Orchard Beach. Some call this the Canadian Riviera, and more often than not the language spoken here is French. Lovely fine white sand beaches with a total length 3,320 yds. Bathhouse. Fee for parking.

Parsons and Crescent Surf beaches; Rte. 9 to Parson's Beach Rd., Kennebunk. You get to these two pretty beaches along a private way owned by the Parson family. Total is 1,700 yds.; no facilities; limited parking.

Pine Point and Grand beaches; Rte. 9, Scarborough. Two fine white sand beaches and sand spit totaling 2,500 yds. Facilities nearby; fee for parking.

Scarborough Beach; Rte. 207, Scarborough. This is a barrier beach and dunes that protect a freshwater marsh. It's so popular among swimmers and surfers that it often fills to overflowing by noon on a hot day; 2,060 yds.; picnic tables, grills, bathhouse, fishing; fee for parking.

Wells Beach; Rte. 1 to Mile Rd., then left onto Atlantic Ave., Wells. Motels and condos line the beach; 4,000 yds.; facilities; fee for parking.

Winslow Memorial Park; Rte. 1 onto South Freeport Rd. (at the Big Indian) and follow to Staples Rd., South Freeport. Nestled in the middle of a pretty, immaculate town-run park and camping area, this is another great beach for the family. The small, man-made beach is sheltered although untended by a lifeguard. Picnic tables, playground, rest rooms; entrance fee charged.

BERRY & APPLE PICKING

Wild blueberries, wild red and black raspberries, and berries of the cultivated kind, including strawberries, somehow taste better in Maine.
Maybe it's because spring here is usually a long, cold, and damp affair. Maybe
it's because you get to pick them yourself, sneaking a taste now and then to
determine whether the big ones or smaller ones are sweeter this year.
Whatever the reason, berry season in Maine is heavenly, beginning with
strawberries in late June to early July, and with wild blueberries in late July
right through August Down East.

Good wild berrypicking spots, like fishing holes, are well-guarded secrets
passed down from parent to child. Better-known berry spots are the tops of
Blue Hill and *Schoodic Mountain*. Knowing those two will put you ahead of
millions of visitors, but get there early. If you want to do better than that, we
recommend you find a local family willing to adopt a berry picker.

Here are some places that, for a fee, will let you pick cultivated berries to
your heart's content. We've also listed a few apple orchards for fall visitors in
search of a crisp Mac or Cortland. Call ahead for picking prospects.

Hilltop Raspberry Farm (207-737-4988; Post Rd., Bowdoinham). Raspberries.
July 15–Oct. Daily 9–6.

Jordan's Farm (207-799-1466; 21 Wells Rd., Cape Elizabeth). Strawberries. End
of June through August 1. Mon.–Sat., 7–7.

Juniper Edge Strawberries (207-725-6414; 532 Harpswell Rd., Rte. 123,
Brunswick). Strawberries. June 15 to end of season. Daily 8:30–5:30.

Maxwell's Farm (207-799-3383; off Rte. 77 near Two Lights, Cape Elizabeth).
Strawberries. Mid-June–mid-July. Mon.–Sat., 7 a.m.–8 p.m. Closed Sun. Call
ahead.

Prouts Strawberries (207-666-5604; Brown Point Rd., Bowdoinham). Strawberries. Late June–mid-July. 7 a.m.–dusk. Closed Sundays.

Spiller Farms (207-985-2575; store: 207-985-3383; E-mail, SpillerFarms@Juno.
com; Rte. 9A, Wells Branch). Strawberries and raspberries. June 10 to end of
season. Apples. Hours fluctuate.

Whistling Wings Farm (207-282-1146; 427 West St., Biddeford). Raspberries.
July to Labor Day. Daily 8–5.

BICYCLING

DeLorme Mapping Company offers an inexpensive pamphlet titled
Bicycling. It can be found at bookstores and large supermarkets in the
magazine/ map/recreation areas. Another excellent guide for cyclers is *25
Bicycle Tours in Maine* by Howard Stone (Back Country Publications, P.O. Box
175, Woodstock, VT 05091). Both books offer excellent maps and directions for
touring cyclists.

Some of the best cycling in Maine is on coastal byways.

Herb Swanson

Bike clubs, whether off-road or touring, come and go. In the last few years, however, the *Casco Bay Bicycle Club* has maintained a steady following of all kinds of cyclists. Their information line (207-828-0918) will astound you with choices. Or you can write to them at: 84 Gloucester Road, Cumberland 04121. Otherwise, the best bet for updates on new groups, trails, tours, and races is to call the local bike shop. Often one shop in town will be the hub for roadies, while mountain bikers will call the other one home. All are friendly.

For a recap of the state's bicycling laws, see "Bicycling" in the Recreation section of Chapter Four, *Midcoast*. Meanwhile, here's a list of bike stores where you can locate a spare part, get a repair or check in to see where folks are cycling these days. A few also offer bikes for rent.

Allspeed Bicycles (207-878-8741; 1041 Washington Ave., Portland).

Back Bay Bicycle (207-773-6906; 333 Forest Ave., Portland).

Bicycle Habitat (207-283-2453; 294 Main St., Saco).

Brad's Bike Rental and Repairing (207-766-5631; E-mail, peaksmerc.com; 115 Island Ave., Peaks Island).

Breton's Bike Shop (207-646-4255; www.bretonsbikeshop@cybertours.com; Rte. 9B, Wells).

Cape-Able Bike Shop (207-967-4382; www.mnetwork.com/cape-able bike; 83 Arundel Rd., Kennebunkport).

CycleMania (207-774-2933; 59 Federal St., Portland).

Haggett's Cycle Shop (207-773-5117; 34 Vannah Ave., Portland).

Joe Jones Ski and Sports (207-885-5635; E-mail, Joejones.com; 456 Payne Rd., opposite Wal-Mart, Scarborough).

L.L. Bean Bicycle Dept. (207-865-4761; www.llbean.com; Main St., Freeport).

Quinn's Bike Shop (207-284-4632; 140 Elm St., Biddeford).

Rodgers Ski and Sport (207-883-3669; 332 Rte. 1, opposite Scarborough Downs, Scarborough).

Wheels and Waves (207-646-5774; Rte. 1, Wells).

BIRD WATCHING

Biddeford Pool (Rte. 208, Biddeford). A one-mile wide tidal basin and broad mud flats at low tide. There is excellent bird watching here, because many species of shore birds stop here en route to northern and southern climes. Open Mon.–Fri., 8–4:30.

Maine Audubon Society (207-781-2330; www.maineaudubon.org; 20 Gilsland Farm Rd., Falmouth). The Gilsland Farm Sanctuary is home to the society, as well as whoever stops by. More than 60 acres of salt marsh, fields, and forest also serve as a workshop and touring ground for naturalists. There is a great bookstore for naturalists here, with the best selection of optics and guides around. Early morning bird walks and the children's discovery room are open to the public. Weekend programs. Mon.–Sat. 9–5 p.m.; Sun. 12–5 p.m.

Rachel Carson National Wildlife Refuge (207-646-9226; 321 Port Rd., Wells). This famous refuge includes 5,000 acres of salt marsh, white pine forest, and many, many birds. It is managed by the U. S. Fish and Wildlife Service, which offers limited access to birders and naturalists interested in viewing extensive bird life. Maps and guides to the preserve are available.

Scarborough Marsh Nature Center (207-883-5100; www.maineaudubon.org; E-mail, smnc@maineaudubon.org; Pine Point Rd., Scarborough). The Maine Audubon Society operates an education center on this 3,000-acre saltwater marsh. They offer guided tours, including Full Moon Canoe tours during the summer when participants can experience the marsh at night. There's also a self-guided tour (you follow directions in a pamphlet available at the center). You can rent a canoe for your trip through the marsh on your quest for birds until 4 p.m. Art programs and walks are available for kids. In the early morning on Wednesdays, a bird-watching walk is offered. Open 9:30–5:30.

Seapoint Beach (Seapoint Rd., Kittery). Good bird-watching on a tiny peninsula that sticks out into the Atlantic Ocean, just southwest of Brave Boat Harbor.

Webhannet River Marsh (off Rte. 1, Wells). Good birder's vantage for spotting shore birds and migrating waterfowl.

Wells National Estuarine Research Reserve (207-646-1555; Laudholm Farm Rd., Wells). This reserve has seven miles of trails on estuaries, rivers, and beaches. Wednesday mornings there is bird banding at 8 a.m. Children's programs. Visitor's center, 10–4 p.m. Sun. 12–4 p.m.. Trails, 8–5 p.m. Parking fee July and August.

BOATING

CANOEING AND SEA KAYAKING

Kittery Rent-All & Sales (207-439-4528; Rte. 1, Kittery). Canoe rentals.

L.L. Bean Outdoor Discovery Program (207-865-4761, ext. 26666; Main St., Freeport). Throughout the summer, the L.L. Bean store staff gives canoe and kayak lessons on a nice, easy stretch of the Royal River in Yarmouth. The academic wing of the outdoor store also hosts an annual Sea Kayak Symposium in July.

Maine Island Kayak Co. (207-766-2373 or 800-796-2373; 70 Luther St., Peaks Island 04108). Trips and instruction.

Maine Island Trail. 207-596-6456; www.mita.org). The waterway is a kind of Appalachian Trail for boaters. It begins with islands in Casco Bay and follows the coast Down East past Machias, a distance of 325 miles. See sidebar on page 175.

Paddleworks USA (207-833-5342; E-mail, H2O@H2outfitters.com; Rte. 24, Harpswell).

Scarborough Marsh Nature Center (207-883-5100; www.maineaudubon.org; E-mail, smnc@maineaudubon.org; Pine Point Rd off Rte. 1, Scarborough). Hourly canoe rentals and self-guided canoe tours of the marsh. Also guided tours, including "full-moon" tours during the summer. The center is open from 9:30 a.m.–5:30 p.m.; last canoe rental at 4. Open from mid-June until Labor Day.

CHARTERS & RENTALS

From the bow of the Friendship sloop Edna.

Herb Swanson

Edna (207-967-8809; Schooner Wharf, Kennebunkport). Capt. Richard Woodman is an obliging captain known to perform many ceremonies at sea for his guests aboard his pretty schooner. He's done weddings, burials, and an occasional "pirate cruise" complete with eye patch. Two-hour and four-hour crewed sails, two-person minimum; private charters also negotiable.

Palawan (207-773-2163; www.sailpalawan.com; E-mail, palawan@nlis.net; Long Wharf, Portland). Half-day, full-day, and evening trips aboard a gorgeous vintage 58-foot ocean racing sloop.

SAILING LESSONS

Spring Point Sailing School (207-799-3976; www.smtc.net; Southern Maine Technical College, South Portland). Classes for beginning sailors, including private lessons by appointment.

BOWLING

Big 20 Bowling Center (207-883-2131; Rte. 1, Scarborough). 20 candlepin lanes.
Vacationland Bowling Center (207-284-7386; Rte. 1, Saco). 32 candlepin lanes.

CAMPING

There are hundreds of private and public campgrounds along the coast. Many offer priceless views of the water at campers' prices. Some are no bigger than a modest parking lot. Others are mammoth. Because the summer camping season is short in Maine, we recommend calling well ahead for reservations. For a complete list of private campgrounds, contact the *Maine Campground Owners Association* (207-782-5874; www.campmaine.com; E-mail, info@campmaine.com; 655 Main St., Lewiston 04240). The *Maine Tourism Association* also publishes a statewide travel information planner. Call or write for one (207-623-0363 or 800-533-9595 out-of-state; www.mainetourism.com; E-mail, metainfo@mainetourism.com; P.O. Box 2300, Hallowell 04347).

Recompense Shores Camp Sites (207-865-9307; Burnett Rd., Freeport). Tent and RV campsites, showers, electrical hookups, and one of the best views in the area. Next door is a state-run organic beef farm.
Winslow Memorial Park (207-865-4198; Staples Point Rd., Freeport). Small, municipally run park with camp and picnic sites and a lovely man-made beach.

CROSS-COUNTRY SKIING

Most of the areas listed below are unstaffed. Remember that it can be unsafe to ski alone. Stay on the trails, and be prepared for Maine's mercurial weather. Also, don't forget to carry out your trash. Call beforehand for snow and trail conditions.

Bradbury Mountain State Park (207-688-4712; 6 miles west from the Freeport exit of I-95, Pownal). From the top of Bradbury Mountain (460 feet) you can see past L.L. Bean to the ocean. Ten miles of trails; two difficult paths, two intermediate, and four trails for beginners. Trail maps are available at the entrance.

Gilsland Farm (207-781-2330; Gilsland Farm Rd., Falmouth). This is the home of the Maine Audubon Society. Three-and-a-half kilometers of trails through their country backyard. Open dawn to dusk.

Mast Landing Sanctuary (207-781-2330; Upper Mast Landing Road, Freeport). Also owned and operated by the Maine Audubon Society. Five kilometers of foot trails and canoe ways wind through estuaries, forests, and orchards. Open from dawn to dusk.

Valhalla Country Club (207-780-8200; Valhalla Rd., Cumberland). In winter, you can check out the snow conditions right from Interstate 295 at this week-end-only free touring center on a rolling golf course. Peak Performance, a local recreational outfitter, also offers lessons and equipment rentals.

Vaughan Woods State Park (207-384-5160; Old Fields Rd. off Rte. 236, South Berwick). 4.5 miles of snow-covered hiking trails that take you by Salmon Falls River and Cow Cove. Two miles are classified "easy," the other four miles are more difficult.

Wolfe's Neck Woods State Park (Wolf Neck Rd, Freeport). This small park is officially closed during the winter, but skiers like to ski the snow-covered walking trails which wind for about 4 miles through the woods and follow along the edge of Casco Bay and the Harraseeket River.

FAMILY FUN

There's recreation and then there's recreation. When you get tired of going to the beach, the perfect remedy is a stroll down *the boardwalk at Old Orchard Beach* where you can get your fortune read, ride the Ferris wheel, and eat more than one man's share of fried things — French fries, fried clams, and fried dough. If you're somewhere else on the coast and looking for family fun, herewith is some more good stuff, kids.

Aquaboggan Water Park (207-282-3112; Rte. 1, Saco). Can't miss it. Kids love it. Water slides, splash pools for tots, bumper boats, races cars, shuffleboard. A real fun time. Daily.10 a.m.–6 p.m.

Fun-O-Rama (207-363-4421; E-mail, funorama@nh.ultranet.com; 7 Beach, York Beach). Arcade.

Funtown'splashtown U.S.A. (207-284-5139 or 800-878-2900; Portland Rd., Saco). Need we say more? Open at 10 a.m.

Jellystone Park (207-324-7782; Rte. 109, Sanford/Wells). Family camping at Yogi Bear's place! Wacky fun all night long!

Maine Narrow Gauge Railroad Co. & Museum (207-828-0814; www.data-maine.com/mngrr; 58 Fore St., Portland). This train is immensely popular with travelers young and old. A well-preserved two-foot narrow gauge train follows about 1.5 miles of track on Portland's Eastern Prom. Train rides and tours of the adjacent museum are available seven days a week, mid-May–mid-Oct.

Pirate's Cove Adventure Golf (207-934-5086; First Street, Old Orchard Beach). 36 holes. "Explore the wonderful and mysterious hideout of pirates!" 9 a.m.–11 p.m.

Westerly Winds (207-854-9463; 771 Cumberland St., Westbrook). Pitch n' Putt golf course, driving range, miniature golf, and pitching machines for hardball and softball. Swimming, tennis and basketball courts.

York Wild Kingdom (207-363-4911; www.yorkzoo.com; Rte. 1, York). Contained wild animals and more.

FISHING

If you want to learn how to fish, you can learn from the pros at "fly fishing school." L.L. Bean's *Outdoor Discovery Program* every year offers intense fly fishing instruction in addition to frequent free programs about fishing. For more information about those classes call the outdoor school (207-865-4761 or 800-341-4314, ext. 26666; www.llbean.com).

DEEP SEA FISHING BOATS

Bunny Clark (207-646-2214; www.bunnyclark.com; Perkins Cove, Ogunquit). Mid-March–mid-November. Full- and half-day trips as well as 12-hour "fishing marathons."

Ugly Anne (207-646-7202; Perkins Cove, Ogunquit). April–November. Half-day trips only July–Labor Day. Full-day trips April–July and Sept.–Nov.

GOLF

The first golf courses built in Maine were built along the coast at the turn of the century, just as the game was beginning to take hold in this country. The 18-hole course at *Kebo Valley Club* in Bar Harbor, built in 1892, has the distinction of being the oldest operating golf grounds in America. Mark Twain, who once said that "Golf is a good walk spoiled," learned how to play golf at a course in York County. Former President George Bush continues to master the intricacies of the game on a course in York County.

Many of the courses listed here are set right on the shore. If you don't make par, at least you've scored a great view. Call for current rates and hours and reservations.

Biddeford-Saco Country Club (207-282-5883; Old Orchard Rd., Saco). 18 holes, 6,200 yds., par 71, cart and club rental, pro shop, clubhouse, lessons, snack bar.

Cape Arundel Golf Club (207-967-3494; Old River Rd., Kennebunkport). 18 holes, 5,869 yds., par 69. Cart and club rental, pro shop, clubhouse, lessons.

Dutch Elm Golf Course (207-282-9850; Brimstone Rd., Arundel). 18 holes, 6,230 yds., par 72. Cart and club rental, pro shop, clubhouse, lessons.

Freeport Country Club (207-865-4922; Old County Rd., Freeport). 9 holes, 2,955 yds., par 36. Cart and club rental, pro shop, clubhouse.

Old Orchard Beach Country Club (207-934-4513; www.dunegress.com; Ross Rd., Old Orchard Beach). 9 holes, 2,762 yds., par 36, cart and club rental, pro shop, clubhouse.

Pleasant Hill Country Club (207-883-4425; 38 Chamberlain Rd., Scarborough). 9 holes, 2,400 yds., par 34. Cart and club rental, pro shop, clubhouse, snack bar.

Riverside Municipal Courses (207-797-3524 or 207-797-5588; 1158 Riverside St., Portland). Two courses: 18 holes, 6,520 yds., par 72; and 9 holes, 3,152 yds., par 36. Cart and club rental, pro shop, clubhouse, lessons.

Sable Oaks Golf Club (207-775-6257; 505 Country Club Dr., South Portland). 18 holes, 6,359 yds., par 70. Cart and club rental, clubhouse, pro shop, snack bar, lessons.

South Portland Municipal (207-775-0005; 155 Wescott Rd., South Portland). 9 holes, 2,171 yds., par 33. Cart and club rental, pro shop, snack bar.

Val Halla Golf Course (207-829-2225; Val Halla Rd., Cumberland). 18 holes, 6,200 yds., par 72. Cart and club rental, pro shop, clubhouse, lessons.

Webhannet Golf Club (207-967-2061; Kennebunk Beach). 18 holes, 6,136 yds., par 69. Cart rental, pro shop, lessons. Call 24 hours in advance.

Willowdale Golf Club (207-883-9351; Willowdale Rd., Scarborough). 18 holes, 5980 yds., par 70. Cart and club rental, pro shop, snack bar.

HARNESS RACING

Standardbreds pulling a two-wheeled sulky and driver compete against each other for your betting pleasure. There's only one harness racing track on the coast of Maine — *Scarborough Downs* (207-883-4331; exit 6 off the Maine Turnpike, Scarborough, just southwest of Portland). It also happens to be the largest of its kind in New England. Races run Wed, Fri., and Sat., 7:30 p.m.; Sun. 2 p.m. The season varies; call for schedule.

HEALTH CLUBS

Here is a list of health clubs along the South Coast. Health clubs come and go. Call first to find out about guest and visitor policies, and check the phone book for new clubs that may have opened.

Maine Coast Fitness (207-883-3858; 605 Rte 1., Scarborough). Weights, lifecycles, stair masters, and fitness machines.

The Racquet and Fitness Center (207-775-6128; 2445 Congress St., Portland). Racquetball, tennis, aerobics, weights, fitness machines, lifecycles, spin bikes, and sauna.

Saco Sport and Fitness (207-284-5953; 329 North St., Saco). Pool, sauna, whirlpool, racquetball, aerobics, weights, lifecycles, stair masters, and fitness machines.

Union Station Fitness (207-879-9114; www.unionstationfitness.com; 274 St. John St., Portland). Aerobics, weights, treadmill, stair master, lifecycles, rowing machines, Versa climber, spin bikes, cardio kick-boxing, and Nautilus.

YMCA (207-283-0100; Alfred Road Business Park, Biddeford). Aerobics, fitness machines, Bio climbers, Nautilus, rowing machines, lifecycles, pool, and sauna.

YMCA (207-874-1111; 70 Forest Ave., Portland). Pools, sauna, squash, racquetball, aerobics, fitness machines, and basketball gym.

YWCA (207-874-1130; 87 Spring St., Portland). Pool, aerobics, sauna, weights, yoga, water aerobics, and self defense.

HIKING AND WALKING

A good, heart-pounding hike is hard to come by in the relatively flat terrain of the South Coast. The best hiking on the Maine coast is midcoast near Camden and in Acadia National Park. Still, there are some lovely walks in this region.

Back Cove, Portland. This 3.5-mile walk around Back Cove in Portland is a popular one on a warm spring or summer evening. What's that smell? Baked beans? That's the B & M Baked Bean factory across the way putting the final touches on a new batch of the sweet beans.

Bradbury Mountain State Park, Pownal. A little north and west of Freeport on Rte. 9, this small state park is a great place to get out of the car and stretch the legs. You'll get a good view of Casco Bay and the White Mountains from the summit of this small, bald mountain.

Marginal Way, Ogunquit. Begin near Rte. 1 in Ogunquit and follow the paved footpath over cliff and ledges all the way to Perkins Cove. It's about a mile and is perfect for a morning constitutional or an evening sunset stroll.

Rachel Carson National Wildlife Refuge, Wells. Follow the signs off Rte. 9 to parking area and trail head. This is another short and pretty walk rich with coastal flora and fauna. The refuge borders the Wells National Estuarine Sanctuary, a 16,000-acre preserve.

Wolfe's Neck Woods State Park, Freeport. Just a few miles from the commercial craziness of downtown Freeport, this is truly a cool haven in the spring and summer. The 200-acre state park is on a small peninsula jutting into Casco Bay. The park has four miles of well-marked trails that lead along Casco Bay past Googins Island (where a pair of osprey return from South America to nest every year) through a stand of white pine and along the Harraseeket River.

HORSEBACK RIDING

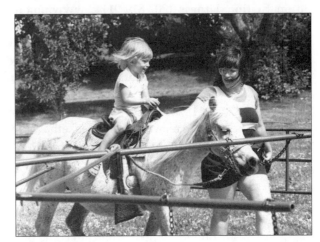

The thrill of learning to ride a pony.

Diana Lynn Doherty

Bush Brook Stables (207-284-7721; 463 West St., Biddeford). Lessons, boarding, indoor riding arena.

Highland Dressage Center (207-797-6207; 75 Babbidge Rd., Falmouth). Lessons, training, riding, driving, boarding, indoor and outdoor rings.

Horseback Riding Plus (207-883-6400 or 800-883-6499; longhorneq@aol.com; Scarborough). Public trails.

MOTORCYCLING

Annually, motorcycle clubs do a lot of socializing in Maine. During the summer of 1997, around 5,000 motorcyclists rolled into Portland for a Harley Davidson convention. Bikers enjoy the beauty of Maine's back country roads and the excitement of the downtown water district. Also during a recent season, bikers went on a lobster run in Brunswick, a surf and turf run from Biddeford, held a swap meet in Portland and a Halloween Party in Hallowell. See a local bike shop for scheduled gatherings.

The state urges all riders to wear helmets, though helmets are *required* only for passengers under 15, those driving with a learner's permit, and those who have had their licenses less than one year. The law requires lights to be on during the day as well as at night.

NATURE PRESERVES

The state may seem vast and unpopulated to visitors from the north and south, but the fact is that less than four percent of Maine's lands are publicly held. That makes Maine 47th in the union in the preservation of public access lands. Three groups are actively trying to increase the supply of lands protected from commercial development.

The Maine chapter of the *Nature Conservancy* (207-729-5181; www.tnc.org; Fort Andross, 14 Maine St., Suite 401, Brunswick 04011) has been able to convert more than 103,000 acres of Maine wilderness to protected preserves since it was founded in 1956 at the urging of naturalist Rachel Carson. The group's recent projects included a close study of the saltwater ecosystem of Cobscook Bay, one of the most biologically diverse ecosystems on the East Coast — the group's first research and preservation efforts focused below the tidal waterline. The Nature Conservancy owns and manages more than 20,000 acres of nature preserves, including 50 Maine islands and several coastal preserves. Day use of the Conservancy's lands are welcome, including the string of nature preserves called the *Rachel Carson Sea Coast*.

The *Maine Audubon Society* (207-781-2330; P.O. Box 6009, Falmouth 04105) operates several nature centers on the coast as well as inland. Founded in the early 1970s by Peggy Rockefeller and Tom Cabot, the *Maine Coast Heritage Trust* (207-729-7366; 169 Park Row, Brunswick 04011) has worked to preserve and protect more than 66,000 acres through conservation easements. That includes 173 entire islands and 250 miles of shoreline.

These and several smaller conservation organizations have established a network of nature preserves that grace the coast like pearls on a loosely strung necklace. Beginning in the South Coast with the *Wells National Estuarine Sanctuary* and the *Rachel Carson National Wildlife Refuge*, these few small preserves are rich with avian and plant life, and they are fragile havens for birdwatchers, ecologists, and the garden variety of nature lover. Spring, summer, and fall are good times to walk the trails and observe nature in action. Many of the preserves turn over their trails to cross-country skiers in the wintertime (see below).

East Point Sanctuary, Biddeford Pool. A 30-acre sanctuary on the largest tidal pool in Maine. Two trails ring the water and give views of nesting and migratory birds as well as harbor seals at high tide.

Fore River Sanctuary, Portland. A 76-acre preserve on the Fore River Estuary. This small pocket of nature includes a portion of the old Cumberland and

Oxford Canal and Jewel Falls, the city's only waterfall; 2.5 miles of nature trails lead through hemlocks, red oaks, and white pine.

Gilsland Farm, Rte. 1, Falmouth. The headquarters for Maine Audubon sits on 60 acres of salt marsh just minutes from Portland with 2.5 miles of trails. Good walks, great cross-country skiing, and one of the region's best selection of natural history books in the society's gift shop. Open year round.

Laudholm Farm, a working saltwater farm in Wells.

Herb Swanson

Laudholm Farm, Wells. Part of the Wells Reserve that also links the Carson Refuge, this is a saltwater farm that boasts soils more fertile than the richest Iowa farmland. More than 300 years ago the first European farmers in the New World tilled land like that found at Laudholm Farm. Visitors can tour buildings and grounds to get a taste of this endangered agricultural tradition.

Mast Landing Sanctuary, Freeport. Another of the small refuges set aside by Maine Audubon, this one winds through the hills, fields, woods, and salt marshes near busy downtown Freeport. There are self-guided nature walks, and you can tent, camp, and picnic here.

Rachel Carson National Wildlife Refuge, Rte. 1, Wells. The naturalist summered on the coast, and during her lifetime she was instrumental in establishing the national environmental movement with the writing of environmental classics including *Silent Spring* and *The Edge of the Sea*. Her estate was willed to the Sierra Club and the Nature Conservancy. Today, this refuge is a living reminder of her crusade — and a wonderful place to observe nature. The mile-long trail built by volunteers in 1988 is handicap accessible.

Refuge at Brave Boat Harbor, Seapoint Rd., Kittery Point. Small refuge on a tidal inlet with good bird watching and an interesting trail through a salt marsh.

Scarborough Marsh Nature Center, Scarborough. Maine Audubon operates this nature center on the coast's largest saltwater marsh. Self-guided nature walk, as well as several special events and educational programs. You can rent a canoe here, too, to visit marsh animals in their natural habitat. This is a great way to "get into" coastal biology.

Wells National Estuarine Research Reserve, Rte. 1, Wells. An educational and research facility set on 1,600 acres of coastal marshland and woods with seven miles of nature trails. There are guided nature, birding, sky watch, and wildflower tours in the summer. Admission is free, but there is a nominal fee for guided tours and parking in July and August.

Wolfe's Neck Woods State Park, Freeport. This small park is truly one of nature's gems. Well-marked, self-guiding nature trails through coastal woods on Casco Bay and the Harraseeket River. Lovely picnic area. Nominal fee in summer time.

ROCK CLIMBING

In spite of this being the rock-bound coast, rock climbing is not one of the most popular pastimes. Consequently, good rock climbing spots have not yet been well mapped. The coast of Maine offers climbers both challenges and solitude. On the South Coast, there are really only two climber's hangouts that we know of: *Fort Williams Park* in Cape Elizabeth just south of Portland and the *Maine Rock Gym* (207-780-6370; www.climbingusa.com; 127 Marginal Way, Portland). The gathering place for the lithe athletes, the gym has been such a hit that they built a climbing tower outside. For further information or gear, call or stop by one of the nearby sporting goods stores (see "Sporting Goods" in *Shopping*, below).

SEASONAL SPORTING EVENTS

Beyond the annual events mentioned in the above categories, the coast has dozens of events that lure sportsmen and women from around the world. Following are a few favorite events you should know about.

Beach Olympics, mid-August. On the beach in Old Orchard (207-934-2500). Kids and adults enjoy this three-day event to benefit the Maine Special Olympics. Round-robin volleyball, water-balloon races, ice cream eating contests, and more. Live music and entertainment at night.

Great Inner Tube Race, early August. On the river in Ogunquit. (207-646-2939 for information).

Kite Flying Contest, early Sept. On the beach in Ogunquit (207-646-2939).

Peaks Island-to-Portland Swim, early Aug. Strong-armed swimmers often finish the 2.4 mile swim from Peaks Island beach to East End Beach in Portland in under one hour (contact YMCA, 207-874-1111).

Sand Building Contest, mid-July. On the beach in Ogunquit, the time of this contest is governed by the tides (phone 207-646-2939 for information).

SKATING

If it has to do with water — frozen included — it's available on Maine's coast. Skating is popular on the coast during the winter. Outdoor listings are free. Indoor listings cost a couple of dollars. Call for times and fees.

The Arena (207-283-0615; Alfred Rd., Industrial Business Park, Biddeford). July 31–April 14. Indoors.

Deering Oaks Park (207-874-8793; State St. and Park Ave., Portland). December–February. Outdoors.

Mill Creek Park (207-767-7651; Cottage Rd., South Portland). December–February. Outdoors.

North Yarmouth Academy Ice Arena (207-846-2384; Rte. 1, Yarmouth). Indoors. Mid-Oct.–late Dec., Jan.–Mar; Sunday afternoons, 3:40–4:40 p.m.

Payson Park (207-874-8793; Baxter Blvd., Portland). December–February. Outdoors.

Portland Ice Arena (207-774-8553; 225 Park Ave., Portland). July through April. Indoors.

Yarmouth Community Services Park (207-846-9680; Main St., Yarmouth). Check out the skating nearby on the Royall River, too. December–February. Outdoors.

SURFING

A surfer and kayaker ride the waves off Kennebunk Beach.

Herb Swanson

It's a South Coast sport. That's where the best waves are, and, in the fine tradition of Moon Doggie and Gidget, that's where the best beaches are. Don't plan on sunbathing when you surf. The truth is that the best surfing is in the fall and winter. Even then surfing here is mostly for beginners. Here are some prime surf apprentice spots.

Fortune Rocks, Biddeford. Surf on the incoming tide. Then the waves are steep, hollow, and break to the right.

Gooch's Beach, Kennebunkport. Best surfing is at low to mid-tide. The steep, thick waves break both right and left.

Moody Beach, Wells. Best waves at high tide. They break close to shore.

Old Orchard Beach, Old Orchard Beach. There is a designated surfing area on the north side of the pier.

Wells Beach, Wells. Surfing best during the incoming tide. The waves break both right and left over sandbars.

York Beach, York Beach. Best waves are at low to mid-tide, and they break right and left.

TENNIS

Biddeford (207-283-0841; Memorial Park, May St.). Three courts with night lights. Also Clifford Park, Pool St., has two courts.

Falmouth (Tennis of Maine, 207-781-2671; 196 Rte. 1, Falmouth). Six indoor courts.

Kennebunk (207-985-6890; Parsons Field, Park St.). Two courts, plus four courts at Kennebunk High School.

Ogunquit (207-646-3032; Agamenticus Rd.). Three courts.

Old Orchard Beach (207-934-2500; www.oldorchardbeachmaine.com; Emerson Cummings Blvd. and First St. near high school). One court; plus three clay courts at Ocean Park and two more at Memorial Park.

Portland (207-874-8793; Deering Oaks Park). Eleven courts, and six more across town at Deering High School; four courts on the Eastern Promenade; four courts at Payson Park on Baxter Blvd.; the Racket & Fitness Center (207-775-6128; 2445 Congress St., Portland).

Wells (207-646-6171; www.cybertours.com/~congdonsresort; E-mail, congdonsresort@cybertours.com; Congdon's Resort, Rte. 1). Three courts.

York Recreation Area (207-363-1040; Organug Rd.). Four courts; two at the high school and two with night lights at the middle school.

WHALE WATCH

Indian Whale Watch (207-967-5912; The Landing Restaurant, Ocean Ave., Kennebunkport).

Odyssey Whale Watch (207-775-0727, 207-642-3270, or 800-437-3270; Long Wharf, Commercial St., Portland).

WINDSURFING

This is not an easy sport to learn. It's even harder in the ocean. Lakes are the place for lessons. *Back Cove* in Portland is a popular spot. It's lake-like enough to learn on, and the wind can blow like the ocean in a storm. *Pine Point* in Scarborough is another good spot.

SHOPPING

Maine these days is known for its outlets as well as its inlets. The outlet trail stretches north and eastward from Kittery all the way to Ellsworth, near Bar Harbor. Maine's outlets may be traced back in history to the first L.L. Bean store in Freeport, a shopping mecca for hunters, fishermen, and outdoors people. The descendants of L.L. Bean, the man who invented the Maine Hunting Boot, still keep shop in Freeport on Casco Bay and in two "factory stores," one in Ellsworth and another in Freeport.

Mainers have been commercially adept since the early 1600s. The Pilgrims of Plymouth Colony sent their most industrious members north to establish a fur trade out of Bagaduce (now known as Castine) on the Blue Hill peninsula. They paid off the debts for their voyage in just a few years, evidence of the resources they found there.

The earliest trade, both with Europe and their fellow colonists, was in furs and lumber, then ships and granite. Later, coastal residents began selling manufactured goods to the rest of the world: fabric woven in textile mills to the south; shoes from leather tanned and handsewn at factories inland; paper made at pulp mills on many of the state's rivers; and herring and sardines canned at factories Down East. Not all the commerce was one-sided. Mainers were world-class shoppers, and during the 18th and 19th centuries world travelers — ship captains and merchants filled their homes with riches from Europe, the Far East, and ports to the south.

Shoes, paper, lumber, and seafood still comprise much of the industrial and commercial base for the state. Yet since the days the "rusticators" discovered Bar Harbor and summer resorts began to sprout up along the coast and inland, much of the state's economy has focused on catering to seasonal residents and tourists. Shops and roadside stands sell everything from paintings, artwork, and nautical gear to T-shirts, balsam sachets, blueberry pottery, and lobster magnets — everything to remind the visitor that they have been here.

Antiques, pottery, and other handcrafts are especially big here. Until the past decade, many of the stores along the coast would close after the tourists went home on Labor Day. Now, in towns like Ogunquit and Kennebunkport, they are open all year long.

ANTIQUES

Carolers in Victorian dress in Portland's Old Port.

Herb Swanson

Shopping for antiques on the coast is almost as popular as outlet hopping, but slower paced. To really know who has what and what it's selling for, pick up a copy of the *Maine Antique Digest,* the bible for coastal and inland antique shoppers. It's published in Waldoboro and can be found at most newsstands in the state.

Antiques on Nine (207-967-0626; 73 Western Ave., Rte. 9, Kennebunk). American and continental furniture, architectural elements, art, and textiles — even old garden accessories.

The Barn at Cape Neddick (207-363-7315; Rte. 1, Cape Neddick). Recognized for its selection of American country furniture, accessories, and folk art.

The Farm (207-985-2656; Mildram Rd. off Rte. 1, Wells). Fine English antiques from the 18th and 19th centuries and oriental porcelain. Yankee magazine calls this one of the best in New England.

F.O. Bailey (207-774-1479; 141 Middle St., Portland). Great showroom and a terrific mix of stuff from rustic pottery to highly polished highboys.

Kenneth & Ida Manko (207-646-2595; on Seabreeze, one half mile off Eldridge Rd., Moody). An intriguing selection of Americana and folk art, including old weathervanes.

MacDougall-Gionet Antiques Associates (207-646-3531; Rte. 1, Wells). For more than forty years dealers — now there are 60 — have gathered in an old barn to show and sell formal and country period antiques.

Portland Architectural Salvage (207-780-0634; archsal3@aol.com; 253 Congress St., Portland). Alice, the proprietor, usually has an ear glued to a cordless phone as she calls all over the state chasing down a good bargain.

We've found many fine things to take home from here, from Tuscan garden ornaments to eight foot doors for our old Victorian parlor.

R. Jorgensen Antiques (207-646-9444; Rte. 1, Wells). Eleven rooms of period furniture and antiques from North America, the British Isles, France, and Scandinavia. This is the place for serious antique shoppers.

Red Wheel Antiques (207-865-6492; 275 Rte. 1, Freeport). We think some of this mix of old dishes, tools, glassware, lamps, military items, and paraphernalia is overpriced. Still, we keep going back to find that occasional bargain. On summer weekends, it becomes an open air flea market.

Riverbank Antiques (207-646-6314; Wells Union Antiques Center, Rte. 1, Wells). If we had a fortune, we'd consider spending a considerable portion of it here on old statuary, antique pots, and other stuff for our garden.

Auctions on the Coast

If you're looking for antiques or just a Victorian knick-knack to take back to your Aunt Pearl, auctions provide the chance to cut out the middleman and get a feel for the worth of something by competing against professional buyers. Estate auctions are even more fun, because they give you a truer sense of time and place than many historic homes or museums. Most of the auction houses listed below will be glad to put you on their mailing lists. The *Maine Sunday Telegram* and *The Maine Times* often run notices of upcoming auctions in their classified sections. Another source of auction notices, the *Maine Antique Digest* has auction news and an entertaining column of auction gossip complete with photographs.

South Coast

F.O. Bailey Antiquarians (207-774-1479; 141 Middle St., Portland).

Southerland Auctions (207-829-3063; Yarmouth). Thursday nights year round.

Midcoast

Andrews and Andrews (207-338-1386; 71 Cross St., Northport).

Downeast/Acadia

Dawson's Auctioneers and Appraisers (207-526-4600;Swans Island; www. dawsonsauction.com; E-mail, dawson1@idt.net).

BOOKSTORES

Friends who visit Maine love our bookstores. While many are small mom-and-pop affairs, they cater to a literate clientele. Several are known for their specialties — like women's studies or New Age essays or fine old volumes only a bibliophile could love. Others you can count on for having a good translation of Homer as well as the top ten from *The New York Times Book Review* section. Maybe it's the long winter, and the fact that people here really do curl up by the fireplace with a good book. A couple of years ago Maine's preeminent weekly, *The Maine Times*, surveyed its readers and found they read, on average, fifty books a year. Herewith is a list of bookstores we have frequented and like. If you're into old books, you may request a directory of dealers by contacting the Maine *Antiquarian Booksellers Association* (207-443-1510).

Allen Scott Books (207-774-2190; E-mail, allenHScott@msn.com; 97A Exchange St., Suite 303, Portland). Old, used, and rare books bought and sold. Good browsing for a rainy day.

Bookland (207-772-4045;1 Monument Way, Portland). The biggest volume bookseller in Maine, and for periodical junkies, the place to go to get Italian *Vogue*. (They also have stores in Brunswick, Freeport and other locations on the coast.)

Books Etc. (207-774-0626; E-mail; leaf@gwi.net; 38 Exchange St., Portland). This is one of our favorite Maine bookstores. Travelers take note, they have an excellent Maine and travel book selection.

Carlson & Turner Antiquarian Books (207-773-4200 or 800-540-7323; E-mail, swilson@maine.rr.com; 241 Congress St., Portland). We love to survey these dimly lit shelves. Ask to be put on their mailing list to receive their annual collectors' calendar.

Eartha, *the giant globe at the DeLorme Map Company.*

Herb Swanson

DeLorme Mapping Company (207-846-7000; www.delorme.com; 2 DeLorme Drive, Yarmouth). This is the shiny new home of a favorite place of ours, just off Rte. 1 on the way to Freeport. A dozen or so years ago, DeLorme began charting the state's wilderness — urban and otherwise — from every possible point of view. Now they chart the world, and they do it with satellites, computers, and automobile navigation systems. Cool. If you love maps, globes, or computers, you'll love this place. Check out *Eartha*, the giant globe in the lobby.

Harbour Books (207-846-6306; 438 Rte. 1, Yarmouth). Books for children and mariners, as well as general books.

Harding's Book Shop (207-646-8785; Rte. 1, Wells). A book collector's paradise with old and rare books, maps, and prints.

Kennebunk Book Port (207-967-3815; www.kbookport.com; 10 Dock Square, Kennebunkport). Books sold in an old rum warehouse.

The Store at Maine Audubon Society (207-781-2330; www.maineaudubon.org; 118 U.S. Rte 1, Falmouth). A good collection of books for those interested in natural history.

CLOTHING

Amaryllis (207-772-4439; 41 Exchange St., Portland). Unusual women's clothing, shoes, and hats.

Dock Square Clothiers (207-967-5362; Dock Square, Kennebunkport; and 207-646-8548; Perkins Cove). Classic, natural-fiber clothing for men and women sold at two locations.

Joseph's (207-773-1274 or 207-773-4454; 410 Fore St., Portland). The men's and women's clothing stores are as haut as Maine gets.

Levinsky's (207-774-0972; 516 Congress St., Portland). This is a bargain-hunter's institution among tight-fisted Mainers, so much so the store had been immortalized in the pages of *Down East* magazine. This is a good place to outfit the kids for school.

GIFTS & SOUVENIRS

Animal Instinct (207-646-7728; www.animalinstinct.com; E-mail, toys@animal instinct.com; Main St., Ogunquit). Bear collectors alert! Great stuffed animals, puppets, dolls, and toys for the young and young at heart.

Brass Carousel (207-646-8225; 3 Oarweed Lane, Perkins Cove). Virginia metal crafts, brass, jewelry, decorative accessories, kites, and Beanie Babies.

Brick Store Museum Shop (207-985-3639; 105 Main St.; Kennebunkport). Antique reproduction toys including a jacks set, rag doll kit, and old-time picture book. The shop also has grown-up gifts.

Compliments (207-967-2269 or 800-249-2269; E-mail, complimats@aol.com; Dock Square, Kennebunkport). An unusual gallery of outré pottery, mirrors, jewelry, lamps, and objets d'art. The "Time Bomb" clock with sticks of "dynamite" is worth a look alone.They also carry the Kate Libby calendar.

Dock Square, a retail and social focal point of Kennebunkport.

Herb Swanson

Dunne Roman (207-780-6456; 428 Fore St., Portland). This store, in an Old Port warehouse, is absolutely gorgeous and the perfect place to find a gift for that eccentrically elegant aunt or friend of yours. At the time of this writing, they were expanding to a second floor.

Indrani's (207-775-1901; 7 Moulton St., Portland and 149 Maine St., Brunswick). Indrani Dennen grew up in Africa, and she has brought some of the most beautiful traditions from that continent to Maine, including handsome wedding baskets which tell a story about the women who wove them.

Lighthouse Depot (207-646-0608; Rte. 1, Wells). Maine is almost as well known for its lighthouses as for its lobster. Here there are two floors of lighthouse memorabilia ready to go home with you.

Nestling Duck Gift Shop (207-883-6705; 350 Pine Point Rd., Scarborough). A collection of New England gifts, including candles, stoneware, jewelry, and Maine-made crafts.

Port Canvas (207-967-2717 or 800-333-6788; 9 Ocean Ave., Kennebunkport). Canvas suit bags, carpetbags, satchels, duffles, totes, raincoats in a variety of sizes and colors. Custom orders taken too.

Something's Fishy (207-774-7726; 22 Exchange St., Portland) Irresistibly ticky tacky, this is where we go to get ticky tacky lobster and lighthouse souvenirs for out-of-town family and friends.

HOME FURNISHINGS

Birdwatcher and Gardener (207-865-4882; 148 Main St., Freeport). Lately, we have spent as much time decorating the outside of our home as the inside. This lovely store is an excellent place to begin. We love their Maine-made fountains and birdfeeders. Plus they have a great collection of garden tools, field guides, and nature books.

Chaudier Cookware Factory Store (207-865-4448; 124 Main St., Freeport). Made in Prince Edward Island in Canada, this cookware is fabulous, and it can be difficult to find on this side of the border. This is one of only three Chaudier stores in the United States.

Cuddledown of Maine (207-865-1713; 231 Rte. 1 South, Freeport). Their down comforters and pillows have been made right here in Maine for 25 years. They also sell beautiful blankets, sheets, and other home furnishings at this true factory outlet where you can get up to 70 percent off catalog prices.

Decorum (207-775-3346; E-mail, decorum@tiac.com; 231 Commercial St., Portland). Old house fanatics travel for hundreds of miles to find nifty, well-made stuff for the house, including reproduction hardware.

Heritage Lanterns (207-846-3911 or 800-544-6070; www.heritagelanterns.com; 25 Yarmouth Crossing Dr., Yarmouth). Handcrafted reproductions of 18th-, 19th-, and early 20th-century lanterns, sconces, chandeliers, and lamps.

Maine Cottage Furniture (207-846-1430; www.mainecottage.com; E-mail, info@mainecottage.com; Lower Falls Landing, Rte. 88, Yarmouth). Furniture in colors that will appeal to modern day rusticators. Also, lighting, vintage-cloth pillows, linen and sofas.

The Whip & Spoon (207-774-4020 or 800-937-9447; www.whipandspoon.com; E-mail, wspoon/@maine.rr.com; 161 Commercial St., Portland). From Cuisinarts to lobster potholders, what to stock for the well-kept kitchen.

JEWELRY

Fibula (207-761-4432; 50 Exchange St., Portland). The showcases here are like the who's who of Maine jewelry making: Werner Reed, P.B. Las, Elizabeth Pryor, Sally Webb, Daniel Gibbings, and the shop's owner, Edie Armstrong, who makes beautiful custom wedding bands, earrings, bracelets, and necklaces at her workbench right in the store.

Geraldine Wolf Antique Jewelry (207-774-8994; 26 Milk St., Portland). Pretty baubles from the past, as well as antique china and decorative art.

Swamp John's (207-646-9414; Oar Weed Rd., Perkins Cove, Ogunquit). They've been making and selling jewelry, including rings, earrings, and pins of Maine tourmaline, for more than two decades.

NAUTICAL EQUIPMENT

Chase Leavitt & Company (207-772-3751 or 800-638-8906; 10 Dana St., Portland). Half a block away from Portland's "working" waterfront, this old-fashioned marine store caters to pleasure boaters, with a good selection of charts, marine hardware, navigation equipment, and foul-weather gear.

POTTERY

Delilah Pottery (207-871-1594; 134 Spring St., Portland). Tucked into a tiny bubble gum pink antique saltbox, this lively potter's studio and store is just packed full of whimsical pottery and sculpture. We especially love their off-beat holiday ornaments.

Maine Potters Market (207-774-1633; www.mainemade.com; 376 Fore St., Portland). Local potter's cooperative featuring stoneware, porcelain, and earthenware. An interesting mix of traditional to funky one-of-a-kind pieces.

Pottery by Peg & Dick Miller (207-846-4981; 19 Smith St. off Rte. 88, Yarmouth). The Millers fashion their wheel-thrown, slab, shingle, and coil pottery from local materials including native clay, beach sand, wood ashes, seaweed, clam, and mussel shells. Then they fire it in their own kiln. Their glazes are lead-free and all of their works are oven proof and dishwasher safe.

OUTDOOR & SPORTING GOODS

Eastern Mountain Sports (207-772-3776; www.easternmountainsports.com; Maine Mall., So. Portland). Clothing, footwear, and gear for campers and hikers.

Kittery Trading Post (207-439-2700 or 888-587-6246; www.kitterytradingpost. com; E-mail, info@kitterytradingpost.com; Rte. 1, Kittery). Just as Freeport's outlets grew up around Bean's, the shopping mecca here seemed to spring from the roots established by this rambling outdoor store full of canoes, sleeping bags, parkas, and pocketknives.

L.L. Bean (207-865-4761 or 800-221-4221; www.llbean.com; E-mail, llbean@ llbean.com; Main St., Freeport). The big daddy of all outdoor stores in Maine. The store stays open 24 hours every day of the year. The best time to shop — if you can stay awake — is in the wee hours. Then you have more time to chew the fat with the staff, who often have great stories to tell about fellow customers and their own outdoor exploits. (See sidebar on page 112.)

Liquid Dreams Surf Shop (207-641-2545; 365 Rte.1, Ogunquit). Surf stuff, skateboards, and clothing. They also rent.

Surplus Store (207-775-0201; 28 Monument Sq. on Congress St., Portland). Before there were Marshalls, Loehman's, and shopping warehouses, surplus stores were the place to buy discounted jeans and old army fatigues. This store has all that, plus a good selection of respectably inexpensive camping and fishing gear.

Herb Swanson

You can take the kayaks for a test ride at L.L. Bean.

L.L. Bean

The lore that surrounds L.L. Bean is almost as numerous as the items sold in the Maine company's mail order catalog, but here are some salient Bean facts.

L.L. Bean was born Leon Linwood Bean in 1872, a name he changed soon after the turn of the century to Leon Leonwood.

- He was orphaned in 1884.
- He invented the Maine Hunting Shoe in 1911.
- He sent potential customers his first mailing in 1912, a small circular with an illustration and description of the Maine Hunting Shoe.
- In 1951, he threw out the keys to his famous store, making it one of the first stores in America to stay open 24 hours a day, 365 days a year.
- Since then the store has closed only four times: two Sundays in 1962 before the town fathers granted L.L. Bean dispensation from the state's new blue laws; the day in 1963 when President John F. Kennedy was assassinated; and the day L.L. Bean died in 1967.

CHAPTER FOUR
Where the Rocky Coast Begins
MIDCOAST

Herb Swanson

Storybook Camden Harbor, one of busiest and prettiest small harbors in Maine.

Midcoast is the point where visitors to the coast have to make choices. It's where little-known detours often can be more rewarding than heading off to better-known vacation spots such as Bar Harbor, Portland, and the beaches of the South Coast. Dozens of peninsulas stretch their rockbound fingers into the Gulf of Maine, each one a destination in itself where a quiet fishing village, an ages-old lighthouse, or a sparkling sand beach awaits the adventurer. For example, just a little to the southeast of Brunswick are the **Harpswells**, skinny stretches of land that stretch into Casco Bay and are connected by bridge to the rounded and rocky terrain of **Sebascodegan, Orrs,** and **Bailey Islands**. Making your way to the edge of Mackerel Cove on Bailey Island is only a matter of about 15 miles, but it can seem like time-traveling through decades. There's also **Cundy's Harbor** off on its own; a fishing village so heavily populated with photographic subjects that local stores do a brisk business selling film.

The Midcoast abounds in cultural destinations as well. Bowdoin College is the overwhelming presence in **Brunswick**, but there's much more here than just the school, including the Peary-MacMillan Arctic Museum and the Maine State Music Theatre. This is also where Harriet Beecher Stowe wrote *Uncle Tom's Cabin*.

Bath is a city of ships and shipbuilding that hugs the shores of the Kennebec, a deep and navigable waterway that has an ocean-like feel to it — as if it were capable of handling any oceangoing vessel large or small. During World War II, Bath built more destroyers than all the shipyards in the entire Japanese empire. Not far from here is the **Phippsburg** peninsula, the cradle of Maine civilization, and its shipbuilding industry.

A launching at Bath Iron Works, one of Maine's active ship-building centers.

Herb Swanson

Across the Kennebec is **Georgetown Island**, a sprawling network of summer communities and fishing villages with names like **Robinhood, Five Islands, Marrtown,** and **Arrowsic.** Robinhood Cove, which cuts into the island's northeastern side, is often filled with the yachts of summering residents, and Reid State Park at the outermost reaches of the Sheepscot River is a wonderful family park with one of the better beaches in the Midcoast.

Wiscasset has billed itself as the "prettiest village in Maine." That title is disputable, but the town's location where Rte. 1 crosses the Sheepscot River makes the town's charm readily visible to anyone traveling up the coast. Adding to Wiscasset's romance are two old schooners lodged haphazardly on the west bank of the river. The *Hesperus* and the *Luther Little* once carried cargo between Boston, Haiti, and Portugal. They were two of thousands of ships that plied the seas until well into the 1920s. Today they are one of the most photographed sites in Maine.

Formerly a trading center, and later a hub of shipbuilding activity, **Boothbay Harbor** today is mostly about boats, activities attached to boats, and people who find the boating way of life appealing. The shady streets of the town, at the tip of a rocky peninsula, are lined with summer-people-minded shops and a wealth of art galleries. The pretty harbor is jam-packed with boats to rent, boats to hire, boats to envy, and boats to drool over and make one consider Captain Kidd's occupation. (The notorious pirate also liked to summer here and reportedly left a buried treasure on nearby **Damariscove Island.** Treasure hunters are still trying to locate the fabled store.) This is also the port of call for Windjammer Days and the Friendship Sloop Races, two famous Maine boaters' events.

Within half an hour's drive you can see the great boats being built in **East Boothbay.** Nearby are the summer retreats of **Newagen** (on **Southport Island**) to the west and **Ocean Point** to the east.

MIDCOAST

statute miles

0   10   20

Orono

Penobscot River

Bangor

95

Brewer

15

7

ALT 1

Bucksport

1

Waterville

95

Kennebec River

Maine

Stockton Springs

Penobscot

175

177

Belfast

Searsport

Castine

Northport

Sedgwick

SOUTH COAST

3

Islesboro

Little Deer Isle

Augusta

Islesboro I.

Deer Isle

17

Union

Lincolnville

Deer I.

495

Camden

North Haven I.

DOWNEAST/ACADIA

Rockport

North Haven

95

Waldoboro

Rockland

North Haven

Newcastle

1

Vinalhaven

Wiscasset

Thomaston

Owls Head

Vinalhaven I.

Damariscotta

Friendship

Spruce Head

Brunswick

1

Edgecomb

Bristol

Port Clyde

Tenants Harbor

Penobscot Bay

Westport I.

Topsham

Bath

East Boothbay

Muscongus Bay

Merepoint

Phippsburg

Boothbay

New Harbor

Mantinicus I.

Harpswell

Cundys Harbor

Southport

Pemaquid Point

Center

Orrs I.

Sebasco

Newagen

Monhegan I.

S. Harpswell

Popham Beach

Bailey I.

Small Point

Casco Bay

For centuries Native Americans summer camped here and left behind giant piles of oyster shells, a feat which today is celebrated at the annual **Damariscotta** River Oyster Festival. Not far off Rte. 1, you can still see one of the great shell heaps where the Damariscotta River and the inland Great Salt Bay meet.

Here is another one of those famous coastal junctures, where travelers can push on toward **Rockland** and **Camden** or veer off the main road onto picturesque Rte. 129. This road runs down the Pemaquid peninsula along the river to **South Bristol**, a fishing village, and **Christmas Cove**, a yachting basin so named by Captain John Smith, who anchored here on Christmas Day in 1614. Rte. 130 picks up in the fishing village of **New Harbor** and meanders on through the historic peninsula to **Pemaquid Point**, where there is one of Maine's most stunning lighthouses — **Pemaquid Light**. This spot shows off the Maine coast at its stormy best with the power of the ocean pounding against the rockbound coast. Rte. 32 takes you back up along Muscongus Sound through pretty **Round Pond** to **Waldoboro**.

Waldoboro was settled by Germans in the mid-18th century, and today is famed for two of the state's culinary landmarks — Moody's Diner and Morse's Sauerkraut. The first five-masted schooner was built here in 1888.

From here, **Friendship** is just a short trip down Rte. 220, which skirts the western shore of the Medomak River. It's hard to believe Friendship exists. Where are the shops, the hotels, the gas stations, restaurants? Here on beautiful, isolated **Hatchet Cove** are a few summer homes, a handful of lobster boats, and a Friendship sloop or two, that famous gaff-rigged working boat now prized by wealthy modern-day sailors. Rte. 97 leads past **Cushing**, another quiet fishing village, made famous by painter Andrew Wyeth.

From **Thomaston**, home of the state prison, you can veer off onto Rte. 131, which leads down yet another peninsula filled with history. **Tenant's Harbor** looks simple, but look again. Those are mighty big yachts anchored so casually in the harbor. Southwest from here is **Port Clyde**, once called Herring Gut. Port Clyde is the point of departure for the hour-long boat ride to Monhegan, eleven miles off the coast. Measuring only one mile by $1/2$ mile, **Monhegan** literally is besieged with painters and the salt breezes alternately smell of turpentine. The dark forests and dramatic cliffs make the island a hiker's paradise as well.

Once known for its quarried lime rock that was shipped to the four corners of the earth, **Rockland** today bills itself as the lobster capital of the world. It is the Penobscot Bay region's central working town, and its harbor is filled with lobster boats and commercial fishing boats that regularly fish the waters of the Grand Banks. Rockland is a bustling town that has become gentrified with artists' studios, galleries, and moderately expensive restaurants that clearly aim to serve tourists. It also is a hub of the windjammer trade, and from here ferries regularly travel to **Vinalhaven**, **Matinicus**, and **North Haven.**

Sitting fifteen miles out in Penobscot Bay, Vinalhaven flourished when gran-

Lobster boats in the harbor off Vinalhaven.

Herb Swanson

ite was quarried here. Today the island has a tenacious year-round population of lobstermen and fishermen and a dedicated coterie of summer residents who seem to like keeping the secret of this island to themselves. To the north is the small and exclusive summer community of North Haven on North Haven Island. Windjammers and large pleasure boats often anchor in Pulpit Harbor where passengers can catch a glimpse of the large seaside estates owned by the island's reclusive summer residents.

In striking contrast there is the quiet, tiny island of Matinicus. Approximately 100 people make their living here, most of them lobstering and fishing the outer waters of Penobscot Bay. It takes about two hours by ferry to ply the 23 miles of water to the island. Dedicated birders often opt to charter a local boat and keep going another five miles to Matinicus Rock, where nesting puffins often can be seen.

Just off Rte. 1 before **Camden** is **Rockport**, a pastoral village where Galloways munch in green meadows and actors, photographers, and boat builders live in mansions by the sea. Rockport was also the home of Andre the Seal; today a statue on the harbor commemorates him.

The storybook beauty of Camden was captured in the film *Peyton Place*. Today it's considered the shoppers' resting place between Freeport and Bar Harbor. Expensive shops cram the old-fashioned town center. The town is part of a miniature filmmaking boom and movie stars and movie crews frequently can be seen at work or relaxing over lunch at Camden's restaurants.

This pretty town is a worthwhile destination, although it can be a hard town in which to find a parking space. Space in the harbor is also scarce. Luxury yachts moor next to giant windjammers that ferry passengers on weeklong cruises; and on a busy summer day it seems possible to walk from boat to boat from one side of the harbor to the other. When here, be certain to visit Merryspring, a breathtaking public garden, and one of the most famous horticultural sites of New England.

Lincolnville Beach just to the north offers an expansive view of Penobscot Bay. This is also where you catch the ferry to **Islesboro**, the exclusive summer community three miles off shore.

The towns along this part of the coast keep promising to be the next Camden. The fact each is still waiting to be discovered makes this a wonderful place to visit. Antiques and sea captains' homes abound. Beautiful old houses with ocean views are still more than reasonably priced. There are art galleries, theater groups, and restaurants for big city palates in **Belfast**.

The deepwater port of **Searsport** at the head of Penobscot Bay was once known in ports around the world. The town still has the grand waterfront houses to prove it; many of them now converted to inns and bed and breakfasts. Today it bills itself as the antique capital of Maine.

MIDCOAST: LODGING

A s in every chapter, the lodgings we recommend represent places we either have stayed at, visited and toured, or that have been recommended and written up by well-traveled friends and family. Certainly, they are not the only places to stay, but they are a reliable list of choices. Whether quiet and beautiful enclaves or places well situated for sightseeing and recreational opportunities, many are worth staying for two or more nights. Several inns listed have restaurants; sometimes they are included in the *Dining* section of this chapter.

For alternative listings, you can contact the **Maine Tourism Association** (P.O. Box 2300, Hallowell, ME 04347; 207-623-0363 in Maine; 800-533-9595 out-of-state and Canada; E-mail, metainfo@mainetourism.com). Every year they publish the *Guide to Inns & Bed & Breakfasts*, a list of inns and B&Bs by region. All of the listings are written and paid for by the owners, so you should take their content with a grain of salt. The **Maine Innkeepers Association Food & Lodging Guide**, with advertising from hotels, motels, and inns throughout the state, is available at most tourist information centers, or from the association (305 Commercial St., Portland, ME 04101; 207-773-7670; www.maineinns.com; E-mail, info@maineinns.com).

MAINE COAST LODGING NOTES

R ates: Rates can vary widely off season and in season. They generally increase close to Memorial Day and are highest from July through the leaf season in mid- to late October. Special packages are often available for two or more nights stay, and frequently there are even better values during the off season. If breakfast and/or dinner is included with the price of a room, we do not alter the rate category, we just note that the room rate includes one or more meals.

Inexpensive	Up to $65
Moderate	$65 to $125
Expensive	$125 to $180
Very Expensive	$180 and up

These rates exclude Maine state lodging tax or individual hotel service charges that may be added to your bill.

Credit Cards: Several lodging places we recommend in this book do not take plastic. If they do not, they almost always take personal or travelers' checks. Following are credit card abbreviations:

AE — American Express	DC — Diner's Card
CB — Carte Blanche	MC — MasterCard
D — Discover Card	V — Visa

Minimum Stay: Many inns and B&Bs require a minimum stay of two or more nights during the summer season. We have noted minimum stays when possible, but it's best to check when making room reservations.

Deposit/Cancellation: To reserve a room on the Maine coast, it is generally necessary to make a deposit to cover the first night of your stay — and some places may require up to 50 percent of the cost of the intended stay. Cancellations often must be made at least seven to 10 days in advance. Ask about the inn's policy when you make reservations.

Handicap Access: Many of the inns and B&Bs in this book have yet to comply with federal regulations regarding handicap access. We have noted handicap access is available in inns, B&Bs, and hotels where the owners can guarantee at least one room with access.

Other Options: For information on camping, from tents to RVs, see the section entitled "Camping" in this chapter. If you plan to camp with an RV, be sure to make reservations well in advance. If you plan on tent camping, most of the national and state parks and national forests campgrounds are available on a first-come, first-serve basis.

Bath

INN AT BATH
Innkeeper: Nicholas
  Bayard.
207-443-4294.
www.innatbath.com.
E-mail: innkeeper@
  innatbath.com.
969 Washington St., Bath
  04530.
Open: All year.
Price: Moderate to
  Expensive.

This old house was built in 1810 when Bath was a booming shipbuilding town. One of the most striking characteristics of this handsomely restored Greek Revival home is the twin parlors with a marvelous marble fireplace and filled with antiques and striking family pieces. There are seven comfortable and roomy guest rooms, all with private bath, TVs, VCRs, air-conditioning, and telephones. Several have fireplaces and king- or queen-sized beds. Two double Jacuzzis can be found resting

Credit Cards: AE, D, MC, V.
Handicap Access: Partial.

next to wood-burning fireplaces in two of the guest rooms. Two of the rooms adjoin and can be made into suites. Our favorite is the River Room, formerly a hayloft in the attached barn, which now has exposed old wood beams and a woodburning fireplace to take the chill off an autumn evening. A full breakfast is included. Children over five welcome. Pets welcome. No smoking.

Belfast

BELFAST HARBOR INN
Innkeepers: Michael and
  Jamie Schnetzer.
207-338-2740 or
  800-545-8576.
www.belfastharborinn.com.
E-mail: stay@belfastharbor
  inn.com.
Rte. 1, Belfast (mailing
  address: RR # 5, Box
  5230, Belfast 04915).
Open: All year.
Price: Moderate to
  Expensive.
Credit Cards: AE, D, MC, V.
Handicap Access: Very
  limited.

We discovered this inn by accident and were pleasantly surprised. It is just the thing for weary coastal travelers. Large — 61 rooms — comfortable, and clean, this is an efficiently run roadside inn just about midway between Belfast and Searsport. We liked it because 24 of the rooms are non-smoking, and because the deck right outside our back door was a great place to convene for a gin and tonic after long day (there's no restaurant or bar here; its BYOB). Best of all, the inn sits at the edge of a large expanse of green lawn that leads all the way down to the shore of Penobscot Bay. Ask for a room on the waterside of the inn. Dogs are welcome, but should not stay in rooms alone and are charged $5.

Boothbay Harbor

THE GREENLEAF INN
Innkeeper: Jeff Teel.
207-633-7346 or 888-950-
  7724; fax 207-633-2642.
www.greenleafinn.com.
65 Commercial St.,
  Boothbay Harbor 04538.
Open: Year round.
Price: Moderate.
Credit Cards: MC, V.
Handicap Access: Yes.

We stumbled upon this bright and airy inn on our last trip to Boothbay and not a moment too soon. It is a nice, quiet refuge in a busy, often honky-tonk, tourist town. You certainly can't beat the location or the views. The 150-year old white cape with trim black shutters is perched on the side of a hill above the harbor and smack dab in the middle of town just a short walk from the town's galleries, fudge shops, and other tourist town lures. The inn has five comfortable guest rooms, all with queen-size beds, cable TV, private baths, and harbor views. Two guest rooms are on the ground floor. A full breakfast is always offered and if you're lucky, you'll be here on the day Jeff serves his gingerbread waffles or his banana French toast. Breakfast is served inside near the new flagstone fireplace or on the pretty front porch that overlooks Boothbay's bustling harbor. No pets. Children over 12 welcome.

Brunswick

CAPTAIN DANIEL STONE INN
Innkeeper: William R. Bennett.
207-725-9898 or 800-267-0525.
www.uswelcome.com/ maine/captdan.htm.
10 Water St., Brunswick 04011.
Off Rte. 1.
Open: All year.
Price: Moderate to Expensive.
Credit Cards: AE, DC, MC, V.
Handicap Access: Yes.

The Captain Daniel Stone Inn mixes old and new to appealing effect. The "old" is the Federal-style home from which the inn gets its name (Capt. Daniel Stone owned it). The "new" refers to the wings that have been added in recent years. Rooms and suites have modern conveniences like cable TV, VCRs, and cassette players. Furnishings are period reproductions. No two of the 34 rooms are alike. Some are done in pine, others in mahogany. Several have whirlpool baths and brass beds. The inn also has a popular restaurant, the Narcissa Stone (named for the captain's daughter) and serves lunch and dinner, in the summer on an outdoor veranda. A light breakfast is included in the price of the room.

CAPTAIN'S WATCH BED AND BREAKFAST AND SAIL CHARTER
Innkeepers: Donna Dillman and Ken Brigham.
207-725-0979.
2476 Cundy's Harbor Rd., Brunswick 04011.
Open year round; by reservation in winter.
Price: Moderate.
Credit Cards: MC, V.
Handicap Access: Limited.

Perched atop a high bluff, this former Civil War "Union Hotel" affords long views over a small working harbor and beyond to ledge, islands, rivers, and bays. The Captain's Watch is an elegant, unpretentious Greek Revival home decorated with family antiques and collections of old china and quilts. All five bedrooms have private bath and overlook the water or secluded woods. Breakfast is included. Outside smoking only. We vow to one day take advantage of the B&B's sail charter on *Symbian*, Donna and Ken's 37-foot sailboat. Ken is a Coast Guard licensed captain and takes guests out for day trips and week-long cruises. Limited availability for children.

Camden

LODGE AT CAMDEN HILLS
Innkeepers: The Burgess Family.
207-236-8478 or 800-832-7058.
P.O. Box 794, Rte. 1, Camden 04843.
Open: Year round.
Price: Moderate to Very Expensive.
Credit Cards: AE, D, MC, V.
Handicap Access: Yes.

The Lodge at Camden Hills offers modern, quiet, clean, efficiently run lodgings to travelers who want a location close to Camden, but away from the traffic and bustle. The Lodge is a small, comfortable motel with several efficiency cottages that sit on a landscaped hillside north of Camden. It's been here for years, although the Burgess family undertook a major renovation and modernization of the lodge during the early 1990s. Everything is spanking new and rooms now provide the amenities that are increasingly in demand by upscale travelers. Many of the private cottages have their own decks, Jacuzzis, and fireplaces. All of the 20 rooms have private baths, cable TV, air conditioning, telephones, and refrigerators. No smoking. Children welcome. No pets.

MAINE STAY INN
Innkeepers: Peter and
   Donny Smith and Diana
   Robson.
207-236-9636.
www.mainestay.com.
E-mail: innkeeper@
   mainestay.com.
22 High St. (Rte. 1),
   Camden 04843.
Open: All year.
Price: Moderate.
Credit Cards: AE, MC, V.

The Maine Stay is one of our favorite inns. Intimate, trim, and quiet, the inn is an early 18th-century farmhouse that sits on two acres in the heart of Camden's historic district. There are eight bedrooms in the main house and the attached carriage house; six have modern, private baths; two share a bath. The largest room now has a wood-burning stove, and two guestrooms have fireplaces. One is located in a suite complete with a large sitting room and queen-sized bed. Out back there is a majestic four-story barn and gardens which the innkeepers expand and improve every year. Capt. Peter Smith is a retired navy pilot, and the house is full of things the Smiths have picked up on their travels — including a tonsu, a 300-year-old Samurai warrior's chest. There are two parlors, each with a fireplace with matches on the mantel and wood and paper ready to be burned when you want to take the chill off. Every morning, breakfast is cooked on an old Queen Atlantic black stove and served on Spode china at a long pine farm table. Usually it's "something eggy one day, something not the next," says Donny. Tea is served in the afternoon. No smoking. Children seven and older.

NORUMBEGA
Innkeeper: Murray Keating.
207-236-4646.
www.norumbega.
   com.
E-mail: norumbega@
   acadia.net.
61 High St., Camden 04843.
Open: All year.
Price: Expensive to Very
   Expensive.
Credit Cards: AE, D, MC, V.

The Norumbega is a stone castle on a hill by the sea that was built about a century ago. Since it opened as an inn a few years back it has become a favorite of honeymooners — perhaps because of its brooding, romantic presence, strong colors, and Victorian antiques scattered everywhere on lovely birds-eye maple floors. Or maybe it's the kitchen where hungry romantics will find a constant supply of fresh-baked cookies, fresh fruit, and other surprises. Altogether there are 13 guest rooms, including the penthouse. (It's really the attic done over into a luxe suite. It offers the best views in the house; it is also the most expensive room at the inn — and perhaps in the entire state.) All rooms have private baths. Almost all the beds are king-sized. Five of the rooms have fireplaces and impressive views. The library suite is just that — with books lining the shelves of the balcony which skirts the bedroom. Outside there are stately elms and well-kept gardens. For those who love theatrics, the inn hosts "Murder by the Sea" some weekends. Guess who-

The Norumbega, with its brooding castle-by-the-sea looks, is a favorite among honeymooners and Texans.

Michael Loomis

dunit, and you could win two nights for you and a friend. The manager told us Texans also like to stay here, and we can understand why. Everything here seems scaled to suit a Texan's grand style. No smoking.

THE OWL AND THE TURTLE HARBOR VIEW GUEST ROOMS
Innkeepers: The Conrads.
207-236-9014.
P.O. Box 1265, 8 Bay View, Camden 04843.
Open: All year.
Price: Inexpensive to Moderate.
Credit Cards: D, MC, V.

This small bed and breakfast is on the floors above Camden's favorite bookstore, right on the harbor in downtown Camden. There are three rooms, each with bath or shower, and million-dollar mountain or harbor view. The accommodations are modest, but a good value. Breakfast includes homemade muffins. No smoking

WHITEHALL INN
Innkeepers: The Dewing family.
207-236-3391 or 800-789-6565.
P.O. Box 558, 52 High St., Camden 04843.
Open: Late May to late October.
Price: Moderate to Expensive.
Credit Cards: AE, MC, V.

This is a fine, sprawling old Yankee inn with an interesting history. The main house began as a fine white Greek Revival sea captain's home built in 1834. It became an inn in 1901, and with many additions has become a favorite coastal retreat. Camden born poet Edna St. Vincent Millay was "discovered" here by a guest. Between the main inn and two smaller "cottages" across the street, there are 50 guest rooms; 42 with private baths. (All three buildings are on the National Register.)

Discover Maine like it used to be at the Whitehall Inn.

Herb Swanson

Guest rooms and spacious common areas, decorated in colonial colors, are quiet, gracious, and comfortable but not deluxe. There are no televisions, but there are books, games, puzzles, a piano, and tennis on the inn's private courts. Tea is served at 4 p.m. We imagine this is how our Yankee ancestors sought relaxation in simpler days, and it feels pretty good. The dining room offers a good wine list and a good menu which changes daily (jackets required). Full breakfast included; dinner additional. Modified American plan available. Children welcome.

Capitol Island

ALBONEGON INN
Innkeepers: Kim and Bill Peckham.
207-633-2521.
Capitol Island 04538.
Open: Memorial Day through mid-October.
Price: Inexpensive to moderate.
Credit Cards: No. Cash, personal or traveler's checks accepted.

We suspect that life at the Albonegon is just like Maine used to be, years ago before motor cars really took over the coast. It's tucked right up against the water on a pretty little tree-covered island not too far from Southport Island and Boothbay Harbor. The rooms are all Yankee elegance with white painted wood walls and narrow beds with old-fashioned quilts and coverlets. The common rooms downstairs really make you want to sit down by the big stone fireplace, read a book and maybe chat up the other guests as they come and go. A continental breakfast of homemade muffins, breads, and coffee cake is served in an airy dining room overlooking Boothbay Harbor and Linnekin Bay. Our friend Elizabeth, a recent convert to kayaking, tipped us off to this place, a favorite resting place for fellow paddlers. In its earliest years, before Capitol Island was connected to the mainland by bridge, windjammers would stop and leave guests off for long, relaxing stays.

East Boothbay

FIVE GABLES INN
Innkeepers: Mike and Dee
  Kennedy.
207-633-4551 or
  800-451-5048.
www.fivegablesinn.com.
E-mail: info@fivegables
  inn.com.
P.O. Box 335, Murray Hill
  Rd., East Boothbay 04544.
Open: Mid-May through
  late Oct.
Price: Moderate to
  Expensive.
Credit Cards: MC, V.

This cream-colored inn is perched on a hillside overlooking pretty Linekin Bay near Boothbay Harbor. Airy, uncluttered, and made cozy with country craft accents, the Five Gables is a restful retreat in an otherwise bustling tourist region. All 16 rooms have private baths and water views; five have working fireplaces. Borrow the inn's golf clubs and hit a few. Or take afternoon tea on the porch overlooking the lush cottage garden. No smoking. Children over eight welcome.

Harpswell

HARPSWELL INN
Innkeepers: Susan and Bill
  Menz.
207-833-5509 or
  800-843-5509.
www.gwi.net/~harpswel.
141 Lookout Point Rd.,
  RR1, Box 141, Harpswell
  04079.
Open: All year.
Price: Moderate.
Credit Cards: MC, V.
Handicap Access: Partial.

A shipbuilder built this home for himself, his family, and the raft of shipwrights busily building boats not far from his door. It's a beautiful old home with white clapboards, black shutters, and more windows than anybody would ever want to clean. Susan and Bill Menz moved here from Houston. Bill is a Bowdoin alumn and many alumns as well as parents of Bowdoin students stay here. The downstairs is filled with furniture they've picked up in their travels to China and Europe. There are 14 bedrooms, eight with private bath. There's the Bowdoin Room, of course. There are also two luxury suites in the cottage—one with a Jacuzzi and both with kitchens (breakfast is not included with these rooms). Breakfast in the main house may include quiche, homemade muffins, and French toast. Children over ten in the main house; children of all ages welcome in the cottages. Smoking on the porch or grounds.

Islesboro

DARK HARBOR HOUSE
207-734-6669.
P.O. Box 185, Main Rd.,
  Islesboro 04848.
Open: Mid-May to
  Mid-October.
Price: Expensive to Very
  Expensive.

The Dark Harbor House is a yellow clapboard Georgian mansion built for a wealthy banker on an Islesboro hillside at the turn of the century. The inn has spacious, summer-elegant rooms, and a well-deserved reputation as a restful staging ground from which to explore Islesboro, enclave of the rich and famous. The inn has ten guest rooms and two suites; all rooms have private baths and several have balconies. Antiques are everywhere. The service is impeccable. The dining room offers a creative menu. A full breakfast is included; dinner is additional.

Monhegan Island

TRAILING YEW GUEST HOUSE
Innkeeper: Marian Choiffi.
207-596-0440.
Monhegan Island 04852.
Open: Mid-May to mid-Oct.
Price: Inexpensive.
Credit Cards: None; personal and travelers' checks accepted.

Monhegan is an island famous for its simple way of life, its views, and the number of renowned artists who for more than a century have stayed there, hoping to capture and carry away the island's peculiar light on canvas. The Trailing Yew fits right in, a spartan collection of rustic white clapboard houses clustered around a lawn where guests gather before dinner to play horseshoes. The 37 rooms are clean and well kept. Minimal electric lighting is provided by generator to most rooms through part of the day and evening; after the generator is turned off, you can read or play cards by oil lamp or candle. Breakfast and a hearty family-style dinner are included with the cost of the room. Limited smoking. Children and pets welcome.

Newcastle

THE NEWCASTLE INN
Innkeepers: Rebecca and Howard Levitan.
207-563-5685.
www.newcastleinn.com.
60 River Rd., Newcastle 04553.
Open: All year.
Price: Moderate to Expensive.
Credit Cards: MC, V.
Handicap Access: Limited.

This handsome inn and restaurant is just off Rte. 1 as you drive into Damariscotta and head down the road for Pemaquid Point Lighthouse. It is also a great stopping point on the route up the coast to Camden, Bar Harbor, and beyond.

The 14 rooms are well-appointed and comfortable, all with private bath; eight are in the main house, while six are in the carriage house. Since the Levitans became innkeepers, the Newcastle has since undergone major renovations. There are two upscale rooms with king beds — one has a fireplace while the other holds a Jacuzzi; another Jacuzzi is in a suite with a queen canopy bed. In several of the rooms you can lie on your pencil-post bed and gaze at the Damariscotta River. Five of the guestrooms have fireplaces. The kitchen turns out three- and five-course meals that have won so many fans that the inn now has two dining rooms. The common room, with its stenciled floor, fireplace, and high-backed antique wing chairs, is a great place to relax with fellow guests. There's also a sunporch with comfortable lawn chairs and views of the Damariscotta River. Children over 12 welcome. No smoking. Breakfast is included. People also come here to cross-country ski.

New Harbor

THE BRADLEY INN
Innkeepers: Warren and
  Beth Busteed.
207-677-2105 or
  800-942-5560.
www.lincoln.midcoast.com
  /~bradley.
3063 Bristol Rd., Pemaquid
  Point, New Harbor
  04554.
Season: Year round.
Price: Moderate to
  Expensive.
Credit Cards: AE, MC, V.

Built in the late 19th century, the building was "literally gutted" in the late 20th century, brought up to the standards of the modern leisure traveler, and filled with nautical pictures, charts, and huge ship models. There are 16 rooms, all with private bath. There's also a cottage across the croquet court. From the top floor, the cathedral-ceilinged rooms look out onto John's Bay and the gardens. A hearty continental breakfast is included. Dinner, additional, is open to the public. So is the pub which boasts a granite-topped bar and attracts a mix of guests and local residents. Non-smoking rooms available.

GOSNOLD ARMS
Owners: The Phinney
  Family.
Summer 207-677-3727;
  winter 561-575-9549.
www.gosnold.com.
Northside Rd., Rte. 32,
  New Harbor 04554.
Open: Mid-May to
  mid-Oct.
Price: Moderate to
  Expensive.
Credit Cards: MC, V.

The Gosnold Arms is the type of old Maine inn that people like to visit again and again. In its first incarnation this was a saltwater farm. It has also served as a summer boarding house for Smith College students (it still has a Please No Men Permitted Upstairs sign), and it's easy to imagine the exuberant voices of Smith women ringing in the hallways and across the inn's broad green lawn. The Gosnold sits at the entrance to New Harbor, not far from splendid Pemaquid Point and its lovely lighthouse. There are accommodations for 40 to 50 guests (every room has its own bath) spread out among the farmhouse, the three-story barn, and 10 separate cottages. One of the cottages is a former steamboat freight office; another is a steamboat cabin. The dining room seats 80 — or you can take your meal on the porch and watch as working and pleasure boats pass by. Dinner is real Yankee fare — fresh seafood, beef, and homemade desserts. We haven't eaten here, but with this view, you almost can't lose. Breakfast included, dinner additional. Smoking in the cottages and on the ground floor. Children welcome.

HOTEL PEMAQUID
Owners: Skip and Cindy
  Atwood.
207-677-2312.
3098 Bristol Rd., New
  Harbor 04554.
Season: Mid-May to
  mid-October.

This Victorian inn sits almost at the very end of the Pemaquid peninsula, not far from the famous lighthouse. The main house is an old-style hotel with eleven rooms; seven with private baths. The inn's parlors are jam packed with dark period furniture, flowered curtains and upholstery, and

Price: Inexpensive to
    Moderate.
Credit Cards: None, but
    personal and travelers
    checks are accepted.
Handicap Access: Yes.

an idiosyncratic collection of Victoriana and other "stuff" including a check signed by glamor goddess Marilyn Monroe. Our favorite room is the Chauffeur's Quarters, a sunny ground floor guest room with a private bath that is decorated in not-too-fussy shades of rose. The hotel annex offers a comfortable suite with a kitchen, living room, and cable TV. The hotel also rents four-unit bungalows and operates a five-unit motel with clean, nicely appointed rooms for budget-conscious travelers. Cottages can be rented on a weekly basis. Breakfast is not included, although the coffee pot is always on. No smoking in the main house, but smoking allowed in one of the bungalows and in the motel.

Newagen

NEWAGEN SEASIDE INN
Innkeepers: Peter and
    Heidi Larsen.
207-633-5242 or
    800-654-5242.
E-mail: seaside@wiscasset.
    net.
P.O. Box 29, Rte. 27 South,
    Newagen 04576.
Open: Mid-May through
    early October.
Price: Moderate to
    Expensive.
Credit Cards: MC, V.
Handicap Access: Yes.

Pronounced "new wagon," this resort inn sits on 85 acres at the southern tip of Southport Island six miles from Boothbay Harbor. The inn retains a '40s look and feel that makes you think of Bing or Bob on the set of a favorite old movie. On inclement days you can hear the foghorn — one guest said if it wasn't turned off he was leaving. (One person's romance is another's nightmare.) Most of the 26 rooms have an ocean view; all have private baths. During the day you have a choice of activities — tennis, horseshoes, badminton, volleyball, rowboats, fishing, swimming in the saltwater pool or heated freshwater pool. Almost any good day in season you can hear that quiet, comforting pock pock of the ball being batted back and forth. The dining room serves all three meals, and the owner screened in a portion of the porch so you can dine *al fresco,* sans bugs. Breakfast included; other meals additional.

Phippsburg

EDGEWATER FARM B&B
Innkeepers: Bill and Carol
    Emerson.
207-389-1322.
www.virtualcities.com/ons
    /me/c/mec2701.htm.
Rte. 216, Phippsburg 04562.
Season: Year round.

The Emersons have converted this 1800 farmhouse into a lovely bed and breakfast, and because the owners have green thumbs, the breakfast table and afternoon snack often include bounty from their orchards and organic gardens. The five guest rooms are comfortable and pretty; one has a private bath. This is a good place to stay for bicy-

Price: Moderate.
Credit Cards: MC, V.
Handicap Access: Yes.

clists and kayakers touring the peninsula. There are several great white sand beaches nearby including those at Popham Beach State Park. If you prefer warmer water however, the B&B has an enclosed swimming pool. No smoking.

Rockland

CAPT. LINDSEY HOUSE INN
Owners: Capts. Ken and Ellen Barnes.
207-596-7950 or 800-523-2145.
www.midcoast.com/ ~lindsey.
E-mail: lindsey@midcoast. com.
5 Lindsey St., Rockland 04841.
Open: Year round.
Price: Moderate to Expensive.
Credit Cards: AE, D, MC, V.
Handicap Access: Yes.

This is the place to stay if you're off on a windjammer cruise (the owners offer discounts to windjammer passengers) or ferrying to the islands from Rockland Harbor. A mustard-painted 1837 brick house on a quiet side street, this was first a sea captain's home. Since then it has housed the local water company (the water company's giant safe, too big to remove, remains as a topic of conversation in one of the sitting rooms). Today it is an inn, owned by two sea captains, Ellen and Ken Barnes — former theater folk who also offer cruises on their schooner *Stephen Taber* or their motor vessel *Pauline*. Right next door is the Waterworks, a pub owned by the Barnes and worth checking out. Local windjammer crews like to hang out in between cruises, and you can sample the best Maine microbrews on tap. The inn has a pleasant, professional air about it, and it seems bigger than it is — big enough to give guests plenty of elbow room and privacy. There are nine rooms, all freshly decorated with unusual lamps and furnishings collected from around the world and covering a range of styles from masculine plaids and stripes to Art Deco. All the beds are big and firm with down comforters and tapestry bedspreads. Every room has a private bath, air conditioning, television, and telephones. If you've borrowed one of the inn's paperbacks from their library and haven't finished it, they insist you take it with you. No smoking. Children over ten welcome.

Rockport

THE SAMOSET RESORT
General Manager: James H. Ash.
207-594-2511 or 800-341-1650.
www.samoset.com.
220 Warrenton St., Rockport 04856.
Off Rte. 1.

The Samoset is one of the places where Mainers like to stay — quite possibly because the resort offers so much for a population that tends to be physically active. Ten kilometers of great cross-country skiing in the winter; golf in the summer on an 18-hole course which was extensively revamped in 1994 and 1995. Year round there is tennis (indoor

The Samoset, Rockport, summer of 1917.

Samoset

Open: All year.
Price: Moderate to Very
  Expensive.
Credit Cards: AE, D, DC,
  MC, V.
Handicap Access: Yes.

and outdoor courts), racquetball, indoor and outdoor pools, bicycles, basketball, fitness room with Nautilus, croquet, badminton, volleyball, and horseshoes. How do they fit all this in? The resort sits on an ample 230 acres that stretches to the water. Although the resort was established more than 100 years ago, few vestiges of the old Yankee inn remain. The rooms are modern, and comfortable after a hard day at play. There is a restaurant on the premises called Marcel's, or you can venture into Rockport, Rockland, or Camden to give yourself a break from all that activity. While everything's deluxe, including the rooms, off-season package deals make it affordable for everyone. Meals are additional.

Searsport

**THE WILLIAM & MARY
INN**
Innkeepers: William and
  Mary Sweet.
207-548-2190.
Rte. 1, Searsport 04974.
Open: All year.

In 1774 Capt. Perry Pendleton sailed into town and built a log cabin just across the street from what is now the William & Mary Inn. More than 50 years later, the captain's granddaughter, Prudence, moved into this elegant home on a hill just two miles northeast of Searsport center. The inn is

Price: Inexpensive to
Moderate.
Credit Cards: None;
personal and travelers'
checks accepted.

named for its owners — former history teacher Bill and his wife Mary Sweet. They have redone the house to emphasize its architectural features — including the wonderful six-on-six windows. There are three guest rooms with pencil-post beds and reproduction wallpapers; each has its own bathroom tucked into former closets. Breakfast every morning is served in a style befitting this elegant New England home at the Chippendale table in the dining room.

Sebasco Estates

SEBASCO HARBOR RESORT
Owner: Bob Smith.
207-389-1161 or
800-225-3819.
www.sebasco.com.
E-mail: info@sebasco.com.
Rte. 217, Sebasco Estates
04565.
Off Rte. 209 near
Phippsburg.
Season: May through
October.
Price: Moderate to Very
Expensive.
Credit Cards: AE, D, MC, V.

Sebasco Lodge is a friendly, oddball collection of structures situated on 600 acres at the southeastern tip of the Phippsburg peninsula near Popham Beach State Park. It offers families and recreation-minded travelers a feeling for how people relaxed — and socialized — 40 years ago. In fact, the Lodge calls the busy months "our social season," and daily activities center around meals served in the large spit-and-polish dining room where jackets are suggested, but not required. Twice a week, everyone moves their socializing outdoors, weather permitting. There's the Sunday poolside blueberry pancake breakfast. Tuesday, everyone's outside again for the weekly lobster picnic. In between, there's plenty of appetite-building activities for guests of all ages: nine holes of golf, swimming in the saltwater swimming pool, playschool for the kids, tennis, shuffleboard, canoeing, lawn bowling, sail and motor boat rental, bingo, and evening dance socials with live music. The cottages and lodge are clean and comfortable, but not luxurious; there have been major renovations, and the gazebo is a welcome fixture. The meals are wholesome and plentiful. Rates for the modified American plan (breakfast and dinner) are available.

Stockton Springs

THE HICHBORN INN
Innkeepers: Nancy and
Bruce Suppes.
207-567-4183 or
800-346-1522.
http://members.aol.com/
hichborn.

It is quiet around this carefully restored former shipbuilder's house that is on the National Register of Historic Places. With high ceilings, handsome Victorian furniture, fireplaces, down quilts, fine linens, and fresh-ground coffee, this is a wonderful home base for those exploring nearby

P.O. Box 115, Church St., Stockton Springs 04981.
Open: All year.
Price: Inexpensive to Moderate.
Credit Cards: None; travelers' and personal checks accepted.

Fort Point State Park (a great spot for biking), antiquing in the as-of-yet undiscovered Stockton Springs or enjoying a nice quiet stop outside busy Mount Desert Island. The inn is small. There are five guest rooms with private and shared baths and views of Stockton Harbor. You can have breakfast in your room, or venture downstairs for Belgian waffles with real maple syrup, homemade bagels, or "Dutch babies" — eggy, oven-baked pancakes that guests fill with fresh fruit in season or the Suppes' homemade raspberry jam. Breakfast included. No smoking.

Tenants Harbor

EAST WIND INN
207-372-6366 or 800-241-8439.
www.eastwindinn.com.
E-mail: info@eastwind.com.
P.O. Box 149, Tenants Harbor 04860.
Open: Early April–late Nov.
Price: Inexpensive to Expensive.
Credit Cards: AE, D, MC, V.

The main house of the East Wind is a former sea captain's home, and most of the rooms in the inn, its downstairs restaurant, and the wide porch offer fine views of Tenants Harbor. The inn is a staple for regular visitors. The 15 guest rooms in the main house are filled with antiques and have a spartan Yankee quality. Six of those rooms have private baths. There are 10 more rooms in the modern "meeting house," and all of those have private baths. There is also a cottage that houses three apartments. One is a full apartment, another a two bedroom, and still another a studio. All three have kitchens. The restaurant, Windows, serves breakfast and dinner, and is a favorite among local residents and business people.

Vinalhaven

THE FOX ISLAND INN
Innkeeper: Gail Reinertsen.
207-863-2122 or in winter 850-425-5095.
www.bbonline.com/me/foxisland.
P.O. Box 451, Carver St., Vinalhaven 04863.
Open: Memorial Day–mid-Sept.
Price: Inexpensive.
Credit Cards: AE, D, MC, V.

This once was an island home; now it is a small village inn that offers guests comfortable lodging in a homelike setting. There are four lovely, clean single and double rooms with shared baths and a restored three-room suite with a private bath. Gail serves breakfast and lets guests use the kitchen — a nice option for picnickers and those made hungry by the sea air. There are also bikes for guest use. Children over six welcome.

Waldoboro

ROARING LION
Innkeepers: Bill and Robin
  Branigan.
207-832-4038.
995 Main St., Waldoboro
  04572.
Open: All year.
Price: Inexpensive.
Credit Cards: None.

In a town that's world famous for sauerkraut and sausage, this very inexpensive inn is an anomaly. It has built a reputation for accommodating vegetarians and other people on special diets. Built at the turn of the century, this was originally a tourist home that once refused to give breakfast to traveling salesmen. There are four rooms at the inn. One has a private bath and a queen-sized bed; two have double beds and one has twin beds. One of the double-bed rooms has a fireplace. The rooms without a private bath share a private bath and a half bath. Downstairs there are four tables in the dining room, and every morning they serve fresh coffeecake, muffins, and other homemade breads to their guests, all with healthy sides of homemade jams and jellies. Ask for the sourdough pancakes — made from sourdough starter nurtured for more than 22 years. The Branigans are big on gardening, and homegrown flowers are everywhere. No smoking. Children of all ages are welcome.

Wiscasset

SQUIRE TARBOX INN
Innkeepers: Karen and Bill
  Mitman.
207-882-7693.
1181 Main Rd., Westport
  Island, Wiscasset 04578.
Open: May through late
  Oct.
Price: Moderate to Very
  Expensive.
Credit Cards: AE, D, MC, V.

Karen and Bill Mitman met while working at the Copley Plaza Hotel in Boston, and although this handsome, beautifully kept farmhouse inn with its pastoral setting may seem charmingly rustic, there is nothing less than polished about the service. The main house has wide colonial floorboards, an interesting mix of antiques, and four guest rooms with private baths and working fireplaces (two are not air conditioned); the barn has seven romantically removed bedrooms and private baths. The barn dates from 1763 and includes a homey common room and a woodstove. Breakfast and dinner, served in a simple paneled and brick dining room with fireplace, are excellent. Beyond hospitality and good food, the primary products here are distinctive goats' milk cheeses — the inn and its restaurant (see Dining, below) operate in the midst of a working dairy farm complete with its own herd of purebred Nubian goats. Borrow the inn's bikes and pedal off to explore the rolling countryside. No pets — they would disturb the goats; no children under 12.

MIDCOAST: DINING

Dining out in the Midcoast can be a down home lobster-in-the-rough experience. Or you can find yourself in a tiny four-star gem in an old meetinghouse. Midcoast is also where you'll find the famous Moody's Diner, where a slice of pie is the next best thing to heaven. A list of Midcoast restaurants follows; some famous, some not-so-famous; places we found out about by badgering reluctant residents and neighbors; places we liked and places we didn't but were out-voted, plus places written up and sent in by friends, all experienced or professional eaters. It's a list long enough to get you up or down the coast and back next summer.

Prices, restrictions, etc. are similar throughout the coast of Maine. We've repeated them here for convenience's sake. Restaurants' serving times and seasons were accurate when we made the final survey for this guide. As with all things, times, phone numbers, and sometimes addresses are subject to change according to the changing seasons and demands of the economy. Call first. If you can, make reservations. Things can get pretty busy at the great places, especially during July and August. Many restaurants, even white tablecloth ones, don't take reservations, though. So if you're really hungry, plan to arrive early enough to stake a good place in line.

The price range we list is meant to reflect the cost of a single meal, usually dinner, unless the review talks about breakfast or lunch. What we've tried to represent as a typical meal is an appetizer, entree, dessert, and coffee, although several of the places we review are not appetizer places. We do not include the price of alcohol or other drinks in the estimated cost.

Dining Price Code:

> Inexpensive — Up to $10
> Moderate — $10–20
> Expensive — $20–30
> Very Expensive — $30 or more

Credit Cards:

> AE—American Express   DC—Diner's Club
> CB —Carte Blanche   MC—MasterCard
> D —Discover Card   V—Visa

Bath

KRISTINA'S
207-442-8577.
160 Center St., Bath.

Kristina's is consistently on everyone's list of coastal favorites, and for good reason.

Closed: January.
Price: Moderate to
  Expensive.
Cuisine: American eclectic.
Serving: B, L, D, SB.
Credit Cards: D, MC, V.
Special Features: Bakery
  takeout.

Upstairs, the low ceiling, modern dining room is casual and lounge-like; downstairs is bright, homey, and cheerful with butcher-block tables and potted plants. They serve all three meals here, and while it might seem that a breakfast place would be unlikely to make an elegant dinner well, they do. Lunch is a meal of soups, salads, sandwiches, and burgers. Dinner runs from such standards as lamb chops and grilled salmon to more exotic Indian tofu. We like their steamed mussels, garlicky and rich, to start everything off. There's also a light menu that includes quiches and burritos. Stop by the bakery case on the way out the door and grab something good to take on the road. Their pies are good, so are their breads and cookies.

Belfast

90 MAIN RESTAURANT
207-338-1106.
90 Main St., Belfast 04915.
Open all year.
Price: Moderate.
Cuisine: Eclectic.
Serving: L, D, SB.
Credit Cards: AE, D, MC, V.

This place is a mix of Down East, New Age, and New York — a common cultural crossroads in Belfast these days. Clean and woody upstairs and down, they offer just what you'd expect: local natural beef cheeseburgers, macrobiotic buckwheat soba noodles with a sweet and sour ginger sauce, blueberry chicken with a bagel and cream cheese on the side.

Boothbay Harbor

BLUEBERRY BAY
207-338-9656
Rt. 1, Belfast.
Open: Year round.
Price: Inexpensive.
Cuisine: Home cooking.
Serving: B, L, D.
Credit Cards:
Special Features: Pie.
Handicap Access: Yes.

This is a friendly, spanking clean family-style restaurant that sits on the left hand side of Rte. 1 as you head east out of Belfast. The breakfast menu is about a mile long and offers something for everyone—the Lumberjack for big eaters and six of what they call "mini" breakfast for somewhat lighter eaters. At lunch and dinner, you can get boat-fresh seafood grilled, baked, or fried, however you wish. If you're traveling with picky eaters, there's also your basic hot dogs, burgers, chicken, and Italian entrees, too. Finish with the homemade pie. They have about a zillion kinds, but we have a soft spot for the blueberry.

**CHRISTOPHER'S
  BOATHOUSE**
207-633-6565.
25 Union St., Boothbay
  Harbor.

Sitting at a table in Christopher's, with its elegant blond wood interior and solid wine list, you might almost forget that you are in Boothbay Harbor. Let's face it, this town is better known for

Herb Swanson

One of Maine's famed peekytoe crabs.

Open: Year round.
Price: Expensive to Very
  Expensive.
Cuisine: International.
Serving: D year round; L in
  winter only.
Credit Cards: MC, V.
Special Features: Wood
  grill and wine list.

it's activities (shopping, shopping, shopping, and boating) than for fine dining. The menu covers the map with French, Italian, Asian, and Mediterranean accents and, from this continent, a little down home barbecue. There is also excellent Maine seafood cooked simply and well. If you like martinis, start with a smoked scallop martini. If not, try the pan-seared Maine peeky-toe crab cakes. Follow with the lobster succotash, one of the restaurant's signature dishes, and we can almost guarantee you won't have room for dessert.

CRUMPS
207-633-7655.
34A McKown St., Boothbay
  Harbor.
Open: Memorial Day
  through Columbus Day.
Price: Inexpensive
Cuisine: Cream teas and
  wraps.
Serving: Lunch and tea.

This is a little piece of Britain tucked among the candy and souvenir shops on Boothbay Harbor's waterfront. The cozy tea room shares space with an eccentric selection of gourmet foods, arts and crafts, and teapots of various shapes and sizes. They serve an authentic cream tea here, complete with little tea sandwiches, scones, strawberry preserves, and clotted cream. (Their scones are so popular, a brisk mail order business has grown up around them, and they will gladly ship a scone gift box with only 24 hours' notice.) Those with heartier appetites can find solace in a traditional ploughman's lunch or the ubiquitous wrap sandwich in one of several vegetarian or meat-eater's versions.

Brunswick

RICHARD'S
207-729-9673.
115 Maine St., Brunswick.
Closed: Sun.
Price: Moderate.
Cuisine: German, American.
Serving: L, D.
Credit Cards: AE, D, MC, V.
Reservations:
    Recommended.
Handicap Access: Yes.

Richard's is in town, residing in an old steak house. German beers and victuals are the thing here. The beer roster is prodigious, with numerous offbeat selections. And beer is just what one needs to wash down hearty fare like wiener schnitzel, smoked pork chops, sauerbraten, wursts, potato salad, and sauteed cabbage. There's also an American menu for the unadventurous that includes chicken, haddock, and steaks. Located in the old Bowdoin Inn, the interior is brick and wood with high chandeliers, table clothes, flowers, and candles. The wait staff is particularly good-natured. Tortes and strudels for dessert.

ROSITA'S
207-729-7118.
212 Main St., Brunswick.
Open daily.
Price: Inexpensive.
Cuisine: Mexican.
Serving: L, D.
Credit Cards: None.
Handicap Access: Limited.
Special feature: Huevos
    rancheros on Sunday.

Every college town needs a Mexican restaurant and Rosita's is the South of the Border outpost nearest to Bowdoin College. The term "casual" is an understatement here. Beer comes out of a cooler and one orders food cafeteria-style. But the folks behind the counter are eager to please and the place has a friendly feel. All the usual suspects are on the menu: burritos, tostados, nachos, tacos, enchiladas, chili, fajitas, and tamales. Besides the standard beef, pinto bean, and chicken trio, there are chorizo, the spicy Spanish sausage, and black beans, too. Salsas come in hot and mild strengths and the overall firepower of most fixings is quite tolerable. Sunday breakfasts are unusual, featuring bacon and egg tacos and huevos rancheros.

Camden

**CAPPY'S CHOWDER
    HOUSE**
207-236-2254.
1 Main St., Camden.
Open all year. Closed Wed.
    in winter.
Price: Moderate.
Cuisine: American.
Serving: B, L, D; call for
    winter hours.
Credit Cards: MC, V.

Right downtown, the compact size belies the huge staff required to make this place run. They claim sooner or later everyone shows up here, and they run it like they're ready for your arrival, morning, noon, and night. Great chowder, good burgers, a good short stack of ribs, and buoyant pancakes (at breakfast). They also are quite competent with locally caught fish. They're now serving more healthy selections, vegetarian and light items, while at the same time they've

Reservations: Large parties only.
Handicap Access: Limited.

expanded their bakery. Many a time we have stood packed in the doorway or at the bar waiting for a table, or preferably a booth. Even once you've been seated in the varnished and bric-a-bracked joint, you feel like you're a character in a triple-decker sandwich.

THE WATERFRONT
207-236-3747.
40 Bayview St., Camden.
Closed: January.
Price: Moderate.
Cuisine: American; seafood.
Serving: L, D.
Credit Cards: AE, MC, V.
Handicap Access: Yes.
Special Features: View of Camden Harbor.

Camden's harbor may be the most beautiful in the Midcoast region, and the Waterfront is the place to watch it from. In summer, the restaurant opens its roomy terrace to salt breezes — all the better to enjoy your lobster and clams by. Seafood, in some cases with a stylish twist, is the kitchen's hallmark. Fresh fish, crab cakes, crab pie, linguine with sun-dried tomatoes, and fresh scallops share the menu with steaks and specials like breast of chicken with olive oil and blueberry vinegar. At lunch, sandwiches and salads are teamed with chowders and soups. This is a charming spot to while away a couple of hours. Crack open a chablis, dig into a halibut steak, and enjoy the water lapping at the docks.

ZADDIK'S PIZZA
207-236-6540.
20 Washington St., Camden.
Open all year.
Price: Inexpensive to Moderate.
Cuisine: Italian and Mediterranean.
Serving: D.
Credit Cards: MC, V.
Handicap Access: Yes.

Zaddik's is probably the closest thing Camden has to a factory. If they're not busy producing, they're standing ready to produce. Zaddik's stresses the freshness of their ingredients. No vegetables in Number 10 sized cans. They also claim their pizza dough had its origins in Brooklyn and comes to them via Roslyn, Washington, where it won "Best in Eastern Washington State." Personally, that doesn't impress us, but their pizza is actually quite good, although the crust is thick and more chewy than crunchy. The menu also offers tastes of the Mediterranean east of Italy, as well as deep into Mexico, including gyros, humus, quesadillas, etc. There's wide-open space with booths if you prefer to eat in rather than order out.

Damariscotta

THE BREAKFAST PLACE
207-563-5434.
Main St., Damariscotta.
Open year round.
Price: Inexpensive.
Cuisine: Breakfast.

Just across and down the street from the historic steeple and clock on St. Andrew's, this morning coffee and baked goods joint also serves a good egg or two. It's been around for ages, serving as a wakeup stop for the local community. Several

Serving: B.
Handicap Access: Limited.
Specialties: Bakery.

years ago, two ambitious transplants from Connecticut bought it; they've raised the level of baking, but kept the hometown decor. Grab some of their tiny pecan and chocolate tarts for the road.

THE SALT BAY CAFE
207-563-1666.
Main St., Damariscotta.
Open all year.
Price: Inexpensive to
  Moderate.
Cuisine: All American.
Serving: L, D.
Credit Cards AE, D, MC, V.
Handicap Access: Yes.

The Salt Bay serves typical American food with a polite nod towards light and healthy. Big fat comfortable booths, a little too much carpet, non-threatening, been-there-forever help. This is *Murder, She Wrote* look-a-like country, and you can imagine Jessica Fletcher and the police chief sitting at the next booth over while the cook lies on the kitchen floor with a knife in his back. You've had this food many times before. It's a good place to come if you're homesick. Pie and bread pudding for dessert.

East Boothbay

LOBSTERMAN'S
  WHARF
207-633-3443.
Rte. 96, East Boothbay.
Closed: Mid-Oct.–early
  May.
Price: Moderate.
Cuisine: American.
Serving: L, D.
Credit Cards: MC, V.
Feature: Kid-proof dining;
  deck with river view.
Handicap Access: Yes.

Wedged between two old shipyards, this family restaurant is fun. Best of all, there's plenty to keep the kids occupied. The long, paneled dining room has the look of an ocean liner, and just in case you don't get it, lobster traps, buoys, and paddles hang from walls and ceilings. In fair weather, dine on the deck overlooking the Damariscotta River. Otherwise, grab a table in the large dining room. Unlike places that are all gimmicks and no substance, the Wharf has good food and an enthusiastic staff. Tasty biscuits and corn muffins. Savory starters like deep-fried artichokes. Bright salads. And interesting entrees. A mixed grill with kielbasa, sirloin, and chicken is a winner, as is the baked flounder stuffed with chunks of crab. There are occasional disappointments, but these can be avoided by sticking to basics. For dessert, brownie sundaes.

Georgetown

FIVE ISLANDS LOBSTER
  COMPANY
207-371-2150.
Off Rte. 127 at Five Islands,
  Georgetown.
Closed: Mid-Oct.–April.
Price: Inexpensive to
  Moderate.

This working pier happens to be an ideal spot to crack open a lobster and suck down some steamers. Picnic tables on the dock are about it for amenities. But the panorama — sailboats on the Sheepscot River and pine-blanketed islands — more than makes up for it. Order corn, steamers, and lobsters at the pound. Then step next door for

Cuisine: Lobster in the
    rough.
Serving: L, D.
Special Features: Outdoor
    pier dining; BYOB.

coleslaw, french fries, burgers, etc. Five Islands also
makes one of the best lobster rolls on the Maine
coast, so if you're feeling lazy, go for it. They also
specialize in grilled seafood. Dessert runs from
double-dip ice cream cones to homemade blueberry cobbler.

Newcastle

THE NEWCASTLE INN
207-563-5685 or
    800-832-8669.
River Rd., Newcastle.
Closed: Mon., June–Nov.;
    Mon.–Wed. rest of year.
Price: Expensive to Very
    Expensive.
Cuisine: Country gourmet.
Serving: D.
Credit Cards: MC, V.
Reservations: Required.

There's only one seating at the Newcastle Inn
each evening. Such regimentation might be off-
putting if the food were not so good and the experience enjoyable. The small dining room is lighted
by candles and has white linens, fresh flowers, and
classical strains. The five-course meal — there's a
single set menu each night — is $37.50. Possibilities
include Newcastle crab cakes, duck breast with
pear and ginger, or champagne lobster. Dessert
might be an airy souffle or some other creation like
luscious lemon-layered ice cream cake.

New Harbor

**SHAW'S FISH &
    LOBSTER WHARF**
207-677-2200.
Rte. 32, New Harbor.
Open: May to October.
Price: Inexpensive to
    Moderate.
Cuisine: Seafood.
Serving: L, D.
Credit Cards: MC, V.

What a wonderful view. Half the wharf is
given over to fishermen and fishing boats,
the other half to serving a prodigious supply of
seafood, side orders, and pie. Lunch and dinner are
self-service, and you can pick your own table, outside, inside, or down on the wharf, where at night
there's also an outside bar. From the deck upstairs,
you can look down on boats being made ready for
next day's sail. If the young travelers don't want
lobster, there's a wide selection of kid's sandwiches
and three kinds of cookies at forty cents a pop.

Rockland

THE BROWN BAG
207-596-6372 or
    800-287-6372.
606 Main St., Rockland.
Open: Year round.
Price. Inexpensive.
Cuisine: Country eclectic.
Serving: B, L .

This place specializes in the most important
meal of the day, breakfast, and the next most,
lunch. They fresh bake daily an edible still life of
warm croissants, sticky buns, giant blueberry
muffins, and fresh shredded wheat bread toast.
Try a toad 'n holes — shredded wheat toast with
an egg dropped in the center and grilled. The oat-

Credit Cards: MC, V.
Handicap Access: Yes,
  through the back.

meal is also homemade. So is the cinnamon swirl French toast. Also, excellent omelets. Lunch is hearty sandwiches and soups and chowders. Congenial customers line up to place their orders for huevos rancheros, brown bag pockets (their version is scrambled eggs with three cheeses in a whole wheat pita falafel with lemon tahini sauce), a roast beef/boursin sub (the beef is marinated and roasted on the premises), or daily fresh roasted turkey. The owners devote a whole blackboard to their changing dessert menu; their seasonal pies, cheesecakes, puddings, and cookies are all made from scratch.

CAPTAIN'S TABLE
207-596-6870.
Rte. 1, Rockland.
Open year round.
Price: Inexpensive.
Cuisine: American.
Serving: B, L, D.
Credit Cards: D, V.
Handicap Access: Yes.

Driving north into "downtown" Rockland on Rte. 1, don't miss the scruffy-looking residential hotel on your left called the Wayfarer. The hotel's restaurant — the Captain's Table — is where the fishermen eat. From Brobdingnagian stacks of flapjacks to eggs with ham and fish cakes (potato, onion, and flaked fish formed into patties and grilled — delicious), this is the way to keep body and soul together through a morning of sightseeing, sailing, or any more strenuous activity. There are also low-priced lunch and dinner specials, but come in the morning. The Ritz it ain't, but you've been living in the city too long if you can't enjoy this real slice of Maine life.

JESSICA'S
207-596-0770.
2 South Main St. (Rte. 73),
  Rockland.
Open year round.
Price: Moderate.
Cuisine: Bistro.
Serving: D.
Credit Cards: D, MC, V.
Reservations:
  Recommended.

We have a soft spot for Swiss chefs, and chef/owner Hans Bucher has earned his way into that spot with consistently good food, prepared and served well. Jessica's is comfortable and inviting. The menu is a well-reasoned mix of Swiss, French, and Italian items. Lamb Bresale are tender lamb chops glazed with mustard, garlic, red wine, and herbs and served with portabello mushrooms. Bucher also serves a classic bistro steak, with rich tarragon butter melted atop. He rounds out the menu with daily fresh seafood specials and excellent desserts.

Searsport

NICKERSON TAVERN
207-548-2220.
Rte.1, Searsport.
Closed: Call for fall and
  winter hours.

The Nickerson is a favorite in the Midcoast area. Chef Jim Bouras runs a classic American restaurant. The raciest accents you will find are a nod to the French here, a nibble of Thai there.

Price: Moderate.
Cuisine: American.
Serving: D.
Credit Cards: D, MC, V.
Reservations:
   Recommended.
Handicap Access: Limited.

Mostly it's just good food — fresh seafood, roast duckling, lobster, salmon, lamb, veal, and filet mignon — served in the quintessential Maine coast setting, a handsome 1838 captain's home. My mother and father love to stop by here on their frequent trips to the region, and every time they are greeted with a fine meal and good service.

PERIWINKLE'S BAKERY
207-548-9910.
Rte. 1, Searsport 04974.
Season: Year-round except
   January.
Cuisine: Bakery, tea.
Serving: Light lunch.
Price: Inexpensive.
Credit Cards: None.
Handicap Access: No.

This pretty little bakery and tea room, tucked into an old white farmhouse right on Rte. 1, is a good place to stop and catch your wind during a big day of antiquing in Searsport and nearby Belfast. There are plenty of tasty cookies, cakes, pastries, and tarts to sample. They also make good soup and sandwiches on thickly sliced homemade bread, and a nice homemade quiche. Enjoy breakfast, lunch, or tea inside, or outside at one of their roadside picnic tables. These folks used to own a bakery in Philadelphia, and Philadelphia's loss is our gain.

Sebasco Estates

THE WATER'S EDGE
207-389-1803.
Off Rte. 217, Sebasco
   Estates.
Open year round.
Price: Inexpensive to
   Moderate.
Cuisine: Seafood.
Credit Cards: MC, V.

The Water's Edge seems as if it sits perched at the end of the world. It is on the peninsula to the east and south of Phippsburg, and getting there takes a fair amount of winding in, out, and down country roads. There are tables outside where you can eat when the weather warms up. We were there late in the spring, and inside we found a woodburning stove to take the chill off. This place feels authentic with rough-hewn wood, old nautical paintings, and an impressive collection of things that look like they've been washing up on the beach for years. The seafood is fresh from the family's wharf just below. On the day we were there, they had tiny, sweet mahogany clams steamed and served with butter, as well as a fine halibut filet. We finished with bread pudding.

South Harpswell

**DOLPHIN MARINA
   BASIN**
207-833-6000.
Basin Point, off Rte. 123,
   South Harpswell.
Closed for the winter.

This is where the fishermen come to eat out. They're the ones sitting at the counter with meaty burgers piled with ketchup. You can get burgers in the city. Try the chunky lobster stew. Watch lobsterboats or sailboats tie up. Wash it all

Price: Inexpensive to
   Moderate.
Cuisine: Seafood.
Serving: B, L, D.
Credit Cards: MC, V.
Handicap Access: Yes.

ESTES LOBSTER HOUSE
207-833-6340.
Rte. 123, South Harpswell.
Open Memorial Day to
   Labor Day.
Price: Inexpensive.
Cuisine: Lobster.
Serving: L, D.
Credit Cards: AE, D, MC.

down with coffee and a slice of fresh fruit pie in season.

It's about at this point on the coast that travelers have to start making choices about which isthmus or peninsula to explore. The advantage to overcoming any indecision you may have is that once you've acted, you feel like you've taken possession of the place — and its food. Temporary ownership has a terrific taste here. This is the sort of out-of-the-way place where you can watch fishermen work around their boats. It gives you a larger appreciation of that delicious haddock sandwich you're holding. If you want something naturally sweet, try a mess of clams.

It is apparent to serious shellfish eaters that in the great evolutionary scheme of things crustaceans developed shells to protect them from knives and forks.

—Calvin Trillin, *Alice, Let's Eat*

Lobsters in the ocean are the color of seaweed and walk along the floor. "A shoe with legs," is how poet Anne Sexton described them. Lobsters are caught by lobstermen who heave a string of box-shaped wooden or vinyl-coated wire traps over the side of their boat. They bait their traps with fish heads and tails and species that don't normally sell well at the fish market. (Somehow it's not surprising to learn that lobsters are carnivores.) With luck, when the lobstermen returns and pulls up the trap, there will be a legal-sized lobster in it. (A waterlogged trap may weigh as much as 70 pounds.) A "keeper" measures at least 3.25 inches and is no more than 5 inches from its eyes to the beginning of the tail. It may or may not weigh a pound or more.

Lobsters in a pot of boiling water turn red. Before the 1800s, lobsters were in

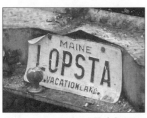

Herb Swanson

A vanity plate on Monhegan Island.

such abundance you could simply pick them off the beach, take them home, and cook them. People who could afford it didn't. Lobsters were considered a low-class food. Nineteenth-century prisoners were forced to eat them three times a week, and on Boston's Beacon Hill the servants ate them, although there was a limit to the number they would eat a week.

Finally, in the mid-19th century, fishermen began lobstering by boat, and scarcity produced demand. In this modern age, the Maine fleet lands an annual lobster catch of approximately 30,000 lbs. or more.

Vinalhaven

THE HAVEN
207-863-4969.
245 Main St., Vinalhaven.
Closed March and April.
Price: Moderate.
Cuisine: Seafood; exotic
regional.
Serving: B, D; call for
schedule.
Credit Cards: MC, V.
Reservations: Yes.

Favored by residents, summer people, and visitors, the Haven has been a popular gathering place for more than a dozen years. The menu changes often to incorporate the day's catch, ripening wild berries, or chanterelles harvested from the surrounding spruce woods. Two dining rooms are open in the summer. The back room offers a more traditional seafood-restaurant atmosphere. The front room, once a storefront, is a favorite place to dine, surrounded by the works of local artists, many of whom are well-known outside of this close-knit community. Haven's has a full bar.

Waldoboro

Try a landmark cream pie at Moody's, the Maine coast's landmark diner.

Herb Swanson

MOODY'S DINER
207-832-7885.
Rte. 1, Waldoboro.
Closed: Fri. and Sat.
between midnight and 5
a.m.
Price: Inexpensive.
Cuisine: Diner food.
Serving: B, L, D.
Handicap Access: Yes.

What distinguishes a really great restaurant is when the locals refuse to leave after it's been discovered by tourists. Everyone shares counter seats and booths at Moody's: Waldoborans, summer people, tourists, fishing boat captains, and yacht owners. The corned beef hash is legendary. The cheeseburgers and meatloaf are too, as is their walnut pie and any one of their cream pies.

Westport Island

THE SQUIRE TARBOX INN
207-882-7693.
Rte. 144, Westport Island.
Closed: Nov.–mid-May;
  open seven days in
  season.
Price: Expensive.
Cuisine: American.
Serving: D.
Credit Cards: AE, D, MC, V.
Reservations: Required.
Special Features: Goat
  cheese made on
  premises; dairy open
  year round.

Dinner is served in the 1763 portion of this pretty farmhouse every night during the busy months. It's a hearty and lavish meal — five courses of good country cooking. The menu changes daily, but you can count on there being plenty of their homemade goat cheese on it — whether it's their spreadable and tasty farmstead chevre (fashioned after French-style goat cheese) or caerphilly, an aged, waxed cheese with a smooth texture and mellow flavor — smoked or plain. You never leave hungry, either, because they fill you up with great vegetables and a selection of dinner meats that can include roast fish, poultry, chops, or their goat salami (it's pretty tasty, too). Desserts include a chocolate torte with peach blackberry sauce and a bread pudding with fresh mango and strawberry sauce.

Wiscasset

LE GARAGE
207-882-5409.
Water St., Wiscasset.
Closed: January.
Price: Expensive.
Cuisine: New England.
Serving: L, D.
Credit Cards: MC, V.
Reservations:
  Recommended.
Handicap Access: Yes.
Special Features: River
  view.

Candelabra, cathedral ceilings, and two half-sunk schooners set the scene at this former auto garage right on the river. The effect is dramatic — especially on one of those gray, misty days for which the Maine coast is famous. As atmospheric as Le Garage is, the food is surprisingly down to earth, with starters like ratatouille; savory charbroiled items like chicken, steak, pork chops; fresh seafood; unusual pastas; light salads, and desserts. Homespun desserts include apple crisp, gingerbread, and birdnest meringue.

MIDCOAST: FOOD PURVEYORS

This section includes a list of food purveyors for the Midcoast region. As in the other chapters, it includes delicatessens that will sell almost anything to go, bakeries, gourmet and ethnic food shops, and beer and wine stores. Visitors will want to note that wine and beer are more readily available than hard liquor.

The Pie State

The feast was a noble feast, as has already been said. There was an elegant ingenuity displayed in the form of pies, which delighted my heart. Once acknowledge that an American pie is far to be preferred to its humble ancestor, the English tart, and it is joyful to be reassured at a Bowden [sic] reunion that invention has not yet failed.'

— Sarah Orne Jewett, *The Country of the Pointed Firs and Other Stories.*

The Maine coast is nothing if not for pie. And it wouldn't take much retooling to change Maine's nickname from the Pine State to the Pie State.

Maybe Maine's having a drowned coast, which resulted from those two tectonic plates crashing together before being smothered by the glaciers, explains why so many people here understand the importance of a good crust and pie a la mode.

Maine even has several filling seasons (see "Berry and Apple Picking" under "Recreation," below).

There are two kinds of Maine pies. Fruit and Cream.

The saying should be, "As American as blueberry pie." The Europeans brought the apples. The blueberries were already here. Cream pies probably were invented in Maine. Somebody looked out the window on a cold wintery day at the snow blanketing a blueberry barren and her thoughts turned to filling.

In 1825, David Robinson, a local ice dealer, supposedly invented ice cream and by extension, pie a la mode. Yorkie's, the best pie place in the history of civilization, flourished in Camden until the last decade. Sigh. Pie gone by.

Here are several pie places, some legendary, some secret and wrangled from friends, and some our own favorites.

South Coast

Hattie's Deli (207-282-3435) in Biddeford Pool. Blueberry.

Spurwink Country Kitchen (207-799-1177, Cape Elizabeth). We're happy to say that even though pastry chef Eileen Esposito is no longer baking there, the wild blueberry pie remains topnotch.

Midcoast

The Brown Bag (207-596-6372; 606 Main St., Rockland). Go with what's in season.

Dip Net Coffee Shop (207-372-6275; Port Clyde). This could very well be the true "son of Yorkie's" (see above).

Kristina's Bakery and Restaurant (207-442-8577; 160 Center St., Bath). Try the orange-walnut.

Moody's Diner (207-832-7785; Rte. 1, Waldoboro). Famous for strawberry-rhubarb since 1927.

Weaver's Bakery (207-338-3540; 19 Main St., Belfast). Any flavor.

Down East/Acadia

The Fisherman's Friend (207-367-2442; School St., Stonington). Bonafide home-made.

The Left Bank Bakery & Cafe (207-374-2201; Rte. 172, Blue Hill). Good pie and good music.

East of Schoodic

Helen's (207-255-8423; Rte. 1, Machias). Her famed strawberry.

BAKERIES

Boothbay Harbor Bagel (207-633-3039; 43 Commercial St., Boothbay Harbor). Toto, we aren't in Brooklyn any more.

Kristina's (207-442-8577; 160 Center St., Bath). Pastries and tortes to fuel your way up the coast. They also make great French toast for a sit-down breakfast.

BREWERIES

Andrew's Brewing (207-763-3305; High St., Box 4975, Lincolnville). Call ahead for directions and to make an appointment for a tour.

Sea Dog Brewing (207-236-6863; 43 Mechanic St., Camden). We like their India ale, although we aren't in love with the pub.

CANDY AND ICE CREAM

The Downeast Ice Cream Factory (207-633-5178; 7 Bridge St., Boothbay Harbor). They make the ice cream, you make the sundaes. They also make homemade candies.

Fun? . . . You Bet! (207-882-9426; Rte. 1, Wiscassett). See it, make it, eat it. That's the motto here. Ice cream, fudge, and saltwater taffy in an interactive environment.

Miss Plum's (207-596-6946; Rte. 1, Rockport). A reporter friend of ours thinks this is the best ice cream on the coast. They also sell sorbet, frozen yogurt, and baked desserts.

Orne's Candy Store (207-633-2695; 15 Commercial St., Boothbay Harbor). Old glass topped counters, saltwater taffy, and countless types of fudge; this could be a movie set.

Round Top Ice Cream (207-563-5307; Bus. Rte. 1, Damariscotta). For years they've made ice cream at this dairy. Now they also make art and music, but you can still find 30 flavors of the good stuff. Look for Round Top at stores and restaurants nearby.

DELIS AND TAKE-OUT

Camden Deli (207-236-8343; 37 Main St., Camden). New York-style sand-wiches, wine and beer, and great desserts.

Eastside Market and Deli (26 Atlantic Ave., Boothbay Harbor, Maine). You get here by walking across the long footbridge at the shallow end of this popular harbor. Once here, you can get everything for a picnic lunch on a whale watch or at the beach. They also have an excellent selection of micro-brews from here and away.

FAST FOOD

Brud's Hot Dogs (East Side, Boothbay Harbor). Hot dogs, fast and inexpen-sive. Since 1948. Sold out of a cart on the east side of town.

Cod End (207-372-6782; near town landing; Tenants Harbor). From Memorial Day through mid-October they serve up fresh, fast seafood, including good lobster rolls and chowder. Take it with you or eat it on their picnic tables.

Lady Millville Store (207-236-6570; 113 Washington St., Rte. 105, Camden). Fresh dough pizza, subs, burgers, hot dogs, even fast food seafood and chicken.

Wasses (207-594-7472; 2 North Main St., Rockland). *The Washington Post* likes their hot dogs. Their "waffles" are pretty good, too — vanilla ice milk, Spanish peanuts, and thick fudge in a crispy waffle cone.

GOURMET FOOD STORES

Ducktrap River Fish Farm (207-338-6280; Belfast). Naturally smoked Atlantic salmon and rainbow trout raised here and at fish farms nearby. Open year round, Monday through Friday. We like their smoked bluefish and scallops best.

Foggy Ridge Gamebird Farm (207-273-2357; West Branch Rd., Warren). They raise, dress, and smoke game birds. They also sell live ones. Pheasants, par-tridges, and quails. Call for an appointment.

Great Eastern Mussel Farms (207-372-6317; Long Cove Rd., Tenants Harbor). They've taken the lowly mussel and cultivated it. Call ahead and ask for a tour of their plant. They'll let you taste them as well.

Kohn's Smokehouse Inc. (207-372-8412; Rte. 131, St. George). They make and sell fine smoked meats and seafood. Bacon, sausage, bratwurst, salami, even poultry. In the winter they're open Monday through Saturday; in the summer seven days a week.

Morse's Sauerkraut (207-832-5569; Rte. 220, Waldoboro)Every once in a while they run a simple ad in the paper that says, "Kraut's ready." Maybe eating sauerkraut wouldn't be considered a chore if it were all as good as the fresh stuff made here. Also available are your knockwurst, bratwurst, kielbasa, and the humble dog. Sandwiches available.

Mystique (207-832-5136; Friendship St., Waldoboro). Open June to Dec. They sell French-style goat cheeses, as well as feta.

State of Maine Cheese Company (207-236-8895; 321 Commercial St., Rockport). Peter Kress, cheesemaker, is responsible for these distinct cheeses: Penobscot cheddar, Katahdin cheddar, Cumberland smoked, Aroostook Jack, and more, all made from all natural Maine milk.

Weatherbird Trading Company (207-563-8993; Elm St. Damariscotta). Pates, imported beers, and French scents in a 1754 saltbox cape.

Wicked Wild Maine Preserves (207-882-7772; Rte. 27, North Edgecomb). Jams and jellies for toast or cooking; some are made with no sugar at all. Especially interesting are their hot sauces and their run-for-water mustard. Call ahead.

HEALTH FOOD AND FARM MARKETS

Belfast Co-op Store (207-338-2532; 69 High St., Belfast). Whole foods, local produce, fresh bread, and other baked goods. Bona fide good things brought to you in a macrobiotic town.

Camden Farmers' Market (Colcord Ave., near Union St., Camden). Every Saturday morning, rain or shine.

Fresh Off The Farm (207-236-3260; Rte. 1, Rockport). Native produce and berries in season; apples and cider in season; natural foods, vitamins, herbs, jams, jellies, maple syrup and candy, pickles, relishes, blueberry syrup, chutney, mustards, dried beans, and local honey year round. Lots of things to take home to your friends.

The Last Stop Poultry Farm (207-273-4029; Rte. 1, Warren). In case you're running low. Fresh native broilers and roasting chickens. Fresh native turkeys. Homemade chicken and turkey pot pies.

School House Farm (207-273-2440; Rte. 1, Warren). Late June through Thanksgiving. Seven days a week. They raise and sell 24 varieties of apples, six of plums, and four of pears. They also have fresh vegetables in season. Fresh homemade donuts as well as their renowned cider donuts in the fall.

Maine Food Festivals

As we said before, Mainers love to eat. They also love to celebrate food. Here is a list of some of the annual food-centered celebrations on the coast. For more information, see individual listings under "Seasonal Events" in the "Culture" sections of Chapters 3–6.

Annual Winter Harbor Lobster Festival (207-963-7638; 800-231-3008 out-of-state). Mid-August. Almost as famous as Rockland's Lobster Festival. The lobster boat races are a main attraction.

Bay Festival, Belfast (207-338-5900). Last week in July. This used to be called the Broiler Festival on account of its being a big chicken town. There used to be so much chicken here, you would think twice before visiting. These days, most chickens have moved out of town, but they still celebrate their broilers.

Maine Lobster Festival, Rockland (207-596-0376). First weekend in August. A parade, pageant, and the world's largest lobster cooker. This festival has been famous for more than 45 years.

Wild Blueberry Festival, Machias (207-255-4402). Mid-August. Two days celebrating one of the state's biggest crops. This is the home of the wild blueberry.

Yarmouth Clam Festival (207-846-3984). Third week in July. Every year for almost 30 years, the folks in Yarmouth pay tribute to the clam. They eat lots of fried ones, then they go take a ride on the roller coaster at the midway.

An inviting window display at a Maine island general store.

State Development Office

MIDCOAST: CULTURE

Realists Robert Henri, Rockwell Kent, and George Bellows painted on Monhegan during the early 20th century. Soon after the turn of the century, painter Charles Woodbury and modernist Hamilton Easter Field established two competing and sometimes feuding painting schools at Perkins Cove in Ogunquit. Their presence drew other artists there through the mid-1900s, including Alfred Stieglitz, Georgia O'Keeffe, Maurice Stern, and Stefan Hirsch. Walter Kuhn, one of the greatest American painters of the 20th century, made his home in Ogunquit, too, although he kept himself aloof from the sometimes raucous antics of the local art colony.

Sculptor Louise Nevelson lived near Rockland for many years. Andrew Wyeth painted his famous canvas *Christina's World* on the site of an old farm near Cushing. In 1991, the Olson family, who owned the three-story farmhouse with gray weathered clapboards, donated the saltwater farm on Hawthorne Point Rd. to the Farnsworth Museum in Rockland. Neil Welliver, whose landscapes hang in the Metropolitan Museum of Art and Museum of Modern Art in Manhattan, has a farm in Lincolnville, northeast of Camden.

Abolitionist and novelist Harriet Beecher Stowe (whose husband taught at Bowdoin) wrote *The Pearl of Orr's Island* in Maine. Edna St. Vincent Millay was born at 198 Broadway in Rockland (the house, a private residence, still stands) and spent much of her childhood in Camden, the subject of many of her poems. For one long and painful year, novelist Jean Stafford (*The Mountain Lion*) and her husband, poet Robert Lowell, lived in Damariscotta Mills. Their marriage hit the rocks there. Later Stafford wrote *An Influx of Poets,* about poets and their quarreling wives and mistresses who came to visit them during their short residence.

In this section we have tried to give you an idea of the people and organizations that give shape to the Midcoast's cultural community. Still it has not been possible to list every historic site and arts organization. For a more complete listing for the area you plan to visit, contact the chamber of commerce for that region (See Chapter Seven, *Information*).

ARCHITECTURE

Several chambers of commerce, including Wiscasset and Belfast offer maps for self-guided walking tours of local historic districts and buildings.

CINEMA

Bay View Street Cinema 9 (207-236-8722; Bay View St., Camden). Seasonal.
Brunswick 10 Cinemas (207-798-3996; Cooks Corner Shopping Center, Brunswick).

The Colonial Twin Cinemas (207-338-1930; 121 High St., Belfast).

Evening Star Cinema (207-729-5486 or 888-304-5486; Tontine Mall, Brunswick).

Harbor Light Cinema (207-633-3799; Rte 27 and Rte. 96, Boothbay Harbor). Seasonal

Strand Twin Cinema (207-594-7266; 339 Main St. Rockland).

GALLERIES

The arts flourish along the coast of Maine; we have featured galleries specializing in the work of Maine artists and of artists who regularly summer here. In the Midcoast, a good place to see what's happening on the art scene is right on Main Street in Rockland. where galleries spring up faster than we can write about them.

Chocolate Church Gallery (207-442-8455; E-mail, chocolate@gwi.net; 804 Washington St., Bath). Part of the lively, regional arts center housed in a grand old church, this gallery features the work of its members and other Maine artists. Tues.–Fri. 10–4; Sat. 12–4.

Icon Contemporary Art (207-725-8157; 19 Mason St., Brunswick). Changing shows of emerging and established Maine and regional contemporary artists. Mon–Fri 1–5; Sat 1–4.

M.H. Jacobs Gallery (207-338-3324 or 888-338-3324; 48 Main St., Belfast). Sells traditional and representational watercolors and acrylics by artist Marvin Jacobs.

Maine Coast Artists (207-236-2875; www.midcoast.com/~mca/; Russell Ave., Rockport). Their annual juried art show is a good introduction to new and rising local talent.Tues.–Sat. 10–5; Sun. 12–5.

O'Farrell Gallery (207-729-8228; E-mail, ofarrell@netquarters.net; 58 Maine St., Brunswick). Works by local artists. Mon.–Sat. 10–5

Round Top Center for the Arts (207-563-1507; liincoln.midcoast.com/~rtca; Business Rte. 1, Damariscotta). This organization sponsors shows of area artists in its Main Gallery, including an annual exhibit of members' work. They also offer alternative looks at the arts with exhibits of quilting and other crafts. Each show is accompanied by a lecture open to the public. Mon.–Sat. 11–4; Sun.–1–4.

GARDENS & GARDEN TOURS

One of our favorite gardens in Maine, Merryspring, can be found in Camden. That's also where you can tour some wonderful private gardens during one of the coast's most popular garden tours. Since 1947, the *Camden*

Open House & Garden Tour has taken place on the third Thursday of July (call 207-236-7714 for information). For further information about regional garden tours, call the chamber of commerce for the area you plan to visit (see Chapter Seven, *Information*). Meanwhile, be sure to visit these excellent gardens.

Merryspring (Conway Rd. off Rte. 1, on the Camden-Rockport town line). A 66-acre nature park with an herb garden, a lily garden, a 10-acre arboretum and more cultivated wonders. Guided tours are available. Open dawn to dusk year round.

Nickels-Sortwell House (207-882-6218; Main and Federal Sts., Wiscasset). The gardens are being restored to their original design (1926) by the Wiscasset Garden Club. The ships captain's house and gardens are well worth the visit. June–Oct. 15. Tours on the hours. Admission charged.

HISTORIC BUILDINGS & SITES

Andre the Seal, honorary Harbormaster of Rockport Harbor, is dead, but his stone image continues to watch over the harbor. Harry Goodridge found Andre when he was a young pup; he raised and trained the seal, who became a local celebrity. The entire state mourned when Andre died in 1986, and his statue is one of the coast's most unusual historic markers. Andre was the subject of the forgettable 1994 movie, *Andre the Seal.*

All along the Maine coast there are many historic homes and sites that date from Maine's earliest days as part of the Massachusetts Bay Colony and are open to the public; many of them are the product of the boom times the maritime industry experienced in the late 18th and early 19th centuries. Some notable Midcoast ones follow, as well as forts and other coastal history hot spots. Many of these charge a nominal fee for admission (between $1 and $5); others are open to the public free of charge. Be aware that seasons, hours, and admission policies frequently change. When possible we have provided phone numbers for your convenience.

Whichever region or regions you are visiting, if you are a serious history buff and want to do some additional research, check in with the *Maine Historical Society* (207-774-1822; 485 Congress St., Portland 04101; www. mainehistory.org; E-mail, ncoming@mainehistory.org); the *Maine Historic Preservation Commission* (207-287-2132; 55 Capital St., 69 State House Station, Augusta 04333-0065; E-mail, kirk.mohney@state.me.us); or the *Society for the Preservation of New England Antiquities* (603-436-3205;Piscataqua Maine Region, 143 Pleasant St., Portsmouth, NH 03801; www.spnea.org). The last will provide you with a free visitors' guide to their historic homes in Maine if you send a self-addressed, postage paid envelope (you'll need two first-class stamps).

BOOTHBAY REGION HISTORICAL SOCIETY
207-633-0820.
Elizabeth Reed House.
72 Oak St., Boothbay
   Harbor.
Season: July–Labor Day,
   Wed., Fri., Sat. 10–4; rest
   of the year Sat. 10–2.

An excellent collection of period photographs depicting the region's daily activities, including fishing, ice cutting, lumbering, farming, shipping, and shipbuilding. Plus early fishing gear, shipwrights' tools, and navigation instruments.

CASTLE TUCKER
603-436-3205
www.spnea.org
Lee and High Sts.,
   Wiscasset.
Season: June–Oct. 15,
   Wed.– Sun. 11–5. Tours
   on the hour.
Hourly tours.
Admission charged.

The coast is rich with boom-and-bust stories, and Castle Tucker is a perfect example. In 1807 Judge Silas Lee decided to build himself a "great house" on the hill overlooking Wiscasset Harbor, and nothing stopped him, not even his bank account. By the time of his death seven years later he had so heavily mortgaged the house that it became the property of his three neighbors. It was bought in 1858 by Capt. Richard Tucker, a third-generation mariner. Today the house is still owned by the Tucker family. It has original Victorian furniture, kitchen, wallpapers, and a handsome elliptical staircase.

FIRST MEETINGHOUSE
207-833-6336 or
   207-833-6322.
Rte. 123, Harpswell
   Center.
Open by request only.
No charge.

Constructed in 1757, this is Maine's oldest meetinghouse, and its earliest congregations included what residents called "praying Indians." The building is still in general use as a town office and is an excellent example of early church architecture.

FORT EDGECOMB
Right off Rte. 1 just past
   Wiscasset Bridge,
   Edgecomb.
Free.

The restored fort with an octagonal, two-story blockhouse was first built in 1808 to protect the port of Wiscasset from its vantage point overlooking the Sheepscot River. Great place for a picnic.

FORT KNOX
207-469-7719.
Rte. 174 off Rte. 1 just east
   of Stockton Springs.
Season: May–Nov.; daily,
   9–sunset.
Admission charged.

Looking west across the Penobscot River from Bucksport, this great granite fort looks like a medieval castle. It was built in 1844 as a defense against the British during the Aroostook War. In 1842, U.S. troops based here tromped north to meet British troops in New Brunswick; the "war" reached a negotiated settlement after some tense posturing on both sides. Today, the fort is the state's most complete historical military structure. It was constructed of granite mined from nearby Mount

A historical re-enactment at Fort Knox near Stockton Springs. The fort was built in 1842 to defend the coast from a threatened invasion by the British.

Tom Hindman

Waldo and named for the first U.S. Secretary of War, who was from the territory that eventually became the state of Maine.

FORT WILLIAM HENRY
Pemaquid Peninsula.
Admission charged.
Season: May–Sept.
  Grounds open year
  round.
Admission charged.

The fort was a hot spot before and during the French and Indian Wars and changed hands — and names — several times. Fort Pemaquid (1632) was looted by pirates; as Fort Charles, it was captured by the French in 1689; Fort William Henry, believed to be New England's first stone fortification, was captured by the Baron de Castine; Fort Frederic was built from the ruins of Fort William Henry in 1729. What you see today is an impressive replica of the fort in addition to the authentic Old Fort House built in 1729. The *Old Burial Ground,* just down the road from here, has graves dating to 1695. Also nearby is an archaeological excavation of the Pemaquid settlement established in the 1620s. A museum with artifacts from the dig is nearby. Many consider this to be one of the prettiest — and most significant — historical spots in Maine.

GENERAL HENRY KNOX MUSEUM
207-354-8062.
Rtes. 1 and 131,
   Thomaston.
Season: May 30–mid Oct.;
   Tues.–Sat. 10–4 , Sun.
   1–4.
Admission charged.

A replica of the 1795 house built by Gen. Henry Knox and his wife, Lucy Flucker. Knox served in President Washington's cabinet as Secretary of War (see Fort Knox, above). In addition to guided tours of the reconstructed mansion, Montpelier offers programs throughout the summer featuring guides in authentic Colonial costumes, an antique fashion show, and an Independence Day celebration with "Henry Knox," and a silver high tea.

JOSHUA L. CHAMBERLAIN HOUSE
207-729-6606.
226 Main St., Brunswick.
Season: June–Aug.,
   Tues.–Sat. 1–4; by
   appointment during the
   rest of the year.
Admission charged.

J oshua Chamberlain led a large life. He won a Congressional Medal of Honor for his defense of "Little Round Top" in the battle of Gettysburg. He accepted the Confederate Army's surrender at the close of the Civil War. He went on to become governor of Maine (1866–1870) and president of nearby Bowdoin College (1871–1883). He occupied this house (built in 1825) while serving Bowdoin. Several rooms have been restored and are on view, as well as a collection of Chamberlain's Civil War memorabilia.

NICKELS-SORTWELL HOUSE
207-882-6218.
www.spnea.org
Main and Federal Sts.
   (Rte. 1), Wiscasset.
Season: June 1–Oct. 15,
   Wed.–Sun.; tours at 11,
   12, 1, 2, 3, 4.
Admission charged.

B uilt in 1807 for Capt. William Nickels, a shipmaster in the lumber trade, this elegant Federal mansion also did service as a hotel. The furnishings are Colonial Revival style. Don't miss the beautiful elliptical stairway, and the wooden inlay work on the facade of the house. The gardens are currently being restored to their original 1926 design.

OLD CONWAY HOUSE
207-236-2257.
www.c.house.home.
   ml.org.
Rte. 1, Camden.
Season: July 1–late Aug.;
   Tues.–Fri. 10–4. May
   and Sept. by
   appointment.
Admission: $3 adults; $2
   seniors; $1 students
   6–18; children under 6
   free.

T he Camden-Rockport Historical Society has restored this old farmhouse, which offers an authentic picture of Maine farm life during the 1700s. There is a blacksmith shop on the premises and a small historical museum.

OLD GERMAN MEETING HOUSE
Rte. 32, Waldoboro.
Season: June–Aug., daily 1–4.
Free.

This meetinghouse, which has a spectacular wineglass pulpit and striking, unpainted square-benched pews, was built in 1772 by the German families that settled the town 24 years earlier. The church was built on the eastern bank of the Medomak River, but later was moved to its current location.

ST. PATRICK'S CHURCH
207-563-3240.
Academy Hill Rd., just off Rte. 1, Newcastle.
Open year round 9 a.m.–sundown.

The oldest surviving Catholic church in New England, St. Patrick's was dedicated in 1808 and served a small group of Catholics who had emigrated from Ireland. The early Federal-style church was designed by architect Nicholas Codd and built from locally fired bricks. The pews and colored glass window date from 1896, but mass has been served continually from the altar since 1808. Be sure to check out the Paul Revere church bell.

SKOLFIELD-WHITTIER HOUSE
207-729-6606.
www.curtislibrary.com/pejebscot.htm.
161 Park Row, Brunswick.
Season: Late May–Early Oct., Tues.–Sat. tours at 10, 11:30, 1 and 2:30.

Three generations of prominent Brunswickians resided in this handsome 17-room home. They were doctors, mariners, and educators, and the house remains pretty much as it was when the family last lived here in 1925. Maintained by the Brunswick Historical Society.

WALDOBOROUGH HISTORICAL SOCIETY
Rte. 220, just south of Rte. 1, Waldoboro.
Season: July and Aug., daily 1–4:30.
Admission free.

This is three buildings — a schoolhouse, a barn, and a small museum — in addition to an 1819 pound where stray livestock were impounded. The barn houses displays of old toys, period clothing, china, and glass, as well as a library and a reconstructed 19th-century kitchen and Victorian-style bedroom.

LIBRARIES

Farnsworth Art Museum Library (207-596-6457; E-mail, farnswth@midcoast. com; 352 Main St., Rockland). A collection of art reference materials, including books, magazines, and videotapes in a handsome Greek Revival setting. Call for library hours.

Southport Memorial Library (207-633-2741; Cape Newagen). Home of one of the largest butterfly collections in the country. Open all year. Tues.and Thurs. 9–11, 1–4, 7–9; Sat.1–4.

Stephen Phillips Memorial Library (207-548-2529; www.acadia.net/pmmu-seum; E-mail, pmmlib@acadia.net; Church Street, Searsport). Part of the Penobscot Marine Museum. Open April–Nov., Mon.–Fri. 9–4; Dec.–March, Tues.–Fri. 9–4.

LIGHTHOUSES

If you'd like to learn more about lighthouses, visit the *Shore Village Museum* in Rockland (see "Museums," below). It has one of the largest collections of lighthouse material in the country.

As far as Maine lighthouses go, *Grindle Point Light,* built in 1935, is young. Today the building on Isleboro houses the *Sailor's Memorial Museum.* It is open mid-June through Labor Day. Call the Islesboro Town Hall for more information (207-734-2253).

Marshall Point Light (1895) in Port Clyde is home to a collection of lighthouse memorabilia. Open June–Sept., Sat. 10–5, Sun.–Fri. 1–5; May and Oct., Sat.–Sun 1–5.

A ferry ride away, the keeper's house at *Monhegan Island Light* (1824) is worth a visit because it now serves as a museum that contains exhibits of the island's native plants, wildlife, and Native American artifacts.

Owls Head Light sits on a park called the U.S. Lighthouse Reservation (near Thomaston). The light was built in 1826 and is located at the head of the Saint George Peninsula on West Penobscot Bay. Although Owls Head Light is only 26 ft. high, it can be seen from 16 miles at sea.

Pemaquid Lighthouse Park (Lighthouse Rd. off Rte. 130, Pemaquid Point) is a good place to relax for a picnic. The lighthouse was built in 1827, and the keeper's house has been converted to an art gallery and museum featuring exhibits about saltwater fishing.

You can walk on the breakwater 7/8 mi. to the *Rockland Lighthouse* (take Rte. 1 north to Waldo Ave. and Samoset Rd.). A favorite fishing spot is at the end of the breakwater under the lighthouse.

MUSEUMS

BOOTHBAY RAILWAY VILLAGE
207-633-4727.
E-mail, lincoln.midcoast.com/~railvill.
Rte. 27, Boothbay.
Season: Mid-June to Columbus Day, daily 9:30–5.
$7 adults; $3 children.

They have recreated a quaint New England village and its transportation system on eight acres here. There are more than 24 buildings of historical exhibits and 60 vehicles on display, including a steam locomotive, which for 15 minutes carries you back to a simpler time on 1.5 miles of narrow-gauge track. A doll museum is on the premises.

**BULL MOOSE
RAILROAD**
207-338-2931.
11 Water St. off City
Landing, Belfast.
Season: June–mid-Oct.,
several one-hour runs a
day. Call for schedule.
Admission charged.

The Belfast & Moosehead Lake Railroad (nick-named "Bull Moose") was founded in 1867 to carry lumber from inland Maine to the coast. That plan was short-circuited only a few years later when B&ML RR decided to hook up with the Maine Central Railroad just 33 miles inland. These days, the line is operated by the City of Belfast, and its mixed freight and passenger runs are shorter. Visitors are invited to ride the rails for a one-hour excursion along the coast several times a day.

**FARNSWORTH
MUSEUM**
207-596-6457.
www.wyethcenter.com
or www.farnsworth
museum.org.
E-mail: farnswth@
midcoast.com.
356 Main St. P.O. Box 466,
Rockland 04841.
Season: Memorial Day–
Columbus Day, 9–5.
Columbus Day– Memorial
Day, Tues.–Sat. 10–5;
Sun. 1–5.
Admission: $9 adults; $8
seniors; $5 students over
18.

One of our favorite museums, the story behind the Farnsworth is nearly as fascinating as its collection. The citizens of Rockland were stunned in 1935 when their neighbor Lucy Copeland Farnsworth left $1.3 million and instructions that the money be used to build a library and one-room art museum. The mystery? During her lifetime, Ms. Farnsworth had never been known to be an art lover. With a little finagling, the Farnsworth legacy became one of the best regional collections in the country. The home of this collection is a well-kept complex with the museum, an excellent art library, and the Farnsworth Homestead (1850), a gorgeous Greek Revival home with original high-Victorian furnishing and decor. The focus of the museum's permanent collection is on American art and includes work by the Wyeths, Winslow Homer, John Marin, Fitz Hugh Lane, Edward Hopper, Neil Welliver, and sculptor Louise Nevelson. The Farnsworth has undergone a capital campaign for the construction of a 2-part Farnsworth Center for the Wyeth Family in Maine. The addition will include a renovated Pratt Memorial Church featuring works by Jamie and N.C. Wyeth, and a new wing showing pieces by artist Andrew Wyeth.

FRIENDSHIP MUSEUM
Call the town office for
more information:
207-832-7644.
Rte. 220 and Martin's Point
Rd., Friendship.
July–Labor Day, Mon.–Sat.
noon–5.
Donations welcome.

A one-room brick schoolhouse dedicated to the history of the Friendship sloop.

MAINE MARITIME MUSEUM
207-443-1316.
www.bathmaine.com.
243 Washington St., Bath.
Open year round 9:30–5
   except Thanksgiving,
   Christmas and New
   Year's Day.
Admission: $8 adults;
   $5:50 children 6 to 17;
   $24 per family.

With an abundance of interpretive and hands-on exhibits, ships you can climb aboard, and a museum-sponsored narrated cruise along the waterfront, this is a great museum for visitors of every age. The core of the museum is the Percy & Small Shipyard (open late spring through late fall), the only surviving shipyard in the country where large wooden sailing ships were built at the turn of the century. It is also home to the *Sherman Zwicker*, a Grand Banks fishing schooner, visiting historic boats that stop in during the warm months.

MUSICAL WONDERHOUSE
207-882-7163.
www.musicalwonder
house.com.
18 High St., Wiscasset.
Season: Late May–late
   Oct., daily 10–5.
Admission: $1 general
   admittance fee.
   One-hour guided
   presentations: $12
   adults; $10 seniors
   and children under 12.
   Three-hour guided
   presentations available
   by appointment only:
   $30 per person, $50
   per couple.

For more than 30 years, travelers and music lovers from around the world have made their way to view Danilo Konvalinka's marvelous collection of restored music boxes and musical instruments on display in a handsome Greek Revival ship captain's home. Many are works of art and are capable of playing complicated songs with a wide range of notes. Some date from 1750. There are pocket boxes and floor models. He also keeps player pianos and other mechanical musical treasures. Konvalinka also buys, sells, and repairs music boxes. Ask about the candlelight concerts.

OLD COUNTY JAIL & MUSEUM
207-882-6817.
www.pchmaine.vs3.net.
Rte. 218, Federal St.,
   Wiscasset.
Season: July–Aug.,
   Tues.–Sat. 11–4.
Admission: $2 adults; $1
   children.

An unusual view of life in the 19th century. Visitors can peruse prisoners' cells with original graffiti. The jail was built in 1811, has granite walls 41 inches thick, and saw service as recently as 1953. Inside the jailer's house there is a display of early American tools, costumes, artifacts, and changing exhibits about local history.

OWLS HEAD TRANSPORTATION MUSEUM
207-594-4418.
www.ohtm.org.

An interesting collection of pioneer aircraft, automobiles, engines, motorcycles, bicycles, and carriages — almost anything that moves. The museum has guided tours of these conveyances, all

Rte. 73, Owls Head.
Season: May–Oct., daily
    10–5; Nov.–April 10–4.
Admission: $6 adults; $4
    children under 12; under
    6 free. $16 family. Special
    events: $7 adults; $5
    children under 12.
Members: free.

**PEARY-MacMILLAN
ARCTIC MUSEUM**
207-725-3416.
Hubbard Hall, Bowdoin
    College, Brunswick.
Open Tues.– Sat. 10–5; Sun.
    2–5. Closed holidays.
    Guided tours available
    during the academic
    year; call to schedule.

of which are run from time to time. Some planes
and vehicles operated on weekends.

Admirals Robert E. Peary and Donald B.
MacMillan were both graduates of Bowdoin
College, and this museum commemorates their
joint explorations. Peary was the first man to reach
the North Pole on April 6, 1909; MacMillan was
Peary's chief assistant on that expedition. Exhibits
include the log and a sledge from the 1909 expedition, as well as displays of Inuit art and artifacts
from Labrador and Greenland that MacMillan
gathered on subsequent expeditions to the north.

The Penobscot Marine Museum

*The Penobscot Marine Museum is housed in several period buildings in Searsport, which
during the 1800s was a lively port and home to hundreds of ships' captains. The museum has
one of the largest collections of marine paintings in the world.*

**PENOBSCOT MARINE
MUSEUM**
207-548-2529.
www.acadia.net/
    pmmuseum.
Church St., Searsport.

At the height of the shipping industry in Maine
during the 19th century, ten percent of
America's deep water shipmasters lived in
Searsport. They brought mementos of the world
back to this pretty little town. This museum, con-

Season: Memorial Day–mid-Oct.: Mon.–Sat. 10–5; Sun. 12–5.
Admission: $6 adults; $5 senior citizens; $2 children 7–15; under 6 free.

sisting of nine buildings restored or converted to individually themed galleries, is a terrific place to spend the day. It is home to one of the largest collections of marine paintings in the state, including ship portraits commissioned and painted in the ports of Europe and China. The Old Town Hall is devoted to the description of the great Down Easters, the square- rigged vessels built in Maine during the late 1800s. The museum sponsors annual events, concerts, lectures, and readings by Maine authors.

SHORE VILLAGE MUSEUM
207-594-0311.
104 Limerock St., Rockland.
Season: June–mid-Oct., daily 10–4; by appointment the rest of the year.
Donations.

This small, lively museum situated on an old Rockland street is crammed to the rafters with an odd and ever growing assortment of historical materials: the world's largest selection of lighthouse paraphernalia from old candle-powered lights to the latest solar-powered lenses; Coast Guard memorabilia; uniforms, weapons, and papers concerning the Maine soldiers who fought in the Civil War; and the Llewella Mills collection of 34 dolls dressed in period costumes from the Middle Ages to the Gay '90s (she was a sea captain's daughter).

WALKER ART MUSEUM
207-725-3275.
Bowdoin College, Brunswick.
Open year round. Tues.–Sat. 10–5; Sun. 2–5.
Closed Mondays and national holidays.
Free.

A beautiful Greek Revival building houses the museum's permanent collections including ancient Mediterranean art and European and American paintings, sculpture, drawings, prints, and photos. Of special interest are the selection of Colonial and Federal portraits and paintings by Winslow Homer, John Sloan, and Rockwell Kent. The museum also regularly features changing art exhibits.

MUSIC

Harps, dulcimers, brass quintets, jazz quartets — the coast is home to dozens of musical groups and festivals every year. Below we've listed two large Midcoast organizations. But be warned, there are many more. For a comprehensive schedule of musical events for the area you plan to visit, contact the local chamber of commerce (see Chapter Seven, *Information*).

BAY CHAMBER CONCERTS
207-236-2823 or 888-707-2770.

This group has brought music to mid-coast Maine for nearly 40 years. The summer season runs from mid-July through August, and includes twice

The Hallowell Community Band performs on the green in Boothbay Harbor.

Herb Swanson

www.midcoast.com
/~bccmusic.
P.O. Box 191, Camden
04843.
Season: Winter series:
Sept.–June; summer
series July and Aug.
Tickets: Winter $5–$12;
Summer $7–$17.

**ROUND TOP CENTER
FOR THE ARTS**
207-563-1507.
http://lincoln.midcoast.
com/~rtca.
Bus. Rte. 1, Damariscotta.
Open year round.
Tickets: $8–$14 for music
and theater events.

weekly lectures and concerts with the Vermeer Quartet and guest artists. The organization also promotes the music of young performers with five prizes to Maine musicians and its Next Generation program in August. During the winter the group sponsors monthly classical and jazz concerts by world-renowned artists. All concerts take place at the renovated Rockport Opera House.

The Round Top was a dairy farm in a former life. The cows are long gone, but you can still enjoy 30 flavors of the ice cream made here. Now the farm's main product is music, theater, arts, and crafts, taught and put on display. Business has been so good they can hardly restore and convert the old farm's buildings fast enough to accommodate the growth. During the warm weather many of their concerts, children's and adults' plays, art and crafts shows, lectures, and workshops are staged outside. Come winter, activities move indoors. One of their most anticipated events is the annual Festival Day and Concert on the Lawn in July. This event is fun for everyone, with children's activities and crafts in the morning and orchestra or brass quintet music in the evening. People sprawl out on the lawn with blankets and picnic baskets for a jam-packed day of fun and enjoyment.

Seasonal Music

Annual Bluegrass Festival (207-725-6009; www.thomaspointbeach.com; Thomas Point Beach, Brunswick). This Bluegrass music fest is the finale to a long season of camping, music, and fun. Take in just a day of this country music with a twang or stay for the whole weekend. Date: Labor Day weekend. Admission: $15–$30, day; $65–$80, weekend (music and accommodations); children under 12 free.

NIGHTLIFE

The Blue Goose (207-338-3003; Rte. 1, Northport). Contradancing.

Gilbert's Publick House (207-236-4320; Bay View Landing, Camden). Live music and dancing Thurs., Fri., and Sat. nights.

Gray's Wharf (207-633-5629; Pier One, Boothbay Harbor). Seafood dining offering the "best lobster roll around." Open year round with entertainment five nights a week throughout the summer and on weekends in winter months.

SCHOOLS

What is culture, anyhow? We raise the question because maybe this section on schools suggests an answer. Here you will find schools not only for painters and musicians but also schools for fly fishermen and ocean navigators.

Learning how to pull together on one of Outward Bound's pulling boats.

Courtesy of Outward Bound

Hurricane Island Outward Bound School (207-594-5548 or 800-341-1744 out-of-state; hious@outwardbound.org; Mechanic St., Rockland). Courses lasting 5 to 26 days are offered, as well as semester courses lasting 72 days in Penobsot Bay, Greenville, and Newry. There are sessions year-round for every age and both sexes; they focus on sailing, rock climbing, dog-sledding, and outdoor problem-solving. Prices are a bit steep. An international program begun in Wales, O.B. challenges participants to do things they never thought they could do and then pushes them just a little further. For details, write Box 429, Rockland 04841.

Maine Coast Art Workshops (207-372-8200; P.O. Box 236, Port Clyde 04855). Throughout the summer, five-day workshops with recognized artists are held here on the St. George peninsula, taking advantage of the surrounding natural setting. Sixteen workshops to choose from; tuition is about $360.

The Maine Photographic Workshops

Students at the Maine Photographic Workshops take a break on a field trip to Monhegan Island.

Maine Photographic Workshops (207-236-8581; www.meworkshops.com; Two Central St., Rockport). Photography, cinematography, television production, acting, and other related courses for the aspiring or experienced visual artist. All are taught by established professionals from around the country and the world. The workshop also operates an excellent gallery on the premises and a good retail store with photographic equipment and accessories.

Penobscot School (207-594-1084; www.midcoast.com/~pnobsct/; 28 Gay St, Rockland 04841). Founded in 1986, this non-profit school began as one woman teaching French to area children. Today the school offers 10–12 week classes in conversational Russian, Japanese, Spanish, French, Italian, and German 'and the occasional intensive weekend course in Russian, Italian, French, Spanish, Chinese, and German — most taught by native speakers. During the summer they teach English as a second language and provide informal cultural events for the community.

Shelter Institute (207-442-7938; www.shelterinstitute.com; 38 Center St., Bath 04530). As featured on *Good Morning America,* the Shelter Institute teaches its international student body how to make their houses energy efficient from the ground up. They sell all energy related products and house an incredible home builder's library. Classes year round.

Watershed Center for the Ceramic Arts (207-882-6075; 19 Brick Hill Rd., Newcastle). This is a Yaddo for the clay set. Big time and up-and-coming potters come here to get away from it all and devote themselves to their craft. They also teach the general public the secrets of handbuilding, wheel throwing, glazing, and firing.

SEASONAL EVENTS

Arts & Crafts Festival (207-236-4404; Public Library, Bok Amphitheater, Camden). Crafters from all over show and sell their work. Mid-July and again in October.

Fall Foliage Festival (207-633-4727; Boothbay Railway Village, Boothbay Harbor). Leaves, music, crafts, food, and fun for the family. Mid-October.

Fishermen's Festival (207-633-2353; Boothbay Harbor). Miss Shrimp Contest, lobster boat races, chowder contest, and other great fisherman things, all to benefit the Fishermen's Memorial Fund. Late April.

Maine Festival (207-772-9012; www.mainearts.org; Thomas Point Beach, Brunswick). More than 600 artists and craftsmen on site. Folk Arts Village highlighting music and crafts traditional to Maine, plus bands and performers from other parts of the country. Early August.

Maine Highland Games (207-364-3063; www.mint.net/bravehrt; Thomas Point Beach, Brunswick). People of Scottish ancestry show their colors. Bagpipe bands, highland dancing, food, border-collie demonstrations, and clan exhibits. Third Saturday in August.

Military Aviation Airshow (207-594-4418; Transportation Museum, Owls Head). Fly-bys and demonstrations of armed forces aircraft. Late June.

Rockland Maine Lobster Festival (207-596-0376; Public Landing, Rockland). Just about everything to do with lobster, including lots to eat. Early August.

Windjammer Days (207-633-2353; Boothbay Harbor). For more than thirty years this windjammer parade has attracted an international crowd. Also antique boat parade, concerts, and exhibitions. Late June.

THEATER

Belfast Railroad Maskers (207-338-9668; Maskers Railroad Theatre, Belfast). Wide assortment of comedies and dramas.

Camden Civic Theatre (207-236-2281; Camden Opera House, Rte. 1, Camden). Musicals.

Iron Horse Dinner Theater (207-338-2931; 11 Water St. off City Landing, Belfast). Actually, it's dinner, theater, and a train ride.

Maine State Music Theatre (207-725-8769; www.msmt.org; Pickard Theater, Bowdoin College, Brunswick). Topnotch musicals with resident professional talent who for nearly 40 years have belted out great show tunes. June–Aug.

Studio Theater (207-442-8455; Center for the Arts at the Chocolate Church, 804 Washington St., Bath).

The Theater Project/Young People's Theater (207-729-8584; www.col.me.us/theater; 14 School St., Brunswick). This theater company puts on more than seven productions a year featuring dramas, contemporaries, and musicals. The Young People's Theater has classes for school aged children and productions involving both kids and adults from the community. Tickets: $12 adults; $6 kids.

MIDCOAST: RECREATION

BEACHES

Crescent Beach; Crescent Beach Rd., Owl's Head. Popular swimming beach near summer colony. Length, 1,100 yards. Nearby facilities; limited parking.

Pemaquid Beach Park; off Rte. 130, New Harbor. About a half-mile long and backed by dunes. There's a bathhouse, picnic tables, restrooms. Entrance fee.

Popham Beach State Park; Rte. 209, Phippsburg. Not only fine sand, but a fine beach. In fact, one of the finest. More than two miles long; there are picnic tables, rocky outcrops and tide pools, and plenty of parking, which fills up quickly on a hot day. Entrance fee.

Reid State Park; Rte. 127 to Seguinland Rd., Georgetown. A half-mile open barrier spit, this is another great beach. There's a salt marsh, sand dunes, rocky ledges, tidal pools, a bathhouse, picnic tables, fireplaces, and a snack bar. Decent parking. Entrance fee.

Sandy Point Beach; Stockton Springs. About a mile long; there's not much here except beach. No facilities and little parking.

A young visitor enjoys Thomas Point Beach in Brunswick.

BERRY & APPLE PICKING

Wild blueberries abound in Maine, and more often than not, you'll stumble on a patch if you're out hiking on a mid- to late summer's day. If you don't plan to hike, check out one of these farms where for a fee, you can pick cultivated berries to your heart's content. Call ahead for picking prospects.

Hilltop Raspberry Farm (207-737-4988; Post Rd., Bowdoinham). Raspberries. July 15–Oct. Daily 9–6.

Juniper Edge Strawberries (207-725-6414; 532 Harpswell Rd., Rte. 123, Brunswick). Strawberries. June 15 to end of season. Daily 8:30–5:30.

Prouts Strawberries (207-666-5604; Brown Point Rd., Bowdoinham). Strawberries. Late June–mid-July. 7 a.m.–dusk. Closed Sundays.

Spear Farm & Greenhouse (207-273-3818; Rte. 1, Warren). Strawberries. Call for information.

BICYCLING

First, here's what The Law says:

• You need to have brakes so you can stop within a reasonable distance. (Seems fair.)

• You need a headlamp if you're riding at night; night being that time when cars by law should have their headlights on.

• The headlamp has to produce a white light someone in front of you can see from at least 200 ft.

• You need a rear red reflector visible from at least 200 ft. and reflector strips on your bike pedals and handlebars.

• Helmets are not the law for cyclists in Maine. However, we strongly suggest them. Coastal paved roads, dirt roads, and trails open to cyclists are often narrow and winding as they follow the terrain. Traffic at the height of summer can make those byways even more dangerous. Wearing a helmet will help protect you from injury should you hit a bad piece of road or path. It also could save your life should you encounter a car wanting more than its share of the road. We'd also like you to consider that biking — and any other outdoor activity in Maine — requires paying careful attention to weather conditions. Be sure to dress properly. Even if it promised to be a warm day, take along a windbreaker that will help you ward off a sudden damp fog.

Now, here's a roundup of biking on the coast.

There are three highways closed to cyclists: the Maine Turnpike, the interstate highway system and Rte. 1 between Brunswick and Bath.

Otherwise, go crazy. Great areas to pedal on the Midcoast include: the stretch of **U.S. Rte. 1 between Belfast and Bucksport** which is littered with old sea captains' homes; the perimeter of **Megunticook Lake** and on to Lincolnville around **New Harbor** and the **Pemaquid Peninsula**.

Several chambers of commerce offer bike tour maps of their areas, including the Rockport-Camden-Lincolnville Chamber of Commerce. (See "Tourist Information" in Chapter Seven, *Information*.) If you want to make your own way, the state publishes excellent, inexpensive highway maps. Write for information from the Maine Department of Transportation, State House Station 16, Augusta, 04333-0016. Margaret Vandebroek is the state's bicycle coordinator.

DeLorme Mapping Company offers an inexpensive pamphlet titled *Bicycling*. It can be found at bookstores and large supermarkets in the magazine/map/recreation areas. Another excellent guide for cyclers is *25 Bicycle Tours in Maine* by Howard Stone (Back Country Publications, P.O. Box 175, Woodstock, VT 05091). Both books offer excellent maps and directions for touring cyclists.

BICYCLE DEALERS

You're on the road bright and early on your first day, and bam, you hit a bump, wipe out, and break a spoke. That's not to say the roads and trails in Maine are any rougher than those you're used to at home. We just say it to remind you that accidents do happen, and to let you know that help is not far away.

Here's a list of bike shops on the coast. Several rent bikes; all repair them. Some are great places to go to replace the water bottle you left behind, as well as pick up information on roads and trails favored by local cyclists, tours, and clubs.

Bath Cycle and Ski (207-442-7002; Rte. 1, Woolwich; E-mail, bikeman.com).

Birgfeld's Bicycle Shop (207-548-2916; www.agate.net/birgfelds; E-mail, birgfelds@agate.net;). Web site may change in near future.

Brunswick Bicycles (207-729-5309; 11 Center St., Brunswick).

Fred's Bicycle (107-236-6664; Chestnut St., Camden).

Maine Sport (800-722-0826; www.mainesport.com; Rte. 1, Rockport).

BIRD WATCHING

The black-billed cuckoo taps out his hollow message in code. . . .

— E. B. White

FOR EXPERIENCED BIRDERS

Bird life in the woods, bogs, ponds, open lands, rocks, and beaches of the Maine coast is amazingly rich. Though there are few year-rounders, innumerable birds drop by. Maine is the last stop for many migrants, both from the north in winter and from the south in summer.

Accordingly, human migrants from the north will be attracted in late summer to the abundant shorebird life of marshes and mudflats like *Scarborough Marsh* and *Biddeford Pool*, where they may hear the coocoo of the least bittern or catch sight of a little blue or a black crowned night heron, a snowy egret, glossy ibis, or even a marbled godwit.

Southern birders, on the other hand, will head well-bundled in winter for a shore lookout like *Quoddy Head* to see flying murres, kittiwakes and other alcids, a swimming harlequin duck, or a king eider. Or they may hope to see a northern three-toed woodpecker in the spruce forests along the rocky northeastern shore, the year-round habitat of gray jays, northern ravens, and boreal chickadees.

Any birder north of Portland will look for bald eagles nesting. All will want to visit the extraordinary flocks of ocean birds that breed in early summer among the more than 2,000 sheltering islands and the plankton-rich waters fed by the icy Labrador Current. The puffin is the most famous; other notable breeds include black headed gulls, razorbills, black guillemots, and Leach's petrels, hard to spot because they fly at night.

Arctic terns arrive in mid-May like a snowstorm over the sea. In late summer they're off east again over the Atlantic, starting their incredible annual trip through Europe and Africa to the Antarctic. All these nesting creatures pose the birder's familiar dilemma: how to observe the birds without disturbing their habitat.

The ferry from *Bar Harbor to Yarmouth* is an excellent place from which to observe coastal bird life. So are many shorter ferry rides (See "By Ferry" in Chapter Two, *Transportation*, and "Whale Watching," below). Take a boat ride around *Matinicus Rock* (offshore from Matinicus Island), the southernmost known breeding place for puffins on the East Coast. *Seal Island* near Machias has pathways and blinds set up for birders and is worth a special trip in June. You can land for a few hours but not stay overnight.

Wonderful places to see the fall migration of shore birds are the quiet beaches near the Canadian border. One birder we've heard of spotted 100 species in one day in *Dennysville* on the Dennys River. The *Lubec and Eastport flats* host an enormous number and variety of traveling sanderlings, sandpipers, knots, willets, and other beach feeders.

FOR NON-BIRDERS

If you've never watched birds, Maine raises your awareness of them. As your car crosses an inlet or shallow river your eye is suddenly caught by a four-foot-tall great blue heron — still as a post, ankle deep in running water, coiled to spear his lunch on a six-inch yellow beak. On a Maine beach you see a familiar flock of sandpipers do their tiny quickstep all together, slow down to stoop and feed together along the curl of a retreating wave, soar away together with a flash of white along each wing. It's hard to imagine these tiny creatures may have spent the winter in Palm Beach and have Arctic plans for the summer.

Keep watching. You might see among them one with longer legs or, higher up the beach, a plumper bird with a reddish back looking under seaweedy pebbles. A fellow beachgoer with binoculars will tell you the plump one is a ruddy turnstone and the tall one a yellowlegs. If you ask to borrow the binoculars to see the color of the long-jointed legs, you've taken the first step to a new interest.

Irresistible in harbor waters in winter are the diving buffleheads, chunky little black and white birds that tip up like toys, all in one motion. In tidal inlets and freshwater ponds you see not only birds shaped like farm ducks but also swimming birds of less familiar shape, maybe one with a tuft of feathers on the top or back of the head, a grebe or merganser.

Finally, there are the sea birds on the rocky shores. Even if you haven't learned to distinguish the soaring seagulls from the smaller terns that hover and dive along the surf, you may want to take the boat to *Matinicus* in June or July. Then you can tell friends back home you've seen the unmistakable puffin, standing tall like a penguin on its large orange feet, its back black, its round stomach white, its broad beak blue, yellow, and red.

FOR ALL BIRDERS

If you want to know the latest action on the wing call the *Maine Audubon* bird alert hotline at 207-781-2332. The hotline operates 24 hours a day. Daily.

Wooden Boats

Pleasure boats and working boats come and go in all shapes and sizes in Maine, but there's something particular about a wooden boat. Museums are devoted to the wooden boat, and a magazine industry flourishes here thanks to wooden boats. There are also schools to help keep the craft of wooden boat building alive. Best of all you can still look out at the harbor — or practically anyplace else on the coast — and see them in abundance.

In spite of all the extra work wooden boats demand of their owners, many Mainers would not go down to the sea in anything else. They are a living part of the sea. A boat, said someone probably before the invention of fiberglass, is a hole in the water into which you throw money. Nowhere else do people throw money into their wooden boats so willingly as in Maine.

The wooden boat has as important a place in Maine's history as the glacier. The Passamaquoddy Indians cruised the coast in birch bark canoes. The graceful lines of those canoes still live in the famed Old Town canoes made in Bangor. The first wooden ship built in America was constructed in Maine by the colonists of Popham Colony in 1607. It was a 30-ton pinnace called the *Virginia*, and it carried cargo between England and Virginia for 20 years.

At first, Maine boat builders relied on the forests at their back door. As lumber along the South Coast became scarce, more boat builders moved Down East to take advantage of cheaper building materials. The industry grew. Soon it seemed like the whole coast was one big shipyard, building good, cheap cargo ships.

The earliest Maine ships were built in the tradition of their British forebears, but by the time of the Revolutionary War, Maine shipwrights had developed their own designs and style of shipbuilding. Speed became important to the merchant marine, and shipbuilders responded with the sleek, fast clipper ship; 83 clippers were built and launched in the state during the mid-1800s. The last of the famous wooden cargo ships built in Maine was a three-masted square rigger ship called the Down-Easter that was almost as fast as the clipper, but had a deeper, more spacious hull and enabled merchants to haul more with every trip.

Schooners were also built in Maine. Merchants prized them because they were even larger than the clippers and Down-Easters and more economical to operate. Today they operate out of Rockland and Camden serving the tourist trade (See "Windjammers," below).

The end of the wooden boat as a merchant trading vessel came with the invention of the steamers. Steamships didn't rely on changeable winds and currents. They ran on time, and even the fastest clipper couldn't compete. Ironically, renowned Bath shipbuilder Arthur Sewall built the first steel sailing vessel, *Dirigo I*, in 1894. It weighed more than 2,800 tons.

Maine wooden boat builders took a new tack, building smaller boats for fishermen and pleasure sailors. The style of boat often depends on where it comes from: Peapods come from Penobscot Bay; Quoddy boats from Passamaquoddy Bay; the pretty, gaff-rigged Friendship Sloops from the town of Friendship on Muscongus Bay. There were also punts built to navigate a harbor or any small, calm waterway; dories to ferry people and small loads to and from shore; and pulling boats that were manned by oarsmen who literally hauled large ships that had been becalmed on windless water. Today those same pulling boats are used by Outward Bound students, their courses set on personal development.

For an invigorating taste of Maine's wooden boat heritage hard at work, watch the *Friendship Sloop Races,* held every year in late July in Rockland. Sponsored by the Friendship Sloop Society, the sloop races are really a week of wooden boat activities, including three days of racing and events at the Maine Maritime Museum in Bath. For more information, contact the Rockland-Thomaston Chamber of Commerce (207-596-0376). Also in Rockland are the spectacular *Schooner Days,* a three-day festival with all the trimmings — food, entertainment, arts, and marine demonstrations — crowned by the Parade of Sail, which features more schooners every year, including the National Historic Landmark *Stephen Taber.*

Windjammer enthusiasts head to Boothbay Harbor in late June for *Windjammer Days.* The festival includes concerts, a boat and a street parade, fireworks, and a chance to tour visiting military vessels. The Boothbay Harbor Chamber of Commerce has all the information (207-633-2353; P.O. Box 356, Boothbay Harbor, 04538).

Smart enough to realize that you can't get too much of a good thing, the Rockport-Camden-Lincolnville Chamber of Commerce (207-236-4404) promotes another windjammer fix later in the summer. Pretty Camden Harbor hosts *Windjammer Weekend* every Labor Day weekend, when over two dozen wind-jammers from ports along the mid-coast are on display — except for the *Victory Chimes,* which at 132 feet is the largest windjammer in the fleet and too big to stick around after the parade.

All of the beaches listed above come with birds. Following are a few places well worth looking into. Some are full-fledged nature preserves or refuges. Others are just great spots for locating birds. When possible, we have provided addresses and phone numbers.

Hog Island Audubon Camp (Muscongus Bay). Osprey drop in here, so do eagles. Audubon annually sponsors two six-day field ornithology sessions. The Todd Wildlife Sanctuary on the island hosts a variety of nesting birds. Workshops include a one-day trip to Matinicus Rock. For more information, see "Schools" in *Culture,* earlier in this chapter.

Salt Bay (Rtes. 215 and 1 through Damariscotta Mills, Newcastle, and Damariscotta). If you don't want to leave your car, Salt Bay is a good spot. Rte. 215 borders the bay along its southwest edge; Rte. 1 leads along the bay to the east. Birds like to rest and feed in the large shallow bay and its mud-flats laid bare at low tide.

Swan Island (Merrymeeting Bay near Richmond). The state operates this 2,000-acre preserve and allows a few visitors to camp at shelters in the path of a wide variety of migrating and nesting birds, including the Canada or wild goose. Tours are available, provided you obtain the necessary (and inexpensive) permit. Write Swan Island Reservation Clerk, Maine Department of Inland Fisheries and Wildlife, 8 Federal St., Augusta 04330.

BOATING

Boating on Maine's shore was once exclusively the activity of members of the Abenaki tribe cruising the coast in well-made birch bark canoes. Today few people venture on saltwater in modern fiberglass and aluminum canoes, let alone birch bark. Most recreational boating is now done in sailboats, motor boats, and kayaks. Some will argue that ferries — a way of life for many Mainers — are also a form of recreational boating. They certainly are a good way to gain access to some of the best sights on the coast (See "By Ferry" in Chapter Two, *Transportation*.) Windjammers and sightseeing cruises to view puffins and whales are two types of boating we list later in this chapter.

Whatever boat you choose, watch the weather. Spring often brings weather systems moving through the Gulf of Maine at a fast clip. Summer fogs can last for days. Fall and winter nor'easters can combine driving winds and rain with a high tide to make life on the water miserable if you are unprepared.

CANOEING AND SEA KAYAKING

Canoeing is rare off the Maine coast these days. Most boaters prefer something larger or smaller and more self contained. Where canoeists reign is on the small inland waterways, fresh and saltwater ponds, and salt marshes.

Extended solo sea kayak trips are not the stuff for amateurs. It's not so much the kayak as the elements that can cause problems. Weather changes quickly, currents and tides can be dangerous and tricky. Knowing how to handle your kayak properly will give you an edge out on the water. You can learn the basics in a couple of hours on a few weekends. You begin with wide, stable kayaks, then you learn how to flip. After a while, it won't feel too tippy. A great reference for kayakers is *Sea Kayaking Along the New England Coast* (AMC Books, $14.95). It contains an excellent round-up of information on everything about coastal kayaking conditions throughout New England, including the *Maine Island Trail* (see sidebar below).

The following places offer gear, lessons, rentals, and two hour to five-day trips.

Dragonworks (207-666-8481- RR1, Box 1186, Bowdoinham 04008) Boats, tours, instruction on Merrymeeting Bay.

H2Outfitters (207-833-5257; E-mail, H2O@H2outfitters.com; P.O. Box 72, Orrs Island 04066). Canoe and kayak instruction for groups or individuals, as well as three-hour guided tours of waters near Bailey and Orrs islands. Classes offered year round.

Island Hopping (603-466-2721; www.outdoors.org; or write Summer Workshop, P.O. Box 298, Gorham, NH 03581). The Appalachian Mountain Club offers experienced canoeists the chance to spend three days exploring the water routes the Abenaki Indians used as they traveled among the islands of Penobscot Bay.

Maine Sport Outdoors School (800-722-0826; www.mainesport.com; Rte. 1,

Rockport 04856). Sea kayaking guided tours from two-hour harbor trips to six-day excursions, and all levels of instruction from beginners' clinics to five-day trips. They also rent sea and lake kayaks, canoes, and bicycles (see "Bicycling").

Tidal Transit Ocean Kayaking Co. (207-633-7140; 49 Townsend Ave., Boothbay Harbor). Instruction and custom trips for sea kayakers. Guided tours.

Maine Island Trail

The Maine Island Trail Association was founded in 1988. The waterway is a kind of Appalachian Trail for boaters. It begins with islands in Casco Bay and follows the coast Down East past Machias, a distance of 325 miles. The trail includes 77 islands where travelers can put ashore and camp for the night. Thirty are privately owned islands; the rest are owned by the state and governed by the Bureau of Parks and Lands.

"What makes the Maine Island Trail a pleasure is its 'connect the dots' character, the 'dots' being islands. Without access to islands along the way, there would be no trail," wrote kayaker Michael Burke in *Yankee* magazine.

Members have access to prudent use of the islands on the trail — as well as a stewardship handbook and guidebook. Members receive a copy of *The Maine Island Trail Book*, a guidebook packed with charts and information. There are about 2,000 members of MITA, 300 of whom regularly monitor usage and erosion on forays to islands they have "adopted."

For information about the organization, contact the Maine Island Trail Association; 207-596-6456; www.mita.org; P.O. Box C, Rockland, ME 04841.

CRUISING

For the sailboat or motorboat cruiser, the coast could be considered a paradise. There are hundreds of deepwater anchorages, beautiful fishing villages like Jonesport, and quaint, albeit sophisticated, towns such as Camden (a true pleasure sailor's town). Islands make for great side trips. The smallest are great places to anchor and enjoy a swim on a warm summer day and lobster on the rocks; the largest offer almost all the amenities of the mainland.

An excellent guide for pleasure boaters in Maine is *A Cruising Guide to the Maine Coast* by Hank and Jan Taft (International Marine Publishing; Camden, ME; $32.50). It's packed with charts, tips, and history for those viewing the coast from the water. If you don't have your own boat, here is a list of dealers who sell and rent sailboats and motorboats.

CHARTERS & RENTALS

There are not a lot of people willing to rent you their boats. More are willing to take you. Boat people are like that.

Sloop Surprise (207-372-6366; www.eastwindinn.com; Tenants Harbor). Capt. Steve Daley sails his Friendship sloop from the East Wind Inn's pier around the islands of Tenants Harbor. Up to six people. Daily.

S<small>AILING</small> L<small>ESSONS</small>

Bay Island Yacht Charters and Sailing School (207-596-7550; Bay Island).

Chance Along Community Sailing Center (207-338-6003or 800-286-6696; 278 High St. Belfast). Lessons to get around the harbor or down the coast. Rentals from Sunfish to 23 ft. boats; half day, full day , or weekly rates.

Sawyer's Sailing School (207-783-6882 or 800-372-8465; www.boatshow.com/ captainbob.html; E-mail, bobsails25@aolcom; Dolphin Marina, S. Harpswell). One and three-day instructional cruises aboard a 25-foot sloop.

BOWLING

Candlepin Lodge (207-863-2730; Vinalhaven). Six candlepin lanes.

Columbus Club Bowling Bowl (207-725-5241; 7 Dunlap Rd., Brunswick).

Oakland Park Bowling Lanes (207-594-7525; Rte. 1, Rockport). 12 candlepin lanes.

Yankee Lanes of Brunswick (207-725-2963; Bath Rd., Brunswick). 32 tenpin lanes.

CAMPING

*Camping in beautiful
Camden Hills State Park.*

Herb Swanson

Midcoast offers dozens of private and public campgrounds, often with great views of the water at campers' prices. Sizes and facilities vary, and the season is short; we recommend calling well ahead for reservations. After

Labor Day weekend most Midcoast campgrounds become lovely, quiet, and wonderfully available.

As in all of coastal Maine, for a complete list of private campgrounds, contact the *Maine Campground Owners Association* (207-782-5874; www.camp-maine.com; E-mail, info@campmaine.com; 655 Main St., Lewiston 04240). The *Maine Tourism Association* also publishes a statewide travel information planner. Call or write for one (207-623-0363 or 800-533-9595 out-of-state; www.mainetourism.com; E-mail,metainfo@mainetourism.com; P.O. Box 2300, Hallowell 04347).

Camden Hills State Park (207-236-3109; www.state.us.m/doc/prkslnds/reser; two mi. off U.S. Rte. 1). Often this lovely campground is full. It's near one of the most popular seacoast towns in Maine, as well as within striking distance for hikers headed up Mount Battie. You should have a reservation to make sure you have a spot during July and August. But you're almost certain to get one the rest of the season if you arrive before 1 p.m. Showers. Nominal fee. Open May 15–October 15.

FISHING

People have fished in Maine's waters since before recorded history. Tribes of the Algonquin nation used to erect weirs — traps of net and wood that fish swim into, but can't get out of — in the bays and inlets of the coast. The Portuguese are believed to have fished here long before the coast of Maine was first "discovered" by the British and French. The cold waters off the coast were famous for their abundant supply of bluefish, striped bass, mackerel, and tuna. Today, the waters are not as populated as they once were. Commercial fisheries during this and the last century have depleted much of the natural supply of saltwater fish.

While large schools of fish are now rare on the coast, there are many opportunities both for salt and freshwater fishing. Former President Bush's fishing tackle master Bob Boilard, one of the most knowledgeable sports fishermen in the Saco Bay area, suggests bottom fishing for cod, pollock, and mackerel. Well-known spots for saltwater fishing are Boothbay Harbor; the waters off Rockland; and Passamaquoddy Bay near Eastport.

Beach and shore fishing is also popular in the fall when sunbathers have left; Popham Beach near where the Kennebec River empties into the Gulf of Maine near Bath is a good spot to try your luck.

If you're a competitive fisherman or you like to be there when the pros weigh their fish, there are two saltwater tournaments held on the coast. *Tuna Tournament & Small Fish Rodeo* usually takes place from July to August. Fair game includes codfish, bluefish, mackerel, and cusk. For more information contact the Boothbay Chamber of Commerce (207-633-2353) or Breakaways

Sports Fishing (207-633-6990; E-mail, breakaway@lincoln.midcoast.com; P.O. Box 4, Boothbay Harbor 04538). *The New England Bluefish Open* is held every year in mid-August in the waters near Bath. For more information, contact Eastern Sports Fishing (207-443-8940; ww.gwi.net/~espnbo/; 118 Front St., Bath 04530).

When your taste runs more to trout and bass, try the rivers near the coast. Late spring and early summer are traditionally good seasons for freshwater fishermen. Then hungry fish come to the surface to feed on insects and their larvae.

Freshwater fishing licenses may be bought at the Kittery Trading Post in Kittery, L.L. Bean, and Peregrine Outfitters in Freeport, as well as many other Maine sporting goods stores (no licenses are required for saltwater sport fishing). The rate for a one-day license is about the price of a movie. The longer you plan to fish, the cheaper it gets. Junior licenses are available for those ages 12 to 16. For more information call or write the *Department of Inland Fisheries and Wildlife* (207-287-8000; 284 State St., 41 State House Station, Augusta 04333). They also can give you dates for the freshwater fishing season and send maps showing waters open and restricted to fishing.

DEEP SEA FISHING BOATS

Breakaway (207-633-6990; E-mail, breakaway@lincoln.midcoast.com; Pier 6, Fisherman's Wharf). Sport fishing charters. Full- or half-day trips.

GOLF

Many of the courses listed here are set right on the shore. If you don't make par, at least you've scored a great view. Call for current rates and hours and reservations.

Bath Golf Country Club (207-442-8411; Whiskeag Rd., Bath). 18 holes, 6,260 yds., par 70. Cart and club rental, pro shop, clubhouse, lessons.

Boothbay Region Country Club (207-633-6085; Country Club Rd., Boothbay). 9 holes, 2,668 yds., par 35. Cart and club rental, pro shop, clubhouse.

Brunswick Golf Club (207-725-8224; River Rd., Brunswick). 18 holes, 6,600 yds., par 72. Cart and club rental, pro shop, clubhouse, lessons. On weekends, private until 10 a.m.

Bucksport Golf Club (207-469-7612; Duckcove Rd., Bucksport). 9 holes, 3,352 yds., par 36. Cart and club rental, pro shop, clubhouse, lessons, snack bar.

Goose River Golf Course (207-236-8488; 50 Park St., Camden). 9 holes, 3,049 yds., par 35. Cart and club rental, pro shop, clubhouse, lessons.

North Haven Golf Club (Iron Point Rd., North Haven). 9 holes, 2,060 yds., par 35. Cart and club rental, lessons.

Northport Golf Club (207-338-2270; Bluff Rd., Northport). 9 holes, 3,047 yds., par 36. Cart and club rental, pro shop, clubhouse, lessons.

Rockland Golf Club (207-594-9322; Old County Rd., Rockland). 18 holes, 6,121 yds., par 70. Cart and club rental, pro shop, clubhouse, lessons.

Samoset Resort (207-594-1431 or 800-341-1650, ext. 511; www.samoset.com; Warrenton St., Rockport). 18 holes, 5,620 yds., par 70. Cart and club rental, pro shop, clubhouse, lessons.

HEALTH CLUBS

The Maine Event (207-729-0129; 126 Main St., Topsham). Pool, aerobics, weights, racquetball, sauna, whirlpool, fitness machines, and lifecycles.

The Maine Pines Raquet & Sport (207-729-8433; 120 Harpswell Rd., Brunswick). Tennis and racquetball, walleyball, yoga, karate, squash, fitness center, baby sitting.

Oceanside Health and Fitness (207-338-1692 or 800-626-1692; 9 Field St., Belfast). Fitness machines, weights, aerobics, and lifecycles.

Samoset Resort (207-594-2511 or 800-341-1650; Waldo Ave., Rockport). Pools, hot tubs, sauna, weights, lifecycles, fitness machines, and aerobics.

Trade Winds Health Club (207-596-6889 or 800-596-6889; 2 Parkview Dr., Rockland). Pool, sauna, whirlpool, steambath, Nautilus, weights, fitness machines, lifecycle, stairmasters, and treadmill.

Women's Fitness Studio (207-729-5544; 21 Standwood, Brunswick). Aerobics, Nautilus, spa services, yoga, aerobics, childcare.

YMCA (207-443-4112; 26 Summer St., Bath). Aerobics, pool, whirlpool, sauna, racquetball, weights, and basketball gym.

YMCA (207-633-2855; Townsend Ave., Boothbay Harbor). Pool, aerobics, weights, racquetball, sauna, and cardiovascular equipment.

YMCA (207-236-3375; 50 Chestnut St., Camden). Aerobics, racquetball, weights, pool, sauna, and fitness machines.

HIKING AND WALKING

Some of the best hiking on the Maine coast is found in the Midcoast. DeLorme Mapping Company offers an inexpensive booklet titled *Hiking: Volume 1 Coastal & Eastern Region*. It is available in most bookstores and larger supermarkets and has several routes mapped with experience levels clearly marked. Here are some of the more popular Midcoast hikes and walks:

Bald Rock Mountain, Lincolnville. From the summit, you can see Mount Desert and the Penobscot Bay islands. From Ski Lodge Rd., this is an easy ascent on a well-traveled path to the top. It is a one-half mile walk with an elevation gain of 1000 feet.

Monhegan Island. Take the Burnt Head trail along the 150-foot cliffs and through Cathedral Woods — one of the few existing stands of virgin pine in Maine. This is a good day trip. The island has about 17 miles of hiking trails and is ruled by walkers (no vehicles are allowed). Ferries leave for Monhegan from Boothbay Harbor, New Harbor, and Port Clyde.

A view of Lake Megunticook from the Camden Hills.

Herb Swanson

Mount Battie, Camden. There aren't many prettier walks than this one. From various lookouts you can see Mount Desert Island, Blue Hill Bay, Camden village, harbor, coast, and Megunticook from the mountain's exposed summit. There's also a stone tower at the top. This walk is even prettier in the fall when the leaves change. A park nature trail joins with a short, steep trail that climbs parallel to the auto toll road. One-mile climb with a 600-foot elevation gain.

Mount Megunticook, Camden. The highest of the Camden Hills, the ridge is ascended by park trails from several directions. The views are more limited on this walk, but there are several good vistas from exposed ledges en route. The Megunticook Trail offers the most direct ascent. It begins near the park entrance and passes a grotto and stream, then rises steeply to Ocean Lookout and panoramic views. Base to Lookout is a one-mile climb with an elevation gain of 1,100 feet.

Mount Megunticook/Mount Battie, Camden. More ambitious walkers can plan to do both hills in one day. The trip begins at the parking lot, continues over Mount Megunticook, across to Mount Battie, and back to the parking area. The total walk is about 4.5 miles, and the top of Mount Battie is a great place for a picnic.

Ragged Mountain, Camden. An easy trail that weaves in and out of the trail and ski lift at Snow Bowl. The elevation gain is about 400 feet, and the trail is about one mile from base to summit.

HORSEBACK RIDING

Cherrydale Horse Farm (207-443-6782; Old Brunswick Rd., West Bath). Trails, boarding.

Gallant Morgan Horse Farm (207-443-4170; Days Ferry Rd., Rte. 128, Woolwich). Lessons, boarding, training, indoor facilities, tack shop, girls' riding camp.

Hill-N-Dale Farm (207-273-2511; 626 Western Rd., Warren). Lessons, trail rides, indoor arena, day camp, and carousel tack shop.

Ledgewood Riding Stable (207-882-6346; 432 Bradford Rd., Wiscasset). Trail rides.

Fall Foliage in Maine

Leaf peeping is relatively new to Maine. For years, devoted foliage aficionados have chosen New England neighbors to the south and west of Maine. That wasn't for any lack of color, say state tourism officials, but merely because the state had failed to promote the fall season. The truth is the coast does have a lovely foliage season, and it is often less crowded than coinciding seasons in New Hampshire and Vermont.

The change begins almost immediately after Labor Day, when the temperature begins to drop. The big change comes about a month later, when warm days and cool nights cause trees to begin storing energy to get them through the winter. Trees extract sugars, starches, and other nutrients from their leaves, causing leaves to turn from green to red, yellow, and orange. First trees inland change, then those on the coast.

Down East from Acadia to Washington County is the first region on the coast to turn — generally around the end of September or early October. The western coast stretching from Kittery to Bucksport usually turns about a week later. Peak foliage usually lasts for about three to four weeks. This can all change from year to year, depending on the prevailing temperatures, the rainfall and other weather factors. For an inside tip on color conditions, call the **Foliage Hotline** (207-582-9300; out-of-state 800-533-9595) after September 15. The state publishes a leaf peepers' guide with several coastal leaf routes between 100 and 250 miles long; ask for it at any of the state information centers listed in Chapter Seven, *Information*.

If you want to find your own way, here are some tips on colorful routes. *St. George's Peninsula* near Port Clyde usually has great color. So does the *Blue Hill Peninsula*. *Acadia* is a favorite spot, particularly if you drive the park loop road or hike up Cadillac or the other Mount Desert hills.

The *Camden Hills* are another excellent site for autumn foliage. The *Saco River* near Biddeford and the *Royal River* in Yarmouth are two great canoe trips for viewing the foliage. One of our favorite sights is the *blueberry barrens* that cover the hillsides way Down East. As the weather cools, they turn a brilliant scarlet. We also think the shortcut (See "Shortcuts" in Chapter Two, *Transportation*) on Rte. 182 between *Ellsworth and Cherryfield* is one of the prettiest autumn drives in New England.

NATURE PRESERVES

Fernald's Neck Preserve, off Rte. 52, Camden-Lincolnville. Four miles of trails through woods, bog, and along 200-ft. cliffs on a 315-acre preserve near Lake Megunticook. Managed by the Nature Conservancy.

Josephine Newman Wildlife Sanctuary, Rte. 127, Georgetown. A 119-acre preserve on the ocean with more than two miles of natural trails. The sanctuary is bounded on two sides by salt marsh and contains a small pond. Managed by Maine Audubon.

Lane's Island Preserve, Vinalhaven. The Nature Conservancy manages a 43-acre refuge here made up of rolling moors and shoreline pounded by rough surf. Trails lead to several beaches. Access is by a stone causeway from Vinalhaven (a car ferry from Rockland services the island of Vinalhaven).

Merryspring (Conway Rd. off Rte. 1, on the Camden-Rockport town line). A private foundation manages this 66-acre nature park. While there are several cultivated gardens, the park also features a 10-acre arboretum and the group's ongoing efforts to preserve native wildflowers.

Rachel Carson Salt Pond Preserve, Rte. 32, Bristol. Part of the Rachel Carson Sea Coast, the network of protected lands willed to the public by the late naturalist Rachel Carson. A great place to observe marine life from the point of view of a tidal pool. Good views of Muscongus Bay. A map published by the Nature Conservancy (207-729-5181) points out interesting rock formations along the shore.

Robert P. Tristram Coffin Wildflower Sanctuary, Rte. 128, Woolwich. The New England Wildflower Society owns and operates this 180-acre refuge. It is home to more than 200 species of flowers, grasses, trees, and other plants. Nature trails follow the edge of Merrymeeting Bay.

PUFFIN WATCHING

Their feathers once graced the heads of fashionable women during the 19th century, so much so these colorful sea birds were almost plucked from the species list. Their eggs were also a favorite meal of gourmands. Also known as sea parrots because of their colorful curled beaks, their population is on the increase with help from their friends at the Audubon Society, which launched a major campaign in 1973 called *Project Puffin*. The project has been successful to date, although puffins may never reach their pre-1800 population. The society relies on private donations to fund the repopulation. To make one, write to Project Puffin, National Audubon Society, HC 60, Box 102-P, Medomak, ME 04551.

The struggle to repopulate puffin colonies off the coast is understandable. Puffins prefer to nest on the remote islands stretching from mid-Maine to Canada. They don't reproduce until after their fifth year, and each mating pair produces only one egg each year. Today puffins flourish to the north in Newfoundland, Iceland, and Britain. In Maine, colonies of the birds nest on Matinicus Island, Machias Seal Island, Eastern Egg Rock in Muscongus Bay, and Seal Island in Penobscot Bay. Early summer is the best time to see them. Several tour boat operators split ticket sales with the National Audubon Society, which watches over these puffin sanctuaries.

Hardy III, **Hardy II Tours** (207-677-2026; www.gwi.net/~hardy; E-mail, hardy@gwi.net; Rte. 32, New Harbor).

Mary Donna, **Offshore Passenger & Freight** (207-366-3700; Maine State Ferry Service, Rockland).

Pink Lady, **R. Fish and Son** (207-633-3244; Pier 1, Boothbay Harbor).

SEASONAL SPORTING EVENTS

Beyond the annual events mentioned in the above categories, the coast has dozens of events that lure sportsmen and women from around the world. Following are a few favorite events you should know about.

Friendship Sloop Days and **Friendship Sloop Races**, late July in Friendship. Beautiful wooden boats compete for attention and prizes (contact the Friendship Sloop Society, 207-354-8036).

The Great Schooner Race, early July. Sponsored by the Maine Windjammer Association, this all-day race begins at North Haven and ends in Rockland (contact the Rockland Chamber of Commerce, 207-596-0376).

Maine Retired Skipper's Race, mid-August. You have to be at least 65 to enter (contact the Retired Skipper's Race Committee, Castine, 207-326-8579).

The Monhegan Island Yacht Race, mid-August.

Owls Head Transportation Rally, early August. Planes, high-wheeled bicycles, and automobiles. More than 300 of them (contact the Owls Head Transportation Museum, 207-594-4418; www.ohtm.org).

Schooner Days, early July (Rockland area Chamber of Commerce, 207-596-0376).

Windjammer Days, late June. Windjammers of all shapes and sizes (contact the Boothbay Harbor Chamber of Commerce, 207-633-2353).

Windjammer Weekend, late August. Parade of sail, fireworks, day sails (contact the Camden Chamber of Commerce, 207-236-4404).

SKATING

Brunswick Parks & Recreation (207-725-6656; on the Mall, Brunswick). December–March. Outdoors. Free.

Camden Snow Bowl Ski Area (207-236-3438; www.camdensnowbowl.com; Hosmer Pond Rd., Camden). Open December–March. Outdoors. Free.

SKIING

DOWNHILL SKIING

There are not many people who come to the coast to go downhill skiing; the state's biggest ski areas are inland near Bethel and Rangeley. But you can be one of the few to escape the crowds and feel the ocean breezes at the *Camden Snow Bowl* (207-236-3438; www.camdensnowbowl.com; Camden). The vertical drop is about 950 feet, the mountain has ten trails and is serviced by a double chairlift and two T-bars. Best of all, lift tickets are inexpensive.

CROSS-COUNTRY SKIING

Cross-country on the coast is another story. There are dozens of summer hiking trails that are converted to cross country ski trails with the first snow-fall. Almost every town along the coast has a park and trails that cross-country skiers take over in the wintertime. We've listed some of the better-known areas, but you can find out more by contacting the local chamber of commerce where you plan to visit.

Wherever you ski, remember that it can be unsafe to ski alone. Stay on the trails, and be prepared for Maine's mercurial weather. Also, don't forget to carry out your trash. Call beforehand for snow and trail conditions.

Camp Tanglewood at Camden Hills State Park (207-789-5868; off Rte. 1, Lincolnville). Ten miles of ungroomed trails, graded for entry level to the most skilled skiers. Ask for a map available at the gate. January through March, dawn to dusk.

Samoset Ski Touring Center (207-594-1431; www.samoset.com; P.O. Box 78, Rockport). 4.5 kilometers of groomed trails split evenly between entry level and more difficult.

TENNIS

For a tennis vacation try these resorts: The *Samoset Resort* (207-594-2511 or 800-341-1650; www.samoset.com; Rockport) has both indoor and outdoor courts, so you can play year round; *Sebasco Estates* (207-389-1161 or 800-225-3819) near Phippsburg boasts two courts with a great view of the ocean; the *Whitehall Inn* (207-236-3391 or 800-789-6565; www.whitehall-inn.com; 52 High St, Camden) is an old-style Yankee resort with tennis courts perched on a hillside above Penobscot Bay.

Below are some public and private courts where play is free or at least available to visitors for a small fee. In addition to those listed, call the local town hall for the location of other free municipal tennis courts. Also several motels and hotels make their courts available to the traveling public for a small fee. **Bath** (207-443-8360; Congress Ave.). Four courts with night lights.

Boothbay Harbor (207-633-2855). Two courts.

Brunswick (207-725-6656; Stanwood St. Courts). Five courts with night lights; bring change. The Pines of Maine (207-729-8433; 120 Harpswell Rd.).Six indoor courts.

Damariscotta (207-563-3477; YMCA). Two indoor courts.

WHALE WATCH

Whales are frequent summer visitors off the coast of Maine. Finbacks, pilots, minkes, rights, and humpbacks cruise the coast along the continental shelf. From early spring through late fall from shore you can see whales from *East Quoddy Head Lighthouse, West Quoddy Head Lighthouse* and *West Quoddy State Park* looking out toward Grand Manan Island. The Gulf of Maine is also home to dolphins, harbor porpoises, seals, osprey, storm petrels, puffins, and other sea birds (see "Birdwatching", above) and fishermen. Charter season runs from the summer into mid-September or October. Reservations are recommended.

The Acadian Whale Watcher (207-288-9794 or 800-247-3794; 52 West St., Bar Harbor).

Whale Watcher Inc. (207-288-3322 or 800-508-1499; www.atlantiswhale.com; 1 West St., Bar Harbor).

WINDJAMMERS

Today the only cargo these sea trains carry are tourists. Life on a windjammer was never the cruise it is today. Work for the crew was never optional; private cabins were unheard of for all but the captain; and there were never gourmet meals served at respectable hours.

At 132 feet and capable of carrying 44 passengers, the *Victory Chimes* is the biggest of the windjammer fleet (no wonder many of those passengers hail from Texas). The *Lewis R. French*, built in 1871, is the oldest. *Angelique*, a steel-hulled ketch launched in 1980, is the youngest member of the fleet. That new ships still are being built and the industry is prospering is testament to the enjoyment windjammers provide. The newest windjammers are built true to old ways, only with a few added comforts. In fact, most of the old fleet has been rebuilt or refurbished to serve the cruise business in the style to which its tourists are accustomed. Some of the old ones are still pushed by yawl boats to open water.

Every year near Rockland, home to much of the fleet, there is an annual *Great Schooner Race* in early July. People with timely reservations take part. There are Windjammer Days in Boothbay Harbor around the end of June, and *WoodenBoat* magazine's annual sail-in during mid-September.

If you aren't lucky enough to visit during one of these events, there are always the cruises. They last from three days in the off-season to six days during the summer. Most windjammer cruises cost between \$325–\$650. On some windjammers you can take a two-hour ride for less than \$20 per person. For more information about the old sailing vessels, you can contact the Maine Windjammer Association, 800-807-9463 or www.midcoast.com/~sailmwa.

American Eagle (Capt. John Foss; 207-594-8007 or 800-648-4544; www.mid-coast.com/~schooner; P.O. Box 482, Rockland 04841).

Angelique (Capts. Mike and Lynne McHenry; 207-785-3020 or 800-282-9989; www.midcoast.com/~sailypc; Box 736, Camden 04843).

Appledore (Capt. Andrew Grainger; 207-633-6598; www.fishermanswharf inn.com; Fisherman's Wharf, Boothbay Harbor 04538). Two and a half hour cruises to the outer islands. June through September.

Appledore (207-236-8353 or 800-233-PIER; Sharp's Wharf, Camden 04843). Four two-hour sails daily, late June through mid September. Three daily, mid-September through mid-October

Grace Bailey (Owners Ray and Ann Williamson; 207-236-2938 or 888-MWC-SAIL; www.midcoast.com/~mwc; E-mail,mwc@midcoast.com; Maine Windjammer Cruises, P.O. Box 617, Camden 04843).

Heritage (Capts. Doug and Linda Lee; 207-594-8007, 800-648-4544, or 800-542-5030; www.midcoast.com/~schooner; P.O. Box 482, Rockland 04841).

Isaac H. Evans (Capt. Ed Glaser; 207-594-8007 or 800-648-4544; www.mid-coast.com/~schooner; P.O. Box 482, Rockland 04841).

J & E Riggin (Capt. John Finger; 207-594-1875 or 800-869-0604; Box 571, Rockland 04841).

Lewis R. French (Capt. Dan and Kathy Pease; 800-469-4635; www.midcoast.com/~windjam; E-mail, windjam@midcoast.com; Box 992, Camden 04843).

Mary Day (Coastal Cruises, Owners Steve Cobb and Barry King; 207-236-2750 or 800-992-2218; www.midcoast.com/~maryday; E-mail, maryday@mid-coast.com; P.O. Box 798, Camden 04843;).

Mercantile (Owners Ray and Ann Williamson; 207-236-2938 or 888-MWC-SAIL; www.midcoast.com/~mwc; E-mail,mwc@midcoast.com; Maine Windjammer Cruises, P.O. Box 617, Camden 04843).

Mistress (Owners Ray and Ann Williamson; 207-236-2938 or 888-MWC-SAIL; www.midcoast.com/~mwc; E-mail,mwc@midcoast.com; Maine Windjammer Cruises, P.O. Box 617, Camden 04843).

Nathaniel Bowditch (Capt. Gib Philbrick; 207-273-4062 or 800-288-4098; www.midcoast.com/~natbow/; E-mail, natbow@midcoast.com; P.O. Box 459, Warren 04864).

North Wind (Capt. John Nugent ; 207-236-2323; P.O. Box 432, Camden 04843).

Roseway (Capt. John Nugent; 207-236-4449 or 800-255-4449; www.midcoast. com~roseway; E-mail, roseway@midcoast.com; Yankee Schooner CruisesX, Box 696, Camden 04843;).

Stephen Taber (Capts. Ken and Ellen Barnes; 207-236-3520 or 800-999-7352; www.midcoast.com/~kbarnes/; E-mail, kebarnes@midcoast.com; Windjammer Wharf, 70 Elm St., Camden 04843). This is the only windjammer to be listed on the National Historic Register.

Summertime Cruises Inc. (Capt. Bill Brown; 800-562-8290; 115 South Main St., Rockland, 04841).

Surprise (207-236-4687; Drawer H, Camden 04843). Owners Jack and Barbara Moore.

Sylvina W. Beal (Capt. Steven F. Pagels; 207-288-4585 summer, 207-546-2927 winter; Downeast Windjammer Cruises, P.O. Box 8, Cherryfield 04622). Sails out of Boothbay Harbor.

Timberwind (Capt. Rick Miles; 800-759-9250; www.schoonertimberwind.com; Box 247, Rockport, ME 04856;).

Victory Chimes (Capt. Kip Files and Paul DeGaeta; 207-594-0755 or 800-745-5651; P.O. Box 1401, Rockland 04841). Three- and six-day cruises on the state's largest windjammer, built in 1900.

Wendameen (Capt. Neal Parker ; 207-594-1751; www.midcoast.com/wendameen; Box 252, Rockland 04841;). Overnight cruises on a 67-foot schooner.

MIDCOAST: SHOPPING

ANTIQUES

In Midcoast Maine, most antique shopping is done between Belfast and Searsport; though you will find lots of great finds in other areas; it just isn't as concentrated an experience.

Anywhere on the coast, to really know who has what and what it's selling for, pick up a copy of the *Maine Antique Digest*, the bible for coastal and inland antique shoppers. It's published in Waldoboro and can be found at most newsstands in the state.

Apex Antiques and Design Service (207-338-1194; 208 High St., Belfast). Eclectic mix of American and formal furniture, painted furniture, and custom-designed quilts.

Restored brick shop fronts on Water Street in Eastport.

Herb Swanson

Avis Howell's Antiques (207-338-3302; corner of Pearl and Court, Belfast). Avis has collected and sold Shaker furniture for more than a quarter of a century.

Captain Pinkham's Emporium (207-548-6465; www.sphynx.com/jonesport-wood; E-mail, captt@mint.net; 34 Main St., Searsport) Old tools, furniture, old books, old paintings. This is just the kind of place you can make a "find."

The Ditty Box (207-882-6618 or 207-563-7510; Rte. 1 at the No. Edgecomb–Newcastle town line). Antiques and collectibles including old samplers, china, Currier & Ives prints, and American country furniture.

F. Barrie Freeman (207-442-8452; Quaker Point Farm, West Bath). Old American maps. They also specialize in printed Americana and ephemera.

The Palabra Shop (207-633-4225; 85 Commercial Street, Boothbay Harbor). Moses bottles, antique dolls, books, primitives, nautical collectibles and American jewelry.

Searsport Antique Mall (207-548-2640; Rte. 1, Searsport). About 20 dealers gather here in the heart of Maine's antique mecca.

Wee Barn Antiques (207-354-6163; $4^1/_2$ Georges St., Thomaston). Gwen Robinson and Lee-Ann Upham have gathered a fun collection of antique "smalls," glass, furniture, jewelry, and silver.

AUCTIONS

Andrews and Andrews (207-338-1386; 71 Cross St., Northport).

A flea market in Searsport. Flea markets, yard sales, and garage sales yield some of the coast's best selections of antiques and other treasures.

Tom Hindman

BOOKSTORES

In addition to the following listing, if you're into old books, you may request a directory of dealers by contacting the Maine Antiquarian Booksellers Association (207-443-1510).

ABCDef (207-236-3903; E-mail, abcbks@midcoast.com; 23 Bayview St., Camden). Used, rare, and out of print books.

Canterbury Tales Books (207-338-1171; 52 Main St., Belfast). Books for all ages, in addition to topographical maps.

The Fertile Mind Bookshop (207-338-2498; 105 Main St., Belfast). New and "recycled" books and a book and cassette rental collection.

Maine Coast Book Shop (207-563-3207; Main St., Damariscotta). Penguin novels and coffee table books, as well as a full selection of paperback and hardcover books.

The Maine Writers Center (207-729-6333; 12 Pleasant St., Brunswick). More than 1,800 works by Maine writers, publishers, and small presses are represented, as well as Maine-related books. This is the home of the Maine Writers Alliance, a non-profit organization that sponsors seminars and workshops.

Owl & Turtle Bookshop (207-236-4769 or 800-876-4769; www.midcoast.com/~owlturtl; E-mail, owlturtl@midcoast.com; 8 Bay View St., Camden). Not only do they encourage browsing, but if you get really absorbed in something, they have a few rooms available upstairs at the guest house. They specialize in children's and nautical books.

Thomaston Books & Prints (207-354-0001 or 800-300-3008; E-mail, thombook@midcoast.com; 105 Main St., Thomaston). Books for kids, adults, and everyone in between, plus limited edition prints and art posters.

CLOTHING

Coyote Moon (207-338-5659; 54 Main St., Belfast; coyote@acadia.net) Natural fiber clothing and funky, New Age-like gifts.

Theo B. Camisole and Company (207-763-4297; 391/2 Main St., Camden). There's nothing like great lingerie, and here is some of the best we've seen. Pretty, lacy things and soft cotton terry robes.

COLLECTIBLES

Duck Trap Decoys (207-789-5363; www.duck-trap.com; E-mail, ducktrap@ midcoast.com; Duck Trap Rd. off Rte. 1, Lincolnville Beach). Hand-carved decoys by Walt Simmons and 32 other carvers. Furry animals, too. Prices range from under $10 to several thousand.

Ducktrap Bay Trading Co. (207-236-9568 or 800-560-9568; E-mail, ducktrap@ tidewater.net; 28 Bayview St., Camden). Decoys, ships' models, carvings, prints, and original art.

Ye Olde Coin Shop and Fine Jewelry (207-338-2663; E-mail, yocslrc@agate.net; 64 Main St., Belfast). A collector's mix including old comic books and collectors' supplies. If there has to be an Ye Olde anything, then, okay, this place.

CRAFT SUPPLIES

Halcyon Yarn (207-442-7909 or 800-341-0282; www.halcyonyarn.com; E-mail, service@halcyonyarn.com; 12 School St., Bath). You can tell how long and cold the winter is by the quality of the local yarn shop. If you knit, spin, or weave or you know someone who does, check this place out.

The Cat's Meow (207-548-2546 or 888-388-MEOW; www.catsmeowdoll-clothes.com; Rte. 1, Searsport). Patchwork quilts. Calicoes and solids. Also quilting supplies and doll clothing.

GIFTS & SOUVENIRS

Enchantments (207-633-4992; 16 McKown St., Boothbay Harbor). Crystals, herbs, incense, and books. Gifts and stuff for the metaphysical crowd.

Granite Hall Store (207-529-5864; Round Pond). An old-fashioned country store in an historic building. Penny candy, antiques, and woolens. Closes after Christmas.

The Leather Bench (207-236-4688; 34 Main St., Camden). Great leather bags, belts, wallets, and clothing. Whenever a movie is filmed anywhere nearby, this is where the crew comes to get those cool leather jackets with their movie's name on it.

Maine Gathering (207-236-9004; hmgall@agate.net; 21 Main St., Camden). Contemporary and traditional crafts by Maine residents with an extensive selection of Maine Native American baskets.

Narragansett Leathers (207-563-5080; Main St., Damariscotta). Leather goods — bags, belts, briefcases — handmade right here.

The Right Stuff (207-236-9595; 38 Main St., Camden). A gift and home store crammed with attractive reproductions, period lighting, and country-style accessories.

The Sheepskin Shop (207-273-3061; Rte. 90, Warren). If it can be made from sheepskin, these folks have it: seatcovers, gloves, footwear, hats, purses, blankets, rugs, and chamois cloth. A good shopping stop on the shortcut past Rockport to Camden.

HOUSEWARES

The Store (207-594-9246; 435 Main St., Rockland). Set in the heart of Rockland's old fashioned Main Street, this is an upscale kitchen store where

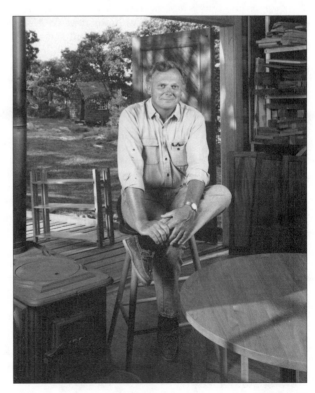

Master cabinetmaker Thomas Moser.

Maine Cabinetmakers

What is it about Maine and cabinetmakers? Ever since Thomas Moser quit his teaching job at Bates College to make his signature Shaker-style tables and chairs, dozens of other fine cabinetmakers have sprung up nearby. Some have worked in Moser's workshops. Here are a few of the cabinetmakers we know about in residence on the coast.

South Coast

Green Design Furniture Co. (207-775-4234 or 800-853-4234; www.greendesigns. com; E-mail, info@greendesigns.com; 267 Commercial St., Portland) Doug Green has designed a line of contemporary cherry furniture that is handsome and innovative, so much so *Time* magazine named him designer of the year.

Thos. Moser (207-774-3791 or 800-862-1973; www.thosmoser.com; 149 Main St., Freeport). The most famous of Maine's cabinetmakers, Moser was instrumental in making Shaker furniture fashionable again.

Midcoast

David and Susan Margonelli (207-633-3326; 780 River Rd., Edgecomb). Fine handmade furniture.

Studio Mnemosyne (207-389-2027; HC 31 Box 323, Popham Beach). Jerry Moser designs and builds modern hardwood furniture with plenty of right angles.

Thomas C. Hinchcliffe — Cabinetmaker (207-326-9411; Rte. 176, Blue Hill). Hinchcliffe uses old woods and 18th-century joinery to make handmade copies of antique chairs, tables, cupboards, and armoires.

William Evans, Cabinetmaker (207-832-4175; 804 Main St., Waldoboro). Reproductions, restorations, and contemporary furniture.

Windsor Chairs (207-789-5188 or 800-789-5188; Rte. 1, Lincolnville). They make chairs. Windsor chairs. Watch them work. They also make other furniture, providing it complements their Windsors.

East of Schoodic

Jim's Smoked Salmon & Fine Woodworking (207-853-4831; 37 Washington St., Eastport) Jim's fly fishing boxes, humidors, and jewelry boxes are almost as good as his smoked seafood. This may sound like an odd combination to you, but here in Maine, it's thoroughly logical. Also, custom-built guitars and island tours.

you can find the perfect corkscrew or whatever other essential you need to make your vacation complete.

Village Store & Children's Shop (207-633-2293; 20 Townsend Ave., Boothbay Harbor). Gifts for the home, made here in Maine and elsewhere.

Well-Tempered Kitchen (207-563-5762; 122 Atlantic Highway; Waldoboro). Okay, we admit it. We have a soft spot for a good kitchen store, because you never know when you're going to find those perfect custard dishes or that sweet little sauce pot.

JEWELRY

A Silver Lining (207-633-4103; 21 Townsend Ave., Boothbay Harbor). Blueberry pendants and other originally designed memories of the Maine coast in metals past cast in sterling, gold, copper, brass, titanium, or gold electroplated.

NAUTICAL EQUIPMENT

Bohndell Sails (207-236-3549; Commercial St., Rockport). They've been making sails since 1870, which is nothing sailors around here don't know.

Hamilton Marine (207-548-6302 or 800-639-2715; East Main St., Searsport). Everything you need for your sailboat or motor boat. Should your radar — or any other nautical doodad — break down in some exotic far off port, call these guys. They ship replacement parts and hardware daily via UPS.

POTTERY

Andersen Studio (207-633-4397 or 800-640-4397; Rte. 96 and Andersen Rd., East Boothbay). Clay rendered and glazed to resemble seals, gulls, and ducks. Also stone-ware vases and bowls.

Edgecomb Potters (207-882-6802; Rte. 27, Edgecomb). Chris and Richard Hilton founded their potter's studio in 1976. Today their staff produce striking and functional pottery for the home, and the Hiltons manage three stores, including one on School St. in Freeport and another on Exchange St. in Portland's Old Port.

OUTDOOR & SPORTING GOODS

Maine Sport (207-236-7120 or 888-236-8797; www.midcoast.com/~mainespt; Rte. 1 Rockport). They sell and rent mountain bikes, sea kayaks, canoes, camping gear, backpacks, and fishing equipment. They also serve as a true factory outlet for Moss tents.

CHAPTER FIVE
Where the Mountains Meet the Sea
DOWNEAST AND ACADIA

Rte. 175 off Rte. 1 just past **Bucksport** takes you down The Blue Hill Peninsula to **Castine**. This former trading post is one of the most attractive towns on the coast, with its tree-lined streets, grand homes, and spectacular views of **Holbrook Island Sanctuary**, **Isleboro**, and **Cape Rosier**, where authors Helen and Scott Nearing built their own Walden. The Maine Maritime Academy is in **Castine** and so is its training

Herb Swanson

Stonington Harbor.

ship, the *State of Maine*, which is open for tours when in port. Rte. 15 to **Stonington** on **Deer Island** at the end of the peninsula is a good hour and a half off Rte. 1 and prefers it that way. The fishing industry is very much alive here. The mail boat leaves here for **Isle au Haut**, Acadia National Park's least-visited outpost, which it shares with a small community of fishermen and farmers.

Blue Hill, named after the nearby blueberry-crested mountain, has abundant views of Mount Desert Island. This is obviously ample inspiration, because it is a thriving center for artists and writers who live here and in nearby villages including **Brooklin** and **Sedgwick**. It is also the sight of the annual Blue Hill Fair, made famous by local writer E. B. White in *Charlotte's Web*. Surry, on pretty Rte. 172, which leads up to Ellsworth, may be the only village of its size with its own opera company.

If only the French explorer Champlain had known what he had discovered when he first set eyes on **Mount Desert Island** and its rounded mountains almost 400 years ago. Today Mount Desert, which includes **Bar Harbor** and most of **Acadia National Park**, is the most visited place in Maine. Visitors come here to walk the famed carriage trails, built in the early part of this century as a kind of social lifeline connecting the homes of summer residents like the Rockefellers and the Pulitzers. They also drive the twenty-mile Park Loop Road along Frenchman's Bay and the road to the top of Cadillac Mountain, where they watch the sun go down from Sunset Point, which has been renamed Blue Hill Overlook by park officials to help reduce overcrowding at dusk. The hike up Cadillac is usually a lovely, lonely climb because so many of the park's visitors prefer to travel by car. **Bar Harbor** a lively, unabashedly tourist town, somehow manages to keep its dignity. Maybe the stately Victorian townhouses lining the streets, many converted to small inns and bed and breakfasts, keep check on the proliferating T-shirt and souvenir stores. Maybe also because the people who get the most out of their visit here only stop mountain climbing, biking, canoeing, and kayaking long enough to grab a bite and a good night's rest. If you like it quieter, there are the civilized charms of tea at the Jordan Pond House in Acadia and the famous Mount Desert gardens bursting in bloom at the height of summer. There also are more secluded island spots like **Northeast Harbor, Hulls Cove, Southwest Harbor** and **Bass Harbor**, and the islands — including **Little Cranberry Island**, the lovely home of the tiny village of **Isleford**. Or do what many Mainers do, and visit in the spring, fall, and winter — when the island is less crowded.

DOWNEAST AND ACADIA: LODGING

LODGING NOTES

Rates: As elsewhere in coastal Maine, rates can vary widely between off season and in season, generally increasing close to Memorial Day and peaking from July through the leaf season in mid- to late October. Special packages are often available for two or more nights stay, and frequently there are even better values during the off season. If breakfast and/or dinner is included with the price of a room, we do not alter the rate category, we just note that the room rate includes one or more meals.

Inexpensive—Up to $65
Moderate—$65 to $125
Expensive—$125 to $180
Very Expensive—$180 and up

These rates exclude Maine state lodging tax or individual hotel service charges that may be added to your bill.

Credit Cards: Several lodging places we recommend in this book do not take plastic. If they do not, they almost always take personal or travelers' checks. Following are credit card abbreviations:

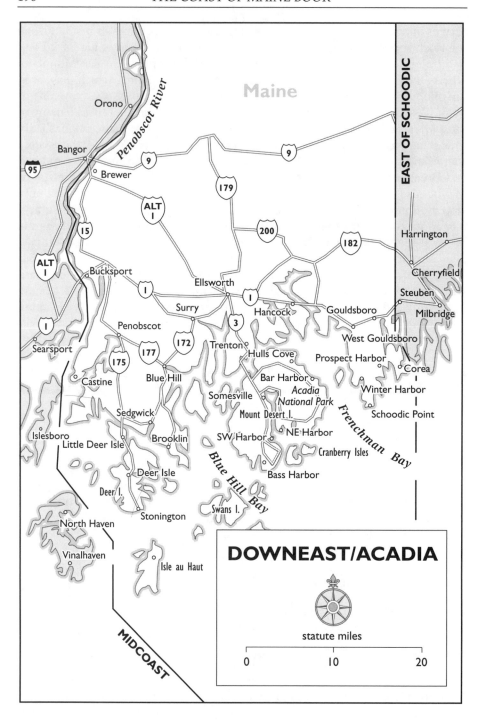

DOWNEAST/ACADIA

statute miles

0   10   20

AE — American Express   DC — Diner's Card
CB — Carte Blanche   MC — MasterCard
D — Discover Card   V — Visa

Minimum Stay: Many inns and B&Bs require a minimum stay of two or more nights during the summer season. We have noted minimum stays when possible, but it's best to check when making room reservations.

Deposit/Cancellation: To reserve a room on the Maine coast, it is generally necessary to make a deposit to cover the first night of your stay — and some places may require up to 50 percent of the cost of the intended stay. Cancellations often must be made at least seven to ten days in advance. Ask about the inn's policy when you make reservations.

Handicap Access: Many of the inns and B&Bs in this book have yet to comply with federal regulations regarding handicap access. We have noted handicap access is available in inns, B&Bs, and hotels where the owners can guarantee at least one room with access.

Other Options: For information on camping, from tents to RVs, see the section entitled "Camping." If you plan to camp with an RV, be sure to make reservations well in advance. If you plan on tent camping, most of the national and state parks and national forests campgrounds are available on a first-come, first-serve basis, although some advance reservations may be made for Acadia National Park during the summer season.

Another alternative for a stay in the Bar Harbor area is the *American Youth Hostel* (Kennebec St., Box 32, Bar Harbor, ME 04609; 207-288-5587). Members may find lodging there during the summer season for a minimum fee. Reservations are suggested. From September to mid-June the hostel moves to 122 Cottage St., Bar Harbor 04609; 207-288-3855.

For alternative listings, you can contact the *Maine Tourism Association* (P.O. Box 2300, Hallowell, ME 04347; 207-623-0363 in Maine; 800-533-9595 out-of-state and Canada; E-mail, metainfo@mainetourism.com). Every year they publish the *Guide to Inns & Bed & Breakfasts,* a list of inns and B&Bs by region. All of the listings are written and paid for by the owners, so you should take their content with a grain of salt. The *Maine Innkeepers Association Food & Lodging Guide,* with advertising from hotels, motels and inns throughout the state, is available at most tourist information centers, or from the association (305 Commercial St., Portland, ME 04101; 207-773-7670; www.maineinns.com; E-mail, info@maineinns.com).

Bar Harbor

BREAKWATER
Owners: Tom and Bonnie Sawyer.
207-288-2313 or 800-238-6309.

Only a few blocks from downtown Bar Harbor, and right on the shore, this English Tudor estate feels miles and eras away. On the National Register, this is the former summer cottage of John

45 Hancock St., Bar
   Harbor 04609.
Open: Mid-April to early
   November.
Price: Expensive to Very
   Expensive.
Credit Cards: AE, MC, V.
Handicap Access: Yes.

Innes Kane, great-grandson of John Jacob Astor. (The Astors still can be seen around town.) This was how the wealthy "rusticators" must have vacationed in Bar Harbor — in the grand style to which they were accustomed. The parlors and game rooms offer the decor and furnishings one would expect at a private, turn-of-the-century hideaway: substantial, overstuffed sofas; broad, open hearth fireplaces; wood paneling; gleaming wood floors, and a grand pool table. The guest rooms are impressive — all of them large enough to spread out in and furnished with antique and reproduction furniture and great beds — sleigh beds, mansion beds, iron valanced canopy beds — every one big and comfortable. All six chambers have their own fireplaces and private baths. Four have ocean views. Abigail's Chamber has views of the courtyard and rose garden. Breakfast is included and is served in the formal dining room. A complimentary tea hour and hors d'oeuvres are provided in the afternoon.

The Inn at Canoe Point on the shore of Frenchman Bay in Hulls Cove is a quiet spot on busy Mount Desert Island.

Inn at Canoe Point

INN AT CANOE POINT
Innkeepers: Tom and
   Nancy Cervelli.
207-288-9511.
www.innatcanoepoint.
   com.
E-mail: canoe.point@
   juno.com.
P.O. Box 216, Bar Harbor
   04609.
Off Rte. 3.
Open: all year.

Closeted away in the garret room of the Inn at Canoe Point on Hull's Cove, one is apt to feel like the heroine of a Brontë novel. Despite its Tudor trappings and the pounding surf below, the five rooms are stylishly modern. Lots of pillows, sleek subdued fabrics, white walls, and beds as comfortable as the one at home. The master suite has a gas fireplace. Down in the parlor, the look is polished as well — dark wood floors, a flickering fireplace, handsome chairs. In summer, a substantial and deli-

Price: Moderate to Very
Expensive.
Credit Cards: D, MC, V.

cious breakfast is served on the porch: homemade blueberry pancakes, quiches, muffins. Later in the afternoon, refreshments are served as well. Set in a wooded area on the edge of a small cove, the inn has a commanding view of Frenchman Bay, and exploring the rocky outcropping is a favored pastime among guests. Though the feeling is remote, Bar Harbor is minutes away. We would love to come stay here with our cross-country skis in the winter. No smoking. No young children.

THE LEDGELAWN INN
Owner: Nancy Cloud.
207-288-4596 or
  800-274-5334.
66 Mount Desert St., Bar
  Harbor 04609.
Open: Mid-May to late Oct.
Price: Moderate to Very
  Expensive.
Credit Cards: AE, D, MC, V.
Handicap Access: Some of
  the rooms in the Carriage
  House.

A short walk from downtown, this large, red-shingled Victorian summer cottage is homier and more inviting than many of the Bar Harbor "cottages" we have visited. But this 1904 mansion seems as if it were built to accommodate company and lavish parties. All the ornately decorated rooms in the inn and the Carriage House next door provide the proper retreat. Most of the beds are queen-sized, several are kings. Some have whirlpool tubs, sauna, fireplaces, and sitting areas. They all have private baths and mostly original furnishings. The sweeping staircase says come on up, and there are bowls of red apples in the common room. There's a pool out back and bar in one corner of the living room (open 4 p.m. to midnight). The inn also offers a breakfast buffet for a nominal fee. No smoking. Pets and children are welcome.

**MIRA MONTE INN &
  SUITES**
Owner: Marian Burns.
207-288-4263 or
  800-553-5109.
www.miramonteinn.com.
E-mail: mburns@acadia.net.
69 Mount Desert St., Bar
  Harbor 04609.
Open: Early May through
  late October.
Price: Moderate to
  Expensive.
Credit card: AE, D, MC, V.
Handicap Access: Yes.

A winner of Maine's innkeeper of the year award, Marian Burns has restored this gracious 1865 mansion to its former glory and filled it to the rafters with antiques. There are thirteen spacious and elegant rooms, all with private baths, air-conditioning, televisions, and telephones. Nine of the rooms have fireplaces. Two additional suites have double whirlpool baths, queen canopy beds, fireplaces, bay windows with window seats, and cooking units. These suites can be rented for the week during the winter. The grounds are beautifully kept, and the library is a good place to relax after a day scouring the island for fun. This is a restful place — and one of our favorite stopping places on the coast. The Mira Monte offers a glimpse of what Bar Harbor must have been like during the grand old days. Full breakfast buffet is included. Smoking allowed on the room balconies only.

Blue Hill

THE BLUE HILL INN
Innkeepers: Mary and Don
  Hartley.
207-374-2844 or
  800-826-7415.
www.bluehillinn.com.
E-mail: mary@bluehillinn.
  com.
P.O. Box 403, Union St.
  (Rte. 177), Blue Hill
  04614.
Open: Mid-May to late
  Nov.
Price:Expensive to Very
  Expensive.
Credit Cards: MC, V.
Handicap Access: Limited.

This place is no newcomer to innkeeping; the lovely old clapboard and brick building framed by stately elms and handsome gardens has been an inn since 1840 (before that it was a private residence). It is, in fact, the oldest continuously operating inn in the state and, like much of the rest of Blue Hill, is listed on the National Register of Historic Places. There are 11 guest rooms, all furnished with period antiques, many with fireplaces. Every one has a private bath; two have ceramic tile floors. The newest suite features a king-sized canopy bed, cathedral ceiling, raised hearth, large bathroom, and full kitchen. You might as well plan to take advantage of the works while staying here. Dinner (see the entry in "Dining") is so good, you will regret it if you don't eat here at least once while you're in town. Breakfast and hors d'oeuvres are included and served year round. There is a rate that does not include dinner.

JOHN PETERS INN
Innkeepers: Rick and
  Barbara Seeger.
207-374-2116.
www.johnpetersinn.com.
E-mail: jpi@downeast.net.
P.O. Box 916, Peters Point,
  Blue Hill 04614.
Open: May to Nov.
Price: Moderate to
  Expensive.
Credit Cards: MC, V.

Just a mile out of Blue Hill village, the John Peters is on a sparsely inhabited peninsula known as Peters Point. The inn, built in 1810, is on the National Historic Register. Over the years, there have been changes to the building's exterior and modern conveniences added, but the original structure possesses a great deal of old time charm. It has eight rooms in the main house and six in the carriage house, many with fireplaces, all with warm, country furnishings. Several of the rooms offer a view of the bay. Some have outside decks; all have private baths. Four have kitchens. Breakfast often includes fresh crabmeat or lobster prepared in various ways, including the Seegers' lobster omelette. For those guests who can tear themselves away from the comfort of the inn, a sailboat and canoe are available. No smoking allowed. Children over 12 welcome.

Castine

CASTINE INN
Innkeepers: Tom and Amy
  Gulow.
207-326-4365.
www.castineinn.com

Bright, airy and welcoming, the Castine Inn is the more relaxed of two inns in Castine, and it offers all a visitor could want by way of lodgings in this pretty seaside town — a fine restaurant, harbor

E-mail: relax@castineinn.
com .
P.O. Box 41, Main St.,
Castine 04421.
Open: Early May through
mid-Dec.
Price: Moderate to
Expensive.
Credit Cards: MC, V.
Handicap Access: Yes.

views from many of the 20 rooms, and a perfect location. Perched half-way up the main street that ascends from the town's bustling port, the inn is a good example of the many late-Victorian structures that grace this historic area. There are plenty of spots where you can relax after a walking tour of the historic town: on the lovely front porch among the flowers and rocking chairs; out back in the gardens; in the sitting room with a wood-burning fireplace; or in the sauna. Contemporary and older seascapes and harbor views hang on every wall. The dining room walls have been painted with a mural of the region that is something of a local tourist attraction. The pub is a good place to have a nightcap and maybe meet a captain from one of the many windjammers that anchor in the bay. Breakfast included; dinner additional. No children under five.

**PENTAGOET BED &
BREAKFAST**
Innkeepers: Lindsey and
Virginia Miller.
207-326-8616 or
800-845-1701.
http://media5.hypernet.
com/~PENTAGO/
pentagoet.htm.
E-mail: pentagoet@
pentagoet.com.
P.O. Box 4, Main St.,
Castine 04421.
Open: May to October.
Price: Moderate.
Credit Cards: MC, V.

The Pentagoet, a lovely three-story Victorian, sits right across the street from the Castine Inn and right down the street from the water. There are 15 rooms in the main building and an older colonial structure. There are turrets, balconies, tea rose prints, and a flower-decked porch with rockers. Pentagoet is Old Breton for "on a hill lined with trees leading to the water," an apt description. A full breakfast is included. Afternoon and high teas, hors d'oeuvres, and drinks are usually available to guests; inquire ahead to confirm.

Deer Isle

PILGRIM'S INN
Innkeepers: Jean and Dud
Hendrick.
207-348-6615.
www.pilgrimsinn.com.
P.O. Box 69.
Deer Isle 04627.
Open: Mid-May to mid-
Oct.
Price: Very Expensive.
Credit Cards: MC, V.

There are 13 wide pine-floored guest rooms in this wonderful 18th-century National Register house about 15 minutes' drive from Stonington. Eight have private baths and all are furnished with antiques and Laura Ashley fabrics. There are two parlors where you can read in front of the fire until hors d'oeurves are served and people gather for dinner. Dinner is served in what once was a goat barn. The Hendricks also rent "Ginny's," a cozy vintage house adjacent to the inn. It has two separate units, each includes a bedroom with queen bed, living room (with a pull-out sofa), cable TV, gas stove, kitchenette, and dining area. Ginny's is great for families who seek privacy but still wish to take part in the activity of the inn. They've also added a gift shop — The Rugosa Rose — filled with local products. The food is country inn fare served by well-trained waiters in white jackets. Breakfast may include homemade granola, cheddar omelets, or pancakes. For dinner, first courses have included risotto with nasturtiums, leeks with fennel, and gazpacho with Maine lobster and fresh chervil. Two recent entrees were grilled Stonington scallops with Balsamic butter sauce and garlic mashed potatoes or sauteed crab cakes with mango cilantro vinaigrette and curried couscous. Breakfast and dinner included. Children ten and up are welcome.

Hancock

LE DOMAINE
Owner: Nicole Purslow.
207-422-3395 or
    800-554-8498.
www.ledomaine.com.
E-mail: nicole@
    ledomaine.com.
HC77 Box 496, Rte. 1,
    Hancock 04640.
Open: Late May to mid-
    Oct.
Price: Very Expensive.
Credit Cards: AE, D, MC,
    V.

As one might guess from the name, Le Domaine is less a New England inn and more an *auberge*. From the small parlor with its wicker and floral settees and tiny bar to the handsome dining room dominated at one end by a huge walk-in fireplace, the inn has the look of a Provençal hideaway. There are seven rooms divided between the main inn and a modern annex. All rooms have private baths and most have small balconies or terraces. The inn rooms are smaller and stylishly done with good Italian reading lamps, small libraries, crisp new linens, lounge chairs, and lovely modern baths. Breakfast is a French-American hybrid — crisp, buttery croissants, homemade granola, yogurt, cream, fresh fruit, and honey from the inn's own hives. The inn's restaurant, with an extensive wine list and excellent cuisine, is we believe the finest in all of Maine, and is included in the "Dining" section. Breakfast and dinner are included in the room rate.

Isle au Haut

THE KEEPER'S HOUSE
Innkeepers: Jeff and Judi
    Burke.
207-367-2261.
www.keepershouse.com.
P.O. Box 26, Lighthouse
    Point, Isle au Haut 04645.
Open: May 15 through Oct.
Price: Expensive to Very
    Expensive.
Credit Cards: None, but
    they accept personal
    and travelers' checks.

Isle au Haut is the best kept secret of Acadia National Park, and the Keeper's House is a wonderful place to enjoy this national treasure. Guests ride the mail boat from Stonington — the innkeepers ask you to either amuse yourself all day on the island shore and trails or take the later boat. The stone cottage used to be the home of the lighthouse keeper before it was converted to an inn in 1986, and today the lighthouse, the "oil house" and the "woodshed" have six guest rooms, three shared baths, and are furnished with antiques and comfortable beds with down comforters for cool island evenings. There is no electricity — which makes the candle-lit Keeper's House romantic and cozy. You eat and relax after dinner in candlelight. There is a kerosene lantern in the common room for reading, but usually there's too much talk among guests to concentrate. The room rate includes tea, an exquisite dinner cooked by Ms. Burke (bring your own wine and don't expect red meat), as well as a hearty breakfast and a bag lunch to take with you as you explore the island the next day. Be sure to make your reservations early. Aside from the park lean-tos, this is the only lodging on the island and fills up quite rapidly. If you're lucky enough to book your stay in late August, look for the wild blueberries and raspberries that grow in abundance on the island. Two-night minimum during July and August.

Northeast Harbor

The Asticou Inn in Northeast Harbor on Mount Desert Island.

Herb Swanson

ASTICOU INN
Manager: Joseph Joy.
207-276-3344 or
  800-258-3373.
www.asticou.com.
E-mail: asticou@acadia.net.
P.O. Box 337, Northeast
  Harbor 04662.
Open: Mid-May to mid-
  Oct. Cottages are open all
  year.
Price: Moderate to Very
  Expensive.
Credit Cards: D, MC, V.
Handicap Access: Yes.

The Asticou Inn is in the low-key, wealthy summer town of Northeast Harbor, and it has all sorts of charms — simple furnishings, courteous bellmen, ties and jackets suggested for dinner, unadorned, locally caught halibut, and Grapenut pudding for dessert. It is a sage and weathered-looking place — with 44 rooms it looks like a overgrown summer cottage that is set in the middle of beautiful, well-groomed lawns, and gorgeous gardens. Guests are welcome to the heated pool and the inn's tennis court. Some rates in the summer include breakfast and dinner, while others offer a B&B style breakfast. No children under six. Smoking is allowed, but discouraged. There's a non-smoking area in the dining room and you may smoke in your room.

THE HARBOURSIDE INN
Owner: The Sweet Family.
207-276-3272.
Northeast Harbor 04662.
Open: Mid-June to mid-September.
Price: Moderate to Very Expensive.
Credit Cards: None; personal and travelers' checks accepted.
Handicap Access: Yes.

According to one guest, this inn has a "monastic quiet" to it. The Sweet family likes it that way. The inn was built in 1888, and retains much old-time character. Rooms are furnished with 19th-century pieces and show distinctive touches such as Wedgewood patterned wallpaper, a Wallace Nutting bed, and Gustave Stickly rugs. Each has a private bathroom; most have working fireplaces; some have king- or queen-size beds; some have kitchenettes. All of the guest rooms have telephones. There are three suites with adjoining rooms to accommodate larger families. A short walk from the village, the woods behind the inn are honeycombed with hiking trails that extend into Acadia National Park. Breakfasts are simple: homemade blueberry muffins and coffee or tea. Many visitors come here for extended stays. No smoking.

Prospect Harbor

OCEANSIDE MEADOWS INN
Innkeepers: Sonja Sundaram and Ben Walter.
207-963-5557.
Box 90, Rte. 195, Corea Rd., Prospect Harbor 04669.
Open: May to Nov.; by reservation the rest of the year.
Price: Moderate.
Credit Cards: AE, DC, MC, V.

Set on the Schoodic Peninsula near the farthest reaches of Acadia National Park, this 19th-century sea captain's home is still one of the best bargains on the coast. Spacious, immaculate and quiet, the inn has undergone many renovations since we first visited. Every one of the rooms now has a private bath, and the owners, Sonja Sundaram and Ben Walter, have restored and updated the building. A separate old stage coach inn at the head of the bay has seven rooms, all with private baths, two rooms for receptions, and a full country kitchen. It's perfect for large families and longer term guests. Family reunions are popular here. The main house sits on a beautiful 200-acre preserve just yards away from a lovely private cove and sand beach. The sound of the surf is a great lullaby. Well-behaved children and amiable dogs are welcome. Breakfast and tea included. No smoking.

Southwest Harbor

CLAREMONT HOTEL
Owners: The McCue Family.
800-244-5036.
P.O. Box 137, Southwest Harbor 04679.

This is a wonderful old place, listed on the National Register, with its great, green lawn, clay tennis court, and pier extending out into the sheltered, yacht-dotted harbor. There are 30 simple rooms in the main building and Phillips House, as

Open: Mid-June–mid-October.
Prices: Moderate to Expensive.
Credit Cards: None; personal checks accepted.
Handicap Access: Limited.

well as 12 cottages. This is a traditional summer hotel where you can expect to hear the sound of slamming wooden screen doors and kids, many of whom probably know each other from previous visits. Downstairs in the main house, hanging next to the life preservers, is an eclectic collection of dinner jackets to borrow. These jackets and the fact there are men willing to wear them bear witness to a certain devil-may-care sense of Yankee propriety that can be experienced on the coast of Maine. Ties are not required. The Claremont is renowned for its croquet tournaments. Smoking outside only.

LINDENWOOD INN
Innkeeper: James King.
207-244-5335 or 800-307-5335.
www.acadia.net/ lindenwood.
E-mail: lindenwoodinn@ acadia.net.
118 Clark Point Rd., Box 1328, Southwest Harbor 04679.
Open: All year.
Price: Inexpensive to Very Expensive.
Credit Cards: D, MC, V.

The Lindenwood has been extensively remodeled, expanded, and now has three very private cottages and a piece of the shore. The main house of the inn, located in one of Mount Desert's small, quiet island communities, was a sea captain's home at the turn of the century. The house is flooded with light, while the 16 rooms all have an off-to-themselves feel. Most have harbor views. All have private baths. Some have balconies. The Lindenwood has a heated pool and hot tub for guests to enjoy, as well as a restaurant with fine dining. Breakfast is included for guests staying in the house. No smoking. No pets. No children under 12 in the inn. Younger children are welcome in suites and cottages.

Sunset

The view from the deck at the Goose Cove Lodge in Deer Isle.

Herb Swanson

GOOSE COVE LODGE

Innkeepers: Joanne and Dom Parisi.
E-Mail: goosecove@ hypernet.com.
www.hypernet.com/ goosecove.html.
207-348-2508 or 800-728-1963.
P.O. Box 40.
Deer Isle, Sunset 04683.
Open: May 15 to late October.
Price: Expensive to very expensive.
Credit Cards: AE, D, MC, V.

On a secluded cove off Penobscot Bay, this is a place for rest, relaxation, and supreme dinners. It's the kind of place that people want to keep a secret. That's what the people who told us about it said. There are nine private cottages, all off by themselves and all with ocean views. Four attached cottages are near the lodge. The lodge and annex have eight suites, all with private bath. All are simply furnished and complement the surrounding beauty. Dinner may include scallop and lobster terrine with bacon citrus vinaigrette, or barbecued rack of lamb with mint tomato chutney and savory corn grits. In addition to the requisite simple pleasures, golf, tennis, massage, and a small fleet of kayaks are close at hand. The innkeepers also have a huge telescope and an extensive knowledge of the night sky.

Swans Island

JEANNIE'S PLACE B&B

Innkeepers: Llewellyn and Jeannie Joyce.
207-526-4116.
Box 125, Swans Island 04685.
(Off Bar Harbor).
Open: All year.
Price: Inexpensive.
Credit Cards: None; personal and travelers' check accepted.

A 45-minute ferry ride from Bass Harbor on Mount Desert Island, this simple gabled home has three guests rooms that share a single bath — all with double beds. Two rooms overlook Burnt Coat Harbor. The look is plain, homey, and clean, and everyone is treated as part of the family. Guests are just as likely to answer the phone when you call to book your room. The Joyces also rent a housekeeping cottage with a kitchen. It's available for weekly visits or for the night. There's a full breakfast for those who want it that includes homemade bread and muffins, cereal, eggs, and bacon. They also serve dinner, "if need be." No smoking. No alcohol. Children welcome.

West Gouldsboro

SUNSET HOUSE BED & BREAKFAST

Owners: Kathy and Carl Johnson.
207-963-7156 or 800-233-7156.
www.sunsethousebnb. com.
E-mail: lodging@sunset housebnb.com.

This family-run bed and breakfast offers ocean views from the front bedrooms and views of a freshwater pond and an old millstream from the rear bedrooms. The six rooms, three with private bath, are small and cozy. There is also a full kitchen on the third floor which can combine with three bedrooms to become a suite. The breakfasts are fortifying: French toast from fresh homebaked bread;

HCR 60 Box 62, Rte. 186,
West Gouldsboro 04607.
Open: Year round.
Price: Moderate to
Expensive.
Credit Cards: AE, D, MC, V.

sourdough waffles; fresh herbed goat cheese omelets. Book your winter stay in advance, and you may be asked to stay for a homestyle dinner cooked by Carl, who is an executive chef during the summer at a big deal restaurant in nearby Bar Harbor. In 1994, Carl was named Maine's Chef of the Year by the American Culinary Federation. No pets are allowed. There is one cat in residence. The Johnson family also keeps goats, and guests are invited to the morning milking. No smoking. Bikers take note: the Sunset House is located near the 27-mile bike trail through the Acadia region.

DOWNEAST AND ACADIA: DINING

When you spend the day out on a sailboat in Penobscot Bay, hiking Cadillac Mountain, or scrambling over the surf-rounded rocks at Schoodic Point, you're bound to work up an appetite. The restaurateurs oblige with everything from authentic French cuisine to American fusion. It's no coincidence that some of the finest restaurants in the state of Maine are found in the towns on and near Mount Desert Island. They cater to a hungry and appreciative audience.

We've noted the restaurants' serving times and seasons as they were when we made the final survey for this guide. As with all things, times, phone numbers, and sometimes addresses are subject to change according to the changing seasons and demands of the economy. Call first. If you can, make reservations. Things can get pretty busy at the great places, especially during July and August. Many restaurants, even white tablecloth ones, don't take reservations, though. So if you're really hungry, plan to arrive early enough to stake a good place in line.

The price range we list is meant to reflect the cost of a single meal, usually dinner, unless the review talks about breakfast or lunch. What we've tried to represent as a typical meal is an appetizer, entree, dessert, and coffee, although several of the places we review are not appetizer places. We do not include the price of alcohol or other drinks in the estimated cost.

Dining Price Code:

Inexpensive—Up to $10
Moderate—$10–20
Expensive—$20–30
Very Expensive—$30 or more

Credit Cards:

AE—American Express	DC—Diner's Club
CB—Carte Blanche	MC—MasterCard
D— Discover Card	V—Visa

After the restaurant listings, we have included a list of food purveyors as well. Some are delicatessens that will sell almost anything to go, others are bakeries or gourmet shops, ethnic food, and beer and wine stores. Visitors will want to note that wine and beer are available broadly, but hard liquor can be more difficult to find. Maine sold its state liquor store franchises, and liquor stores are not plentiful.

Acadia National Park

Tea on the lawn at Jordan Pond House in Acadia National Park.

Herb Swanson

JORDAN POND HOUSE
207-276-3316.
Park Loop Rd., Acadia
  National Park.
Closed: Late Oct.–May.
Price: Moderate.
Cuisine: American.
Serving: L, D, afternoon tea.
Credit Cards: AE, D, MC,
  V.
Reservations:
  Recommended.
Handicap Access: Yes.
Special Features: Tea and
  popovers on the lawn.

Yes, this is a touristy spot smack in the middle of Acadia National Park, but every once in a while tourists know the score. With an outdoor patio and a many-windowed dining room, the restaurant makes the most of its location on Jordan Pond. Tea, a repast of meltingly good popovers and raspberry preserves, is served at long tables on the lawn; lunch and dinner can be had on the patio or indoors. So what if the service can be a bit relaxed? Why would you want to rush off anyway? Look for lobster roll, curried chicken salad, sandwiches, and quiches at lunch; steaks, chicken, and lots of seafood at dinner.

Bar Harbor

GEORGE'S
207-288-4505.
7 Stephans Lane, Bar
  Harbor.
Price: Expensive.
Cuisine: Mediterranean
  with ethnic influences.
Credit Cards: AE, D, MC, V.
Serving: D.
Reservations: Suggested.

Behind the First National Bank and the most touristy section of Bar Harbor is George's, an excellent restaurant as well as an excellent alternative to the honky-tonk of the high season in Bar Harbor. The interior is done in rich, very soothing colors. There are several dining rooms with many windows to look out at the canopy of old trees. It's like sitting on the ground floor of a tree house here. The menu is limited, but excellent, and usually includes something on the following order: cream and smoked mussels; and a muscovy duck breast with rhubarb Zinfandel sauce and Ceylon cinnamon. They also serve game: the night we were there, char-grilled elk loin steak with fresh peach and plum salsa. What ports and sherries are to Redfield's (see Redfield's, located in Northeast Harbor) single-malt scotches and single-barrel bourbons are to George's.

**MAINE STREET
  RESTAURANT**
207-288-3040.
297 Main St., Bar Harbor.
Open: Daily.
Price: Inexpensive to
  Moderate.
Cuisine: Family.
Serving: L, D.
Reservations: No.
Credit Cards: D, MC, V.

The local working folks like this place. Partly because you can get it to go, partly because of the price, partly because it offers a little bit of everything. (Believe it or not, some people in Maine sometimes get a little sick of lobster.) In addition to lobster, you can have your soups, your salads, your burgers, your vegetarian dishes, as well as your usual choice of side orders, all served in a location that has a comfortable feeling recognizable everywhere.

THE OPERA HOUSE
207-288-3509.
27 Cottage St., Bar Harbor.
Open: May through Oct.
Price: Moderate to
  Expensive.
Cuisine: Cajun opera.
Serving: B, L, D.
Credit Cards: AE, D, MC, V.
Handicap Access: Limited.

Where else can you listen to opera and eat Chateaubriand Ponselle? In Maine, anyhow. This is what Mainers call dining for adults. This place is so overdone it's come out the other side. The walls are plastered with opera stars and a couple of Norman Rockwells. Restaurant reviewers as far away as Germany have written this place up. All of them feel pretty much the same: Rococo on the half shell and well worth the visit. The owner is from Louisiana, obviously misses it very much, loves Maine as well, and indulges her passions. Have the creme brulee for dessert.

PORCUPINE GRILL
207-288-3884.
123 Cottage St., Bar Harbor.

Antique oak, chic window swags, and oversized black-and-white photos of the Porcupine Islands give the place a big city look. Start with one

Closed: Sun.–Thurs.;
  Oct–June.
Price: Expensive.
Cuisine: Regional
  American.
Serving: D.
Credit Cards: MC, V.
Reservations:
  Recommended.

of the classy cocktails — fresh fruit daiquiris, sparkling cider, peppered vodka. The wine and beer lists are interesting, too. Food is clever and modern: grilled salmon parfait, (otherwise known as, "The leaning tower of Eastport,") with sushi rice and mango salsa; homemade breads like poppy seed dill and cranberry walnut; offbeat salads like a Caesar with garlic fried clams; pork chops with cornbread stuffing, and homemade applesauce. Desserts, like chocolate fudge pie, are a good ending to it all.

Bass Harbor

KEENAN'S
207-244-3403.
Rte 102A, Bass Harbor.
Closed: Mon.
Price: Inexpensive to
  Moderate.
Cuisine: Seafood.
Serving: D.
Handicap Access: Limited.

D on't come here unless you've hiked or biked Cadillac Mountain or something equally deserving. These two former teachers from Massachusetts offer great deals at cheap prices. The decor is late shack. It's a work in progress that leaves you thinking it'll be a long time coming. All of this, of course, adds to the dining experience. All seafood is cooked to order. You can have it baked, broiled, grilled, deep fried, sauteed, steamed, or blackened. The seafood sampler provides enough stuff to open your own fish market. Red beans and rice are also available.

Blue Hill

THE BLUE HILL INN
207-374-2844 or
  800-826-7415.
Union St., Blue Hill.
Closed: Oct. 31–April; open
  Nov. weekends.
Price: Expensive.
Cuisine: Continental.
Serving: D.
Credit Cards: D, MC, V.
Reservations: Required.
Special Features: No
  smoking; six-course prix-
  fixe dinner.

W ith its many chimneys and six-over-six windows, The Blue Hill Inn has been a beacon in the night for travelers since 1840. One cool fall evening before dinner we sat in the common room enjoying warm brie, a glass of Medoc, and a crackling fire. When time for dinner came, we moved to the romantic dining room, candlelit by sconces and an enormous chandelier. The first course, butternut squash and apple soup, was rich and flavorful, warmed by nutmeg and thickened with creme fraiche. The second was a rainbow trout wrapped around a delectably smooth salmon mousseline, surrounded by a light mushroom sauce. After that they offered us a "breather" with grapefruit ice, a tart lead-in to the two main courses: noisettes of lamb, medium rare and juicy, served with sauteed red peppers and shallots; and lemon-and-bourbon-marinated quail with sides of scallions and summer squash. We especially liked the quail. It had no trace of gaminess and was crisp on the outside. We finished with a dark chocolate gateau and good strong coffee for the road. This is an inn as well, and we wished we had made arrangements to stay.

Dining outside at the Firepond Restaurant in Blue Hill.

Herb Swanson

FIREPOND
207-374-9970.
Main St., Blue Hill.
Closed: Labor Day–Mid-Oct.
Price: Expensive.
Cuisine: Classic gourmet; regional American.
Serving: D.
Credit Cards: AE, D, MC, V.
Reservations: Recommended.
Special Features: Screened porch overlooking creek.

Lady Chatterley would have been fond of Firepond. A rushing stream below and rough-hewn wood beams give it the feel of a romantic lair. But with lighted candles and pale linens this is more elegant than anything Lawrence might have dreamed up. The food encourages amorous visions, as well. Homemade breads and rolls, smoked trout, Chef Reeder's pate du jour, or wild mushroom saute. Entrees have included duckling with a raspberry Chambord sauce and milk-fed veal sauteed in white wine with tomatoes and Kalamata olives. For dessert, look for fresh fruit tarts, homemade ice cream, or flourless chocolate cake.

LEFT BANK BAKERY & CAFE
207-374-2201.
Rte. 172, Blue Hill.
Open daily.
Price: Moderate.
Cuisine: Eclectic homegrown; some vegetarian.

The Left Bank has a counterculture feel not unlike those coffeehouses Bob Dylan and Joan Baez used to hang out in. A fieldstone chimney, pine paneling, and windows facing the garden (much of the food is homegrown) make for a rustic dining room. The help, although perfectly polite and efficient, has that I-was-at-Woodstock look.

The Left Bank Cafe, a good place to hear folk music in Blue Hill.

Herb Swanson

Serving: B, L, D.
Credit Cards: D, MC, V.
Reservations:
  Recommended.
Special Features: Bakery
  takeout; live music after
  8 p.m.

Not surprising then that the pickings are wholesome and homespun. Breakfast is a real eye-opener with more than a dozen options — challah-bread French toast, exotically stuffed omelets, pancakes, granola, oatmeal, homemade whole wheat bagels, muffins, cinnamon puffs, smoked salmon, and "home away from home" fries. For lunch try a build-your-own pizza. Dinners may be a vegetable jambalaya, fettuccine Alfredo, or baked haddock.

Castine

CASTINE INN
207-326-4365.
P.O. Box 41, Main St.,
  Castine 04421.
Open: daily May through
  late Dec.
Price: Expensive.
Cuisine: New England
  regional.
Serving: B, D.
Credit Cards: MC, V.
Reservations:
  Recommended.
Handicap Access: Yes.
Special Features: Porch
  dining in good weather.

The restaurant at the Castine Inn is one of the best in Maine. The fare is New England regional — simple cooking with classic underpinnings, a tendency toward seafood, and a good view of the harbor. Chicken and leek pot pie is a specialty here, as are crabmeat cakes with mustard sauce. The menu varies with the seasons, depending upon the harvest of local farmers and fishermen, and always offers half a dozen appetizers (the salmon ravioli with a tomato saffron sauce is excellent). Entrees include a delicious roasted squab with a morel torte. The dessert list is solid, too: raspberry creme brulee, Aunt Becky's blueberry kuchen, assorted sorbets. Service is friendly and efficient. Smoking is permitted only in the pub, where appetizers such as mussel bisque or oysters on the half shell are served. Weather permitting, seating is available on the porch overlooking the handsome gardens.

DENNETT'S WHARF
207-326-9045.
1 Sea St., Castine.
Open: May–early October.
Price: Moderate.
Cuisine: American.
Serving: L, D.
Credit Cards: D, MC, V.
Handicap Access: Yes.

This place boasts the longest raw bar in New England. That may be one reason it's a favorite stop for cruising sailors, Maine Maritime cadets, tourists, and year-round residents. Dollar bills have been stuck to the high, barn-like ceilings, and the waiter says it costs a buck to find out how. The food is as good as the company and about as refined: seafood lasagna, grilled marinated swordfish steak. It can get particularly racy when sailors stop by during the regatta season. Great homemade desserts and decent coffee.

East Orland

DUFFY'S
207-469-1100.
Rte. 1, East Orland.
Open all year.
Price: Inexpensive.
Cuisine: American.
Serving: B, L, D.
Handicap Access: Yes.

Home-style food, muffins the size of softballs and a clientele that looks like a reunion of Norman Rockwell models. The silverware doesn't match and the chairs wobble. No extra charge for that. The motto on the menu says succinctly: "We here at Duffy's are a native orientated restaurant. We aren't fussy and we're certainly not fancy. If you are, Ellsworth is 12 miles east and Bucksport is 7 miles west."

Gouldsboro

CHARLIE'S LOBSTER HUT
No telephone.
Rte. 186, Prospect Harbor Rd., Gouldsboro.
Open Memorial Day to mid-Oct.
Price: Inexpensive.
Cuisine: Lobster.
Serving: Takeout.

Charlie would be out lobstering again if he had $100,000 for a boat, but he doesn't. So instead he sells lobsters, crabmeat, clams, and chips out of the cabin he was born in out here by the side of the road. You can get the lobsters live, or cooked in the big blackened half-barrel filled with water that contains his "secret solution." Although you might not think so, people from all over the world have stopped by. This is lobster to the right of rough. People say it tastes better here. Charlie says, "I know how I want it, so it suits me, and that's how I do it for everyone else."

Hancock

The crisp, casual atmosphere belies the serious – and excellent – cooking going on at Le Domaine.

Herb Swanson

LE DOMAINE
207-422-3395 or
   800-554-8498.
Rte 1., Hancock.
Closed: Oct. 15–late May.
Price: Expensive.
Cuisine: French.
Serving: D.
Credit Cards: AE, D, MC, V.
Reservations: Suggested.

Here is excellent French country cooking and an encyclopedic wine list (all French with many obscure regional labels) right in the heart of Down East. Everything that comes out of the kitchen is wonderful — dense rich chicken liver pate (now available by mail order as well), garlicky escargots, rabbit with prunes, stuffed Savoy cabbage. Vegetables (baby string beans and carrots) are from the garden, as are the salad greens. Desserts include Chestnut Coupe (a vanilla ice cream and chestnut parfait), bread pudding, mousses, and tarts. Even the dining room has a Provencal feel. A walk-in fireplace at one end dominates and doubles as a rotisserie. Copper pots, wine maps, and red-and-white linens give the place the feel of a bistro, while dark wood and classical music add an elegant touch. We know several well-traveled people who, if offered a last meal, would choose dinner from Le Domaine.

Little Deer Isle

EATON'S LOBSTER POOL
207-348-2383.
Blastow's Cove, Little Deer Isle.

Eaton's sits on one of those incredibly perfect Maine coves with small islands silhouetted against the horizon at dusk. Indoors or out, bibbed families lay waste to some of Maine's finest: steamed clams, lobster, chowder, French fries,

Open: Mother's Day
   through Oct.
Price: Moderate.
Cuisine: Lobster.
Serving: D.

coleslaw, blueberry pie, and coolers of beer (it's BYOB). When we were kids, Eaton's was exactly the same.

Northeast Harbor

REDFIELD'S
207-276-5283.
Main St., Northeast Harbor.
Open: Mon.–Sat.
Price: Moderate to
   Expensive.
Cuisine: Continental.
Serving: D.
Credit Cards: AE, MC, V.
Reservations:
   Recommended.

Redfield's is very *Town & Country*, usually very crowded and caters to the wealthy summer crowd and local residents wise enough to book their tables well in advance. The wine bar includes an impressive offering of sherries and ports. The menu changes nightly and is the sort you could find in many sophisticated cities — shrimp and pork dim sum with black bean garlic sauce to start, grilled chilled filet of beef with horseradish sauce or loin of lamb with rosemary Provençal sauce for entrees.

Otter Creek

THE BURNING TREE
207-288-9331.
Rte. 3, Otter Creek.
Closed: Tues. except in
   August.
Price: Moderate.
Cuisine: American with
   Caribbean accents.
Serving: D.
Credit Cards: MC, V.
Handicap Access: Partial.
Reservations: Suggested

From the outside, The Burning Tree doesn't look like much. Although it is one of the best on the coast, you might be tempted to drive right by on your way to Northeast Harbor. This place is for those in the know — particularly those who know enough to be impressed by the restaurant's wonderful vegetable garden and compost pile in the back. We've heard Brooke Astor and other members of Mount Desert's old-money summer residents come here. Most dishes take advantage of homegrown herbs. The salmon appetizer is house smoked and served with a corn and caper relish.

They do not serve meat. Southwestern and Caribbean flavors and their characteristic colors predominate. Desserts include ginger orange cheesecake and chocolate applesauce cake with Kahlua frosting.

Southwest Harbor

PREBLE GRILLE
207-244-3034.
14 Clark Point Rd.,
   Southwest Harbor.
Closed: Sun., Mon. in the
   off season.

The place to eat in Southwest Harbor, this small, on-the-street spot offers the same famed crab cakes as its sister restaurant, The Fin Back in Bar Harbor. They share the same pink and turquoise color sense. Grilled polenta, baked asiago cheese,

Price: Moderate to
	Expensive.
Cuisine: Mediterranean.
Serving: D.
Handicap Access: No.
Reservations: Suggested.

puttanesca — you get the picture. Also, for entrees, they have grilled pork chops glazed with applejack maple syrup and apple chutney. There is a full bar.

Stonington

**THE FISHERMAN'S
	FRIEND**
207-367-2442.
School St., Stonington.
Open 7 days.
Price: Inexpensive.
Cuisine: Seafood, pie.
Serving: L, D.

There's no other place in the world like Stonington, and the Fisherman's Friend is a good place to take it all in. Besides, the food is great, and the fish is certified fresh. Get there early on Friday for the all-day fish fry, just $6.50. Don't forget to get a slice of pie. It and all the other desserts are homemade.

Winter Harbor

CHASE'S
207-963-7171.
Rte. 186, Winter Harbor.
Open daily.
Price: Moderate.
Cuisine: American; New
	England diner.
Serving: B, L, D.
Credit Cards: AE, CB, D,
	DC, MC, V.
Handicap Access: Yes.

Chase's is Maine's answer to the diner: chowder, burgers, sandwiches, and broiled and fried seafood served in a no-nonsense, no-frills setting. The lights are bright and the chairs worn, but the food is right on the mark and the help on their toes. When was the last time you saw waiters carrying three plates on an arm? Among the better picks: broiled fresh haddock, fried clams, chowder, and specials like a fried flounder basket. Bread pudding or pie for dessert. Afterwards, take a spin out to Schoodic Point and work it all off by climbing along the rocks.

**FISHERMAN'S INN
	RESTAURANT**
207-963-5585.
7 Newman St., Winter
	Harbor.
Open May through early
	Dec.
Price: Inexpensive to
	Moderate.
Cuisine: Seafood.
Serving: D.
Credit Cards: AE, D, MC,
	V.
Handicap Access: Yes.

Lobster served seven ways — from boiled and served whole to lobster pie and lobster rolls — and other local seafood, as well as staples like chopped sirloin with mushrooms and a salad bar with limited but crisp vegetables, lettuce, coleslaw, and potato salad. There are no frills in this modest dining room lined with spartan wooden booths and linoleum-topped tables. And the service could have been friendlier. But that was a little easier to overlook at the meal's sweet finale —hot, gingery Indian pudding and a nicely eggy custard pie.

DOWNEAST AND ACADIA: FOOD PURVEYORS

BAKERIES

Bah's (207-326-9510; Water St. behind the Co-op, Castine). Everybody likes to linger over breakfast at this bakery/deli, and then stay on for lunch. Scones, great-looking bread, sweet rolls, and when we were there, boar's meat chili.

Cottage Street Bakery and Deli (207-288-3010; 59 Cottage St., Bar Harbor). You can have a sit-down meal here or you can grab a sweet to go. We weren't nuts about their muffins, but everything else was pretty good.

The Donut Hole (Main St., Winter Harbor). Homemade donuts, pies, and pastries. Also a good spot to grab a grilled cheese, take in the view of Henry's Cove and maybe run into Tom Selleck.

Left Bank Bakery & Cafe (207-374-2201; Blue Hill). Handmade, homemade bagels, peasant bread, good pies, and European pastries are baked fresh here every day.

BREWERIES AND WINERIES

Atlantic Brewing & the Lompoc Cafe (207-288-9392; 34-36 Rodick St., Bar Harbor). A good place to hang out and savor the local flavors. Brewery tours daily.

Bar Harbor Brewing (207-288-4592; Rte. 3, Otter Creek Rd., the Acadia Park Loop near Thunder Hole). Check out their Bar Harbor Peach, which tastes better than it sounds. Tours weekdays in the summer; less frequently during the rest of the year.

Bartlett Maine Estate Winery (207-546-2408; RR 1, Box 598, Gouldsboro). A tasting here is pretty relaxed. Honey wine, apple wine, and wines of pear, blueberry, raspberry. Robert and Kathe Bartlett have been making their fruit wines since 1983. We especially like their dry pear and apple combination. Tours and tastings available.

Down East Country Wines (207-667-6965; Rte. 3, Bar Harbor). More than 40,000 bottles of fruit wines are produced in this old blacksmith's barn. Semi-sweet or medium dry wild blueberry, spiced apple, and blue blush, a blend of apples and blueberries. Tours are available.

Maine Coast Brewing (207-288-4914; 21A Cottage St., Bar Harbor). Tours by appointment.

CANDY AND ICE CREAM

Ben & Bill's Chocolate Emporium (207-288-3281; 66 Main St., Bar Harbor). This is like walking into a cartoon candy store: truffles the size of handballs; lobster ice cream (blechhhh). It's almost pornographic.

DELIS AND TAKE-OUT

Cottage Street Bakery & Deli Café (207-288-3010; 59 Cottage St. Bar Harbor). There's limited indoor seating. They serve a good box lunch which is not in their flyer and their pizza slices are large enough to feed a small family.

FAST FOOD

Bubba's (207-288-5871; 30 Cottage St., Bar Harbor). Soups, sandwiches, and a full bar, for those who choose to linger. You wouldn't guess by the name that this would be a small art deco palace, would you?

The Deacon Seat (207-244-9229; Clark Point Rd., Southwest Harbor). They serve breakfast and lunch here from 5:00 a.m. to 4:30 p.m. every day except Sunday. Eat it as fast as you want.

Epi Sub & Pizza (207-288-3507; 8 Cottage St., Bar Harbor). Homemade calzones, pizza, pasta, and other quick stuff like crabmeat rolls, quiche, and salads.

Seaside Takeout (Town Pier, Seal Cove on Mount Desert Island). Steve Smith serves a dynamite chowder from this tiny joint. The view's not too shabby, either.

FOOD FESTIVALS

Annual Winter Harbor Lobster Festival (207-963-7638 or 800-231-3008 out-of-state). Mid-August. Almost as famous as Rockland's Lobster Festival. The lobster boat races are a main attraction.

GOURMET FOOD STORES

Penobscot Bay Provisions (207-367-2920; W. Main St., Stonington). Let them get you ready for the boat ride to Isle au Haut. Smoked seafood, cheese, fresh fruit salads, good baked goods.

Periwinkles (207-288-9685; 59 Cottage St., Bar Harbor). Wild Maine blueberry jam, relish, syrup, and jelly. Also local cookbooks and other made-in-Maine specialties.

HEALTH FOOD AND FARM MARKETS

Darthia Farm (207-963-7771; West Bay Rd., Rte 186, Gouldsboro). They offer a selection of organic fruits, vegetables, and herbs, as well as homemade jams, vinegars, pesto, yogurt, herb cheeses, and fresh butter.

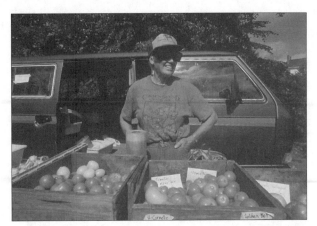

Farmers' market in Blue Hill.

Herb Swanson

Hay's Farm Stand (Rte. 172, Surry Hill, Blue Hill). From July to October, Monday through Saturday, they sell certified organic vegetables, strawberries, raspberries, tomatoes, corn, potatoes, and lamb. They also sell farm sausage, jams, and their homemade Old Goat Soap.

H.O.M.E. (207-469-7961; Rte. 1, Orland). It stands for Homeworkers Organized for More Employment and, in addition to crafts, they sell fresh vegetables in season and storage crops like potatoes and squash. They also have a good selection of locally grown spices, flour in bulk, grains, and dried fruit.

DOWNEAST AND ACADIA: CULTURE

Wealthy summer visitors during the early 20th century would arrive here not just for a day or two's stay. They came for months on end. The artists and musicians followed to decorate the walls of their wealthy patrons' summer homes and play concerts for them and their guests. That — and the breathtaking scenery to serve as inspiration notwithstanding — is why there is such a rich tradition of the arts in this part of the coast. Painters, sculptors, and photographers abound. So do small galleries showing their wares. And almost everywhere in the summer you can hear music.

FILM

Criterion Theatre (207-288-3441; 35 Cottage St., Bar Harbor). Seasonal.

The Grand (207-667-9500; Main St., Ellsworth).

Maine Coast Mall Cinemas (207-667-3251; Maine Coast Mall, Ellsworth).

Reel Pizza Cinerama (207-288-3811; The Village Green, Bar Harbor). Alternative films, pizza, and beer and wine.

GALLERIES

Blue Heron Gallery (207-348-6051; Church St., Deer Isle). A barn full of contemporary crafts including works by faculty members of the nearby Haystack Mountain School with a focus on "functional clay." Open June through September.

Deer Isle Artists Association (second floor, Seamark Bldg., Rte. 15, Deer Isle). Revolving, two-week exhibitions of members' sculptures, paintings, photographs, and drawings. Open June through August.

Leighton Gallery (207-374-5001; Parker Point Rd., Blue Hill). Local critics and those from away rave about this gallery, owned by outdoor sculptor Judith Leighton, which shows her work as well as that of other well-known sculptors and painters. The gallery is happy to be celebrating its 18th year, and opens its season in late May.

Turtle Gallery (207-348-9977; Rte. 15, Deer Isle). Paintings, drawings, prints, sculptures, and contemporary crafts by Maine artists.

GARDENS AND GARDEN TOURS

Azalea Gardens (Rte. 3 and 198, Northeast Harbor, Mount Desert Island). Twenty different varieties of azaleas. They bloom in June. The rest of the year, the garden features native plants and trees and a Japanese sand garden. Open 7 a.m.–9 p.m. daily.

The Black House (Surry Rd., ¹/₂ mi. off Rte. 1, Ellsworth) The formal gardens to the rear of this historic mansion weren't planted until 1903, about 100 years after construction of the house. Following a period of disrepair, the grounds and gardens have been returned to their original state.

Thuya Gardens at Asticou Terraces (Rte. 3, Northeast Harbor on Mount Desert Island). A formal English garden filled with country flowers — zinnias, dahlias, plume poppies, goatsbeards, monkshood. The garden was founded by Joseph Henry Curtis, a Boston landscape architect who summered in Northeast Harbor from 1880 to 1928. 7–7 daily.

The Wild Gardens of Acadia (Rte. 3, Sieur de Monts Spring entrance, Mount Desert Island). Maintained by the Bar Harbor Garden Club, this is an exquisite collection of native plants. Open year round.

HISTORIC BUILDINGS AND SITES

FORT GEORGE AND FORT MADISON
Castine.
Season: Open year round.

Castine played a major role in the military history of the region, trading hands between the colonists and British during the Revolutionary War and after. Much of that military history can be told by these two forts located at opposite ends of the Castine peninsula. The Brits built Fort George in 1779 and only gave it up to the colonists at the close of the war. Excavation has exposed remnants of the old fort making this a great place to scramble over the ramparts.

When the British tried to reassume sovereignty over their former colonies during the War of 1812, this small community was one of their staging grounds. Fort Madison, on the other side of this small town from Fort George, was built in 1811 by the U.S. The British captured it in 1814, renamed it Fort Castine, and held the fort and the town until the close of the war one year later. This town owned park is a good staging ground for a picnic.

THE WILSON MUSEUM
Perkins St., Castine.
Season: Late May–Sept., Tues.–Sun. 2–6.
Admission free.

This is really a series of several historic houses and commercial buildings, including a working blacksmith shop, the *Hearse House* (with 100-year-old summer and winter hearses) and the pre-Revolutionary *John Perkins House* (admission is charged here). The Wilson is home to a collection of prehistoric artifacts from North and South America, Europe, and Africa that stress man's development of tools from the Paleolithic to the Bronze and Iron ages. It also has a collection of ship models, rocks and minerals, and an 1805 kitchen exhibit.

LIBRARIES

Bagaduce Music Lending Library (207-374-5454; www.hypernet.cm/musiclib.html; E-mail, musiclib@hypernet.com; Rte. 172, Greene's Hill, Blue Hill). A music resource with a collection of more than 700,000 items. Open year round: Tues. 10–3; Wed. and Fri. 10–3.

Jesup Memorial Library (207-288-4245; 34 Mount Desert St., Bar Harbor). An interesting collection of historical records of the island's past, including old hotel registers and scrapbooks, some with photos of the island before the 1947 fire. The library is open mid-June through Oct., Mon.–Sat. 1–4 and Wed. 7–9, and by appointment during the winter. Closed holidays.

MUSEUMS

COLLEGE OF THE ATLANTIC NATURAL HISTORY MUSEUM
207-288-5015.
College of the Atlantic, 105 Eden St., just north of Bar Harbor.
Season: Memorial Day–Labor Day, daily 9–5. Labor Day–Columbus Day, daily 10–4.
Admission: $2.50 adults; $1.50 seniors and teens (13–18); $1 children ages 3–12.

In earlier times this lovely granite summer cottage was known as the Turrets. Today it is a museum that offers an environmental perspective on Mount Desert Island. On display are interpretive exhibits about more than 50 species of island animals, plants, and trees. Every day at 11 a.m., there is a free program open to all visitors; and the museum hosts weekly evening lectures on topics regarding the native populations of the island from Native Americans to seabirds and coyotes. Call for a schedule of events.

JACKSON LABORATORY
207-288-3371.
600 Main St., Bar Harbor.
Season: Mid-June–Aug., Call for hours and dates.
No charge.

The Jackson Laboratory was founded in 1929, and since that time has made a name for itself in the world of mammalian genetic research. Currently the laboratory performs research on such varied human maladies as obesity, cancer, AIDS, allergies, diabetes, reproductive disorders, aging, and transplantation rejection. It also raises more than 1,300 genetically unique laboratory mice and sells them to research scientists around the world. They offer a one-hour lecture and multimedia presentation describing the lab's mission and ongoing research every Tuesday and Thursday at 2 p.m.

M.D.I. BIOLOGICAL LABORATORY
207-288-3606.
Old Bar Harbor Rd., Rte. 3 (northwest of Bar Harbor), Salisbury Cove.
Season: July–Aug., Wed. only, 1:30.
No charge.

M.D.I. is a laboratory that conducts research in marine organisms. While most of its work is confined to animals that live in the sea, it has many implications for human health and the environment. Once a week the lab provides the public an opportunity to see what goes on here during a lecture, tour, and video presentation.

MOUNT DESERT ISLAND HISTORICAL SOCIETY
207-244-5043.
Rte. 102, Somesville, Mount Desert Island.
Season: June–Oct., Tues.–Sat. 10–5.
Admission: $1.

Bric-a-brac and other interesting stuff from Mount Desert's past including period clothing, furniture, early household items, sleigh bells, guns from the Revolutionary War days, and old pewter. Tools from the wool, grist, saw, tannery, and barrel stave mills that were operated nearby. Kids will want to see Dr. Nehemiah Kittredge's tooth extractor. It will make them cringe.

MOUNT DESERT OCEANARIUM
207-288-5005.
Two locations: Rte. 3, Thomas Bay, Bar Harbor; Clark Point Rd., Southwest Harbor.
Season: Both mid-May–Oct. 9–5.
Nominal admission.

The two museums are fun stops for any aquatic-minded tourist, particularly the younger ones. The Thomas Bay branch is home to some happy harbor seals, and, at the Maine Lobster Museum, a licensed lobster fisherman will take you aboard a real lobster boat and answer your questions about crustaceans (the organization also offers a guided walk through Thomas Bay Marsh). There is a working lobster hatchery on the grounds where you can see between 5,000 and 10,000 tiny lobsters being raised for future release in the Gulf of Maine.

The Southwest Harbor Oceanarium, located right next to the Coast Guard base, has 20 tanks filled with resident Maine sea life, a touch tank, and an audio-visual exhibit where you can hear whale songs.

ROBERT ABBE MUSEUM OF STONE AGE ANTIQUITIES
207-288-2179.
Rte. 3 near Sieur de Monts Spring, Acadia National Park.
Season: Spring and fall, 10–4; summer, 9–5.
Admission: $2 adults; 50¢ children 12 and under.

This impressive small museum houses a record of Maine's native inhabitants of 11,000 years ago to now. Stone tools, baskets, musical instruments, and ornaments — some as old as 5,000 years — and a canoe made from a single piece of birch bark are among the items that have been brought together from the Frenchman Bay and Mount Desert Island area. During the summer weekends members of the Micmac, Maleseet, Passamaquoddy, and Penobscot tribes demonstrate Native American art such as basket and jewelry making.

STATE OF MAINE
207-326-2255.
Maine Maritime Academy, Castine.
Season: mid-July–late April.
Free.

This is the training ship for students at nearby Maine Maritime Academy. When it is in port, you can go aboard for a free tour and check it out. Call for scheduled times.

WENDELL GILLEY MUSEUM OF BIRD CARVING
207-244-7555.
Herrick Rd. and Main St. (Rte. 102), Southwest Harbor.
Season: Closed at the end of January for the winter. Call for museum hours.
Admission: $3 adults; $1 children; free to members.

Wendell Gilley was a plumber until he decided to turn in the wrench and devote himself to his hobby full time. He carved birds, more than 10,000 of them. Beautiful specimens of airborne nature — wooden eagles, chickadees, ducks, owls, and tiny lyrical songbirds. His birds are in full feather and on view here.

MUSIC

MOUNT DESERT FESTIVAL OF CHAMBER MUSIC
207-276-3988.
Mount Desert Island.
Tuesday concerts from mid-July–Aug.

Since the late '60s the Composers String Quartet, a resident ensemble, has celebrated the works of Haydn, Schumann, Brahms, and Bartók as well as other classical and contemporary composers.

SURRY OPERA COMPANY
207-667-9551.
Surry 04684.
Season: Call for schedule.

Walter Nowick founded this small, amateur opera company in 1984 with high aims — "to promote beautiful music and work toward peace through people-to-people experiences." During the summer of 1991 the group hosted a festival of Russian opera with the Leningrad Amateur Opera Company.

Seasonal Music Events

Annual Bar Harbor Music Festival (212-222-1026; 207-288-5744 after July 1; locations throughout Bar Harbor). This series of classical, jazz, and pops concerts, with an emphasis on young and upcoming talent, celebrated its 30th year in 1996. The Festival has a series of nine or ten concerts, three of which offer a buffet dinner. Admission is $15 adults; $10 seniors and students; $18 dinner and music. Season: Mid-July–mid-August. Call box office for scheduled times and events.

Annual Downeast Jazz Festival (207-594-1837; Rockport). Jazz greats gather every summer for this day of music. A jazz luncheon is offered in the afternoon, with three hours of food and music, while night-time concerts take place separately later in the evening. Admission: $15, afternoon luncheon; $10–$12, evening. Call for more information.

The Arcady Music Festival (207-288-3151; Mount Desert Island High School). Guest artists perform every Mon., Tues., and Thurs. for seven weeks throughout the summer. The season commences in mid-July. Call for locations.

Downeast Dulcimer & Harp Festival (207-288-5653; Agamont Park & Congregational Church, Bar Harbor). Song sharing, workshops, and concerts featuring these traditional American instruments. Early July.

NIGHTLIFE

Left Bank Bakery and Cafe (207-374-2201; Rte. 172, Blue Hill). In addition to serving a great meal (breakfast, lunch, and dinner), these guys serve up good music: Mose Allison, Odetta, Bill Staines, Bill Morrisey, The

Persuasions, Greg Brown, and local Noel Paul Stookey of *Peter, Paul and Mary* fame. Music starts at 8:30 p.m.

SCHOOLS

Haystack Mountain School of Crafts (207-348-2306; P.O. Box 518, Deer Isle 04627). One of the foremost craft schools in the country, Haystack offers two- and three-week sessions for artists and craftspersons working in a variety of media. Evening lectures by faculty and visiting artists are open to the public. Public tours are offered Wednesdays at 1:00 from June to August.

Kneisel Hall School for String and Ensemble Music (207-374-2811; Blue Hill). Summer school for chamber musicians. Kneisel Hall also provides a summer concert festival to the public, featuring student and faculty artists.

Pierre Monteux School for Conductors and Orchestra Players (207-422-3931; Monteux Hall, off Rte. 1, Hancock). Named for the conductor who made his home here, this is where one goes to learn to lead in the musical sense. About 20 gifted musicians take part in this two-week summer program. Six concerts are performed.

At WoodenBoat School in Brooklin, students learn to build traditional wooden craft including canoes, Friendship sloops, and other small boats that have been made in Maine for centuries.

WoodenBoat

WoodenBoat School (207-359-4651; P.O. Box 78, Naskeag Point Rd., Brooklin 04616). Founded by the management at *WoodenBoat* magazine, this is where readers and armchair seafarers come to live out their dreams. The school offers more than 75 courses on topics like navigation, boat building, and sailing for around 700 students every summer.

SEASONAL EVENTS

Relaxing at the Blue Hill Fair, which has been held every year at summer's end for almost a century, and was the inspiration for Charlotte's Web.

Tom Hindman

Blue Hill Fair (207-374-9976; East Blue Hill). This fair was the inspiration for E.B. White's children's classic *Charlotte's Web*. Late August to early September.

THEATER

Acadia Repertory Theater (207-244-7260; Masonic Hall, Rte. 102, Somesville, Mount Desert Island). Modern comedies and dramas every summer for more than 25 years.

Cold Comfort Summer Theater (207-326-4311 or 469-3131; several locations throughout Castine). Comedies, dramas, and other summertime fare. Call for more information.

DOWNEAST AND ACADIA: RECREATION

If ever a landscape were built for fun, this part of the Maine coast is that landscape. Sailing, kayaking, and canoeing among the inlets and islands of

Penobscot, Blue Hill and Frenchman's bays. Hiking, biking, and cross-country skiing on the trails and carriage paths of Acadia National Park. Watching for puffins on Matinicus Island. Just knowing that it's all out there waiting for you can be exhausting.

BEACHES

Sand beach in Acadia National Park is one of the few sand beaches east of Portland.

Courtesy: State of Maine

Lamoine Beach; Lamoine State Park, Rte. 184, Lamoine. Best swimming beach in the area with great views of Mount Desert Island across the bay. Picnicking, camping, no bathhouse, parking, entrance fee.

Sand Beach; off Park Loop Rd., near Cadillac Cliffs, Acadia National Park. Possibly more people have driven by this famed pocket beach than any beach in the country. It's on the Loop Road. There are no facilities. There are so few parking spaces and so many people who want to stop, they sometimes have to close it off during the height of the summer. It's a beauty. The sand is actually shell fragments. Entrance fee to national park.

Acadia National Park

A cadia National Park on Mount Desert Island is the most visited place in Maine. It has more than 100 miles of trails through forests and past lakes; eight climbing peaks, most suitable for family hikes; great biking on old *carriage trails*; camping facilities; wonderful views; good rock climbing, canoeing and cross-country skiing; lovely beaches and the only fjord on the eastern seaboard.

You can wander through the *Wild Gardens of Acadia* and see over 200 species of plants, trees, and shrubs indigenous to the island; climb to the summit of *Cadillac Mountain*, the highest point on the eastern seaboard, and enjoy the grand views, including of Frenchman Bay; swim at freshwater *Echo Lake* or saltwater *Sand Beach*; see the high tide surge at *Thunder Hole*, a tidal cavern carved by wave action with water spouts as high as 40 feet, and sea kayak along the New England coast.

Part of Acadia National Park is on the *Isle au Haut*, a lightly populated island that is eight miles out to sea from Stonington, where there is good hiking, swimming, and fishing.

A third section of Acadia is *Schoodic Point*, at the tip of the Schoodic Peninsula near Winter Harbor, where there are great views of the rocky coastline from hiking trails that ascend to overlooks, and a scenic 13-mile biking loop.

BERRY AND APPLE PICKING

Richard's Orchard (207-667-7287; Oak Point Rd., Trenton). Apples, plums, pears. Call for information.

Silveridge Farm (207-469-2405; McDonald St., Bucksport). Strawberries. Late June to end of season; daily, 8–8, conditions permitting.

BICYCLE DEALERS

Acadia Bike and Canoe and Coastal Kayaking (207-288-9605; www.acadia-fun.com; 48 Cottage St., Bar Harbor).

Bar Harbor Bicycle Shop (207-288-3886; www.barharborbike.com; 141 Cottage St., Bar Harbor).

Southwest Cycle (207-244-5856; Main St., Southwest Harbor).

BIRD WATCHING

Matinicus Rock (Criehaven Township). A mass of granite that rises 60 ft. above sea level is home to the southernmost colony of puffins. It's also favored by many other birds, including the rare razorbill auk.

Stanwood Museum and Birdsacre Sanctuary (207-667-8460; Rte. 3, Ellsworth). A 160-acre sanctuary and museum that is the former home of Cordelia

Stanwood, a famed ornithologist and nature writer. In the museum there are stuffed birds, eggs, and photos any birder will love.

BOATING

CANOEING AND SEA KAYAKING

Coastal Kayaking Tours (207-288-9605, 207-288-8118 or 800-526-8615; E-mail, Acadiafun.com; 48 and 106 Cottage St., Bar Harbor). Canoe and kayak rentals. The store also offers sea kayaking tours for coastal waters.

National Park Canoe Rentals (207-244-5854; www.acadia.net/canoe/index/html; Long Pond, Acadia National Park). There are 30 canoes available, but reservations in July and August are suggested as all canoes are often rented by 9 a.m. Open daily 8:30–5. Paddles, life jackets, and basic instruction provided.

Phoenix Centre (207-374-2113; Rte. 175, Blue Hill). Kayaking only, but they offer special tours like the Fantasy Island escape for two, a romantic weekend led by a guide who sets up camp and prepares fancy meals for you. Their daily guided tours are for a maximum of eight people, and all trips include equipment, gear, instruction, and transportation to the launch site.

Reversing Falls

Maine with its dramatic tides has several good reversing falls, favorite proving grounds for kayakers and canoeists. What makes reversing falls interesting is the water speed and direction change as the tide changes. The rapids run inland as high tide approaches, and they run out to sea as the tide ebbs. Here are some favored by small boaters in Maine:

Bagaduce Falls (Brooksville). It's easy to park and find these reversing falls between Snow Cove and the Bagaduce estuary.

Blue Hill Falls (under Rte. 175 bridge, Blue Hill Falls). The best time to negotiate these rapids, which are only about 100 yds. long, is about 3 hours before high tide. The coast near here also offers some good exploring for people in small boats. Parking is limited, and access to the falls is hampered by traffic. Be careful walking to and from the water.

Damariscotta Reversing Falls (Damariscotta/Newcastle; Rte. 1 bridge or Rtes. 129 and 130 bridges). Two locations to practice your whitewater canoe and kayak skills.

Goose Falls (Brooksville). Reversing falls at outlet of Goose Pond.

Sullivan Falls (Sullivan). Great scenery at these reversing falls between Taunton Bay and Sullivan Harbor.

CHARTERS AND RENTALS

Black Jack Charters (207-276-5043; Northeast Harbor).

Chance Along Sailing Center (207-338-6003; Belfast). Sailboats from Sunfish to day sailers. Half-day, full-day, and week rentals.

Hinckley Yacht Charters (207-244-5008 or 800-HYC-SAIL; www.acadia.net/hyc; E-mail, hyc@acadia.net; South West Harbor). Bareboat sailboat charters to qualified sailors. Thirty boats available from 32 to 50 feet. Reservations suggested.

During the summer on Mount Desert Island narrated nature cruises introduce visitors to the wonders of Maine's birdlife, geography, and seals.

Diana Lynn Doherty

Machias Bay Boat Tours (207-259-3338; Machiasport). Half-day trips around Machias Bay afford views of salmon aquaculture pens on Cross Island, sheep on Chance Island, a lighthouse, and many harbor seals. Visits to Native American petroglyphs. Lobster traps also are hauled onto this 34-foot lobster boat during the tour. Sea kayaking and basic instruction offered as well.

Mansell Boat Rental (207-244-5625; www.downeast.net/com/mansell/mansell.html(boats); E-mail, mansell@downeast.net; Main St., Southwest Harbor). Day sailors and canoes and power boats for the day. Sailing lessons.

SAILING LESSONS

WoodenBoat School (207-359-4651;E-mail, Bernice@woodenboat.com; Brooklin). One- and two-weeklong instructional programs, part of the boat-building school and run by *WoodenBoat* magazine. June–late Sept.

BOWLING

Bucksport Bowling Center (207-469-7902; Rte. 46, Bucksport). 12 candlepin lanes.

Eastward Bowling Lanes (207-667-9228; Eastwood Plaza, Ellsworth). 12 candlepin lanes.

CAMPING

Acadia National Park. There are two campsites in the national park. The larger of the two, **Blackwoods**, is located off Rte. 3, five mi. south of Bar Harbor; www.nps.gov. Call Mistix 800-365-2267 for reservations. Call well in advance. **Seawall**, the other camp, is on Rte. 102A, four mi. south of Southwest Harbor. Sites are first come first serve. Both have attractive, wooded sites, and most amenities during the season (electrical hookups excluded; showers and a camp store are within $1/2$ mi.). Blackwoods is open all year. Seawall is open between Memorial Day and the end of September. Campsites are easier to come by during the off season.

Lamoine State Park (207-667-4778; off Rte. 1 on Rte. 184, Lamoine). This is one of the best-kept secrets for campers visiting Acadia during the high season. While sites in the national park are crammed, there are usually available waterside spots in this pretty little campground with 61 sites, as well as great views of Cadillac Mountain and Mount Desert Island. There's a lovely pebble beach nearby, too.

CLAMMING

How to clam. Get a bucket, a pitchfork or a clamming rake, which looks like a gardener's claw with a long handle — that kind of thing — then go down to the beach, preferably at low tide, when your clam is at its most vulnerable. Stomp on the beach. If you see a stream of water squirt up, start digging. Warning: before you begin, look around for signs warning not to dig because of red tide. Clams and mussels drink in this rust-colored algae and collect it in a concentrated form. Cooking the clam or mussel won't help. If you eat some you can develop paralysis.

CROQUET

Croquet. The game that makes mergers and acquisitions look like sandbox play. If you don't believe it, go watch the annual *Claremont Croquet Classic*, played during early August on the lawns of the Claremont Hotel (207-244-5036; Southwest Harbor). You're invited.

CROSS-COUNTRY SKIING

*There are more than 40 miles
of well-marked cross-country
ski trails in Acadia National
Park on Mount Desert
Island.*

Roy Zalesky

Acadia National Park (207-288-3338; www.nps.gov/acad; Mount Desert Island). Forty miles of well-marked carriage roads and trails. A trail map can be had from park headquarters on Rte. 233. Wilderness facility.

Holbrook Island Sanctuary State Park (207-326-4012; Cape Rosier, Brooksville). Seven miles along wood roads and hiking trails through upland forests and fields offering views of Penobscot Bay.

FAMILY FUN

Odyssey Park (207-667-5841; Bar Harbor Rd., Trenton). Bumper boats, go-carts, mini go-carts. 10 a.m.– 9 p.m.

Pirate's Cove Adventure Golf (207-288-2133; Rte. 3 near Hulls Cove, Mount Desert Island). 36 holes of miniature golf. 9 a.m.– 11 p.m.

GOLF

Bar Harbor Golf Course (207-667-7505; Rtes. 3 & 204, Trenton). 18 holes, 6,667 yds., par 71. Cart and club rental, pro shop, clubhouse, lessons.

Castine Golf Club (207-326-8844; Battle Ave., Castine). 9 holes, 2,977 yds., par 35. Cart and club rentals, pro shop, lessons.

Causeway Club (207-244-3780; Fernald Point Rd., Southwest Harbor). 9 holes, 2,302 yds., par 32. Cart and club rentals, pro shop, lessons.

Grindstone Neck Golf Course (207-963-7760; Grindstone Ave., Winter Harbor). 9 holes, 3,100 yds., par 36. Cart and club rentals, pro shop, lessons.

Island Country Club (207-348-2379; Rte. 15A, Sunset). 9 holes, 3,865 yards, par 31. Pull cart and club rental, pro shop, clubhouse, lessons, clay tennis courts.

Kebo Valley Club (207-288-3000; Eagle Lake Rd., Bar Harbor). 18 holes, 6,131 yds., par 70. Cart and club rental, pro shop, clubhouse, lessons.

Northeast Harbor Golf Club (207-276-5335; Sargent Drive, Northeast Harbor). 18 holes, 5,430 yds., par 69. Cart and club rentals, pro shop, lessons.

White Birches Golf Course (207-667-3621; www.wbirches.com; Rte 1., Ellsworth). 9 holes, 2,800 yds., par 34. Cart and club rental, pro shop, snack bar.

HANG GLIDING

Island Soaring (207-667-7627; Hancock County-Bar Harbor Airport, Trenton). Soar over Mount Desert Island and Acadia National Park. Avoid the crowds and the entrance fee to the Loop.

HEALTH CLUBS

Fitness East Health and Racquet Club (207-667-3341; Rte. 1, Trenton). Pool, tennis, aerobics, racquetball, weights, sauna, whirlpool, lifecycles, rowing machines, Nautilus, and stairmasters.

YMCA (207-288-3511; 21 Park St., Bar Harbor). Aerobics, weights, fitness machines, Nautilus, pool, rowing machines, Nordic track, toning classes, and indoor running track.

HIKING AND WALKING

Blue Hill, Blue Hill. A one-mile climb up a Jeep trail. The path leads through open areas and woods. Look for blueberries. (500 feet.)

A hiker takes in the view.

Herb Swanson

Hiking in Acadia National Park

There are eight climbing peaks in Acadia National Park on Mount Desert Island. All of them are relatively easy. The tallest and most often climbed is Cadillac, probably because most people choose to climb Cadillac in their cars. On foot, it's less crowded, and many of the best sites come before or after you make it to the top. Below we list favorite hikes in the park. You can get trail information at the park entrance.

Cadillac Mountain, Mount Desert Island. This is a gradual climb that belies the fact that it is the highest peak on the coast. From the park loop road it is about 3.5 miles with a 1,200 foot elevation gain. Make it a round trip, and you have an excellent day's hike.

Dorr Mountain, Mount Desert Island. Stone steps lead directly up this mountain passing through woods. There are some great views of Frenchman Bay and Cadillac Mountain from its ledges. Base to summit, this is a 1.5 mile walk with a 1,200 foot elevation gain.

Flying Mountain, Southeast Harbor. Short, brisk climb through pleasant woods to a plateau and outlook, with great views of Somes Sound and Cadillac. (Possible loop, descending via Valley Cove; slippery in spring.) Fernald Cove to overlook, $1/2$ mile; elevation gain 200 feet. (Loop, 1.25 miles.)

Gorham Mountain, Mount Desert Island. This is a great hike for amateur geologists. Combined with a side trip to Cadillac Cliffs, you will walk among overhangs, arches, and caves. From the summit, you can see many of the park highlights, including the Beehive, Sand Beach, Great Head, Otter Cliffs, and The Bowl. If you want to continue on, a trail leads along the ridge to Champlain Mountain. This is a one-mile hike to the summit, with a 500 foot elevation gain.

Pemetic Mountain, Mount Desert Island. This is one of the best hikes on the coast and perhaps the very best on the island. It lets you warm up on a nice, easy stretch, then gets tougher as the trail gets steeper. It passes through what some call a "storybook forest" to great views of Mount Desert's hills and the nearby islands and ocean. The climb begins at Bubble Pond and continues for one mile with an elevation gain of 1,000 feet. You can make this walk into a 3.75-mile loop by following the trail down to Jordan Pond, then the carriage trail back to Bubble Pond.

Penobscot and Sargent Mountains, Mount Desert Island. A wonderfully varied walk with excellent views of Cadillac and the island panorama. This begins tough with a somewhat difficult ascent up Jordan Cliffs, but the rest is relatively easy. After the cliffs, follow the trail from the summit of Penobscot about 1.5 miles past a pretty lake to Sargent, the island's second highest mountain. The climb is about 1,200 feet from Jordan Pond to the top of Sargent.

Schoodic Mountain, Winter Harbor. An easy climb that offers a short backward-looking view of Frenchman Bay and the more populated section of Acadia. It's a winding road to the top of this rocky headland (400 feet).

NATURE PRESERVES

Crockett Cove Woods, Stonington. A 100-acre preserve managed by the Nature Conservancy, this is a good example of an eastern coastal rain forest. It is a great place to visit on a foggy summer day. Self-guided nature trail.

Indian Point-Blagden Preserve, Mount Desert Island. One of the few forested portions of Mount Desert Island that survived the disastrous 1947 fire, this 110-acre preserve is managed by the Nature Conservancy. Pick up a map and guide from the caretaker and explore the intertwined trails leading through spruce, fir, and cedar forests, and along the water. Seals like to sun on nearby islands.

Ship Harbor Nature Trail, Rte. 102A, Mount Desert Island. Thirteen stations describe the geology, flora, and fauna of the island along a 1.4-mile trail. This is a good, self-guided trail for the family. The trail is named for the famous 1739 shipwreck of the Grand Design from Ireland.

The Wild Gardens of Acadia (Rte. 3, Sieur de Monts Spring entrance, Mount Desert Island). Maintained by the Bar Harbor Garden Club, this is an exquisite collection of plants native to Mount Desert Island.

TENNIS

Bar Harbor (207-288-5801; Atlantic Oaks, Rte. 3). Four courts. Night lights.

Trenton (Fitness East Health and Racket Club, 207-667-3341; Rte. 3). One outdoor court.

WHALE WATCH

The Acadian Whale Watcher (207-288-9794 or 800-247-3794; 52 West St., Bar Harbor).

Whale Watcher Inc. (207-288-3322 or 800-508-1499; www.atlantiswhale.com; 1 West St., Bar Harbor).

WINDJAMMERS

Sylvina W. Beal (207-288-4585 summer, 207-546-2927 winter; Downeast Windjammer Cruises, Capt. Steven F. Pagels, P.O. Box 8, Cherryfield 04622).

Whale Watching Inc. (207-288-3322 or 800-508-1499; 1 West St., Bar Harbor 04609). Twenty-one trips a day from whale watching to windjamming.

Young America (207-288-4585 summer, 207-546-2927 winter; Downeast Windjammer Cruises, Capt. Steven F. Pagels, P.O. Box 8, Cherryfield 04622). Sails from Bar Harbor Inn Pier, Bar Harbor.

DOWNEAST AND ACADIA: SHOPPING

ANTIQUES

Dawson's Auctioneers and Appraisers (207-526-4600; www.dawsonsauction.com; E-mail, dawson1@idt.net; Swans Island).

Mayo & Mayo Auctioneers (207-667-2586; Rte. 3, Trenton).

BOOKSTORES

Blue Hill Books (207-374-5632; 2 Pleasant St., Blue Hill). A healthy selection of books about Maine and New England. Books for children. Fiction for adults.

BookStacks (207-469-8982, 888-295-0123; 333 Main St., Bucksport). Over 10,000 book titles, 1,000 magazine titles, books on tape, out of state newspapers, maps and charts. Swiss chocolate and postcards, too.

The Compass Rose (207-326-9366 or 800-698-9366; Main St., Castine). Books and antique prints.

Port in a Storm Bookstore (207-244-4114; Main St., Somesville). This is a wonderful local bookstore, and a great place to spend an afternoon getting your bearings in a vacation town. Check their schedule — they often have local authors in for talks and signings. They also have a very entertaining biennial newsletter, a good music selection, and two amiable bookstore cats.

Sherman's Book Store (207-288-3161; 56 Main St., Bar Harbor). Books, gifts and souvenirs. Also hiking and road maps of Acadia National Park.

Maine Outlets

Maine's outlet trail runs from Kittery to Freeport and on to Ellsworth near Bar Harbor, and you can pick up the trail almost immediately after you cross the state line. Now, the news tells us, the tiny midcoast town of Rockland wants to become the next big outlet town. We'll tell you more about that in our next edition as shopping there develops. Meanwhile, here are a few tips for shopping the Maine outlets.

1. Try to avoid shopping on rainy days. Visitors to the coast like to be outside whenever they can, and whenever they can't — that usually means when it's raining — they like to shop.

2. Outlets have sales. Even outlets have sales, and many times those coincide with sale seasons in regular retail stores (July 4, late summer, and early fall are particularly popular sale times here because of the summer tourist traffic).

3. Not all outlet bargains are real bargains. Many times, there's a reason, good or otherwise, these items did not sell elsewhere.

Ellsworth, the youngest outlet community on the coast, has the smallest selection of stores, but if you're an outdoors person, you'll want to check out the L.L. Bean

---

Factory Store. Unlike their off-price store in Freeport, you occasionally can find significant markdowns on store samples of their sporting equipment — mountain bikes, steppers, tents, stoves, and the like. If you find something you like, grab it. It's usually the only one in stock.

In Kittery, most of the outlets are for products you can purchase at many other outlet havens throughout the country. Anne Klein, Brooks Brothers, Corning/Revere, Timberland, Puma, Capezio, Villeroy & Boch, Crate & Barrel, Dansk, Black & Decker, and more.

It's much more of the same in Freeport in the Casco Bay region, except there you have L.L. Bean. You'll also find an outlet for high-end Maine shoe manufacturer Cole-Haan (The Company Store), Calvin Klein, Reebok, The Gap (upstairs there are some great bargains), Banana Republic, J. Crew, Patagonia, and G. H. Bass (based just south of here in Falmouth). My quality-minded father-in-law especially likes to shop the Ralph Lauren store during their late summer sale. There he finds great bargains on his favorite polo shirts.

Elsewhere on the coast, travelers will find hundreds of true factory stores and outlets, where the goods are made right there — or not far away. Here are some of our favorites:

Big Al's Odd Lot Outlet (207-882-6423; Rte. 1 Wiscasset) Big Al's is a Maine coast tradition that gets bigger every year. From funky gadgets, ugly sunglasses to some just plain weird and tacky stuff, you can find everything and nothing here. Still it's fun to wander the aisles.

The Company Store (207-865-6321; 66 Main Street, Freeport). An upscale "outlet" for Cole-Haan, the high-end shoe manufacturer that has its offices in nearby Yarmouth. Downstairs they stock beautiful shoes. Upstairs it's clothing from around the world.

Cuddledown Factory Store (207-865-1713 or 888-235-3696; 231 Rte. 1 So. Freeport). Lush down comforters, comforter covers, sheets, and other linens sewn at a factory in nearby Portland. Buy them here and save 30 to 70 percent. Or ask to receive their catalog.

Maine State Prison Showroom Outlet (207-354-2535; Rte. 1, Thomaston). Everyone needs an outlet. Handcrafted furniture and gift items usually with a nautical theme. Here you can find patio furniture, lamps, ship's wheel mirrors, hutches, hand carved novelties, desks, and cedar chests. All are at reasonable prices.

The Moss Tent Outlet (at Maine Sport, 207-236-7120 or 888-236-8797; Rte. 1, Rockport). Moss Tents are considered by many experts to be the finest. Firsts, seconds, and discontinued models are sold at up to 30 percent off retail.

Portmanteau (207-774-7276; 191 Middle St., Portland). Elegant tapestry and leather clothing, bags, luggage, and accessories made on the premises.

Tom's of Maine Natural Living Store (207-985-3874; 106 Lafayette Center, Kennebunk). Since we've moved here, we've gotten hooked on their natural toothpaste (no saccharine), so we venture south every once in a while to stock up on toothpaste in slightly battered tubes, shaving cream, shampoo, and other natural personal care items and bathroom staples. Tom Chapell, the founder, graduated from Harvard Divinity School and is looking for new ways to fill the spiritual void in corporate America, as well as prevent tooth decay naturally.

CLOTHING

Darthia Farm (207-963-7771 or 800-285-6234); Rte. 186, West Bay Rd., 1.7 miles off Rte. 1, Gouldsboro). Ikat dyed and handwoven clothing and accessories by Cindy Thayer, as well as hand spun yarns and hand knit items by other local craftspersons. In season you can purchase organic produce raised by Ms. Thayer and her husband on the saltwater farm.

The Grasshopper Shop (207-667-5816; 124 Main St., Ellsworth). Unusual, interesting, and comfortable women's clothing. They also have a shop in Camden.

Water Witch (207-326-4884; Main St., Castine). Jean de Raat sells amazing selection of hats, dresses, sundresses, and other summer weekend clothes made by local tailors and seamstresses from textiles she's gathered on travels around the world. Her sundresses may seem a bit pricey, but they are the kind you'll wear again and again. Want to buy a house in this pretty little town? Ms. de Raat is also the local realtor.

COLLECTIBLES

Belcher's Country Store (207-348-9938; Reach Rd., Deer Isle). They are big on Christmas here, all year round. Antique and collectible tinware, hooked rugs, hand blown glass, ceramics. Recently the owners opened a baby Belcher's on Water St. in Blue Hill.

Dakin's Quality Crafted Miniatures (207-548-6500; 21 Prospect St., Searsport). Wooden Breyer horses, horse show stalls, and accessories.

Downeast Decoys (207-469-2158; Rte. 1, Orland). Antique and old decoys, as well as new ones carved by Bill Conroy. He will appraise yours, if you ask.

Nancy Neale Typecraft (207-244-5192; Steamboat Wharf Rd. off Rte 102, Bernard). Irving Silverman and Nancy Neale began collecting antique wood type in 1969. Today they have the largest selection in the country in a shop near Bass Harbor on Mount Desert Island. In addition, Ms. Neal creates what she calls "framed assemblages" — type collages — for anniversaries, birthdays, and other events. Open by chance or appointment.

GIFTS & SOUVENIRS

Dollhouse Treasures (207-469-7832 or 800-743-7832; Acadia Hwy., East Orland). This store sells miniatures, dollhouses, and toy replicas. Everything's here for the doll lover, including building materials to make your own dollhouse. Know the building code in your own state.

Glass Workbench (800-564-2788; Rte. 1, Lincolnville Beach). Original stained glass designs for windows and gifts.

H.O.M.E. Craft Shop (207-469-7961; Rte. 1, Bucksport). A craft lover's dream, this sprawling store is a cooperative for more than 400 Maine craftspersons — H.O.M.E. stands for "Homeworkers Organized for More Employment." For sale are quilts, toys, jewelry, weaving, pottery, and other handcrafted items, as well as homemade, home-canned goods.

Island Artisans (207-288-4214; 99 Main St., Bar Harbor). Beautiful things, both practical and decorative, made by Mt. Desert Island craftspeople.

U. S. Bells (207-963-7184; Rte. 186, Prospect Harbor). Sculptor Richard Fisher began crafting bells more than 20 years ago. Now his bronze and brass bells are sold around the world. They're in all shapes, all sizes, and for all purposes — including wind chimes for letting you know it's windy and doorbells for letting you know someone is at the door. He also sells beautiful handmade quilts in a "factory outlet" that sits next to the bell foundry.

HOME FURNISHINGS

Harbor Farm (207-348-7737 or 800-342-8003; Rte. 15 just over the causeway, Little Deer Isle). We can't believe this place has been around for more than 10 years, and we hadn't found it until recently. They have almost all the things we like to accumulate from wrought-iron lamps, European and Maine made pottery, to very cool paving stones (imported from England) for our garden.

North Country Textiles (207-374-2715; Main St., Blue Hill). Home textiles and clothing. The cloth is the thing here.

Rooster Brother (207-667-8675 or 800-866-0054; 18 W. Main St., next to Union River Bridge, Ellsworth). Cooking equipment and tableware, plus gourmet foods and wine.

Scottish Lion Blacksmith (207-529-5523; Rte. 32, Round Pond). Blacksmith Andrew Leck's hand-forged iron home accessories include pot racks and fireplace tools.

Sleepy Hollow Rag Rugs (207-789-5987; Rte. 173, Lincolnville Beach). Hand-loomed rag rugs woven on antique looms and sold right in the studio.

Weatherend Estate Furniture (207-596-6483 or 800-456-6483; 6 Gordon Drive, Rockland). Reproductions of lawn furniture first crafted using yacht joinery techniques and considered by many to surpass the originals in style, construction techniques, and durability.

POTTERY

A Potter's Choice (Main St., just past Cottage St., Bar Harbor) A potter opened this shop more than a decade ago to show and sell work she liked by potters she knew. Over the years the collection has grown to include an impressive selection of ceramics, clothing, and jewelry by artists in Maine and through-out New England.

Gull Rock Pottery (207-422-3990; 325 Eastside Rd., Hancock). Tori and Kurt Wray create wheel-thrown pottery decorated with birds, fish, and scenes from nature.

Rackliffe Pottery (207-374-2297 or 888-631-3321; Rte. 172, Ellsworth Road, Blue Hill). Younger than Rowantrees, but just as famous.

Rowantrees Pottery (207-374-5535; Union St., Blue Hill). They've been in business a long time — 50 years. Their glazes, made from locally found minerals, are famous.

OUTDOOR AND SPORTING GOODS

Cadillac Mountain Sports (207-667-7819; 34 High St., Ellsworth and 207-288-4532; 26 Cottage St., Bar Harbor). If you can do it outdoors on the island, you can find the gear and clothing to do it here. They have one of the best selections of sports footwear in the area, including more than 100 types of hiking boots. They have the stuff you need for rock and ice climbing and cross-country and telemark skiing. Open seven days a week throughout the year, and until 11 p.m. during the summer.

L.L. Bean Factory Store (207-667-7753; Rte. 1, Ellsworth). Brighter and more airy than their Freeport bargain basement, this store often has one-of-a-kind bargains on tents, bicycles, canoes, and sleeping bags, as well as outdoor clothing.

Only in Maine

During the Civil War one Maine paper manufacturer ran out of cotton rags from which to make his paper. As legend goes, he began importing the cotton wrapping from Egyptian mummies to use in his factory. Today, Maine entrepreneurs are equally as resourceful when making their livings, if not as ghoulish. Here are two of the area's most unusual producers of one-of-a-kind products.

Bar Harbor Weathervanes (207-667-3868 or 800-255-5025; Rte. 3, Trenton). For centuries weathervanes in the shape of boats and animals have been used by sailors and farmers to tell which way the wind blew. This store serves that tradition with hand wrought copper, brass, or cast aluminum weathervanes by Phil Alley. You can buy a whole cupola.

Joseph Gray Flagpoles (207-359-4448, Reach Rd., Sargentville). Handhewn flagpoles measuring 20' to 40'. Mr. Gray prefers to make his poles from Maine cedar because the wood is naturally water repellent. He'll deliver free of charge within 30 miles.

CHAPTER SIX

Blueberry Barrens and the First Sunrise

EAST OF SCHOODIC

Just east of Mount Desert is the Schoodic Peninsula, the tip of which is part of Acadia National Park, a smaller, wilder version of the main portion of the park. The rest of the peninsula is characterized by an anything-goes feeling. Lobstermen rub elbows with the sons of captains of industry and movie stars. Army personnel venture about, caring for a secretive military installation on the point. Year-round residents

Herb Swanson

A painter enjoying the solitude at Schoodic Point.

like to tell the story of one neighbor who bought a whole fleet of little wooden sailboats and every year rounded up family and acquaintances to compete in friendly regattas.

For the majority of coastal Maine visitors, the world ends at Bar Harbor. Washington County, which extends up to the Canadian border, is thought to be dirt poor, flat, and endless. It's not. In fact, it has a beauty all its own, stark as a blueberry barren, religious, pure. Some people love it the best. It's a great place to explore, scramble over the rocks of the rocky coast, search for rare bald eagles and puffins, or just get away from the hubbub of points south.

Everything up here is out in the open, exposed to the elements, and here they seem more, well, elemental. Like **Jonesport.** It's terrifyingly close to the sea. In the hilly fishing village, weather-beaten clapboard and shingled houses huddle together as if to draw comfort from one another. There's also **Dennysville,** tucked into the countryside on the Dennys River where stately Georgian homes rise up from the rolling landscape and make this look more like the manor-strewn countryside of England than Down East.

Machias, which is Indian for "bad little falls," is the most businesslike of

Machias today is an historical center of the coast. The first naval battle of the American Revolution was fought near here.

towns. It's a get-em-in-get-em-out place where waitresses wait on busloads of people headed out of town almost as quickly as they drive in, no questions asked. Settled by the English in 1633, this was a favorite repair and refueling spot for pirates in the late 17th century. For those American history students who thought the Revolution was a unanimous undertaking by all colonists, think again. Prosperous lumbermen, who understood quite well that England was their best customer, argued for a long while about whether or not to support the revolt. They did, and a few months later nearby **Machiasport** was the site of the first naval battle of the Revolutionary War. Stalwart Mainers, you'll be glad to know, won the skirmish, captured the British armed schooner the *Margaretta* and inspired leaders in Philadelphia to establish a navy.

Lubec sits on a narrow strip of land that juts into Cobscook Bay and is a quiet town with tree-lined streets and wonderful views of the bay. Just down the road is West Quoddy Head, the easternmost point of land in the United States and site of a beautiful state park and a lighthouse that is enshrouded by fog 59 days of the year. Lubec is also the only auto route (via bridge) to Campobello Island, the summer home of President Franklin D. Roosevelt. To get there, you have to go through customs — Campobello is within Canadian territory — although the presidential landmark is operated jointly by the U.S. and Canadian governments. The island is also a birdwatcher's haven, part of the famous Quoddy Loop that extends through northeastern Maine and southeastern Nova Scotia.

Eastport has been described as a city of dreamers, and there are ample examples of the city's saga of boom-and-bust. During the early 1800s, when trade between the United States and England was embargoed, Eastport gloried as a smuggler's port. It was certainly far enough Down East to escape diligent enforcers.

Fishing was, and remains today, the city's main industry. Cod, pollock, haddock, halibut, and herring once flourished in the cold offshore waters, but dur-

NEW BRUNSWICK
CANADA

DOWNEAST/ACADIA

Maine

1

9

214

Penbroke

191

Dennysville

1

Eastport

Campobello
Island

86

9

192

Whiting

Lubec

West Quoddy Head

193

1

UNITED STATES

CANADA

182

Harrington

Columbia Falls

1

Machias

Jonesboro

Machiasport

Bucks Harbor

Cutler

Roque Bluffs

Cherryfield

Steuben

Jonesport

Milbridge

Beals Island

West Gouldsboro

Prospect Harbor

Corea

Winter Harbor

Schoodic Point

Frenchman Bay

EAST OF SCHOODIC

statute miles

0   10   20

ing the past 25 years have dwindled. During the late 1800s to mid-1900s, sardines were big business, and canneries lined the waterfront (sardines are actually small herrings). During the '80s, the bay's sweeping tides and deep coastal waters were discovered to be ideal for farming salmon in offshore pens. Now, every year the town celebrates the domesticated Atlantic salmon with a festival in early September. To the outsider this hillside town, with a startlingly minimal number of gift shops and art galleries, has almost a Wild West feel and is a great place to make home base when exploring the beautiful country that surrounds it.

EAST OF SCHOODIC: LODGING

LODGING NOTES

Rates: Rates can vary widely off season and in season. As mentioned in other chapters, they generally increase close to Memorial Day and are highest from July through the leaf season in mid- to late October. Special packages are often available for two or more nights stay, and frequently there are even better values during the off season. If breakfast and/or dinner is included with the price of a room, we do not alter the rate category, we just note that the room rate includes one or more meals.

> Inexpensive—Up to $65
> Moderate—$65 to $125
> Expensive—$125 to $180
> Very Expensive—$180 and up

These rates exclude Maine state lodging tax or individual hotel service charges that may be added to your bill.

Credit Cards: Several lodging places we recommend in this book do not take plastic. If they do not, they almost always take personal or travelers' checks. Following are credit card abbreviations:

> AE — American Express   DC — Diner's Card
> CB — Carte Blanche   MC — MasterCard
> D — Discover Card   V — Visa

Minimum Stay: Many inns and B&Bs require a minimum stay of two or more nights during the summer season. We have noted minimum stays when possible, but it's best to check when making room reservations.

Deposit/Cancellation: To reserve a room on the Maine coast, it is generally necessary to make a deposit to cover the first night of your stay — and some places may require up to 50 percent of the cost of the intended stay. Cancellations often must be made at least seven to 10 days in advance. Ask about the inn's policy when you make reservations.

Handicap Access: Many of the inns and B&Bs in this book have yet to comply with federal regulations regarding handicap access. We have noted handicap access is available in inns, B&Bs, and hotels where the owners can guarantee at least one room with access.

Other Options: For information on camping, from tents to RVs, see the section entitled "Camping." If you plan to camp with an RV, be sure to make reservations well in advance. If you plan on tent camping, most of the national and state parks and national forests campgrounds are available on a first-come, first-serve basis.

For alternative listings, you can contact the *Maine Tourism Association* (P.O. Box 2300, Hallowell, ME 04347; 207-623-0363 in Maine; 800-533-9595 out-of-state and Canada; E-mail, metainfo@mainetourism.com). Every year they publish the *Guide to Inns & Bed & Breakfasts,* a list of inns and B&Bs by region. All of the listings are written and paid for by the owners, so you should take their content with a grain of salt. The *Maine Innkeepers Association Food & Lodging Guide,* with advertising from hotels, motels, and inns throughout the state, is available at most tourist information centers, or from the association (305 Commercial St., Portland, ME 04101; 207-773-7670; www.maineinns.com; E-mail, info@maineinns.com).

Dennysville

The Lincoln House in Dennysville.

Herb Swanson

LINCOLN HOUSE COUNTRY INN
Innkeepers: Mary Carol and Jerry Haggerty.

The lemon-yellow Georgian-style inn lords over the surrounding rural landscape from a dramatic hillside perch above the Dennys River. Mary Carol and Jerry Haggerty, a professional carpenter

207-726-3953 or
  888-726-3953.
R.R.1, Box 136A, Rte. 86
  and Rte. 1, Dennysville
  04628.
Open: Late May to October.
Price: Inexpensive to
  Moderate.
Credit Cards: MC, V.

and antique restorer (who worked for the Smithsonian), bought the 200-year-old home during the mid-1970s, and have fashioned it into an immaculate and handsome showcase for antique lovers and history buffs. Many of the original features of the National Register home are still intact. The inn has six rooms, two with private baths. Guests may roam the adjoining 100 wooded acres. A stay at the inn includes a full breakfast.

East Machias

**RIVERSIDE INN &
RESTAURANT**
Owners: Carol and Tom
  Paul.
207-255-4134.
P.O. Box 373, Rte. 1, East
  Machias 04630.
Open: All year.
Price: Inexpensive to
  Moderate.
Credit Cards: AE, MC, V.

Dinner at this tiny inn has become so popular, the Pauls have added two dining rooms to accommodate guests six days a week. The inn itself is a pretty 1820 cape-style sea captain's home overlooking the East Machias River. There are three guest rooms, each with private bath. Two are in the main house, while the third is in a neighboring carriage house. The owners have also added a suite with its own kitchen and living room also in the carriage house. The main house rooms are small but elegantly appointed with antique furniture and old linens collected over the years by the Pauls who used to own an antiques store in Newport, Rhode Island. The prix-fixe dinner here, friends tell us, is one of the best and tastiest bargains way Down East (BYOB). Breakfast included, dinner by reservation, is additional.

Eastport

TODD HOUSE
Owner: Ruth McInnis.
207-853-2328.
1 Capen Ave., Todd's
  Head, Eastport 04631.
Open: Year round.
Price: Inexpensive to
  Moderate.
Credit Cards: MC, V.
Handicap Access: Yes.

After a career in Portland teaching and collecting antiques, Ruth McInnis returned home to Eastport where she bought and restored this classic Cape farmhouse, now on the National Register of Historic Places. It was built during the Revolutionary War on the shore of Passamaquoddy Bay. The owner, a storehouse of local history, gladly will take you on a tour and has opened up her library of Maine, Revolutionary, and Civil War history books. The six rooms vary greatly in feel: one has a working fireplace; several are packed with carefully chosen antiques and brimming with historical significance; two are strictly modern with queen-sized beds, cable TV, private modern baths, and kitchenettes. A simple, but ample, breakfast is served in the common room: cranberry muffins, fancy breads, cereal, and some very welcome fresh fruit. Children and pets are welcome. No smoking.

WESTON HOUSE
Owners: Jett and John Peterson.
207-853-2907 or 800-853-2907.
26 Boynton St., Eastport 04631.
Open: All year.
Price: Inexpensive to Moderate.
Credit Cards: None.

The Weston House is a civilized place. The formal parlor, with comfortable sofas and wing chairs, odd lamps, and a dish of pistachios on the coffee table, is the perfect place to curl up with a book as the afternoon wanes. There's also a cheerful back room for watching TV. Breakfast, served in the handsome dining room, is a gourmet affair: pancakes with fruit syrup, fresh baked breads, and whatever else Jett Peterson — a prodigious cook — fancies (Mrs. Peterson will also pack box lunches and make dinner on request). Five comfortable guest rooms are furnished with handsome antiques, floral fabrics, and oriental rugs; some have fireplaces and four-poster beds as well.

Jonesport

RASPBERRY SHORE BED & BREAKFAST
Innkeeper: Geri Taylor.
207-497-2463.
Rte. 187, P.O. Box 409, Jonesport 04649.
Open: April to October.
Price: Moderate
Credit Cards: AE, D, MC, V.

Out of the way in the out of the way fishing village of Jonesport, this small Victorian home offers access to a working way of life which not many people get to see anymore. Watch boats come and go from the deck overlooking the harbor and Moose-a-bec Reach. The gardens here are lovingly tended, the rooms filled with antiques and beautifully appointed. Breakfast may include homemade raspberry jam and dinners local crab cakes with lemon sauce, roasted cornish game, and lobster so fresh, they practically walk over to your plate. Packed picnic baskets are a specialty to be enjoyed on side trips.

Lubec

PEACOCK HOUSE BED & BREAKFAST INN
Owners: Chet and Veda Childs.
207-733-2403.
www.nemaine.com/ peacock_house.
27 Summer St., Lubec 04652.
Open: May through October.

This modest white clapboard house sits on a quiet corner near the far end of Lubec's main street. Step over the threshold and you find yourself at a crossroads where Texas meets New England. The bed and breakfast is named for five generations of the Peacock family who once lived there. It was converted to a lodging house by two Southerners — Chet and Veda Childs who serve up expansive breakfasts of homemade Texas-size muffins, blueberry crepes, or "rum-runners" French toast. Five

Price: Inexpensive to
   Moderate.
Credit Cards: D, MC, V.
Handicap Access: Yes.

small to large rooms, all with private baths, are decorated with a mix of comfortable modern and reproduction furniture. The smallest, the Captain's Cabin, is a cozy single named for Capt. William Trott, who built the house for his bride in 1860. The largest — the Margaret Chase Smith — is named after the Maine senator who was a friend and frequent guest of the previous owners. This room has cable TV. No pets. Children over seven welcome. No smoking.

EAST OF SCHOODIC: DINING

Here is a select list of the region's restaurants, some legends, a few new finds, places we found out about by badgering reluctant residents and neighbors, places we liked and places we didn't but were out-voted, plus places written up and sent in by friends, all experienced or professional eaters. It's a list long enough to get you up or down the coast and back next summer.

We've noted the restaurants' serving times and seasons as they were when we made the final survey for this guide. As with all things, times, phone numbers, and sometimes addresses are subject to change according to the changing seasons and demands of the economy. Call first. If you can, make reservations. Things can get pretty busy at the great places, especially during July and August. Many restaurants, even white tablecloth ones, don't take reservations, though. So if you're really hungry, plan to arrive early enough to stake a good place in line.

The price range we list is meant to reflect the cost of a single meal, usually dinner, unless the review talks about breakfast or lunch. What we've tried to represent as a typical meal is an appetizer, entree, dessert, and coffee, although several of the places we review are not appetizer places. We do not include the price of alcohol or other drinks in the estimated cost.

Dining Price Code:

> Inexpensive—Up to $10
> Moderate—$10–20
> Expensive—$20–30
> Very Expensive—$30 or more

Credit Cards:

> AE—American Express   DC—Diner's Club
> CB—Carte Blanche   MC—MasterCard
> D—Discover Card   V—Visa

Columbia

PERRY'S SEAFOOD
207-483-2045.
Rte. 1, Columbia.
Open all year except two
  weeks at Christmas.
Price: Moderate.
Cuisine: American
  roadhouse.
Serving: B, L, D.
Credit cards: All.
Handicap access: In the
  rear.
Smoking & non-smoking
  rooms.

Perry's Seafood is a straightforward eatery on the east side of Rte. 1, where vacationers re-order the fried onion rings and scallop stew they remember from last year and business people hold their lunch meetings because there's something on the menu for everyone. It's fast, friendly, fresh, generous, and clean. Puddings and pies, even the fillings, are made from scratch by the owner. No false notes here except for the butter. It's not real, but the whipped cream is, and they're probably open to persuasion on the butter.

Eastport

THE BAYWATCH CAFE
207-853-6030.
75 Water St., Eastport.
Open all year.
Price: Inexpensive to
  moderate.
Credit Cards: D, MC, V.

The fact they place Raye's Mustard, some of the best in the world and made right here in Eastport, on their tables means we can forgive them the mozzarella sticks and fried mushrooms and the word, "fixins." Mostly this is all simple, inexpensive, locally grown food which should be consumed on the outside deck overlooking the harbor and out onto Passamaquoddy Bay. Try the Maine chocolate raspberry cake or Nancy's strawberry shortcake for dessert.

LA SARDINA LOCA
207-853-2739.
28 Water St. Eastport.
Open all year.
Price: Inexpensive.
Credit Cards: MC, V.
Handicap Access: Partial.

There are not a whole lot of restaurants in this small border town. But that didn't stop the Maggiani's from deciding Eastport was missing a good Mexican restaurant anyway. Touted as the "Easternmost Mexican restaurant and bar in the U.S.A.," this brightly colored, friendly, successful establishment has been providing tasty tacos, enchiladas, burritos, and "especials" to the locals for years. If you're uncomfortable being easternmost, they also have an extensive "to go" menu.

WACO DINER
207-853-4046.
Bank Sq., Eastport.
Open every day.
Serving: B, L, D.
Price: Inexpensive.

It's tempting to mispronounce the name of this place, but just try it and a dozen people will correct you. Wack-o is the right way to say it, and the name is suitable for this quirky little spot. Lunch counter standards – clam chowder, corned beef hash, grilled frankfurters, fish and chips, and all

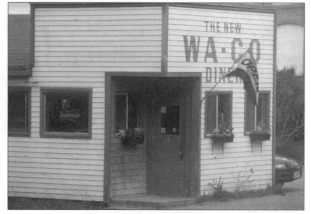

The Waco Diner, a local hangout in Eastport.

Herb Swanson

Cuisine: American diner.
Handicap Access: Limited.

sorts of pies – make up the bulk of the menu, but there are some surprises: scallop stew, tuna noodle casserole, fried clam rolls, homemade English muffin toast, and Grapenut pudding. Best of all, the place looks as if it's been around for eons, with worn vinyl stools, old-timey booths, and counters all crammed in a space the size of a postage stamp. Service may be a little surly, but that only adds to the charm.

Jonesport

SEAFARER'S WIFE
207-497-2365.
120 Main St., Jonesport.
Open all year.
Price: Inexpensive to
  Moderate.
Serving: L, D.
Credit Cards: MC, V.

Two restaurants in one, there's the Seafarer's side and the Old Salt side. The latter is favored by the locals and those who want a quick veal parmesan sandwich or, of course, fish. The Seafarer's Wife requires reservations only for its higher end fare. Baked stuffed lobster tails, scallops in cream sauce, and, simply, chicken with stuffing. Here it's BYOB. We had a bottle in the car, so it worked. If you're curious about the other, there's only a door separating the two restaurants. Whichever you choose, all the fish is fresh from the shores of Great Wass and has no opinion about either restaurant, one way or another.

Machias

HELEN'S RESTAURANT
207-255-8423.
Rte. 1, Machias.
Open all year.

As the tour buses in the parking lot suggest, Helen's, famous coast to coast, is very good at hooking hungry travelers and putting up with any

Price: Moderate.
Cuisine: American.
Serving: B, L, D.
Credit Cards: AE, D, MC, V.
Handicap Access: Yes.

odd request you throw at them. For them it's faster to do it than think about it. All fried foods are cooked in cholesterol-free oil, which means you can then go ahead and get your dose from one of their fine cream pies. The strawberry pie is famous. We had a rib-sticking pork sandwich with home-made mashed potatoes and gravy because Helen's makes you feel that way. That feeling stuck all the way to Eastport. There's good parking.

Machiasport

MICMAC FARM
207-255-3008.
Off Rte. 92, which is off Rte. 1, Machiasport.
Closed: Sun. and Mon.
Price: Expensive.
Cuisine: Country gourmet.
Serving: D.
Credit Cards: MC, V.
Handicap Access: Yes.
Reservations: Required.

This 18th-century farmhouse may be out of the way (that is to say, at the end of a rutted dirt road), but it's worth seeking out for the sheer romance of the place. Flickering candles give a refined glow to the rustic rooms with wide floor-boards and low beams. There are usually five din-ner choices; the night we were there they included filet mignon with Bordelaise sauce; shrimp-or-crab stuffed sole; lobster Graziella cream, and wine and tomato sauce. Desserts are inspired creations on the order of their light-as-air Bavarian cream and meringue glace. Machiasport is dry, so if you want wine or beer with dinner, you'll have to bring your own.

EAST OF SCHOODIC: FOOD PURVEYORS

BAKERIES

The Sugar Scoop (207-546-7048; Main St., Milbridge). Pies, cookies, squares, and a heavenly bakery smell.

CANDY AND ICE CREAM

K-K-K-Katie's (207-454-8446; Rte. 1, Mill Cove, Robbinston). They hand dip all of their homemade chocolates and use recipes from well-loved Passama-quoddy Bay candymakers of old. Check out their Maine potato candy. It's an experience you won't soon forget.

FAST FOOD

The Crossroads (207-726-5053; Rte. 1, Pembroke). Located at the site of an old iron works, this little carry-out attached to a roadside motel serves the best lobster roll around.

GOURMET FOOD STORES

J. W. Raye & Co. (207-853-4451; Rte. 190, Eastport). They've been making mustard here since 1903, first for the sardine canning industry that used to flourish here, now for the mass market. Visit their gift shop or get a tour and learn how they make the stuff at the Mustard Museum

Herb Swanson

Salmon pens on Cobscook Bay near Eastport. Aquaculture is a thriving industry downeast, and many restaurants feature locally raised salmon.

Jim's Smoked Salmon (207-853-4831; 37 Washington St., Eastport). Jim smokes Atlantic salmon raised on farms in Cobscook Bay. He will also wrap your salmon gift in a beautifully crafted wood box that he builds himself. Also, smoked mussels and rainbow and steelhead trout.

Maine Wild Blueberry Company (207-255-8364; Elm St., Machias). These people have the biggest wild blueberry business in the world. You can buy frozen, canned, and dried blueberries right from the factory. They call the dried ones "wild chews." They taste like very sweet blueberries and have the consistency of raisins.

HEALTH FOOD AND FARM MARKETS

Cross Road Farm Stand (Off Rte. 187, Jonesport). Organic isn't a fad here. They've been farming that way for more than 20 years and are certified.

More than 200 types of vegetables, 50 kinds of potatoes, unusual salad greens, squashes, and onions.

EAST OF SCHOODIC: CULTURE

FILM

The Milbridge Theatre (207-546-2038; Main St., Milbridge).

GALLERIES

Eastport Gallery and the Center (207-853-4166 or 207-853-4133; 69 Water St., Eastport). Sculpture, painting, and other media by almost two dozen regional artists. The Arts Center has a series of concerts as well as a theater company. Open June through October.

HISTORIC BUILDINGS & SITES

BURNHAM TAVERN
207-255-4432.
Main St., Machias.
Season:Summer, Mon.–Fri.
9–5; winter by
appointment.
Admission: $2 adults; 25¢
kids.

Revolutionary War afficionados will appreciate the importance of this 1770 gambrel-roofed tavern, the oldest building in the U.S. east of the Penobscot River. This was where local leaders met and planned the first naval battle of the war, in which Machias patriots aboard the schooner *Unity* captured the British schooner *Margaretta*. The building also served as a hospital during the war and a meeting place for local Masons.

RUGGLES HOUSE
207-483-4637.
Just off Main St. (Rte. 1),
Columbia Falls.
Season: June–mid-Oct.,
weekdays 9:30–4:30; Sun.
11–4:30.

Judge Thomas Ruggles did it all; he was a lumber dealer, a store owner, the local postmaster, captain of the local militia, and a judge of the Court of Sessions. His house, designed by Massachusetts architect Aaron Sherman and built in 1818, befits a man of his many talents and high standing in society. The "flying" staircase is a marvel. So is the hand-carved woodwork, which took an English woodworker three years to complete.

LIGHTHOUSES

The light at West Quoddy Head, the easternmost lighthouse in the United States.

Herb Swanson

The boldly striped light at **West Quoddy Head** in Lubec sits at the easternmost point in the U.S. It was built in 1807 and was featured on a 1990 U.S. Postal Service stamp commemorating the 100th anniversary of the Coast Guard.

MUSEUMS

WAPONAHKI MUSEUM AND RESOURCE CENTER
207-853-4001.
Pleasant Point Indian Reservation, Perry.
Season: Mon.–Fri., 9–11, 1–3.
Donations.

The Passamaquoddy Indians were among the tribes that once inhabited Maine shores during the summer. After Europeans settled the coast, their numbers diminished. In 1822 there were 379 Passamaquoddy. Today there are more than 2,000. This museum offers a glimpse of their rich culture through the implements they fashioned from nature — graceful birch bark canoes, handsome ash baskets, snowshoes, clothing, and arrowheads.

Also on exhibit are photographs that document life on the reservation in the past and present. The museum is a repository for a growing collection of books, tapes, dictionaries, and reference books, all of which serve to preserve the Passamaquoddy language. Classes in the tribe's new written language are taught here.

Near the Coast

**ROOSEVELT
    CAMPOBELLO PARK**
Campobello Island, New
    Brunswick.
Free.

Just a stone's throw from Lubec sits the island summer home of former U.S. President Franklin D. Roosevelt. Although on Canadian soil, the historic site is maintained jointly by the U.S. and Canada; the only auto route to the island is via the international bridge at Lubec (a ferry provides access on the Canadian side). The house has been restored and contains many of the Roosevelt family's original furnishings.

MUSIC

**MACHIAS BAY
    CHAMBER CONCERTS**
207-483-6631.
P.O. Box 332, Machias
    04654
Season: July–early Aug.
Tickets: $8 adults; $5
    students; under 12 free.

This group has brought classical chamber music to Machias for almost a quarter of a century. Many of the same instrumental groups that play in Rockport's Bay Chamber series play here in the Machias Congregational Church, which is known for its excellent acoustics. The series of six concerts begins on the first Tuesday evening after July 4.

**STAGE FRONT: THE
    ARTS DOWNEAST**
207-255-1200.
9 O'Brien Ave., Machias.
Season: early Sept.–April.
Tickets: $5–$9.

Folk music from Bolivia, gospel, jazz, classical, and country music. For 13 years Stage Front has been bringing a broad spectrum of music to the Performing Arts Center at the University of Maine, Machias. The group also sponsors theater and dance performances.

SEASONAL EVENTS

Down River Theater Company (207-255-4244; Old Catholic Church, Rte. 1A, Whitneyville). Musical theater from South Pacific to Chicago. Summer.

Eastport Arts Center (207-853-4133; Dana and Water Sts., Eastport). The Center is comprised of three groups: Stage East, a theater company producing three shows a year ranging from Neil Simon's *Rumors* to Charles Dickens's *A Christmas Carol*; the Eastport Gallery featuring art work in a variety of media; and the Concert Series with at least 5 concerts a summer.

The Gathering, Passamaquoddy Tribe (207-853-4001; Pleasant Point Reservation, Rte. 190, Perry). Traditional dances, crafts, lighting the sacred fire. Mid-August.

A ceremonial dance at the annual celebration in Perry; a chance for visitors to experience a mix of old and new customs of the Pasamaquoddy tribe.

Tom Hindman

July 4 and Old Home Days (207-853-4644; Eastport). Every year this small fishing town of 2,000 quadruples in size when everyone who has ever lived here comes to celebrate the easternmost 4th in the country. Great parade. Make sure to make your lodging reservations early. July 1–4.

Salmon Festival (207-853-4644; Eastport). All you can eat, tours of the salmon pens from the water and codfish relays. Early September.

Wild Blueberry Festival (207-255-6665; Centre & Main Sts., Machias). Fish fry, parade, 5-mile run – all to celebrate the wild blueberry harvest. Going on for more than two decades. Mid-August.

EAST OF SCHOODIC: RECREATION

Kayaking in the surf.

Herb Swanson

BEACHES

Jasper Beach; off Starboard Rd., Bucks Harbor. This beach is made up entirely of polished pebbles. It's beautiful, even if it makes for difficult swimming.

Roque Bluffs Beach; Roque Bluffs Rd. off Rte. 1, Roque Bluffs. There's also Simpson Pond next door for freshwater swimming, a playground, picnic tables, grills, a bathhouse, bathrooms, and parking. Sand and shingle beach; 910 yds.

BIRD WATCHING

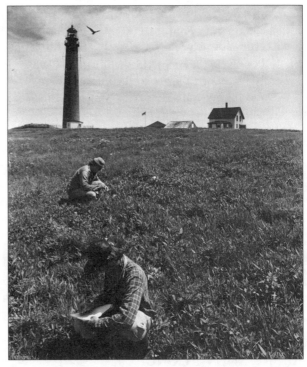

Keeping track of the birds near the lighthouse on Petit Manan, one of the best places in the country to view the European whimbrel.

Tom Hindman

S ome of the best birding in Maine — some may even say the best in the New England — is in Washington County.

Wonderful places to see the fall migration of shore birds are the quiet beaches near the Canadian border. One birder we've heard of spotted 100 species in one day in *Dennysville* on the Dennys River. The *Lubec and Eastport flats* host an enormous number and variety of traveling sanderlings, sandpipers, knots, willets, and other beach feeders. Ducks of many species abound, and eagles are regularly sighted, as well. The *Petit Manan National*

Wildlife Refuge in Milbridge is an excellent perch for dedicated birders. The 1,841-acre preserve includes Bois Bubert, Petit Manan and Nash islands and is said to be one of the best spots in the state to view the whimbrel, a small European curlew. There are nature trails on the mainland. The islands (with the exception of the northern end of Bois Bubert) are open to the public and can be reached by private boat.

CAMPING

Cobscook Bay State Park (207-726-4412; six mi. south of U.S. Rte. 1 at Dennysville). This is a jewel of a campground with 106 camping sites. Most are for tents and many with water views. There are even showers (unusual in a Maine state campground). The 864-acre park has picnic benches, hiking, and cross-country ski trails (see below). Mid-May–mid-October.

McLellan Park (Wyman Rd., Milbridge). Washington County operates this family recreational area. You can camp here. There are also picnicking facilities and hiking trails.

CROSS-COUNTRY SKIING

Cobscook Bay State Park (207-726-4412 for snow and trail conditions; off Rte. 1, Edmunds). Six miles of roads through woods with terrific views of the bay.

Moosehorn National Wildlife Refuge (207-454-3521; Baring). Fifty miles of service roads closed to automobiles in the winter. Moderate to difficult.

GOLF

Great Cove Golf Course (207-434-7200; off Rte. 1 in Jonesboro, Roque Bluffs). 9 holes, 1,694 yds., par 30. Cart and club rental, snack bar, clubhouse.

HIKING AND WALKING

West Quoddy Head State Park, south of Lubec. This is the easternmost point of the United States, an elemental and majestic beginning. A two-mile trail outlines the 100-ft. cliffs and Carrying Place Cove. Several miles out, you can see Grand Manan, looking like a giant humpback whale.

NATURE PRESERVES

Great Wass Island Preserve, Rte. 187, Beals Island. Almost 1,600 acres of land with two wooded trails through spruce and fir forests edging a long, narrow cove. Magnificent views of the ocean and eastern islands. Managed by the Nature Conservancy.

Petit Manan National Wildlife Refuge, Rte. 1, Milbridge. A pleasant trail leads 1.5 miles through a wild blueberry barren and woods to a rugged shoreline. Part of a 1,841-acre refuge that includes Petit Manan Peninsula, Petit Manan, and Nash islands, and part of Bois Bubert Island. The islands – except for the northern end of Bois Bubert – are open to the public and can be reached by private boat.

PUFFIN WATCHING

Barna Norton (207-497-5933; Jonesport).

Seafarer, Butch Huntley (207-733-5584; E-mail, seafarer@nemaine.com; Lubec).

RUNNING

Don't let us stop you. Seriously, *Runner* Magazine readers voted the *Schoodic 10K Road Race* on the Schoodic Peninsula as one of the five best in the country. The terrain is relatively flat, the scenery is beautiful, the air and the light clear.

SEASONAL SPORTING EVENTS

The World's Fastest Lobsterboat Races, early July. Takes place near Moosabec Reach (contact the Jonesport 4th of July Committee, P.O. Box 106, Jonesport 04649; 207-497-2804).

Whales are frequent summer visitors off the coast of Maine.

Tom Hindman

WHALE WATCH

Capt. Butch Huntley (207-733-5584; Lubec). If he can't make it, he'll tell you who can. Butch also does puffin trips.

EAST OF SCHOODIC: SHOPPING

COLLECTIBLES

Nelson Decoys (207-497-5572; School St., Jonesport) Open Monday through Saturday or by appointment, the Downeast Gallery specializes in woodcarvings of songbirds and shorebirds.

The Sow's Ear (207-255-4066; 7 Water St., Machias). An engaging collection of clothing, books, toys, and gifts

POTTERY

Columbia Falls Pottery (207-483-4075; Main St., Columbia Falls). Potters April Adams and Alan Burnham have set up shop in a Victorian country store halfway between Cherryfield and Machias and next to the Ruggles House Museum. You can get a tour of their studio or just browse through their collection of majolica and terra cotta pottery. They also sell baskets, candles, and paintings by Maine artists and crafts people.

Dog Island Pottery (207-853-4775; 224 Water St., Eastport). Functional and decorative stoneware handcrafted by the shop's owner, Barbara Smith.

CHAPTER SEVEN
Practical Matters
INFORMATION

A Maine coast salt water farm.

Herb Swanson

This chapter is meant to be a modest encyclopedia of useful information about the coast of Maine. Visitors can refer to it when planning trips to the coast and when on vacation here. It covers the following topics:

AMBULANCE / FIRE / POLICE

Emergency numbers differ throughout the coast. Here is an abbreviated listing for the major destinations. For other locations, check the local phone listings or dial "0" for operator.

Town	Fire	Police	Ambulance
Bar Harbor	911	911	911
Bath	911	911	911
Belfast	911	911	911
Blue Hill	207-374-2435	207-667-7575	207-374-9900
Boothbay Harbor	911	911	911
Brunswick	911 or	911 or	911 or
	207-725-5521	207-725-5521	207-725-5511
Camden	207-236-2000	911	207-236-2000
Castine	207-326-4322	207-667-7575	207-374-9900
Damariscotta	207-563-3131	207-563-3444	207-563-3200
Eastport	207-853-4221	207-853-2544	207-853-4828
			or 207-853-2771
Ellsworth	207-667-2525	207-667-2133	207-667-3200
Freeport	207-865-4211	207-865-4212	207-865-4211
Jonesport	207-483-2993	800-432-7303	207-497-2385
Kennebunkport	207-967-3323	207-967-3323	207-967-3323
Kittery	911	911	911
Lubec	207-733-4321	207-733-4321	207-733-4321
Machias	207-255-3535	207-255-4033	207-255-3535
Mt. Desert	207-276-5111	207-276-5111	207-276-5111
Ogunquit	207-646-5111	207-646-9361	207-646-5111
Old Orchard Beach	911	911	911
Portland	911	911	911
Rockland	911	911	911
Stonington	207-367-2655	207-667-7575	207-348-2300
Thomaston	911	911	911
Waldoboro	911	911	911
			or 207-832-5211
Winter Harbor	207-963-2222	207-667-7575	207-667-3200
Wiscasset	911	911	911
York	911	911	911

AREA CODE / TOWN GOVERNMENT & ZIP CODES

AREA CODE

Maine's area code is 207.

TOWN GOVERNMENT

Therein Lies a Tale

[from the *Bar Harbor Times*]

CORRECTION

In a news brief in last week's edition of the Times, it was mistakenly reported that Janice Jones-Maxwell was fired from her position as executive director of the Mount Desert Chamber of Commerce after she was charged with embezzling chamber money. In fact, the position of executive director was eliminated due to lack of funds. The *Times* apologizes for the error.

— *The New Yorker*

There are more than 250 cities, towns, villages and "plantations" (see definition below) along the coast of Maine from Kittery to Eastport. There are 16 counties in Maine and eight that line the coast. From west to east, they are: York, Cumberland, Sagadahoc, Lincoln, Knox, Waldo, Hancock, and Washington.

Cities have their own charters and city councils. In Maine you don't have to be big to be a city; if you're big, there's nothing to prevent you from being a town. There are 2,000 city people in Eastport and 10 times that number of townspeople in Brunswick.

During the 19th century the annual town meeting was the social event of the year for most of Maine. Over the course of the day, men managed the town business; women set the noon table. Although more towns are electing officials and hiring professionals to govern and manage their communities, and women are regular fixtures in town hall, the annual town meeting still predominates. At a town meeting, usually held in March, every resident who shows up has as much pull as the person sitting or standing next to him. The government of the towns through the medium of the town meeting has been called the only existing type of "pure" democracy.

In addition to towns and cities, Maine has 33 plantations — a holdover from the time when the region was part of the Massachusetts Bay Colony. Originally intended to be temporary forms of government, many of Maine's plantations, such as Monhegan and Matinicus islands, have annual meetings, do not have home rule powers and are incorporated by county commissioners.

The state government, according to New England tradition, exercises relatively little power over the towns and cities — home rule predominates, in other words.

Don't forget that Maine had a thriving democracy long before European settlers arrived. Today, two Native American reservations, at Old Town near Bangor and Perry outside of Eastport, are self-governed nations and exist outside of U.S. federal jurisdiction.

For more information regarding the governing bodies of Maine's coastal plantations, towns and cities, contact the following town hall offices.

ZIP CODES

Town	Telephone	Zip Code
Bar Harbor	207-288-4098	04609
Bath	207-443-8330	04530
Belfast	207-338-3370	04915
Blue Hill	207-374-2281	04614
Boothbay Harbor	207-633-2144	04538
Brunswick	207-725-6659	04011
Camden	207-236-3353	04843
Castine	207-326-4502	04421
Damariscotta	207-563-5168	04543
Eastport	207-853-2300	04631
Ellsworth	207-667-2563	04605
Freeport	207-865-4743	04032
Jonesport	207-497-5926	04649
Kennebunkport	207-967-4243	04046
Kittery	207-439-0452	03904
Lubec	207-733-2341	04652
Machias	207-255-6621	04654
Newcastle	207-563-3441	04553
Ogunquit	207-646-5139	03907
Old Orchard Beach	207-934-5714	04064
Portland	207-874-8300	04101, 04102, 04103, 04104
Rockland	207-594-8431	04841
Stonington	207-367-2351	04681
Thomaston	207-354-6107	04861
Waldoboro	207-832-5369	04572
Winter Harbor	207-963-2235	04693
Wiscasset	207-882-8205	04578

BANKS

The major banks in Maine and several of the smaller local banks are linked to national and international instant teller machine networks. Following is a list of many of the banks with offices along the coast.

Bank	*Phone*	*Cash Machine Networks*
Bangor Savings Bank	800-432-1591	NYCE, Plus,Cirrus, MasterCard/Visa, American Express, Novus Discover
Bar Harbor Banking & Trust	800-924-7787	Cirrus, Plus, Yankee24 NYCE, Visa
Camden National Bank	800-860-8821	Plus, Honor, NYCE, Cirrus,
First National Bank of Damariscotta	800-564-3195	Plus, Scott 24-Hour, Yankee24, NYCE, MasterCard/Visa
Fleet Bank	800-922-2882	Cirrus, NYCE, Yankee24, MasterCard/Visa
Key Bank	800-635-2265	NYCE, Cirrus, MAC, Maestro
Peoples Heritage Bank	800-295-7400	NYCE, Plus, Yankee24, The Exchange, TX

BIBLIOGRAPHY

BOOKS YOU CAN BUY

AUTOBIOGRAPHY, BIOGRAPHY & REMINISCENCE

Ames, Polly Scribner. *Marsden Hartley in Maine*. Orono, ME: University of Maine Press, 1972. 36 pp., illus., $8.95. Polly Scribner Ames writes about fellow painter Marsden Hartley's final three years living with lobsterman Forrest Young and his wife Katie in Corea, Maine (near Winter Harbor).

Coomer, Joe. *Sailing in a Spoonful of Water*. New York: Picador USA. 256 pp., $22. Coomer, a resident of Eliot, Maine, writes of the revival of his vintage craft *Yonder*, while reflecting on how his life journeys have drawn him again and again to the water.

Small, Constance. *The Lighthouse Keeper's Wife*. Orono, ME: University of Maine Press, 1986. 226 pp., photos, $13.95. Constance Small and her husband Elson tended a Maine island lighthouse for 28 years. This is her wry and moving account of that life.

Tatelbaum, Linda. *Carrying Water as a Way of Life*. Appleton, ME: About Time Press. 117 pp., $9.95. Series of feisty essays chronicling the author and her husband's quest to head back-to-the-land.

FICTION

Landesman, Peter. *The Raven*. New York: Penguin Books. 356 pp., $11.95. Based on the true story of a mysterious disappearance of a pleasure boat, *The Raven*, and its 36 passengers off the coast of Maine.

Maine Speaks. Maine: Maine Writers and Publishers Alliance. 464 pp., $19.95. An anthology of works by writers whose lives have been touched by Maine. E.B. White, Tim Sample, Ruth Moore, Steven King, and more.

McCloskey, Robert. *Blueberries for Sal*. New York: The Viking Press, 1948. 55 pp., illus. $4.99.

_____. *One Morning in Maine*. New York: The Viking Press, 1952. 64 pp., illus. $4.99. Two of the best books about Maine to read, for adults as well as children.

Monroe, Judith W. *Widdershins*. Durham, NC: Crone's Own Press, 1989. 240 pp., $9.95. Quirky, comic feminist novel about a group of women on a Maine island who discover their own power and independence.

Phippen, Sanford, Charles G. Waugh, and Martin Greenberg, eds. *The Best Maine Stories*. Camden, ME: Yankee Books, 1994. 320 pp., $12.95. Short stories set in Maine written by some of America's most famous authors from Henry James to Caroline Chute.

HISTORY

Judd, Richard W. *Common Lands, Common People*. Cambridge: Harvard University Press. 335 pp., $35. The history of conservation ethics in northern New England.

Kurlandsky, Mark. *Cod*. New York: Walker and Company. 276 pp., $21. Spanning thousands of years and four continents, this book is a biography of the fish that changed the world and was a staple of the Maine fishery for centuries.

Rich, Louise Dickinson. *The Coast of Maine*. Camden, Maine: Down East Books, 1993. 400 pp., index, illus., photos. $14.95. A wonderfully rambling history of the coast from the Ice Age to the mid-1970s, punctuated with the author's idiosyncratic interpretations of historical facts.

PHOTOGRAPHIC AND PAINTING STUDIES

Joseph, Stanley and Lynn Karlin. *Maine Farm: A Year of Country Life*. New York:

Random House, 1991. Photos, $32.50. Beautifully photographed, warmly told account of life on a saltwater farm.

Skolnick, Arnold ed. *Paintings of Maine.* New York: Clarkson/Potter Publishers, 1991. 123 pp., illus., $27.50. Luscious reproductions of paintings of Maine by artists including Georgia O'Keeffe, Winslow Homer, Andrew Wyeth, and Edward Hopper.

Tragard, Louise, Patricia E. Hart, and W.L. Copithorne. *A Century of Color*: Ogunquit, Maine's Art Colony 1886–1986. Ogunquit, ME: Barn Gallery Associates, 1988. $24.95 Interviews and commentary from 100 years in the southern Maine art community.

RECREATION

Getchell, Dave and Kate Cronin. *The Maine Island Trail Book.* Rockland, ME: Maine Island Trail Association, 1991. The Maine Island Trail Association publishes this guidebook packed with charts and information for its members. It's worth joining just to get tips about touring the coast from the water. For information, or a copy of this great book, write to: Maine Island Trail Association, 60 Ocean St., Rockland, ME 04841.

Gibbs, David and Sarah Hale. *Mountain Bike! Maine.* Birmingham, AL: Menasaha Ridge Press, 1998. $12.95. This book is the only comprehensive reference for mountain bikers looking to get off the beaten trail in Maine. Hale and Gibbs detail 78 great rides, many of them within 10 miles of the coast.

Isaac, Jeff and Peter Goth. *The Outward Bound Wilderness First-Aid Handbook.* Lyons & Burford, 1991. 252 pp., index, illus., $14.95. A must-have for anyone discovering the coast by kayak, canoe, sailboat, foot or bike.

Taft, Hank. *A Cruising Guide to the Maine Coast.* New York: McGraw-Hill Publishing, 1994. 400 pp., illus., $39.95. The definitive guide for ocean-going travelers.

Peirson, Elizabeth C. and Jan Erik Peirson. *A Birder's Guide to Maine* Camden: Down East Books, 1996. 400 pp., illus., $19. The Maine coast is a wondeful place to bird, and this is the book birders will want at their side to distinguish teals from mergansers.

Venn, Tamsin. *Sea Kayaking Along The New England Coast.* Boston: Appalachian Mountain Club, 1990. 240 pp., maps, photos, $14.95.

BOOKS YOU CAN BORROW

Brault, Gerard. *The French-Canadian Heritage in New England.* Hanover and London: University Press of New England, and Kingston and Montreal: McGill-Queen's University Press, 1986. 264 pp., index, illus.

Caldwell, Bill. *Maine Coast.* Portland: Guy Gannet Publishing Co., 1988. 398 pp. Two collections of a journalist's rambling monologues about the people he has met and places he has visited.

Caldwell, Erskine. *Midsummer Passion and Other Tales of Maine Cussedness.* Camden, ME: Yankee Books. 192 pp. Fifteen short stories Erskine Caldwell wrote while living in Maine.

Carson, Rachel. *The Edge of the Sea.* New York: Houghton Mifflin Company, 1955. The famous naturalist and ecologist's essays on the coast. If you like this, you'll enjoy her other books, *The Sea Around Us* and *Silent Spring.*

Coffin, Robert Tristam. *Saltwater Farm.* New York: Macmillan, 1939. 114 pp., illus. Poetry by the premier poet and prose writer of Maine's middle coast.

Conkling, Philip. *Islands in Time.* Camden, ME: Down East Books, 1981. 222 pp., illus. Former Outward Bound naturalist, now head of the Island Institute, provides a lyrical history of Maine's coastal islands from an ecologist's point of view.

Doty, C. Stewart, ed. *The First Franco-Americans. New England Life Histories from the Federal Writers Project,* 1938–1939. Orono, ME: University of Maine Press, 1985. 163 pp., photos. Collected interviews of first-generation immigrants from Acadia and Quebec.

Eckstorm, Fannie Hardy. *Indian Place Names of the Penobscot Valley and the Maine Coast.* Orono, ME: University of Maine Press, 1978. An interesting journey through Maine by way of Penobscot Indian language and legend.

Federal Writers' Project of the Works Progress Administration, State of Maine. Maine: *A Guide 'Downeast.'* Boston: Houghton Mifflin Co., 1937. 458 pp., index, illust, photos. Try to get hold of this thick volume or the revised version, which was published in 1970 by Dorris Isaacson and the Maine Historical Society. It is a thorough account of all Maine: its history, natural wonders, and recreation.

Jewett, Sarah Orne. *The Country of the Pointed Firs.* Boston and New York: Houghton Mifflin Company, 1929. 306 pp.

Leeker, Robert and Kathleen R. Brown, eds. *An Anthology of Maine Literature.* Orono, Me: University of Maine Press, 1982. 260 pp. A collection of works by native and out-of-state writers, including Nathaniel Hawthorne, Henry David Thoreau, Harriet Beecher Stowe, Sarah Orne Jewett, and Kenneth Roberts.

Monegain, Bernie. *Natural Sites: A Guide to Maine's Natural Phenomena.* Freeport, ME: Delorme Mapping Company, 1988. 48 pp., index, maps, photos.

Monegain, Bernie. *Coastal Islands: A Guide to Exploring Main's Offshore Isles.* Freeport, ME: DeLorme Mapping Company, 1988. 48 pp., index, maps, photos, $4.95.

Pierson, Elizabeth Cary and Jan Erik Pierson. *The Birders Guide to the Coast of Maine.* Camden, ME: Down East Books. Birds that nest and visit, summer and winter, on the coast and its islands.

Shain, Charles and Samuella Shain. *The Maine Reader.* New York: Houghton Mifflin Company, 1991. Illus. Four hundred years of Maine through the eyes of explorers, writers, painters, and photographers.

Williamson, William D. *History of the State of Maine* (2 vols.) 1602-1820, 1832.
An overview of Maine's history and geography before it became a state.

Willis, William, ed. *Journals of Rev. Thomas Smith and Rev. Samuel Deane, 1849.*
The author of this book was a Portland minister whose record of daily life during the Revolutionary War is interesting in its thoroughness.

CLIMATE, WEATHER , & WHAT TO WEAR

Digging out after a snowstorm in Cape Porpoise.

Herb Swanson

Whoever once said "character takes four seasons to make" must have been familiar with the seasons of coastal Maine. The seasons only serve to add drama to the already variable landscape from Kittery to Eastport.

Maine seasons go by their own timetable. Spring bulbs will often bloom as late as mid-June. Summer generally remains temperate throughout July and August. The cool days of autumn frequently extend well past the foliage's fall, and although it has been known to snow up to 70 inches in one winter (it snowed that much in Portland during the winter of 1970–71), harsh northern winter winds are usually softened by warmer ocean temperatures.

The state's climate is governed by the "prevailing westerlies," the belt of eastward-moving air that encircles the globe at the middle latitudes. The westerlies and warm currents of the Atlantic ensure that prolonged hot and cold spells are rare, although coastal weather — with the added moisture from the ocean — can be extremely changeable. Fogs frequently descend upon the coast, and are a reason why Maine mariners are famed the world over for their navigational skills. There are an average of 59 foggy days every year at Quoddy Head Light near Lubec.

What to Wear in Maine

Rainy days are tough on pedestrians, but I grew up in Maine, so I have no qualms about wearing really dorky clothes when it rains.

— Al Daimon, Maine's "walking" newsman,
quoted in *Casco Bay Weekly*

As I write this, I am wearing heavy long underwear, wind pants, three layers of insulation under a water-resistant jacket, wool socks, a wool hat and fingerless gloves. I look ridiculous, especially since it is now early June. But I'm on a small boat, and it is wicked cold out here .

— Jeff Isaac, Maine sailor

One could say fashion is a stranger to Maine. Dressing for a visit to the coast of Maine has everything to do with form and function. Versatility and comfort are respected. Strict formality is highly unusual, and probably transplanted from somewhere else. Any color is okay as long as it is brown, green, or gray.

Knowing how to dress for coastal weather requires understanding the relationship between wind, water, and land. The overall climate of Maine is Northern Temperate with cold winters and warm summers. The effects of the ocean can significantly moderate the weather on the islands and for a few miles inland, depending on the direction of the wind. The water off the coast is part of an upwelling of the Labrador Current that has its origin under the polar ice cap. Although the water has traveled hundreds of miles to get here, it still feels like icebergs. The air — or wind — passing over coastal waters is cooled and humidified before it arrives ashore.

On a typical sunny summer day, warm air rises over the mainland and the cool and dense air over the ocean is drawn in to replace it. This produces the summer southwesterly sea breeze. Temperatures along the immediate coast and islands will reflect that of the ocean, which only reaches 60 degrees by late summer. Approaching the coast on a hot day you can feel the air temperature drop 10 or 15 degrees, and often a thick fog will roll in.

If you're headed for the shore, carry a jacket and a pair of long pants, no matter what the TV weather personality says. This is especially true if you're boarding a boat. Rain is almost always associated with larger and more predictable weather systems. Unless a frontal passage or storm system is expected, you can leave your foul-weather gear in the trunk.

Clothes should be loose and comfortable for scrambling over rocks and through spruce and raspberry bushes. Garments should be versatile enough to handle rapid changes in temperature. Shorts are fine for strolling or trail hiking during the day when it's warm. If you're going any distance, bring wind pants for protection against the sea breeze and bugs. Summer nights are almost always cool. A medium-weight sweater will get plenty of use. If you cannot bring all of them, choose wool or fleece over cotton. Those fabrics will keep moisture away from your skin, and therefore keep you warmer.

Hiking shoes are also a good idea. Maine is really just a very thin layer of topsoil over a very thick layer of coarse-grained granite. Since you don't want to damage the soil layer, most of your walking will be on the rocks. The soft soles of sandals and sneakers are quickly worn smooth by avid hikers. One of the most useful items is a pair of knee-high rubber boots. The tide range in Maine runs from eight to 20 feet, exposing thousands of tidal pools and clam flats for exploring. Bare feet would be shredded by shells and barnacles, and sneakers can get lost in the mud. A good pair of "worm boots" can make your whole trip. Add a cozy pair or two of socks, and they're great for snow, too.

Never mind what the calendar says, fall can begin on the coast during the third week of August. By this time, summer has lost its grip. Increasingly frequent cold fronts bring the prevailing winds to the west and northwest. With the wind off the land, temperatures reflect the cooling mass of the North American continent.

This is a great time to visit Monhegan or Vinalhaven, because summer-like conditions often extend well into the fall on the islands. While the mainland cools, the islands' temperature is moderated by the still-warm ocean water.

For fall and winter travel in coastal Maine, bring everything from shorts to winter gear, and expect to change often. Good foul-weather gear is essential unless you plan to spend a lot of time indoors. When an approaching winter storm swings the wind to the south or east, the breeze brings relative warmth. Wind off the water can melt the snow out from under your cross country skis as fast as it fell. The day can seem downright balmy, until the next front sends the temperature plummeting. Precipitation can alternate quickly between rain and snow as the conflicting land and ocean air masses meet.

Spring on the coast can be a real tease. The ocean is very reluctant to warm up. This creates a drastic difference between inland and coastal temperatures and an even more drastic difference between your expectations and reality. You pull out your bathing suit, head for the beach and find that the water is still 43 degrees. The key is to expect it. Remember your fall and winter wardrobe? Bring it. If the wind is off the water, you'll need it. Away from the shore, or with a shore breeze, you can lie around with as little on as at a summer picnic. It all depends on the wind.

Summer temperatures on Maine's coast range from 60 to 90 degrees, with the steadily warmest temperatures around 80, in mid- to late July. Even when the temperature climbs during the day, coastal nights are almost always cool and comfortable. Autumn generally brings sunny days, cool nights, and a brilliant display of fall foliage colors ranging from vivid golds (birches, poplars, and ginkgos) and oranges (mountain maples, hickories, and ashes) to dazzling scarlets (red maple, red oak, and sassafras).

Frosts and freezing temperatures can occur from October to May, although Portland experiences only 132 freezing days every year and is usually only 4 degrees cooler than Boston. The coast receives about 46 inches of precipitation annually. Of that precipitation, it snows only 15 or 20 days, and there are only 10 to 20 thunderstorms every year.

Meteorological extremes do occur. There was "the year without summer" in

---

Fogs in Maine

E. B. White gave us one of the best descriptions of a Maine fog in his
1948 *Atlantic Monthly* essay titled "Death of Pig."

*We had been having an unseasonable spell of weather — hot, close days,
with the fog shutting in every night, scaling for a few hours in midday, then
creeping back again at dark, drifting in first over the trees on the point, then
suddenly blowing across the fields, blotting out the world and taking possession of houses, men, and animals.*

1816 when it snowed in July. Hurricanes strike the coast about once every
decade. The coast also experiences what have become known as "100-Year
Storms," when severe wind and weather peak with high tide, creating tides 10
to 20 feet higher than normal. More common are "Nor'easters," coastal storms
that come up the coast and pummel it with high tides, heavy rain — or snow
— and gale force winds.

People who enjoy reading about the weather will want to look for The
Weather Report column in the weekly newspaper *Maine Times*. The rambling
weather and natural life accounts are gathered from residents who regularly
observe the great outdoors from their windows onto the harbor or field.
People from all places along the coast and inland give colorful reports of
"flaming swamp maples" or a jack-in-the-pulpit discovered while out looking
for mushrooms or pulling up the boat.

For frequently updated coastal and marine weather information, call the
National Weather Service, 207-688-3210.

GUIDED TOURS

G uided and sightseeing tours on the coast of Maine can be divided into
three categories. You can travel by bus or trolley in many of the more
popular destinations such as Ogunquit, Kennebunkport, Portland, and Bar
Harbor. You can travel by water on regular guided boat cruises, including
whale, seal, and puffin tours. You can also travel by air in a small plane
because there are many small private airstrips and flying services along the
coast. In this section we will discuss guided land and air tours. For lists of
ocean-going guided tours, including windjammer cruises, whale, puffin watch
tours, and harbor tours, see entries in the "Recreation" section of each area
chapter.

South Coast

During the summer months, the *Ogunquit Chamber of Commerce* operates a free, unnarrated trolley that covers the town's high spots from Perkins Cove to the west and Footbridge Beach to the east. The four trolleys — all named after garden flowers — operate daily from Memorial Day weekend through Columbus Day.

The *Intown Trolley Company* in Kennebunkport (207-967-3686) has provided old-fashioned narrated tours of the seaport for more than 10 years, including historical notes, a drive-by of the Bush family summer home at Walker Point and stops at the Franciscan monastery, major inns, hotels, and shopping. There is a nominal fee for the service, and the fare is good for the entire day. The Intown Trolley leaves from the bottom of Ocean Ave. near Dock Sq. during July and August, and it is good to line up 15 minutes before scheduled departure.

As you head up the coast, on-land tours are harder to come by. The best opportunities are for chartered bus, taxi, and van tours operated by various companies. One of those is *Custom Coach of Portland* (800-585-3589; E-mail, ridealimo@aol.com) which provides personalized tours for groups ranging from one to fifty people. They are based in Portland, but will go anywhere in the state of Maine, 24 hours a day. Custom Coach also will lease a van, limousine, or bus to larger groups. *Mainely Tours* (207-774-0808; www.goportland. com/tours) offers 90 minute guided tours of downtown Portland. Guides will point out historical sites while traveling from the city streets to the rocky coast at Portland Head Light. $12 adults, $11 seniors, $6 kids. Also call Mainely Tours for more information on their land & sea and Kennebunkport tours.

Town Taxi (207-772-0111) and *ABC Taxi* (207-772-8685; E-mail, com221@ webtv.net) in Portland offer similar, custom tour service. You can book one of their Chrysler taxis for $20 an hour.

Greater Portland Landmarks (207-774-5561; www.portlandlandmarks.org) provides downtown walking tours every Fri. and Sat. at 10 a.m. from July–late Sept. Tours meet in Monument Square, Portland and highlight the city's architectural history. The tour guides are lively and the price is right $7 (includes $1.50 donation to Save The Observatory).

Midcoast

Guided tours in the Midcoast are just as difficult to come by. Bill Sweet, a retired schoolteacher and history buff, was born and raised on Mount Desert Island. He operates the *Sweet William Tour Guide Service* (207-288-5443; 207-548-2190 in winter) in Bar Harbor. Cost for each two-and-one-half hour step-on guide service is $75 per coach. Bill will take you through Bar Harbor and Acadia. Park admission is not included with the fee. It's important to book in advance during July and August.

If you want to view the region by air, *Downeast Charter Flights* (800-752-6378) offers seats aboard their $1^1/_2$ to 2 hour fire patrol flights conducted for the state of Maine. These two daily flights promise a good chance to actually see a fire as well as up to a third of the state. The fare is $50. They are also available for charter.

Down East / Acadia

One of the best ways to see Bar Harbor and Acadia without having to deal with the summer traffic is on *Oli's Trolley* (207-288-9899), a one-hour or two-and-one-half hour ride. The old-fashioned brown bus seats 40 and travels the park loop with stops at Cadillac Mountain and Thunder Hole. The guided tour also includes Sieur de Mont Spring, Otter Cliffs, and a running historical narrative of Mount Desert Island from prehistoric times through present day. Six daily tours run from May through mid-October. The summer months are busy, and reservations are encouraged. The bus leaves from downtown Bar Harbor in front of the post office.

To view Acadia by air, *Acadia Air* (207-667-5534; acadiaair@acadia.net.), which operates out of Bar Harbor Airport in Trenton, offers several scenic flight tours for under $50 per person with two person minimum. The shorter, less-expensive flights fly over Acadia, Deer Isle, and Stonington in a Cessna 172. Longer flights go down the coast for views of Castine and Camden harbors. Acadia Air operates scenic flights on demand from June 1 through mid-October. The rest of the year tours can be arranged by appointment.

Jeff Miller and his drivers will take you on a tour of Bar Harbor in his *Lobster Bike* (207-288-3028), a pedicab disguised as a seven-foot-long Maine lobster. The comfortable cushioned seat sits at the front of this oversized tricycle and holds two adults or four kids. Go ahead, it's fun. $5 for 10 minutes. Evenings. Reservations taken but not required.

HANDICAPPED SERVICES

A lmost all state and national parks in Maine provide access and facilities for the physically impaired. Most motels and hotels also have rooms easily accessible to the handicapped, although many historic buildings and inns have either not yet complied with or are exempt from the Americans with Disabilities Act. We have tried to provide information on individual restaurants, inns, and bed-and-breakfast establishments that are accessible in the reviews listed the four coastal regions. To confirm, please call ahead.

To find out more about tourist facilities for the handicapped, contact the *Maine Tourism Association,* P.O. Box 2300, Hallowell, ME 04347; 207-623-0363 in state and 800-533-9595 out-of-state.

HOSPITALS

South Coast

BIDDEFORD

Southern Maine Medical Center 1 Medical Center Dr., Biddeford 04005; 207-283-7000; Emergency Room open 24 hours.

PORTLAND

Maine Medical Center, Brighton Campus 333 Brighton Ave., Portland 04102; 207-879-8000; 9–9 walk-in clinic.

Maine Medical Center 22 Bramhall St., Portland 04102; 207-871-0111; Emergency Room open 24 hours.

Mercy Hospital 144 State St., Portland 04101; 207-879-3000; Emergency Room open 24 hours.

YORK

York Hospital 15 Hospital Dr., York 03909; 207-363-4321; Emergency Room open 24 hours.

Midcoast

BATH

Bath Health Care Center 1356 Washington St., Bath 04530; 207-443-5524; Non-life-threatening care. 7 a.m.–10 p.m.

BELFAST

Waldo County General Hospital 118 Northport Ave., Belfast 04915; 207-338-2500.Emergency Room open 24 hours.

BOOTHBAY HARBOR

St. Andrews Hospital 3 St. Andrews Ln., Boothbay Harbor 04538; 207-633-2121; Emergency Room open 24 hours.

BRUNSWICK

Parkview Hospital 329 Maine St., Brunswick 04011; 207-729-1641; Emergency Room open 24 hours.

DAMARISCOTTA

Miles Memorial Hospital Bristol Rd., Damariscotta 04543; 207-563-1234; Emergency Room open 24 hours. Also a walk-in clinic from 8-8

ROCKPORT

Penobscot Bay Medical Center 6 Glen Cove, Rockport 04856 ; 207-596-8000; Emergency Room open 24 hours.

Down East/Acadia

BAR HARBOR

Mount Desert Island Hospital 10 Wayman Ln., Bar Harbor 04609; 207-288-5081. Emergency Room open 24 hours.

BLUE HILL

Blue Hill Memorial Hospital Water St., Blue Hill 04614; 207-374-2836. Emergency Room open 24 hours.

ELLSWORTH

Maine Coast Memorial Hospital 50 Union St., Ellsworth 04605; 207-667-5311. Emergency Room open 24 hours.

East of Schoodic

MACHIAS

Down East Community Hospital Upper Court St., Machias 04654; 207-255-3356; Emergency Room open 24 hours.

LATE NIGHT FOOD AND FUEL

Fishermen's floats and lines. The fishing village of Jonesport is in the background.

Herb Swanson

The coffee pot is always on all night at the service desk at L.L. Bean, the famous store that remains open 24 hours every day, including Christmas and Thanksgiving. If you need more than coffee — say fuel for your car or your body — here is a short list of notable late-night or all-night stores, restaurants, and gas stations.

South Coast

Cumberland Farms (food market and fuel), 207-780-8032, 801 Washington Ave., Portland. Open 24 hours.

Denny's Restaurants (food), 207-774-1886, 1101 Congress Ave., Portland (Congress St. exit off Rte. 295). Open 24 hours.

Howell's Auto Truck Stop (food and fuel), 207-439-2466, Rte. 1 bypass, Kittery. Open 24 hours.

Midcoast

Cappy's Chowder House (food), 207-236-2254, 1 Main St., Camden. Daily 8 a.m.– 1 a.m.

Christys Market, 207-338-3779, Rte. 1, Belfast. Open 24 hours.

Red's Eats (food), 207-882-6128, Rte. 1, Wiscasset. Open Mon.–Thur., 11 a.m.– 11 p.m.; Fri.– Sat., 11a.m.– 2 a.m.; Sun., noon–6 p.m.

MEDIA

Tr. [Trooper] Joseph Tibbets investigated a burglary at a private camp in Twp. 24. The only item stolen was a hand-operated well pump, however, a chain saw was used to gain entrance through the door.

—*The Downeast Coastal Press*, Sept. 16, 1991

The news business on the coast of Maine is dominated by two major newspaper companies, which publish the *Bangor Daily News* to the north and the *Portland Press Herald* and *Maine Sunday Telegram* to the south. To really learn about the area is to read about it through the eyes of the people who live and work here. For that reason, we recommend reading one of the several flourishing weeklies published on the coast.

Down East, based in Camden, is the granddaddy of Maine magazines, but during the past decade dozens of younger magazines have sprung up, from *Ocean Navigator*, rumored to have been Walter Cronkite's favorite magazine, to *WoodenBoat*, *National Fisherman* and *Coastal Fisheries News*. Many of these reflect the mariners' lifestyle. Then there are specialty magazines and newspapers like *Maine Antique Digest*, a thick tabloid packed with articles on art, antiques, and Americana, where to get it, and if you missed it, what it went for. The *Maine Times* (800-439-8866, 9 Union St., Hallowell 04347) is a great place to look for coastal summer rentals — despite its moving inland from Topsham. It's also a good source for those interested in Maine's liberal agenda. Following is a roundup of the media you will find on the coast.

South Coast

NEWSPAPERS

Casco Bay Weekly, 800-286-6601, 561A Congress St., Portland 04102;www.cascobayweekly.com; free weekly. Great for entertainment news and the skinny on the state's largest city. A worthy alternative to the big daily.

Journal Tribune, 800-244-7601, P.O. Box 627, Biddeford 04005; www.journaltribunel.com; daily. Known as a photographer's paper, and a pleasant place to do serious journalism.

Portland Press Herald/Maine Sunday Telegram, 800-894-0031, P.O. Box 11350, Portland 04104; www.portland.com. The state's biggest daily.

York County Coast Star, 207-485-2961, P.O. Box 979, Kennebunk 04043; weekly. Founded in 1877; several reporters for this aggressive tabloid have gone on to work for the *Boston Globe* and other big papers.

The York Weekly, 207-363-4343, 17 Woodbridge Rd., P.O. Box 7, York 03909; www.yorkweekly.maine.com.

MAGAZINES

Golf Course News, 207-846-0600, 106 Lafayette St., Yarmouth 04096; www. golfcoursenews.com. Trade tabloid for the greens crowd.

Gourmet News, 207-846-0600; 106 Lafayette St., Yarmouth 04096; E-mail, editors@gourmetnews.com. Trade magazine for the fancy food industry.

National Fisherman, 207-842-5608; 121 Free St., Portland 04101; www.nationalfisherman.com. A color glossy founded in 1903, they cover commercial fishing and boat building, as well as other marine-related stories.

Ocean Navigator, 207-772-2466; 18 Danforth St., Portland 04101; E-mail, navigatorpublishing@compuserve. com.

Salt Magazine, 207-761-0660; 19 Pine St., P.O. Box 4077, Portland 04102; www.salt.com. Journalistic interviews and studies of the "real people of Maine"; great photos.

RADIO

WBACH-FM, 207-967-0993, 106.3; Kennebunk; Classical.

WBLM-FM 102.9; 207-774-6364; Portland; Album-oriented rock, classic rock.

WCYY-FM 92.9; 207-774-6364; Portland; New rock.

WGAN-AM 560; 207-774-4561; Portland; Talk, Imus, news, sports.

WHOM-FM 94.9; 207-773-0200; Portland; Easy listening.

WJBQ-FM 97.9; 207-775-6321; Portland.

WMEA-FM 90.1; 800-884-1717; Portland; Public radio.

WMGX-FM 93.1, 207-774-4561; Contemporary and classic hits.

WMPG-FM 90.9; 207-780-4424; Portland; Full service, eclectic.

WPOR-AM 1490; 207-773-8111; Portland; Country.

WPOR-FM 101.9; 207-773-8111; Portland; Country.

WRED-FM 96; 888-700-9560; Saco; eclectic.

WTHT-FM 107.5; 207-797-0780; Portland; Country.

WYNZ-FM 100.9; 207-774-4561; South Portland; Oldies.

WZAN-AM 970; 207-774-4561; Portland; News and talk.

TELEVISION

Maine Public Television Channel 10; 207-783-9101, Lewiston, PBS.

UPN Channel 35; 207-772-3535, Portland, UPN

WCSH-TV Channel 6; 207-828-6666, Portland, NBC.

WGME-TV Channel 13; 207-797-9330, Portland, CBS.

WMTW-TV Channel 8; 207-775-1800, Portland and Auburn, ABC.

WPXT-TV Channel 51; 207-774-0051, Portland, Fox.

Midcoast

NEWSPAPERS

The Boothbay Register, 207-633-4620, 95 Townsend Ave., P.O. Box 357, Boothbay Harbor 04538; boothbayregister.maine.com; weekly.

Brunswick Times Record, 800-734-6397, Industry Rd., Brunswick 04011; www. timesrecord.com.

The Camden Herald, 207-236-8511, Box 248, Camden 04843; cherald@courier-pub.com; weekly.

Coastal Journal, 800-649-6241, 99 Commercial St., P.O. Box 575, Bath 04530; cjournal@gwi.net.

The Courier-Gazette, 207-338-5411, 1 Park Dr., P.O. Box 249, Rockland 04841; cgmail@courierpub.com; published Tuesday, Thursday and Saturday.

Lincoln County News, 207-563-3171, Box 36, Damariscotta 04543; lcn@lincoln. midcoast.com; weekly.

The Lincoln County Weekly, 207-563-5006, P.O. Box 1287, Damariscotta 04543; lcwmail@courierpub.com.

The Republican Journal, 207-338-3333, Box 327, High St., Belfast 04915; prjmai l@agate.net; weekly.

Waldo Independent, 207-338-5100, 107 Church St., Belfast 04915; weekly.

MAGAZINES

Down East Magazine, 800-766-1670, Box 679, Camden 04843; www.downeast. com. Bills itself as the magazine of Maine; two-thirds of their 85,000 reader-ship live out of state.

Maine Antique Digest, 207-832-4888, 911 Main St., P.O. Box 1429, Waldoboro 04752; www.maineantiquedigest.com.

Maine Boats and Harbors 207-236-8622; 21 Elm St., P.O. Box 758, Camden 04843; www.maineboats.com.

Rod & Reel, 800-766-1670, P.O. Box 370, Camden 04843; www.flyfishers.com.

WoodenBoat, 207-359-4651, P.O. Box 78, Brooklin 04616; www.woodenboat. com. Beautiful to look at. Covers the design, building, care, preservation, and use of wooden boats, whether commercial or pleasure, old or new, sail, or power.

RADIO

WJTO-AM 730; 207-443-6671; Bath, ABC; Oldies.

WMEH FM 90.9; 207-941-1010; Bangor; Classical.

WRKD-AM 1450; 207-594-1450; Rockland; Talk, news, sports, big band/nos-talgia.

Down East/Acadia

NEWSPAPERS

The Bar Harbor Times, 800-479-3312, P.O. Box 68, 76 Cottage St., Bar Harbor 04609; bhtmail@downeast.net; weekly.

Castine Patriot, 207-326-9300, P.O. Box 205, Castine 04421; weekly.

The Ellsworth American, 800-499-2576, 30 Water St., P.O. Box 509, Ellsworth 04605; www.ellsworthamerican.com; weekly. One of America's truly great small-town papers.

The Ellsworth Weekly, 207-667-5514, P.O. Box 1122, Ellsworth 04605.

Island Ad-Vantages, 207-367-2200, P.O. Box 36, Stonington 04681; weekly.

The Weekly Packet, 207-374-2341, Main St., Blue Hill 04614; weekly.

RADIO

WDEA-AM 1370; 800-640-4941; Ellsworth; Big band.

WERU-FM 89.9; 207-469-6600; East Orland; From cool to kewl, good stuff.

WEZQ-FM 92.9; 800-640-4941; Ellsworth; Adult soft and easy hits.

WKSQ-FM 94.5; 207-667-7573; Ellsworth; Adult contemporary, light/soft rock.

WWMJ-FM 95.7; 800-640-4941; Ellsworth; Oldies.

East of Schoodic

NEWSPAPERS

Machias Valley News Observer, 207-255-6561, P.O. Box 357, Machias 04654; weekly.

The Quoddy Tides, 207-853-4806, 123 Water St., Eastport 04631; qtides@ nemaine.com; bimonthly.

RADIO

WALZ-FM 95.3; 888-855-2992; Machias; Adult contemporary.

WQDY-FM 92.7; 207-454-7545; Calais.Adult contemporary.

REAL ESTATE

If, after visiting the coast, you decide you want to own a piece of it, you can write to the *MaineReal Estate Commission*, 35 State House Station, Augusta

Looking out onto Jordan Pond in Acadia National Park.

Herb Swanson

04333 (207-624-8515) for a list of real estate agents in the areas you like. The fee is $30. That office also can provide names of agents who handle seasonal rentals in coastal areas.

Also, good references for those looking to rent or own along the coast are the *Maine Times* and *Down East* magazine. During late spring, the *Maine Times* publishes a special summer vacation guide with classifieds for rental properties. The supplement is usually available all summer at newsstands throughout the state. *Down East* runs a monthly real estate classified section as well. See "Media," above, for further information about these publications.

ROAD SERVICE

Portland

AAA Maine 425 Marginal Way, 04104; www.aaane.com; Mon.– Fri. 8:30–6, Sat. 9–1. 207-780-6800 or 800-482-7497.

South Portland

AAA Maine 443 Western Ave., 04106; www.aaane.com; Mon.– Fri. 9–6, Sat. 9–1. 207-775-6211 or 800-336-6211.

TOURIST INFORMATION

Which way to Acadia?

There are several publicly funded information centers and state agencies that provide visitor information. In addition, most chambers of commerce will gladly send packets of information to people planning a stay in their area. Here is an abbreviated list of agencies and chambers for coastal Maine.

FISHING AND HUNTING REGULATIONS

Dept. of Inland Fisheries and Wildlife 207-287-8000; www.state.me.us/ifw; E-mail, webmaster_isw@state.me.us; 284 State St., Augusta 04333;.

VISITOR INFORMATION

Maine Tourism Association 207-623-0363; 800-533-9595 out-of-state and Canada; www.mainetourism.com; E-mail, metainfo@mainetourism.com; P.O. Box 2300 Hallowell 04347.

South Coast

Convention and Visitors Bureau of the Greater Portland Visitor Information Center 207-772-5800; www.visitportland.com; E-mail, cbb@cybertours.com; 305 Commercial St., Portland 04101.

Freeport Merchants Association 207-865-1212; www.freeportusa.com; E-mail, freeportcc@maine.com; P.O. Box 452, Freeport 04032.

Kennebunk-Kennebunkport Chamber of Commerce 207-967-0857; www.kkcc. maine.org; E-mail, kkcc@maine.org; P.O. Box 740, Kennebunk 04043.

Kittery Information Center 207-439-1319; I-95 and Rte. 1, P.O. Box 396, Kittery 03904.

Kittery Outlet Association 888-KITTERY.

Ogunquit Chamber of Commerce 207-646-2939; www.ogunquit.org; P.O. Box 2289, Ogunquit 03907.

Old Orchard Beach Chamber of Commerce www.oldorchardbeachmaine. com; E-mail, family_fun@oldorchardbeachmaine.com; P.O. Box 600, Old Orchard Beach 04064.

Portland's Downtown District 207-934-2500; www.portlandmaine.com; E-mail, pdddid@javanet.com 207-772-6828; 400 Congress St. Portland 04101.

Wells 207-646-2451; www.wellschamber.org; E-mail, wellschamber@wells chamber.org; P.O. Box 356, Route 1, Wells, ME 04090.

Yarmouth Information Center 207-846-0833; U.S. Rte. 1/Exit 17, I-95, P.O. Box 1057, Yarmouth 04096.

Yorks 207-363-4422; www.yorkme.org/; E-mail, york@gwi.net; 571 U.S. Rte 1, York, ME 03909.

Midcoast

Bath-Brunswick Area Chamber of Commerce 207-725-8797; www.midcoast-maine.com; E-mail, ccbbr@horton.col.k12.me.us; 59 Pleasant St., Brunswick 04011.

Belfast Area Chamber of Commerce 207-338-5900; www.acadia.net /belfast /8; E-mail, belfast@acadia.net; P.O. Box 58, Belfast 04915.

Boothbay Harbor Region Chamber of Commerce 207-633-2353; www.booth-bayharbor.com; E-mail, seamaine@boothbayharbor.com; P.O. Box 356, Boothbay Harbor, 04539.

Camden-Rockport-Lincolnville Chamber of Commerce 207-236-4404; www. camden me.org; E-mail, chamber@camdenme.org; P.O. Box 919, Camden 04843.

Damariscotta Region Chamber of Commerce 207-563-8340; www.orcc.org; E-mail, drcc@tidewater.piet; P.O. Box 13, Damariscotta 04543.

Rockland/Thomaston Area Chamber of Commerce 207-596-0376; www. mido-cast .com/~rtacc; E-mail, rtacc@midcoast.com; P.O. Box 508, Rockland 04841.

Down East/Acadia

Acadia National Park Headquarters 207-288-3338; www.nps.gov/acad; P.O. Box 177, Bar Harbor 04609.

Bar Harbor Chamber of Commerce 207-288-5103; www.barhaborinfo.com; E-mail, bhcc@acdia.net; P.O. Box 158, Bar Harbor 04609.

Blue Hill Chamber of Commerce, P.O. Box 520, Blue Hill 04614.

Deer Isle-Stonington Chamber of Commerce, Stonington 04681; 207-348-6124.

Ellsworth Area Chamber of Commerce 207-667-2617; w2.downeast.net/ eacc/; E-mail, eacc@downeast.net; P.O. Box 267, Ellsworth 04605.

Mt. Desert Region 207-276-5040; P.O. Box 675, Northeast Harbor, 04662.

East of Schoodic

Eastport Area Chamber of Commerce 207-853-4644; www.nemaine.com/east-portcc; E-mail, eastportcc@nemaine.com; P.O. Box 254, Eastport 04631.

Machias Bay Area Chamber of Commerce, 207-255-4402; P.O. Box 606, Machias 04654.

IF TIME IS SHORT

With its ins and outs, the coast of Maine extends more than 3,000 miles. Even in a direct line, it is a five- or six-hour drive end to end. If your time is limited, you're traveling from the south, and you want to capture the flavors of the rocky coast, we recommend you use Portland as a home base and explore north and southward from there. Portland itself is a comfortable and interesting small city, and in addition to its attractions it is an easy drive north to Freeport and south to Kennebunkport, Ogunquit, and Maine's best sand beaches. If you're traveling from points north, we suggest your home base be Bar Harbor. It's the getting off point for Acadia National Park and its northeasternmost reaches on the Schoodic Peninsula. From either point, there's plenty of lobster, hiking, biking, shopping, cross country skiing, and rocky coast to be found.

What we really hope? That you will use our book to customize your own itinerary.

INNS

Mira Monte Inn (207-288-4263; 69 Mount Desert St., Bar Harbor). If you think of the Rockefellers, the rocky coast, and Acadia National Park in one breathe, you've got a good picture of the Mira Monte. This is everything Bar Harbor is and was about.

The Pomegranate Inn (207-772-1006; 49 Neal St., Portland). This is the city at its best and most eclectic. Great breakfast, amazing style, and smack in the middle of the city's historic West End.

CULTURAL ATTRACTIONS

Portland Museum of Art (207-773-2787; 619 Congress Ave., Portland). Designed by I. M. Pei, this is the oldest and most impressive art collection in Maine, with works by Van Gogh, Picasso, Degas, the Wyeths, and Winslow Homer.

Thuya Gardens at Asticou Terraces (Rte. 3, Northeast Harbor on Mount Desert Island). A formal English garden filled with country flowers — zinnias, dahlias, plume poppies, goatsbeards, and monkshood designed by landscape architect Joseph Henry Curtis. *The New York Times* describes Thuya Gardens as an "accidentally available private retreat left over from another time."

SHOPPING

Exchange St. in Portland is the upscale downtown district near the city's working waterfront, with brick sidewalks, boutiques and art galleries, ethnic specialties, and funky stuff in general. Only 20 miles north on Rte. 295, you'll find **Freeport,** home of the great L.L. Bean and where the world shops when it's in Maine.

The shopping hub of Bar Harbor is at the intersections of **Main and Cottage Streets,** just up from the harbor. There you'll find a proliferation of small stores from T-shirt joints to upscale galleries filled with art and handicrafts. Just over the bridge in Ellsworth, we suggest you stop in at the **L.L. Bean Factory Store,** where you can take home bargains from the famous outdoors store and catalog merchant.

RESTAURANTS

Fore Street (207-775-2717; 288 Fore St., Portland). In an old warehouse, this lively Portland restaurant is great if you like dinner as theater — the kitchen and large, wood burning grill and ovens are at the center.

Le Domaine (207-422-3395 or 800-554-8498; Rte 1., Hancock). If you're going to be in the area two nights, you should have at least one dinner at the impeccably French country inn.

RECREATION

Acadia National Park (207-288-3338; Mount Desert Island). This is a year's worth of recreation in a weekend: 100 miles of trails through forests and past lakes; eight climbing peaks; great biking on old carriage roads; wonderful water view; good rock climbing, canoeing and cross-country skiing; a small sand beach; the tallest mountain; and only fjord on the eastern seaboard.

Portland Sea Dogs (207-879-9500; Hadlock Field, Park St., Portland) The Double A affiliate of the Florida Marlins. This is family entertainment at its best, and the intimate, friendly stadium is usually filled to capacity. Call well in advance for your tickets. Don't worry, there's not a bad seat in the house.

Index

LODGING BY PRICE CODE

DINING BY PRICE CODE

RESTAURANTS BY CUISINE

SOUTH COAST

American
Alisson's, 53
Arrows, 54
Back Bay Grill, 56
Boone's Famous Restaurant, 56
Billy's Chowder House, 61
Buffleheads, 52
Cape Neddick Inn, 49
Carson's Family Restaurant, 60
Della's Catessen, 57
15 Independence, 50
Flo's Hotdogs, 61
Hurricane, 54
Jackie's Too, 55
Jameson Tavern, 50
Katahdin, 58
Norm's Bar BQ, 58
Pepper Club, 58
Port Bake House, 59
Spurwink Country Kitchen
Three Dollar Dewey's, 59
Walter's Cafe, 59
York Harbor Inn, 61

Caribbean
Cotton Street Cantina, 57

Continental
Chebeague Inn, 49
Cornforth House, 60
Jonathan's, 55

Eclectic
15 Independence, 50

French
Joseph's by the Sea, 55

Italian
Roberto's, 55

Maine/New England Regional
Arrows, 54
Back Bay Grill, 56
Fore Street, 57
Harraseeket Inn, 50
Jonathan's, 55
Joseph's by the Sea, 55

Seafood
Billy's Chowder House, 61
Boone's Famous Restaurant, 56
Buffleheads, 52
Cap'n Simeon's Galley, 53
Carson's Family Restaurant, 60
Chauncey Creek Lobster Pound, 53
Jameson Tavern, 50
Harraseeket Lunch & Lobster, 52
Hurricane, 54
Street & Company, 59

Thai
Thai Garden, 52

Vegetarian
Three Dollar Dewey's, 59

MIDCOAST

American
Blueberry Bay, 135
The Breakfast Place, 138
The Brown Bag, 141
Cappy's Chowder House, 137
Captain's Table, 141
Kristina's 134
Lobsterman's Wharf, 139
Moody's Diner, 144
The Newastle Inn, 140
Nickerson Tavern, 141
Periwinkle's Bakery, 142
Richard's, 137
The Salt Bay Cafe, 139
The Squire Tarbox Inn, 145
The Waterfront, 138

Continental/Bistro
Jessica's, 141

Eclectic
The Brown Bag, 140
Kristina's, 134
90 Main Restaurant, 135

German
Richard's, 137

International
Christopher's Boathouse, 135

SOUTH COAST

statute miles

0   10   20

NEW HAMPSHIRE

MAINE

Maine

Saco River

Piscataqua River

Androscoggin River

Lewiston
Auburn

Topsham

Brunswick

Freeport

South Freeport

Merepoint

Harpswell Center

S. Harpswell

Yarmouth

Cumberland

Gt. Chebeague I.

Falmouth

Gt. Diamond I.

Bailey I.

Long I.

Portland

Peaks I.

Casco Bay

South Portland

Scarborough

Cape Elizabeth

Higgins Beach

Old Orchard Beach

Prouts Neck

Saco

Biddeford

Biddeford Pool

Goose Rocks Beach

Kennebunk

Cape Porpoise

Kennebunk Beach

Kennebunkport

Wells

Berwick

Wells Beach

Moody Beach

South Berwick

Ogunquit

Cape Neddick

York Beach

York Village

York Harbor

Kittery

Kittery Point

MIDCOAST

MIDCOAST

statute miles

0   10   20

Penobscot River

Orono

Bangor
95
Brewer

15

ALT 1   Bucksport

1

Penobscot

Stockton Springs

175   177

Belfast   Searsport
Castine

Northport   Sedgwick

Islesboro
Islesboro I.   Little Deer Isle
Deer Isle

Union   Lincolnville
Deer I.

Camden

Rockport   North Haven I.

Waldoboro   North Haven

Newcastle   Rockland

Thomaston   Owls Head   Vinalhaven

Wiscasset   Damariscotta   Vinalhaven I.

Friendship   Spruce Head

Edgecomb   Bristol
Tenants Harbor

Brunswick   Westport I.   Port Clyde

Topsham   Bath   East Boothbay

Merepoint   Phippsburg   Boothbay   New Harbor   Mantinicus I.

Harpswell   Cundys Harbor   Southport   Pemaquid Point

Center   Orrs I.   Sebasco   Newagen

S. Harpswell   Monhegan I.

Bailey I.   Small Point   Popham Beach

Casco Bay

Waterville

Maine

Kennebec River
95

Augusta

3

17

495

95

1

SOUTH COAST

DOWNEAST/ACADIA

Muscongus Bay

Penobscot Bay

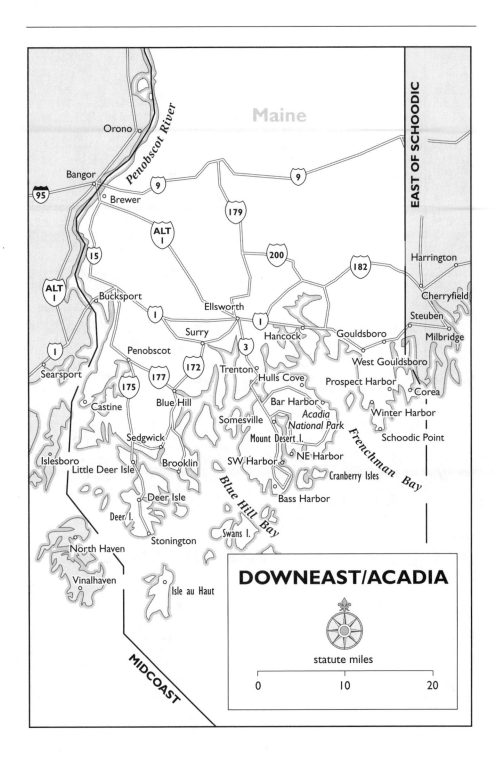

DOWNEAST/ACADIA

statute miles

0   10   20

EAST OF SCHOODIC

statute miles

| 0 | 10 | 20 |

About the Authors

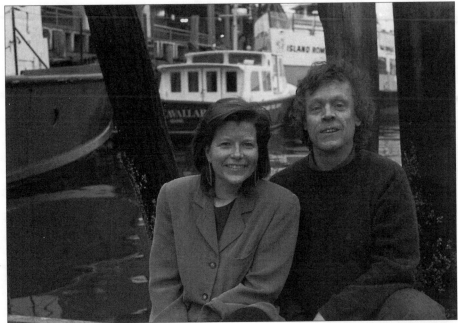

Herb Swanson

Rick Ackermann and Kathryn Buxton live in a 140-year-old home in Portland, Maine's historic West End with their dog, Argos, and their one-year-old daughter, Jane. They have written for *New England Monthly*, *Yankee*, Arthur Frommer's *America on Wheels*, Cognoscenti Map Guides, *Town & Country*, *The Washington Post*, *Variety*, Reuters, and many other newspapers and magazines throughout Maine and the rest of the country.